Vocational Interests

Meaning, Measurement, and Counseling Use

Mark L. Savickas and Arnold R. Spokane, Editors

Davies-Black Publishing
Palo Alto, California

Published by Davies-Black Publishing, an imprint of Consulting Psychologists Press, Inc., 3803 East Bayshore Road, Palo Alto, CA 94303; 1-800-624-1765.

Special discounts on bulk quantities of Davies-Black books are available to corporations, professional associations, and other organizations. For details, contact the Director of Book Sales at Davies-Black Publishing, an imprint of Consulting Psychologists Press, Inc., 3803 East Bayshore Road, Palo Alto, CA 94303; 650-691-9123; Fax 650-988-0673.

03 02 01 00 99   10 9 8 7 6 5 4 3 2 1
Printed in the United States of America

Library of Congress Cataloging-in-Publication Data
Vocational interests: meaning, measurement, and counseling use / Mark L. Savickas and
    Arnold R. Spokane, editors,—1st ed.
        p.   cm.
    Includes bibliographical references and index.
    ISBN 0-89106-126-6
    1. Vocational interests.   I. Savickas, Mark.
    II. Spokane, Arnold R.
    HF5381.5.V55   1999
    158.6—dc21

                                                            98–51047
                                                            CIP

FIRST EDITION
First printing 1999

Contents

CHAPTER ONE

Introduction

Reconsidering the Nature, Measurement, and Uses of Vocational Interests

Mark L. Savickas and Arnold R. Spokane

SEVENTY-SIX YEARS AGO, E. K. Strong began his trailblazing work at Stanford University on the measurement of vocational interests. Few single constructs have so dominated a subfield of modern psychology as interests have preoccupied vocational psychologists. We can think of no better point of departure for this comprehensive volume on vocational interests than the timeless questions that Strong himself attempted to answer and with which vocational psychologists still struggle:

> What are interests? What role do they play in human affairs? Can one's behavior be predicted if his [sic] interests are known? How do the interests of men and women, boys and older men compare? To what extent do men [sic] in different occupations differ in their interests? How significant are these differences in interests? Do they result from differences in training and occupational experience or do they arise rather early in life and condition occupational choice? (Strong, 1943, p. 3)

Although vocational psychologists have repeatedly addressed each of these questions during more than seven decades of research, few of us would claim to have the answers. This volume addresses Strong's initial questions as well as several that Strong could not anticipate. We hope to shed additional light on the nature of vocational interests and to catalyze further research into the origins, development, measurement, and interpretation of vocational interests. Whether we resolve the debate on the conceptual nature of interests, as Savickas (this volume) argues that we should, is less crucial than reopening research into those questions we still have about interest theory, measurement, and practice. We must also continue to investigate differences in vocational interests between women and men (Lippa, 1998) as well as the pressing issue of the appropriateness of interest measurement across cultures and among minority groups within a culture (Fouad, 1993).

PLAN OF THE BOOK

To invigorate research on interest measurement and revitalize reflection on interest theory, the Society for Vocational Psychology dedicated its 1997 Biennial Conference at Lehigh University and this volume to the general topic of vocational interests, concentrating on three fundamental questions about conceptualizing, measuring, and using vocational interests: What are vocational interests? How can they be measured? How should counselors use interest measures in career intervention? The present volume devotes a separate section, containing five chapters, to respond in turn to each of these three questions.

Section 1: Conceptualizing Vocational Interests

The five chapters in Section 1 consider the definitions, determinants, and development of vocational interests. The opening chapter, written by Savickas, closely examines definitions and determinants of interest as a state and vocational interests as a trait. The next two chapters, written by Gottfredson and by Holland, provide a more in-depth examination of two putative determinants of vocational interests: genetic influences and personality. The fourth chapter, written by Rounds and Day, examines the structure of vocational interests. The final chapter, written by Swanson, examines how vocational interests develop—that is, change and continue—over the life span. As a group the five chapters in this section thoroughly analyze the nature of vocational interests. This grounding in interest theory should increase readers' appreciation for the issues that complicate research on the measurement of vocational interests, the topic of Section 2.

Section 2: Measuring Vocational Interests

In contrast to the opening section of this volume, which deals with conceptual definitions and theory, Section 2 concentrates on operational definitions and the measurement of vocational interests. The first chapter, written by

Crites, distinguishes between linguistic and empirical definitions of vocational interests and then discusses five operational definitions that researchers and practitioners can use to measure vocational interests. Two of these operational definitions, *inventoried* and *expressed,* have commanded the most attention from researchers. Accordingly, the next two chapters, written by Harmon and by Fouad, scrutinize the research on inventoried interests, whereas the final two chapters in Section 2, written by Spokane and Decker and by Hartung, peruse the research on expressed interests. As a group the five chapters in Section 2 provide a comprehensive summary of research on the measurement of vocational interests by inventories and verbal expressions. This information about the technical problems involved in measuring vocational interests provides a crucial background for appreciating the challenges inherent in interpreting the results of interest assessments and communicating these interpretations to clients, which is the topic of Section 3.

Section 3: Using Vocational Interests in Career Intervention

The chapters in Section 3 each address the importance of communicating interest inventory interpretations to clients in a manner that fosters their occupational self-efficacy, vocational exploratory behavior, and career decision making. The first chapter on counseling practice, written by Tinsley and Chu, reviews the research on interest inventory interpretation and charts directions for future research. After sifting through the research reviewed by Tinsley and Chu, as well as reflecting on his 30 years of experience as a career counselor, Zytowski offers five principles to guide counselors as they communicate to clients the results of interest measurement. In addition to interpreting interest measurements that identify what a client likes to do, many counselors also attend to what a client can do well. Accordingly, the next two chapters in Section 3 address the joint interpretation of interest and ability measures. The first of these two chapters, written by Prediger, deals with ability self-estimates that have objective, external referents, whereas the second chapter, written by Betz, deals with ability self-confidence measures that have more subjective, internal referents. The final chapter in Section 3 takes up the topic of encouraging clients to engage in vocational exploratory behavior. Blustein and Flum use a self-determination model to explain how vocational interests and occupational exploration interact in charting a career course.

Section 4: Current Status and Future Directions

Section 4 concludes the book by presenting two chapters that assess the current status and chart future directions for interest theory, research, and practice. In the first of these complementary chapters, Walsh states seven conclusions that can be drawn from the empirical literature about interests and then considers how the role of vocational interests in career decision making may change as North America becomes a postindustrial society in need of workers who are occupational generalists and team players rather than vocational specialists. In the final chapter Borgen describes a comprehensive model for linking domains of individuality to venues for living. He then uses this heuristic model to organize the book's major themes as well as propose future directions for interest research. Borgen ends his chapter and this volume with an important recommendation for the future of interest theory, research, and practice. He wisely suggests that practitioners and researchers view interests as the facet of individuality that enables people to passionately express their individuality in all of life's venues.

ENDURING QUESTIONS ABOUT VOCATIONAL INTERESTS

In responding to the three general questions that frame this volume, the chapter authors raise many specific questions. We identify these enduring questions as follows: Why are vocational interests a fundamental topic in counseling psychology? How should interest be defined? Do interests motivate or guide behavior? Are interests narrowly defined surface constructs or do they reflect deeper psychological structures such as personality? What is the underlying structure of vocational interests? Do interests change and develop over time? How reliable and valid are contemporary interest measures, especially across social groups and cultures? What is the meaning of disagreements between expressed and measured interests? How do different scaling and norming methods affect inventory results? How does research inform the interpretation of interest inventory scale scores and profile patterns? How can interest inventory interpretations be communicated to clients so as to ensure optimal outcomes? Each of these questions is now briefly introduced, as an advanced organizer for readers.

Why Are Vocational Interests a Fundamental Topic in Counseling Psychology

The nature of interests is one of the defining questions in vocational psychology—indeed in applied psychology generally (Spokane & Jacob, 1996). This topic arguably constitutes the primary difference between counseling and clinical psychology and embodies a set of understandings and capabilities unique to counseling psychology. As Leona Tyler (1992) once asserted, even if the extant specialties in psychology were merged or redefined, the unique roles enacted by counseling psychologists, such as "helping individuals to understand themselves, make important choices, and plan their lives" (p. 342), should be preserved. Career intervention in general and interest measurement in particular must be functions that continue to advance.

How Should Interests Be Defined?

During the first third of this century, before the unparalleled success of interest inventories, counselors measured interests in many diverse ways, including narratives, autobiographies, behavioral indicators, and objective tests (Crites, this volume; Spokane & Decker, this volume; Walsh, this volume). For example, Bingham (1937) wrote about objective interests as "interests manifest" and imagined observing the behavior of a person in a specially arranged museum, watching how much time he or she spent with each exhibit. He realized that this was inconvenient but concluded that "instead of relying solely on what a person says are his [sic] interests, observe, if possible, that in which he [sic] actually takes interest" (p. 67). Bingham then recommended the use of a "behaviorgram" or recorded data collected over time about an individual's activities, he called these "notes of doings clearly indicative of interests." Contemporary counselors' reliance on inventories obscures other approaches to measuring interests. Ironically, Bingham founded the Division of Applied Psychology at Carnegie Institute of Technology that gave rise to the first standardized interest inventories through the work of Yokum and his seminar students Moore, Freyd, and Ream as well as Strong, who worked at Carnegie as the Director of the Educational Research Bureau (Bingham, 1923). It may be time to reexamine the usefulness of measuring vocational interests through tests, activity diaries, manifest behaviors, narratives, and expressed preferences. These measures can augment interest inventories by providing additional perspectives from which to view and analyze clients' career motivation (Hartung, this volume). Furthermore, multiple measures of interests could advance interest theory by framing a comprehensive definition of vocational interests that subsumes operational definitions by inventories, tests, manifest behaviors, autobiographical narratives, and expressed preferences (Crites, this volume; Savickas, this volume).

Do Interests Motivate or Guide Behavior?

In a comprehensive chapter on the nature of interests, Savickas (this volume) notes that interests (a) focus attention, (b) arouse feelings, (c) steer a direction, and (d) involve activity. These motivational properties have been studied historically yet have received precious little attention of late. The exception to the lack of attention to the motivational properties of interests comes in the work of Betz and Hackett on self-efficacy (Betz, this volume; Hackett & Betz, 1981). Walsh (this volume) notes that interests direct constructive behavior, indicate motivation, and reflect a health-oriented, as opposed to pathology-oriented, view of the human condition—a perfect domain for counseling psychology.

In a different vein, Blustein and Flum (this volume) discuss the contextual influences on exploration and the mediating link among interests, contexts, and exploration. They view self-determination as the organizing construct through which individuals experience this mediating influence. Their chapter discusses, in a clear and compelling manner, the nature of interests and relates this driving or directing quality to extant theory on motivation.

Are Interests Narrowly Defined Surface Constructs or Do They Reflect Deeper Psychological Structures?

To the extent that vocational psychologists can relate interests to the mainstream of modern psychology (Savickas, this volume)—to personality theory, learning theory, and social psychology in particular—they can create a better opportunity to construct a comprehensive definition and conceptual framework for understanding vocational behavior and career development.

Holland (this volume) argues, in one of his more eloquent contributions, that vocational interests overlap substantially with personality and are differentiated only by the criterion base embedded in interest inventories.

McCrae and Costa (1997) urge psychologists to consider the possibility that a limited and fundamental set of underlying dimensions or constructs define the human personality. These dimensions are reflected in all personality measures to a certain degree. Emerging evidence suggests that vocational interests also reflect these dimensions (Costa, McCrae, & Holland, 1984; Lippa, 1998; Walsh, this volume). Furthermore, the link between interests and abilities, once believed to be considerable, is still under scrutiny (Prediger, this volume; Walsh, this volume). Prediger frames the most pressing question here: Even if interests and abilities are unrelated in correlational studies using pairs of interest and ability scores, researchers must ask whether using the two scores together provides any unique information. Moreover, Prediger asks whether the self-estimates of ability now embedded in several inventories are valid. Prediger's advice to counselors in combining interest and ability measures is both thoughtful and consistent with the research evidence.

What Is the Underlying Structure of Vocational Interests?

An unusually vigorous series of studies by Rounds and Tracey (Rounds & Day, this volume; Tracey & Rounds, 1995) rekindled enthusiasm for interest measurement research and theory (Lippa, 1998). To the unschooled eye, the understructure of interests may seem like a topic of minor importance. In fact, however, the "structural model" question is a fundamental one for vocational theory construction, psychometrics, genetic psychology, counseling, and research. The comparison of existing structures in Rounds and Day (this volume), then, deals with an enduring issue and provides seminal ideas for future research and practice.

Do Interests Change and Develop over Time?

Several valid methods exist for calculating whether the vocational interests of individuals and of groups remain stable over long periods of time (Swanson, this volume). The question posed here is not whether interests are stable for the majority of individuals over short and long periods of time. The long-term stability of vocational interests in group data was established in a compelling manner in the late 1960s (Campbell, 1971; Hansen, 1988; Swanson & Hansen, 1988; Walsh, this volume)—a finding that has never been refuted. Swanson (this volume) reminds us, however, that despite the overall stability of vocational interests across time, a small but persistent "unstable minority" of individuals exists for whom interests change over time. In addition there is substantial accentuation of interests even within stable profiles and considerable evidence that significant changes in context or career choice induce parallel changes in measured interests (Spokane, 1991). What researchers have never fully examined is the degree of change or elasticity that is possible in vocational interests when they do change. How change is possible in constructs that are heavily genetically determined is yet to be determined. This question should be addressed in future research.

How Reliable and Valid Are Contemporary Interest Measures, Especially Across Social Groups and Cultures?

Can scales and inventories that have been developed on a largely homogeneous White, middle-class culture be bootstrapped to minority subcultures or to non-Western cultures? Of all the questions we pose in this volume, none is more crucial to the future of interest measurement than the question of cross-cultural validity. Most of the chapters discuss the topic of cross-cultural and multicultural validity in some way. The chapters by Fouad (this volume) and Harmon (this volume) are particularly relevant to the twin issues of reliability and validity. Fouad uses Messick's (1995) comprehensive, six-facet model of validity to evaluate interest inventories generally, and she addresses the sixth facet, consequential validity, with considerable clarity, extending her earlier observations (Fouad, 1993; Fouad, Harmon, & Hansen, 1994). Subich (1996) also underscores the importance of examining the cultural validity of vocational assessments. Although there is some disagreement on the applicability of interest inventories across cultures, much of the disagreement rests on the fact that compelling studies addressing the measurement issues involved are just beginning to appear. Thus it may be some time before we can fully appreciate the problems in this area and even longer before we can resolve them. For the present there is no reason to believe that these issues cannot be faced and overcome, as they seem largely psychometric rather than conceptual.

Many of these psychometric problems are sidestepped when counselors assess expressed interests. Hartung (this volume) explains that vocational card sorts offer counselors a culturally relevant supplement or alternative to interest inventories. Whether operationally defining interests with inventories or card sorts, vocational interests and their structure appear to be a valid concept across cultures (Day & Rounds, 1998; Rounds & Tracey, 1996), although the content of those interests may vary from subculture to subculture.

What Is the Meaning of Disagreements Between Expressed and Measured Interests?

It can be argued that measured interests, by virtue of their indirect measurement, tap deep underlying structures, whereas expressed interests are a self-report that taps a more malleable personal preference. This assertion is addressed by Spokane and Decker (this volume), who review the considerable literature on expressed versus measured interests and the meaning of disagreements between these two operational definitions of vocational interests. Differential interpretation of expressed and measured interests should be discussed, because almost all of the major inventories now combine direct and indirect interest scales, and clients will receive information from both scale types. Hartung (this volume) reviews the advantages of using expressed interests in career interventions and describes a variety of specific approaches to helping clients explore the personal meaning of their expressed interests. Together, Spokane and Decker along with Hartung make a strong case for the value of assessing systematically both measured and expressed interests.

How Do Different Scaling and Norming Methods Affect Inventory Results?

Although there are striking differences in the item technology as well as scaling and norming procedures used in various interest inventories (Taber & Spokane, 1998), we know very little about the interchangeability of inventories employing different psychometric options. The Society for Vocational Psychology's biennial conference at Lehigh University provided an excellent opportunity to collect data pertinent to this question, as 118 career counselors completed the *Campbell Interest and Skills Survey*, the *Kuder Occupational Interest Survey*, the *Self-Directed Search*, the *Strong Interest Inventory®*, and the *Unisex Edition of the American College Testing Interest Inventory*. A moderate to high degree of convergent validity was found across the inventories (Taber & Spokane, 1998) despite their differences in construction. A similar conclusion can be drawn from a case study, also emanating from the Lehigh conference, showing how the same five inventories portrayed a single client (Spokane, 1998).

How Does Research Inform the Interpretation of Interest Inventory Scale Scores and Profile Patterns?

The field of interest measurement has, unequivocally, spent almost its entire effort in developing and establishing the psychometric properties of the instruments it has spawned. Research on how to interpret the meaning of interest inventory scale scores and profile patterns has lagged behind, especially during the last quarter century. Admittedly, during the middle of this century vocational psychologists conducted useful research on the correlates and implications of interest inventory scale scores and profile patterns. The then-popular view that vocational interests are dynamic phenomena that express a self-concept and manifest personality resulted in outstanding manuals for interest inventory interpretation, a few of which remain germane today (e.g., Darley, 1941; Gobetz, 1964; Goldberg & Gechman, 1976). Although contemporary vocational and personality psychologists share a renewed concern about the relation between personality and vocational interests (Tokar, Fischer, & Subich, 1998), they had not yet produced much research on interest inventory interpretation. Prediger (this volume) and Savickas (this volume) remind counselors about the importance of research on inventory interpretation—inquiry that links theory and practice—and illustrate that point by discussing the frequent error of interpreting profile elevation as indicating the strength of vocational interests. Hopefully the renewed enthusiasm for investigating relations between personality and vocational interests (Holland, this volume; Walsh, this volume) will prompt more research on the interpretation of interest inventory profiles, research that can only enhance career assessment.

How Can Interest Inventory Interpretations Be Communicated to Clients so as to Ensure Optimal Outcomes?

As Tinsley and Chu (this volume) document with such force and clarity, empirical research tells us almost nothing about how best to communicate to clients our interpretations of their interest inventory scale scores and profile patters during the course of counseling and career intervention. Although guidelines exist (Tinsley & Bradley, 1986; Zytowski, this volume), the practice of communicating inventory interpretations to clients has rarely been subjected to empirical test. Tinsley and Chu call the situation "shockingly inadequate," a conclusion we can only echo. This lacuna in the literature makes case conferences and published case studies particularly useful for counselors who want to increase their skill at interest inventory interventions. For example, the case study (Savickas, 1998) emanating from the Lehigh conference provides a helpful example of how seven expert counselors interpret and use different interest inventories (Boggs, 1998; Prediger & Schmertz, 1998; Prince, 1998; Rayman, 1998; Spokane, 1998; Zytowski, 1998). After reading these case materials, along with the chapters written by Zytowski (this volume) and Tinsley and Chu (this volume), one quickly concludes that, despite their great usefulness, much more could be discovered about how to best communicate interest inventory interpretations to clients. If nothing else derives from our efforts in this volume, we hope that new research will be formulated and conducted to examine the functional utility (Hayes, Nelson, & Jarrett, 1987) of the measures we use so often in counseling.

TOWARD A REVITALIZED RESEARCH AGENDA

The goal for the Lehigh Conference and this volume is to stimulate new research, revised theory, and perhaps innovations in measurement models and inventories. In chronicling the recent accomplishments and current status of interest theory, research, and practice, the chapters collected herein also raise several important questions and offer many suggestions for future research. Although scholarship and practice regarding vocational interests continue to advance at a vigorous pace, more effort should be invested in intervention research, theoretical conceptualization, and construct validation, including mapping nomological networks. We hope this volume contributes to the current renaissance of interest in interests.

REFERENCES

Bingham, W. V. (1923). On the possibility of an applied psychology. *Psychological Review, 30,* 289–298.
Bingham, W. V. (1937). *Aptitudes and aptitude testing.* New York: Harper & Row.
Boggs, K. R. (1998). Career decisions: The *Campbell* and Miss Flood. *Career Development Quarterly, 46,* 311–319.
Campbell, D. P. (1971). *Handbook for the Strong Vocational Interest Blank.* Stanford, CA: Stanford University Press.
Costa, P. T., Jr., McCrae, R. R., & Holland, J. L. (1984). Personality and vocational interests in adulthood. *Journal of Applied Psychology, 69,* 390–400.

Darley, J. G. (1941). *Clinical aspects and interpretations of the* Strong Vocational Interest Blank. New York: The Psychological Corporation.

Day, S. X, & Rounds, J. (1998). The universality of vocational interest structure among racial/ethnic minorities. *American Psychologist,* pp.728–736.

Fouad, N. A. (1993). Cross-cultural vocational assessment. *Career Development Quarterly, 42,* 4–13.

Fouad, N. A., Harmon, L. W., & Hansen, J. C. (1994). Cross-cultural use of the *Strong.* In L. W. Harmon, J. C. Hansen, F. H. Borgen, & A. L. Hammer, *Strong Interest Inventory: Applications and technical guide* (pp. 255–280). Stanford, CA: Stanford University Press.

Gobetz, W. (1964). Suggested personality implications of the *Kuder Preference Record* (Vocational) scores. *Personnel and Guidance Journal, 43,* 159–166.

Goldberg, R., & Gechman, A. (1976). Psychodynamic inferences from the *Strong Vocational Interest Blank. Journal of Personality Assessment, 40,* 285–301.

Hackett, G., & Betz, N. E. (1981). A self-efficacy approach to the career development of women. *Journal of Vocational Behavior, 18,* 326–339.

Hansen, J.I.C. (1988). Changing interests of women: Myth or reality? *Applied Psychology: An International Review, 37,* 133–150.

Hayes, S. C., Nelson, R. O., & Jarrett, R. B. (1987). The treatment utility of assessment: A functional approach to evaluating assessment quality. *American Psychologist, 42,* 963–974.

Lippa, R. (1998). Gender-related individual differences and the structure of vocational interests: The importance of the people–things dimension. *Journal of Personality and Social Psychology, 74,* 996–1009.

McCrae, R., & Costa, P. T. (1997). Personality structure as a human universal. *American Psychologist, 52,* 509–516.

Messick, S. (1995). Validity of psychological assessment: Validation of references from persons' responses and performances on scientific inquiry into score meaning. *American Psychologist, 50,* 741–749.

Prediger, D. J., & Schmertz, E. A. (1998). Ellenore Flood's UNIACT results. *Career Development Quarterly, 46,* 352–359.

Prince, J. P. (1998). Interpreting the *Strong Interest Inventory:* A case study. *Career Development Quarterly, 46,* 339–346.

Rayman, J. R. (1998). Interpreting Ellenore's Self-Directed Search. *Career Development Quarterly, 46,* 330–338.

Rounds, J., & Tracey, T. J. (1996). Cross-cultural structural equivalence of RIASEC models and measures. *Journal of Counseling Psychology, 43,* 310–329.

Savickas, M. L. (1998). Interpreting interest inventories: A case example. *Career Development Inventory, 46,* 307–310.

Spokane, A. R. (1991). *Career intervention.* Englewood Cliffs, NJ: Prentice Hall.

Spokane, A. R. (1998). Risk versus reluctance: Understanding an ambivalent entrepreneur. *Career Development Quarterly,* 370–375.

Spokane, A. R., & Jacob, E. J. (1996). Career and vocational assessment 1993–1994: A biennial review. *Journal of Career Assessment, 4,* 1–32.

Strong, E. K., Jr. (1943). *The vocational interests of men and women.* Stanford, CA: Stanford University Press.

Subich, L. M. (1996). Addressing diversity in the process of career assessment. In M. L. Savickas and W. B. Walsh (Eds.), *Handbook of career counseling theory and practice* (pp. 277–289). Palo Alto, CA: Davies-Black.

Swanson, J. L., & Hansen, J.I.C. (1988). Stability of vocational interests over four year, eight year, and twelve year intervals. *Journal of Vocational Behavior, 33,* 185–202.

Taber, B. J., & Spokane, A. R. (1998). *Comparing five interest inventories: Item commonality and response consistency.* Paper presented at the Fourth Annual World Conference of the American Counseling Association, Indianapolis, IN.

Tinsley, H.E.A., & Bradley, R. W. (1986). Testing the test: Test interpretation. *Journal of Counseling and Development, 64,* 462–466.

Tokar, D. M., Fischer, A. R., & Subich, L. M. (1998). Personality and vocational behavior: A selective review of the literature, 1993–1997. *Journal of Vocational Behavior, 53,* 115–153.

Tracey, T. J., & Rounds, J. (1995). The arbitrary nature of Holland's RIASEC types: A concentric-circles structure. *Journal of Counseling Psychology, 42,* 431–439.

Tyler, L. E. (1992). Counseling psychology: Why? *Professional Psychology, 23,* 342–344.

Zytowski, D. G. (1998). Ellenore's *Kuder Occupational Interest Survey* and Career Search Schedule. *Career Development Quarterly, 46,* 320–329.

CONCEPTUALIZING VOCATIONAL INTERESTS

As a group the five chapters in Section 1 thoroughly examine the nature of interests by scrutinizing the definitions, determinants, and development of vocational interests. The opening chapter, written by Savickas, evaluates definitions of vocational interests and discusses theories about the origin and development of vocational interests. Savickas begins the chapter by examining the etymology and technical definitions of the word *interest*. He then seeks to elucidate the meaning of the state of being interested and to describe theories of vocational interests as a personality trait. After discussing the meaning of interest as a state and trait, he addresses the determinants that govern the origin and development of interests—including genetic influence, experiential learning, ability self-perception, role-model identification, social role accommodation, personality expression, and self-concept implementation. Then, in an attempt to integrate the foregoing material, Savickas describes succinctly interest, vocational interests, and their determinants. He concludes that interests expedite person–environment interactions by uniting subject, object, and behavior into a vital relationship that satisfies needs, fulfills values, fosters self-development, enhances adaptation, and substantiates identity.

The second chapter, written by Gottfredson, addresses the origin and development of vocational interests. Rather than taking stable traits as her starting point, Gottfredson focuses on how interests originate. In this analysis Gottfredson applies quantitative behavior genetics to examine the heritability of vocational interests. She concludes that individuals become who they are through life experiences that emerge from the complex interplay between genes and environments. Genes are expressed and their effects enhanced through experience. According to Gottfredson, genes do not predestine who we become; it is experience that shapes us. Thus optimal development and self-construction depend on adequate opportunities for exploration and experience. Career counseling fosters this exploration and experience by helping clients to discover, develop, and implement their vocational interests.

In the next chapter Holland examines a second major determinant of vocational interests by describing the relation between personality traits and vocational interests. In so doing, he resolutely asserts that interest inventories are also personality inventories. He chronologically marshals convincing evidence from his 50-year career in vocational psychology to document systematic relationships between personality and vocational interests. Along the way he modestly chronicles his own illustrious career as a personologist and vocational psychologist, a career that earned him the 1994 Award for Distinguished Professional Contributions from the American Psychological Association for his accomplishments in career theory, research, and practice. Holland concludes the chapter by sagaciously identifying important topics for future research on connections between personality and vocation.

The final two chapters in this section examine the structure and stability of vocational interests. In the first of these complementary chapters Rounds and Day examine the structure of vocational interests. They assert that this topic is central in vocational psychology because structural models of occupational interests guide the construction of vocational interest scales, schematize theories of person–environment fit, and govern exploration strategies for career counseling clients. Rounds and Day describe and compare the three basic types of models for the structure of interests: dimensional, classificatory, and spatial. They convincingly argue that each model's validity lies in its ability to illuminate the world of work and promote an individual's career development. Accordingly, Rounds and Day wisely advise counselors to select the structural model most useful for a specific purpose, given that several models probably represent the world with equal accuracy (albeit with different lenses in place). In the second half of the chapter Rounds and Day review the research literature, examining similarities among the three models and investigating how well different interest inventories embody the models. They conclude the chapter by describing the Vocational Interest Circle, an integrated interpretive framework for research and practice involving structural models of occupational interests. They suggest that this circle, not the number of categories carved from it, is the key structure.

In the fifth and final chapter in this opening section of the book Swanson examines continuity and change in vocational interests across the life span. She emphasizes the practical importance of this topic in explaining that some degree of interest stability is required if interest inventories are to have predictive validity. Swanson approaches the empirical evidence about interest permanence by first describing four different methods for operationally defining interest stability. She then summarizes the empirical evidence regarding interest stability that has been accumulated using these four methods. Although interests seem to be remarkably stable over time, some individuals do dramatically change their interests. The issue of identifying which individuals will change their interests is addressed next. Swanson discusses variables that seem to relate to change and continuity in an individual's interests and thus may be useful in predicting degree of interest permanence among clients who have responded to an interest inventory. Swanson concludes her chapter and Section 1 by identifying and discussing several important questions that must be addressed by research designed to advance current knowledge about stability and change in vocational interests. The information and perspectives presented in Section 1 prepare readers to appreciate the complexities involved in measuring vocational interests, the topic for Section 2.

CHAPTER TWO

The Psychology of Interests

Mark L. Savickas

AN EXTENSIVE LITERATURE covers the assessment of vocational interests. These studies generally examine the construction, validation, and interpretation of psychometric scales that operationally define vocational interests. The empirical approach to defining interests, sometimes referred to as "dust-bowl empiricism," has succeeded in producing myriad inventories that counselors routinely use to assess the occupational preferences of clients who seek career counseling. Given the extensive empirical research on vocational interests and the proven usefulness of interest inventories, it seems surprising that vocational psychologists have only infrequently attended to definitions of and theories about vocational interests. Because of this relative inattention leading researchers have characterized the literature dealing with the psychology of vocational interests as self-contradictory, confusing, rambling, and formless (Crites, 1969; Darley & Hagenah, 1955; Dawis, 1991; Holland, 1976; Super, 1960). Allport's (1946) comment, written over 50 years ago, remains true today: "One of our greatest defects is our lack of a consistent or adequate theory of interest" (p. 341). Berlyne (1949) observed that although there were some general agreements, "the problem of the definition of interest, let alone that of the psychology of interest, cannot be said to have been solved" (p. 188). The definitions of interest that do appear seem disparate and generally fail to distinguish interest from other motivational constructs. Hypotheses and theories about the origins and development of vocational interests seem riddled with cliches that lack content and cannot be scientifically examined (Holland, 1966). In short, the accumulated literature on vocational interests is more empirical than conceptual, with little connection between linguistic explications and operational definitions.

The disjunction between the definitions provided by conceptual explanations and by empirical measures has slowed progress in theorizing about interest as a psychological construct. Beginning with landmark publications by Bordin (1943) and Carter (1940), even theories of vocational interests have relied on operational definitions of the construct. A half century later, Lent, Brown, and Hackett (1994) continued the tradition of dustbowl empiricism in using an operational rather than a conceptual definition of interest in their self-efficacy theory about the origins and development of career and academic interests. Similar to Strong (1943) and many psychometricians before them, Lent and his colleagues "define vocational interests as patterns of likes, dislikes, and indifferences regarding career-relevant activities and occupations" (p. 88). A conceptual definition of interest that coincides with Bandura's (1997) sociocognitive theory might more completely illuminate relationships between interests and self-efficacy perceptions. Furthermore, using conceptual definitions when constructing interest inventories and theories would link research on vocational interests to mainstream psychology, a link that is still missing 20 years after Holland (1976) criticized vocational psychology for being unable "to draw on the strength of personality and learning theory and vice versa" (p. 523).

Linking conceptual definitions to hypotheses about the origins and development of vocational interests could also enhance practice. For example, this link might improve inventory construction. It also could prompt innovation in career counseling designed to help clients explore their vocational interests. Currently counselors who address the role of vocational interests in their clients' career development seem to rely excessively on interest inventory interpretation as the paramount intervention. Highlighting the role of interests in personality integration, identify formation, and social adjustment might encourage counselors to examine more closely the subjective meaning of interests in a client's life story (Savickas, 1995).

This chapter reviews the literature that addresses conceptual definitions of interest and theories about the origin and development of interests. In so doing, it seeks to elucidate the meaning of interest as a psychological state and to describe theories of vocational interests as a personality trait. The chapter begins with a section that examines the etymology and technical definitions of the word *interest*. The next section deals with interest as a state, and the third section concentrates on interests as a trait. The fourth and final section addresses the determinants of interests by discussing theories about the origins and development of vocational interests as a personality disposition. A brief conclusion attempts to describe succinctly interest, interests, and their determinants. Now let us begin with the etymology of the word *interest.*

DEFINITIONS OF INTEREST

In Latin, *inter est* is the third person, singular, present indicative of *inter sum* which literally means "to be between." In the English language the word *interest* signifies *between, attend,* and *difference* (Onions, 1966). The most basic meanings of *interest* denote intervening between two things. According to the *Oxford Latin Dictionary* (Glare, 1982) the variable that intervenes can be either *space* (i.e., to lie between) or *time* (i.e., to lapse between). Other meanings revolve around *attention:* "to be present as an onlooker"; "to attend as a participant"; and "to be a member of a group." The last set of definitions pertain to *difference:* "there is a difference" and "to be different"; "to make a difference"; and "to be of advantage." Integrating these etymological meanings into a general statement, one could conclude that interest occurs when, in the belief that it will be advantageous to the self, individuals attend to an environmental object and thereby narrow the distance between themselves and that object.

This general definition based on etymology resembles definitions that appear in specialty dictionaries. For example, *A Comprehensive Dictionary of Psychological and Psychoanalytic Terms* (English & English, 1958, p. 271) defines interest as "an attitude or feeling that an object or event makes a difference or is of concern to oneself; a striving to be fully aware of the character of an object." The *Dictionary of Behavioral Science* (Wolman, 1973, p. 199) defines interest as "an enduring attitude consisting of the feeling that a certain object or activity is significant and accompanied by selective attention to that object or activity." Both dictionaries state that interest is required for learning. Essentially these definitions make two claims about the state of being interested: First, interest involves an attitude or pleasurable feeling that evaluates something as beneficial to the self; and second, interest causes one to attend to that object.

In contrast to psychologists, who emphasize attention and feeling, sociologists emphasize potential benefits in their definitions of interest. For example, the *Encyclopaedia of the Social Sciences* (Seligman, 1937, vol. 4) defined interest as "what people actually seek." Similarly the *HarperCollins Dictionary of Sociology* (Jary & Jary, 1991, p. 245) defined interest as "the particular outcomes held to benefit a particular individual or group." For Karl Marx, interest meant economic and political rights and privileges (Barber, 1957). Awareness of these interests is a central component in Marx's concept of "class consciousness," that is, consciousness of the common interests shared by members of a social class. In contrast, American sociologists, such as Small (1905, pp. 197–198), introduced the concept of interest into sociology mainly as a means by which to derive social phenomenon from individual psychological states. For example, MacIver (1937) built a comprehensive theory of society and social relationships on the foundation of interests. He proposed that the psychological construct of interest logically precedes social relationships, associations, and institutions. Defining interests as "objects of consciousness," MacIver designated them as "anything, material or immaterial, factual or conceptual, to which we devote our attention" (p. 12).

The sociologist's orientation toward interest is shared by practitioners of career counseling, who encourage clients to consider interests as a guide in life planning. For example, the definition offered in the glossary of guidance terms by the National Vocational Guidance Association (now the National Career Development Association) (Sears, 1982) concentrates on the use of interests: "Indications of what an individual wants to do and/or reflections of what he/she considers satisfying" (p. 140). Obviously this utilitarian definition ignores the psychological state of being interested and views an individual's interest as a link to society's occupations.

Conceptual definitions of interest, such as those that appear in technical dictionaries, provide a context for examining definitions constructed by vocational psychologists who have studied interest empirically. Certainly the central figure in this literature, and author of the most influential definition of interest, continues to be E. K. Strong. In 1955 Strong essentially accepted the definition of interest in Webster's dictionary: "a propensity to attend to and be stirred by a certain object." Strong extended this definition of interest to include four qualitative attributes. The first two qualities that Strong attributed to interest were persistent *attention* and a *feeling* of liking for an object. The third quality Strong called *direction* because liking steers a person toward an object and dislike steers a person away. Strong's fourth attribute of interest was *activity*, in that an interested person does something regarding the object.

In addition to characterizing interest with these four qualitative features, Strong identified two quantitative attributes of interests, which he called *intensity* and *duration*. According to Strong, "Intensity pertains to preference for one activity rather than another" (p. 138), while duration refers to the interval of time in which overt behavior occurs. Strong (1955) concluded his explication of interest attributes with the following definition:

> Interests are then activities for which we have liking or disliking and which we go toward or away from, or concerning which we at least continue or discontinue the status quo; furthermore, they may or may not be preferred to other interests and they may continue over varying intervals of time. Or an interest may be defined as a liking/disliking state of mind accompanying the doing of an activity, or the thought of performing the activity. (p. 138)

A second influential definition, proposed by Super, addressed the origin and development of interests as a personality trait or disposition. In an encyclopedic book on *Appraising Vocational Fitness by Means of Psychological Tests,* Super (1949) attributed the origin of vocational interests to four sources: heredity, environment, ability, and personality.

> Interests are the product of interaction between inherited aptitudes and endocrine factors, on the one hand, and opportunity and social evaluation on the other. Some of the things a person does well bring him [or her] the satisfaction of mastery or the approval of his [or her] companions, and result in interests. Some of the things his [or her] associates do appeal to him [or her] and, through identification, he [or she] patterns his [or her] actions and his [or her] interests after them; if he [or she] fits the pattern reasonably well he [or she] remains in it, but if not, he [or she] must seek another identification and develop another self-concept and interest pattern. (Super, 1949, p. 406)

In this chapter I use Strong's definition of interest and Super's explanation of interests to examine systematically the meaning, origin, and development of vocational interests. The next major section of the chapter closely examines the qualitative attributes in Strong's definition of a specific interest, whereas the subsequent major section scrutinizes the quantitative attributes that characterize a general group of interests.

ELEMENTS OF INTEREST

The four qualitative attributes that Strong used to characterize interest implicitly summarize the contributions of four major systems of psychology that were prominent early in this century: associationism, structuralism, purposivism, and functionalism. The associationist system of psychology emphasized cognition, the structuralist system emphasized affection, the purposivist system emphasized conation, and the functionalist system emphasized action (Woodworth, 1964). The following four parts in this section of the chapter each examine one qualitative feature of interest by describing the views advanced by the system of psychology that emphasized that feature, beginning with associationism.

The Associationist View: Interest Focuses Attention

Fundamentally interest denotes awareness of and attention to some environmental person, object, or activity. In the first psychological theory about interest, Johann Friedrich Herbart (1891, p. 167) defined interest as an attitude of the mind—a noticing with attention. Without awareness and attention to something, there can be no interest. Accordingly, perceptual psychologists such as Combs and Snygg (1959, p. 168) asserted that interest helps to organize the perceptual field. High interest narrows the perceptual field, whereas indifference widens the field. Kitson (1925, p. 25) emphasized a narrow perceptual field when he defined interest as "being engaged, engrossed, or entirely taken up with some activity because of its recognized worth." McDougall (1929) believed that "interest determines attention . . . that attention can readily be drawn to it and, when so drawn, will usually be sustained and keen, or as we say, concentrated" (p. 274). Roe and Lunneborg (1990, p. 75) emphasized that the attention associated with interest must be automatic or effortless. This assertion harkens back to Herbart's (1891) contention that things that arouse nonvoluntary attention are interesting, whereas things that require attention through voluntary effort are uninteresting.

In his influential theory of education called the doctrine of interests, Herbart (1891) defined interest as a reaction of knowledge that determines the object of attention. The knowledge, which reacts to environmental objects, already exists in the mind, which Herbart called an "apperceptive mass" of former experience organized in groups of related ideas. Herbart identified six of these groups: empirical, speculative, aesthetic, sympathetic, social, and religious. These six interests have been wrongly called "interests" by orthodox Herbartian psychologists, who viewed interest as a mental state and claimed that "the latent group of ideas bearing on any topic constitute an interest in the sense of a permanent disposition of the mind" (Herbermann, Pace, Pallen, Shahan, & Wynne, 1913, p. 75). The true essence of interest, according to Herbart, is the assimilation of a new idea by a predominant ideational group in the mind. When an individual notices an object, the perception evokes in the mind a particular group of ideas that rise above the threshold of consciousness to embrace the new idea. Interest develops, according to Herbart, "when already strong and vivid ideas are hospitable towards new ones since pleasant feeling arise from the association of old and new ideas. Noteworthy past associations motivate apperception of current ones" (Grinder, 1989, p. 8). Assimilation, or the process of apperception, works best when the new idea is partially familiar; foreign or isolated perceptions are difficult to incorporate because the apperceptive mass contains no preexisting group of ideas to welcome the new perception. Herbart's conception of the actual state of being interested involves a basic meaning of interest as an interval of time: "Interest entails a consciousness accompanying attention which persists during the interval between first observation of the new percept and final attainment of the object" (Herbermann et al., 1913, p. 76).

Using the core constructs of interest and association, Herbart's theory stated that education starts with an appeal to students' present interests and then tries to broaden those interests by associating new and varied interests. Herbart's theory prompted educators and psychologists to reconsider their belief that interests were innate; gradually they began to view interest as learned. Herbart's enduring educational doctrine probably explains why dictionaries of psychological terms explicitly state that interest is essential to learning and why interest traditionally has been a central topic in the psychology of learning (Dewey, 1913; Thorndike, 1935a & b). In fact, Herbartian psychology propelled American educators to found in 1895 the National Herbart Society for the Scientific Study of Education (changed in 1902 to the National Society for the Scientific Study of Education).

In her classic book on *Emotion and Personality,* Magda Arnold (1960) also accentuated the relation of interest to curiosity by defining interest as an impulse to know that centers around an object. Arnold believed that "the first movement of the desire to know seems to be attention" (1960, p. 201). She emphasized that an interest is to want to know, not to have or possess. Interest seems to diminish with possession in that an unfinished task is more interesting than a finished one, and a new acquaintance is more interesting than an old friend. Theorists of aesthetics use this concept to assert that works of art, music, and literature best maintain interest when they balance the familiar and novel.

The Structuralist View: Interest Arouses Feeling

Strong's (1955) second qualitative feature of interest describes a feeling, in particular a simple sensation of pleasantness. Several theorists have chosen to emphasize this attribute of interest. For example, Gardner Murphy (1948) explained this conception succinctly when he defined interest as "the attitude with which one attends to anything; the feeling accompanying attention" (p. 989). In the same vein Super and Dunlap (1951) defined interest as the things to which an individual "responds with a feeling of pleasure" (p. 100).

Whether feeling accompanies, causes, or is identical to attention was hotly debated around the turn of the century (Arnold, 1906a; Hebermann et al., 1913). We have already learned that Herbart's associationist theory, although fundamentally identifying interest with the attention, also asserted that a pleasant feeling accompanies this attention (Herbermann et al., 1913, p. 76). Thus orthodox Herbartians viewed interest as a state of consciousness that included an attentive state and an affective feeling. Apparently one of the first writers to challenge this view was John Stuart Mill (1869) who, in arguing that interest is a pleasurable or painful feeling that fixes attention of the mind, depicted interest as a feeling antecedent to attention. Stumpf (1883) articulated the third view, that "attention is identical with interest, and interest is a feeling" (p. 68). The debate about the exact relation of attention and feeling within interest slowly dissipated, and a group of prominent psychologists advanced the ideas that interest is a feeling. The system of psychology most associated with the affective perspective on interest is structuralism.

Adherents to the structuralist system of psychology emphasized the idea that interest is consciousness of a pleasant feeling. Structuralists agreed with associationist psychologists in defining interest as a complex thought with an element of feeling. However, by focusing almost exclusively on the feeling component of interest, structuralists differed from associationists, who emphasized the cognitive aspect of interest. For example, Titchener (1898), a structuralist who defined psychology as the science of consciousness, viewed interest as the feeling that accompanies the state of attention.

Structuralists (now called existentialists) used introspection to study the experience of interest as the feeling accompanying attention. Unfortunately, they concluded that it was extremely difficult to study interest with their method of experimental introspection because their research participants seemed unable to describe their feelings accurately. When their participants tried to attend to the state of being interested, interest itself evaporated. Titchener (1899) described this difficulty, using the following example: "If we wish to get pleasure from a beautiful picture, we must attend to the picture: if, with our eyes on it, we try to attend to our feelings, the pleasantness of the experience is gone" (p. 108). Titchener and other structuralists, however, were able to use indirect methods to characterize interest with three attributes: quality (i.e., pleasant or unpleasant), intensity, and duration. Furthermore, Titchener (1899) differentiated interest from sensation by explaining that blue is in the sky, yet the pleasant feeling about blue is in the individual: "Pleasantness is always within oneself . . . Sensations are the objective and the affections the subjective mental elements" (pp. 103–104).

This structuralist conclusion still merits consideration today because inventories and counselors typically designate an interest using the names of the stimulating objects and activities that engage attention, not the person's experience of or motivation for attending. For example, Fryer (1931, p. 15) wrote that "interests are the objects and activities that stimulate pleasant feeling in the individual." At the same time, Fryer warned counselors that this perspective on interest as an object of attention directs counselors' concentration away from the human drama and philosophy of life that prompt a person to be interested in certain stimulating objects and activities. Fryer implored researchers to examine interest as a subject of experience as well as an object of attention. Unfortunately, most researchers ignored Fryer's sage advice as they experimentally studied interest with inventories.

To this point we have seen that in the early work on interest, associationists and structuralists concentrated on attention and feeling. Later work on interest, conducted by purposivists and functionalists, concentrated on purposeful behavior. Functionalists emphasized behavioral aspects of interest, whereas purposivists emphasized conative or directional aspects.

The Purposivist View: Interest Steers a Direction

The third qualitative element in Strong's (1955) definition of interest involves steering a direction toward or away from an object. Recall that Strong referred to the simple sensation or feeling of interest as *pleasantness*. He preferred to use *liking* when referring to an individual's evaluation of an object. A response of liking connotes appetition or conation, the forte of the purposivist system of psychology.

Adherents to the purposivist system of psychology conceptualized purpose as a molar fact composed of desire and foresight. To exemplify what they meant by a molar fact, they compared purpose to water. Although composed of hydrogen and oxygen, water is a fact in itself. Similarly interest includes attention and feeling, yet, like water, interest is a fact in itself. Gordon Allport (1946) drew this same conclusion when he resolved that interests may be functionally irreducible. Purposivists defined the molar fact of interest, in motivational terms, as an inclination or wish.

Among the first purposivists was Stumpf (1883) who, as noted previously, argued that "attention is identical with interest, and interest is a feeling. That is all there is to it" (p. 68). But later, in response to his critics, Stumpf revised his theory to state that attention and interest are both forms of will. Stumpf (1890) conceived of interest as "attention-exciting" and a feeling of desire that "can pass into a volition as soon as the object seems probable and attainable" (p. 283). George Frederick Stout (1896, p. 166), another prominent purposivist, also equated interest with conation in arguing that interest is a conative tendency.

Probably the first purposivist to formulate a comprehensive psychology of interest as a conative state of liking was Felix Arnold (1906b), who viewed interest as a striving toward an anticipated gratification. Because he viewed striving toward a future state of pleasure as the essence of interest, Arnold (1906b) contended that associationists and structuralists incorrectly identified interest with cognitive meaning or felt worth. Arnold preferred to view attention and pleasant feeling as concomitants of interest. He explained that attention is a process of control and adjustment over a situation. Attention narrows and illuminates the perceptual field, resulting in a state of increased clearness and distinctiveness of an object. Attention is thus concomitant with, yet different from, interest. Similarly Arnold (1906b) distinguished interest from pleasant feeling in asserting that interest is not exactly a feeling of pleasure, rather "interest is potential pleasure in that it may so end" (p. 292). Thus pleasure may be the starting point for interest, but it is not interest as such. If an object pleases yet carries no future reference, there is pleasure but not interest. According to Arnold, "Any situation involving interest is thus seen as to be connected with the future of the self concerned" (p. 295). Because of his belief that interest points a direction ahead into the future, Arnold criticized Herbartian associationists for viewing interest as a system of ideas rooted in the past. He disparaged Herbart's view of interest as a "mere tickling of the sensations for the purpose of rousing attention" (p. 315).

Arnold went to great lengths to distinguish interest from other forms of striving. He differentiated expectation from interest by arguing that expectation involves only a passive waiting for a future pleasure. In contrast, desire involves an active struggle to remove barriers to future pleasure. He called curiosity a "tentative interest" about how something might influence future pleasure. Interest itself, more fully than curiosity, understands how an object will influence future pleasure. Interest incites repeated striving, but with fuller knowledge the striving of curiosity ceases. In the end Arnold defined interest as a "felt bodily attitude, tending serially to realize a future situation" (p. 305). Such interest is typically accompanied by a cognitive representation of the situation to be realized and by feelings of anticipation.

William McDougall, a prominent advocate of purposive psychology, formulated another conative theory of interest, in part to advance the theorizing of Stout. McDougall (1908), objecting to Titchener's narrow view of psychology as the science of consciousness, was the first to proclaim psychology as the science of conduct or behavior. McDougall argued that behavior strives to an end and the individual understands this striving as purpose.

McDougall (1929) denounced Herbart's (1891) theory of interest as an intellectualist doctrine. He objected to Herbart's claim that interest in any object depends on the possession of appropriate knowledge ("apperceptive mass") related to the object. McDougall preferred to link interest to striving rather than to knowing: "Interest is conative rather than cognitive; it depends upon the strength of the conative tendencies excited, rather than upon the extent and variety and systematic organization of the cognitive systems of the mind" (p. 277). McDougall elaborated this distinction as follows:

> Interest, being essentially conative, is a matter of enduring settings of our conative tendencies or impulses, and is therefore determined by our instincts or sentiments. Knowledge about an object is not in itself a condition of "interest"; though such knowledge favors the sustaining of attention; without such knowledge our attention to any object, determined by conative interests, soon wanes; because we quickly exhaust upon it our limited powers of discriminative perception. (p. 276)

Like Arnold (1906a) before him, McDougall acknowledged a relation of attention and feeling to interest. Rather than just calling cognition and emotion concomitants of interest, McDougall hypothesized a temporal order starting with cognitive awareness of an object. The sequence of interest, McDougall believed, starts with attention because "to have an 'interest' in any object is then to be ready to pay attention to it. Interest is latent attention; and attention is interest in action" (p. 277). Thinking about the stimulating object then evokes some conative striving toward the object. In turn, this striving produces a pleasant feeling. In short, McDougall viewed interest as a knowing-striving-feeling cycle.

Vocational psychologists adopted the view of interest as conation in constructing interest inventories that operationally defined interest as a "response of liking" to an object or activity presented as an inventory item (Strong, 1943, p. 6; Super & Dunlap, 1951, p. 100). For example, Fryer (1930) proposed an "acceptance-rejection theory of interest." Fryer's theory stated that interest inventory items (typically objects, people, and activities) are stimuli that cause feelings of attraction or aversion, which are indicated by the direction and strength of the response to the item. Fryer defined interest as a response of acceptance that guides movement toward an exciting stimulus, and aversion as a response of rejection that guides movement away from the exciting stimulus. He viewed acceptance and rejection, the determinants of direction, as qualitative aspects of interest. The quantitative element of interest, according to Fryer (1931, p. 352), involves the degree of acceptance or strength of response. He argued that, once initiated, interest provides its own quantitative energy or motivational drive in proportion to the strength of acceptance.

Strong (1943) also characterized his own view as an acceptance-rejection theory of interest. Strong explained his theory by stating that acceptance incorporates two dimensions: the simple sensation of pleasantness and the conative liking for an object. For Strong (1943) this acceptance or interest guides purposive behavior because the "essence of such behavior is rejecting the wrong and selecting the right" (p. 8). Other prominent interest researchers have underscored the directional element in interest. For example, Paterson and Darley (1936, p. 119) defined interest as "tendencies toward certain forms of activity or toward certain types of contact with people." For Allport (1961, p. 237) interest acts "as a silent agent for selecting and directing whatever is related to that interest." Todt and his colleagues (Todt, Drewes, & Heils, 1994; Todt & Schreiber, 1996) concurred in defining interests as "activating and steering motives (dispositions), which appear generalized as structures of orientation and which appear in a specified manner as preferences of activities" (p. 2).

Tyler (1964) chastised counselors who fail to understand that interest inventories measure the direction of interests, not their strength. She concluded that counselors' most common error in interest inventory interpretation is thinking that the scores indicate "how much" interest a client possesses, when in fact the scores only indicate "what kind" of interests a client possesses. Tyler (1964) urged counselors to remember that interest inventories measure "concepts like direction, pattern of choices, or program for life" (p. 187). She concluded that "At present we have no technique except behavior observation for assessing how strong a person's drive is in the direction in which he [or she] wishes to go" (p. 186).

Because liking is an important element in interest, it bears noting that liking by itself does not constitute an interest. Magda Arnold (1960, p. 200) explained that liking in itself is a sentiment (cf. McDougall, 1929)—that is, a single basic emotional reaction that endures and develops. As examples of sentiments Arnold cited love of home, family, or country. Individuals react emotionally and overtly when presented with these objects. When one experiences a sentiment, that sentiment grows. For example, liking something about one's family makes one love the family more. Arnold contrasted sentiment and interest in stating that sentiment propels one to possess an object, whereas interest propels one to seek to know about it. In fact, possession seems to diminish interest in an object.

The Functionalist View: Interest Involves Activity

Although sharing the purposivists' concern with conation or behavioral tendencies, adherents to the functionalist system of psychology went even further in concentrating on action itself, particularly the function of behavior. Functionalists sought to transform American psychology into the science of how the mind functions—that is, adapts to the environment. While purposivists focused on "why," functionalists focused on "what for" and "how." For example, a prominent European functionalist, Claparede (1930) asked rhetorically, "What is the use of behavior?" and then answered that behavior functions to meet the individual's needs and interests (p. 79). Personologists, such as Allport (1961), also asserted that acting interested involves engagement in a "culturally elaborated activity" (p. 225) and involves "participation with the deepest level of motivation" (p. 107).

Dewey, one of the founders of American functionalist psychology, concentrated much of his early work on the topic of interest. At the 1896 annual meeting of the Herbart Society, Dewey attacked Titchener's science of consciousness. He objected to the introspectivist study of interest as a static, cross-section of momentary excitation. For Dewey (1913), "to be interested in any matter is to be actively concerned with it. Mere feeling regarding a subject may be static or inert, but interest is dynamic" (p. 16). Dewey bolstered his argument by complaining that structuralists studied (a) how to catch attention rather than how to hold attention and (b) how objects arouse energy rather than the "course that energy takes, the results that it effects" (p. 91). As an alternative to introspective analysis of elements of consciousness, Dewey (1896) proposed that the minimal unit of analysis for psychology should be the "reflex arc," meaning a stimulus *and* response and the function they serve. Titchener responded to Dewey's critique by arguing that structuralists studied "is" whereas functionalists studied "is for" (Grinder, 1989, p. 10).

Dewey's attack on structuralism was published as a supplement to the first yearbook of the Herbart Society, *Interest in Relation to Training of the Will* (1903). Eventually Dewey (1913) expanded the monograph into a book, *Interest and*

Effort in Education, which also addressed the controversy between Herbartian psychologists, who advocated using interest to motivate students, and William T. Harris and his followers, who advocated using effort to build students' character. Dewey rejected both claims in concluding that interest leads to effort. Dewey argued that interest signals a first step in ongoing experience, whereas effort brings about the conclusion. Later in the book Dewey criticized Herbartian psychologists for viewing interest as passively arising from the association of ideas. As a functionalist, Dewey (1913) viewed "interest as an activity that moves toward an end" (p. 92). Thus Dewey believed that individuals "take interest" (p. 16) in objects and activities not because they are intrinsically interesting but because they are instrumental in achieving a purpose. Accordingly, the best way to understand an individual's interest is to focus on the function it serves, not on the interest itself.

From analyses based on his reflex arc paradigm, Dewey (1913) concluded that interest signifies an "organic union" among the person, the materials, and the results of action (p. 17). This union means that the individual identifies self with a certain course of action (p. 43). Dewey (1913) wrote that interest marks "an identification in action, and hence in desire, effort, and thought, of self with objects; namely, with the objects in which the activity terminates (ends) and with the objects by which it is carried forward to its end (means)" (p. 90). In the same book Dewey wrote that the "genuine principle of interest is the condition of identification, that is, the identity through action of the growing self with some object or idea" (p. 7).

The emphasis on interest as functional activity was particularly strong at Columbia University, where Dewey taught. For example, at Teachers College, Columbia University, both Thorndike and Kitson championed the functionalist view of interest. Thorndike (1935b) noted that interest as an "active force works forward to evolve, then and there, behavior which the animal would not have displayed except for the presence of the acting want" (pp. 4–5). Kitson (1925) subscribed to Dewey's view of interest as action in resolving that being interested in something "is to endeavor to identify oneself with it" (p. 142). Kitson asserted that interest should be viewed neither as an entity within an individual nor as a thing to catalogue. He propounded the view that interest denotes activity and recommended avoiding use of the noun *interest,* preferring instead the verb form *to be interested.* Kitson (1925) linked the activity dimension of interest to cultivating new interests. To help clients adopt a new interest Kitson advised counselors to "give information and arouse activity" (p. 27). Information about an object can create attention, yet arousing interest is to arouse activity toward the object. Strong (1943) seemed to agree with Kitson's enjoinment about interest as an activity: "Interest is an aspect of behavior, not an entity itself" (p. 8). Or as Strong (1955) explained, the interested person does something to or with an object. Nevertheless, Strong (1943) defended the use of nouns, the names of things, as interest inventory items because "an activity toward or with the object is assumed" (p. 7). And activity, or doing something regarding the object, was the fourth and final qualitative attribute in Strong's (1955) characterization of interest.

Whether or not Strong did so intentionally, his description of four qualitative attributes of the state of being interested succinctly summarized the contributions of four major systems of American psychology that were prominent in the first third of the century: associationism, structuralism, purposivism, and functionalism. In short, these systems of psychology taught us that interest focuses attention, arouses feeling, steers a direction, and involves activity.

INTEREST CAN BECOME INTERESTS

To this point we have scrutinized interest as a psychological construct by examining four qualitative attributes that characterize interest. As a psychological state, interest describes an individual's *position* in relation to a single, specific object or activity. In contrast, a homogeneous group of specific interests constitutes a *disposition*, that is, "a relatively stable and consistent attitude" (Wolman, 1973, p. 103). An interest disposition, or dispositional response tendency, denotes a trait that is "consistent, persistent, and stable . . . and determines to a great extent which stimuli will be perceived (selective perception) and what kind of response will be given selective action" (Wolman, 1973, p. 389). Interests, being plural, are characterized by quantitative attributes. The shift from a singular interest to plural interests involves a move from verb to noun, from state to trait, from percept to concept, and from awareness to self-awareness. Following this logic, interests are characterized by quantitative attributes such as frequency, persistence, habit strength, and intensity.

Interests Recur

Obviously the word *interests* denotes more than a single interest. Consider as an example five states of being interested that Mary Ann experienced last Sunday: She liked changing spark plugs in her car, enjoyed repairing the lawn mower, renewed her subscription to *Road and Track* magazine because she enjoys reading it, thought that a poem she read was inspiring, and had fun fishing at the pond. An observer such as a parent or career counselor might categorize Mary Ann's specific "likes" as follows: mechanics (3), reading (2), and nature (1). The observer might conclude that Mary Ann frequently initiated mechanical interests or that her mechanical interests recur.

Interests Endure

The counselor might do more than just count the frequency of Mary Ann's five interests. She might determine the interval of time Mary Ann spent at each of the five activities. Not only do interests recur, they endure in the sense that individuals tend to extend or continue activities that absorb their attention. This continuation of interests conveys the meaning of duration, one of Strong's (1955) two quantitative elements of interests. Strong's use of the word *duration* coincides well with *interval*, which is a root meaning of the Latin *inter sum*. Allport (1961) addressed duration when he referred to interests as "tension maintained" (p. 223) and defined interest as "a lasting tensional condition" (p. 237). Walter VanDyke Bingham (1937) also emphasized duration when he characterized the behavioral manifestation of interests as persistence at an activity. Bingham asserted that interest prolongs an activity because it yields satisfaction. He emphasized that interests relate to initiation of and persistence in an activity, not successful performance of that activity.

Interests Show Habit Strength

The strength of interests can be measured by the frequency and duration of the habitual response. Habit strength of interests can also be operationally defined by the degree of stimulation required to activate them, as in tachistoscope studies of interests (see Bellido, 1922; Crites, this volume). However, absolute strength, as a quantitative aspect of general interests, has typically been ignored in favor of relative strength of interests. Strong (1955) considered the relative strength of interests, which he called intensity, as the second quantitative attribute of interests.

Interests Compete with Each Other

The intensity of interests is typically addressed in terms of competing interests— that is, ipsatively rather than normatively. A general interest coexists with many other general interests as part of an individual's personality pattern. As a group, general interests can be viewed as "possibility-processing structures" through which prospects may be screened (Tyler, 1978). Thus individuals use their hierarchy of interests to process and choose which of many possible selves to actualize. In so doing, individuals reveal the relative strength or intensity of their interests in "preference for one activity rather than another" (Strong, 1955, p. 138). For example, a sports enthusiast might choose to watch a televised tennis match rather than a football game.

Counselors typically assess the intensity of a general interest (i.e., an interest disposition) in comparison to other similar traits, not as an isolated trait. The rank of a general interest in a hierarchy of general interests indicates its intensity or relative strength. Intensity or relative strength, not habit strength, is shown by interest inventory profiles. Recall that Tyler (1964, p. 186) chastised counselors for mistaking interest inventories as measures of interest strength. In our language herein, this basic mistake involves interpreting profile level as a measure of habit strength. Profile level should be ignored and attention concentrated on profile shape, which does show intensity. Recently Prediger (1998) has empirically shown that, for homogeneous scales, profile level does not indicate strength of interests. Predictions made from profile shape (relative strength of interest) alone are not improved by adding data about profile level (see Gottfredson & Jones, 1993). Prediger hypothesized that profile level reflects the response style of "yea saying versus nea saying," not the strength of interests.

Interests Are Scale Scores

Recall that Strong (1943) operationally defined an interest as a response of liking to an inventory item. Accordingly, interest inventory items each measure a specific interest. Summing these responses produces scores for homogeneous scales, scores that represent general interests as a disposition or trait. Inventories refer to these general interests by distinctive yet similar names. For example, Mary Ann's interests might result in high scores on the Outdoor and Mechanical scales in the *Kuder* (Kuder & Zytowski, 1991), the Realistic scale in the *Self-Directed Search* (Holland, Powell, & Fristsche, 1994), and the Nature, Agriculture, and Mechanical Activities scales in the *Strong Interest Inventory* (Harmon, Hansen, Borgen, & Hammer, 1994).

The empirical scales in interest inventories such as the *Strong* and the *Kuder*, composed of heterogeneous items, depict neither specific interest nor general interests. Instead, these scores indicate similarity or degree of fit between an individual's interest pattern and the interest patterns empirically identified for selected occupational groups such as engineers and psychologists. For example, a score on the Lawyer scale of the *Strong Interest Inventory* indicates how well a client's pattern of choices resembles the choice pattern that characterizes lawyers. Tyler emphasized that an individual's occupational scores on the *Strong* reflect his or her pattern of dislikes or rejections as well as likes. Tyler (1964) considered this to be crucial because these options show "the process by which patterned interests are shaped" (p. 187). Tyler disliked homogeneous interest scales because, in summing like responses while ignoring indifferent and dislike responses, basic interest scales do not reveal an individual's unique life pattern. For Tyler, dislikes are as important as likes in understanding a person, because rejections are important factors in shaping individuality. Tyler preferred interest inventories such as the *Strong* and the *Kuder* because they use "Like," "Dislike," and "Indifferent" responses in their scoring keys. According to Tyler, scores on these empirical scales provide a "representation of the ways in which the individual has dealt with possibilities in the past as they arose. This is a concept difficult to incorporate into trait psychology that has dominated the study of individual differences" (p. 146).

Despite Tyler's criticism, there are important advantages to homogeneous content scales scored only for like responses. Campbell, Borgen, Eastes, Johansson, and Peterson (1968, p. 1) asked rhetorically, "What does it mean to have interests similar to lawyers?" General interest scales address this question because they reflect clusters of related interests and clearly specify the pattern of work activities that an individual likes. Day and Rounds (1997) argued persuasively that because homogeneous scales actually measure interests as dispositional traits, these scales should play a central role in career counseling. Rationally constructed, homogeneous interest scales should be interpreted to heighten a client's self-awareness of general interests; empirical scales can be interpreted to identify occupations that fit a client's interest pattern.

Interests Symbolize the Self

To illustrate how interests become incorporated into self-concepts, let us return briefly to Mary Ann and her mechanical interests. Clearly the two most obvious quantitative elements of Mary Ann's interests are frequency and duration. The number of specific interest(s) that form her "mechanical interests" and the amount of time that she engages in them, taken together, constitute a pattern of response to environmental stimuli. Once Mary Ann recognizes, either by herself or with the aid of an interest inventory interpretation by a counselor, her pattern of responding positively to and persisting at activities involving mechanics, she must choose whether or not to label herself as having "mechanical interests." Choice plays a role in forming general interests because self-conscious pattern recognition requires effort and application. Through self-conscious, recursive thinking Mary Ann actually must choose or refuse to construct a mental representation of herself as having mechanical interests. She may readily add this to her existing self-concepts or resist identifying with stereotypical masculine interests (see Gottfredson, 1996). If Mary Ann adds this self-concept, then her self-representation of a general response tendency incorporates her pattern of mechanical interests into her psychosocial and vocational identity.

The symbolic representation of an interest disposition through language plays a significant role in (a) identifying the pattern, (b) creating self-knowledge, (c) stabilizing the disposition, and (d) possibly deepening and broadening the disposition. Andras Angyal (1941), who like Allport viewed interest as a tension maintained, called interests "symbolic elaborations" of tensional states. He explained that an interest disposition, or interests, is a representative grasp of things: "Interests show the role the object plays in our personality process" (Angyal, 1941, p. 126). Darley and Hagenah (1955, p. 191) implied that interests involve a linguistic encoding that reflect an individual's values and needs "in the vocabulary of the world of work." Gardner Murphy (1948) added to this view when he speculated that the continuity or permanence of interests relates to their verbal symbolization, which provides inner linguistic cues for behavior.

In this section of the chapter we have concluded that general interests recur and endure as well as differ in habit strength and in relative strength or intensity. Also counselors operationally define general interests with scale scores, and individuals may linguistically encode general interests as part of their self-concept systems and psychosocial identities. In the next section we examine conceptions about how these interest dispositions originate and develop.

THEORIES OF VOCATIONAL INTERESTS

The prior two sections of this chapter concentrated on specific interest as a psychological state and general interests as a personality disposition or trait. In this section we consider theories that explain the origin and development of vocational interests as a personality disposition. Recall, from earlier in this chapter, that Super (1949) attributed the origins of vocational interests to four sources:

heredity, learning, ability, and personality. We will examine each of these components in turn, starting with heredity.

Interests Reflect Genetic Influences

Although no author stipulates that genes alone produce interests, many researchers acknowledge that genetic inheritance influences interest development, if in no other way than by placing limits on innate potential. For a review of this literature, and a classic study in itself, consult Betsworth, Bourchard, Cooper, Grotevant, Hansen, Scarr, and Weinberg (1994). From that literature review, and their own empirical study, they concluded that 30% to 50% of variation in vocational interests could be attributed to genetic factors. Linda Gottfredson's chapter in this book offers a comprehensive summary and analysis of current knowledge concerning genetic influences on vocational interests. Accordingly, the topic will not be further elaborated herein.

Interests Are Learned

Super's proposition about learning interests refers to instrumental learning or, as he preferred to call it, experiential learning, rather than Herbart's associative learning. For our purposes herein, experiential learning refers to the principle that people become interested in objects or activities or events for which they have been reinforced. Kitson, Super's mentor, had argued that individuals acquire occupational interests primarily through experience. Kitson (1925) believed that an individual may cultivate many alternative occupational interests, contingent on being "subjected at the proper time to the appropriate stimulations" (p. 21). Strong (1943) agreed with this view and added that an interest emerges following the reward or recognition of abilities when they are successfully used.

   Maslow (1954) traced interest development to need gratification, or "intrinsic requiredness, and the effects of gratification" (p. 117). Roe (1956) advanced this position in her theory about the origin of interests. Patterns of effortless and automatic attention are first determined by how an individual receives satisfaction and frustration. According to Roe, "The modes and degrees of need satisfaction determine which needs will become the strongest motivators. . . . The eventual pattern of psychic energies, in terms of attention-directedness [especially toward or away from people], is the major determinant of interests" (Roe & Lunneborg, 1990, p. 75). Thus parental reinforcement shapes an individual's need pattern as well as conditions preferred interpersonal means for need gratification. The resulting needs and interpersonal deportment then unfold into interests for occupations that promise to satisfy those needs and reward that conduct.

Murphy (1948) explained interests as a symbolic statement summarizing a complex of canalizations and conditioning toward certain objects and activities. By canalization he meant that biological needs become more specific in response to having been satisfied in particular ways. Experience channels general motives into specific motives, especially values. For Murphy, interests reflect connections between inner values and the outer conditioning stimuli of everyday life. Interests, according to Murphy, "are conditioned stimuli pursued because of their relations to goal objects which are valued" (p. 283). Furthermore, interests are dominant conditionings (especially symbolic) because they are overlearned. In comparing interests to values, Murphy suggested that canalization makes values quite stable and difficult to extinguish. In contrast, conditioned interests are quickly extinguished when their relation to a mode of need satisfaction changes. The canalized value, however, remains and seeks another conditioned interest.

Lofquist and Dawis (1969, 1991) also invoked values and conditioning in their instrumental learning theory of interests. Essentially they asserted that interests derive from the interaction of abilities and reinforcement values, two major independent dimensions of personality. Reinforcement value denotes a person's generalized requirements for reinforcers and preference for stimulus conditions that in the past have been reinforcing. Lofquist and Dawis attributed the origin of interests to the combination of learned preferences for activities that individuals have in the past capably executed *and* the reinforcement value in current stimulus conditions. The role of abilities is given even greater prominence in self-efficacy theories of interests.

Interests Result from Self-Perceptions of Abilities

Many of the applied psychologists who first studied ability as a determinant of academic and occupational success also studied interests, often using the same experimental designs. Given the central role of ability testing in applied psychology, it is little wonder that ability was one of the first variables examined in the search for the determinants of interests. For example, Thorndike (1915, p. 394) viewed interests as "an extraordinarily accurate symptom of relative abilities." Like other early theorists, Thorndike believed that individuals become interested in things they do well and for which they have innate ability or aptitude. Apparently Thorndike (1915) conducted the first empirical investigation of the ability-interest relationship. He reported that during the late elementary school period

> The resemblance between interest and ability may safely be placed at about .9 of perfect resemblance. Interests are shown to be symptomatic, to a very great extent, of present and future capacity or ability . . . Interest and ability are bound very closely together. The bond is so close that either may be used as a symptom for the other almost as well as itself. (p. 395)

Critics attacked Thorndike's study because he used subjective ranking methods to estimate abilities. Subsequent studies used objective measures of abilities and typically reported correlations around .25, not .9. For example, Strong (1943) reported that 80% of the correlations between various abilities and scales on the *Strong Vocational Interest Blank* ranged between plus/minus .30, with 97% ranging between plus/minus .40. Darley and Hagenah (1955) elucidated the low correlations between abilities and interests by explaining that people with the same amount of ability differ in their interests and people with the same interests differ in their ability (pp. 58–59).

Today most psychologists agree that ability and interests are independent variables with a small to moderate relationship (Dawis, 1991). The empirical literature suggests that abilities relate to success, whereas interests relate to initiation of, persistence at, and satisfaction with an activity. Despite the empirical evidence, a few scholars have continued to maintain that abilities and interests correlate highly. For example, Allport (1937) wrote, "Psychometric studies have shown that the relation between interest and ability is always positive, often markedly so. A person likes to do what he [or she] can do well" (p. 201). In 1961 Allport again wrote that "ability often turns into interest. It is an established fact that ordinarily people like to do what they can do well (the correlation between abilities and interests is high)" (p. 235). Although Allport's folk wisdom is appealing, Strong's (1943, p. 17) motorboat analogy is more accurate: The motor of abilities determines the boat's speed, whereas the rudder of interests determines the boat's direction.

Currently much attention has focused on subjective estimates of abilities in relation to interests (Prediger, this volume), the approach initiated by Thorndike in 1915. Two pivotal articles in this literature appeared in 1981. After reviewing the literature on the relation of interests to abilities, Barak (1981) concluded that actual abilities do not relate to interests, yet self-estimates or perceptions of abilities do relate to interests. Based on this conclusion, Barak (1981) proposed a cognitive theory that uses four stages to conceptualize the development of interests:

"(a) differential activities and experiences, (b) differential success and satisfaction, (c) mediating cognitions, and (d) differential interests" (p. 10). The important mediators are expected success, anticipated satisfaction, and perceived abilities.

Also in 1981 Hackett and Betz applied Bandura's (1977) self-efficacy theory to the career domain. They proposed that self-efficacy, or skill self-confidence, mediates the processes of career choice and adjustment. In due course Lent, Brown, and Hackett (1994) followed the lead of Barak (1981) and Hackett and Betz (1981) in using the self-efficacy construct to comprehend educational and vocational interests. In their sociocognitive theory of career and academic interest, choice, and performance Lent and his colleagues asserted that people "form enduring interests in activities in which they view themselves to be efficacious and in which they anticipate positive outcomes" (p. 89). This assertion summons to mind Stumpf's (1890, p. 283) proposition that interest turns to volition (or agency, as it is called in self-efficacy theory) when an objective seems probable and attainable. Lent and his colleagues go on to explain that the antecedent perceptions of self-efficacy and outcome likelihood arise from an adolescent's long history of modeling by important figures, vicarious learning, and experiential involvement in diverse activities with different degrees of activity success and differential reinforcement from significant others. Thus, similar to Barak (1981), Lent and his colleagues hypothesized that perceived abilities, expected success, and anticipated satisfaction play a mediating role in the origin of interests.

Interests Arise from Identifications

Although heredity, learning, ability, and personality are probably of equal importance as determinants of interest, theorists have concentrated more research and reflection on the role of personality as a determinant of vocational interests. The literature on personality and interests highlights the constructs of identification, self-concept, and adjustment. First let us consider how the process of identification may shape vocational interests.

As noted in the prior section, self-efficacy theories of interests prominently feature vicarious learning from observing role models. Personality theorists who have considered interest development also conclude that individuals develop interests through identification with role models. During childhood and adolescence individuals select and then observe several role models. At first they imagine themselves acting like their models, merging the self and model in fantasy. Later imagination turns into imitation as individuals strive in reality to behave like their models. This striving leads to role playing of activities and interests, some of which eventually will be selectively integrated into a self-concept.

Kitson (1925) believed that vocational interests involved "identifying of one's self with a vocation" (p. 155). Carter (1940) asserted that individuals identify with groups whom they respect as a means of gaining satisfaction and status. One subjective factor in this adjustment is "satisfaction from the identification of himself [or herself] with some respected group. This identification leads to interest in restricted activities and experiences: to the extent that this is true, the person learns about the vocation and the vocational group" (p. 185). If the person has the ability required to perform these interests, then the interests persist. Super (1963), expressly building upon Carter's contributions, asserted that identification with parents leads to role playing, both imaginative and participative, in which the person tries an interest on for size to determine if it fits his or her own self-concept.

Interests Accommodate Social Roles

Super (1963) focused his own theorizing on how well interests implement a psychological self-concept, especially personal needs and values. Two other theorists have focused their work on how well interests implement a social self-concept, especially pertaining to social role and prestige. From this perspective, interests accommodate social roles, meaning that individuals develop interests that bring them into harmony with society or adapt them to circumstances. Leona Tyler (1951) viewed interests as roles that an individual has accepted. For her, awareness of, and acceptance of, a social role generates likes and dislikes. In a classic article Tyler (1955) supported this assertion in reporting that fourth-grade students generally disliked activities usually associated with the other gender, indicating the influence of social sex roles on interest development.

Linda Gottfredson also concentrated on the role of social adjustment in interest development. Gottfredson's (1996) sociological theory views occupational aspirations as attempts to implement a social self-concept by placing oneself in the broader social order. Accordingly, her theory emphasizes more public variables, such as gender and social class, rather than more private variables, such as needs and values. Gottfredson theorized that individuals use dimensions such as masculinity-femininity, occupational prestige, and fields of work to chart both social space and their own self-concepts. Individuals organize their images of occupations into cognitive maps using these dimensions and then aspire to occupations that correspond to their self-concepts along these same dimensions. In charting a social space within which to locate one's self, individuals rely more on sex-role concerns and perceptions of prestige than they do on interests. Only given an acceptable zone of alternatives relative to gender and prestige do interests emerge as a determinant of occupational aspirations. When compromises must be made, individuals first sacrifice vocational interests, then if forced they sacrifice their place in society, and only as a last resort do they sacrifice their presentation of masculinity or femininity. From this perspective, sex role and prestige shape interest development by circumscribing the range of socially appropriate likes and dislikes.

Interests Are Solutions

Gottfredson's idea that interests reflect an attempt to locate oneself in the social order can be traced back to the work of Carter (1940) and Bordin (1943). These two psychologists advanced the now popular theory that interests, as expressions of personality, represent attempts to adjust oneself to society. Both Holland's idea that interest types reflect adjustive orientations and Super's (1963) idea that occupational choice implements a self-concept manifest this tradition.

Carter and Bordin were concerned, as many counselors are today, that vocational counseling overemphasizes the assessment of clients' interests instead of dialogue about the meaning and implementation of those interests. Carter blamed this situation, in part, on the overreliance on objective interest inventories while ignoring case-history data that provide "subjective or intuitive insights" (Carter, 1940, p. 185) about a client. In an attempt to have clinical insights complement statistical scores Carter advised counselors to view interests as expressions of personality and self-concept.

Carter (1940, p. 185) argued that "in the development of vocational attitudes the young man or woman is attempting a practical adjustment to environmental conditions." They seek to "find experiences which offer some basis for the integration of personality" (Carter, 1940, p. 186). Interests contribute to this integration by developing individuality, identifying the self, organizing activities, maintaining persistence in selected activities, patterning daily life, focusing drives that can be used to make long-range plans, and easing decision making. Thus interests are "solutions to their problems of adjustment" (p. 187). Accordingly, interpretations of interest inventories should attend to personality integration and social adjustment.

Similar to Carter, Bordin (1943) worried that counselors used interest inventory results to predict occupational choice. Bordin also wanted counselors to refocus their attention away from diagnosis and prediction, to concentrate on helping clients implement their motives. As a clinician Bordin recommended using inventory scores to develop insight into a client's motivation: "Deeper insight into the dynamics of interest types should come from the leveling of our research guns at the question of the development of the individual's concept of himself [or herself] as reflected in his [or her] goal-directed strivings and the effects of the barriers he [or she] encounters" (Bordin, 1943, p. 61). Bordin (1943) asserted that vocational interests, as goal-directed strivings, express a self-concept in terms of occupational stereotypes: "In answering a Strong Vocational Interest test an individual is expressing his [or her] acceptance of a particular view or concept of himself [or herself] in terms of occupational stereotypes" (Bordin, 1943, p. 53). Bordin (1943) also proposed the idea that interest inventories are personality inventories because both inventories require individuals to give a picture of themselves.

These classic articles by Carter (1940) and Bordin (1943) advanced the practice of interpreting score patterns on interest inventories for their personality implications. Exemplars of this clinical approach to interest inventory interpretation, still germane today, were published for the *Strong* by Darley (1941) and by Goldberg and Gechman (1976), and for the *Kuder* by Gobetz (1964). Holland (1966), who agreed that interest inventories are personality inventories, advanced the clinical interpretation of interest inventories to its logical conclusion by constructing a personality inventory composed entirely of occupational titles—the *Vocational Preference Inventory* (Holland, 1985).

Interests Express Personality

Viewing interests as personality variables raises the question of how interests fit into the constellation of personality variables that include needs, values, and traits. Unfortunately, as Darley (1943, p. 113) remarked, the complexity of interests, personality, adjustment, and attitudes makes it difficult to distinguish interests from other motivational constructs. A common resolution to this problem is simply to assume that interests develop from personality and then concentrate on how people express their interests in work and leisure roles. As an example of this strategy consider Darley's (1941) assertion that interests are outgrowths of personality development. Later Darley and Hagenah (1955) wrote that "occupational interests reflect, in the vocabulary of the world of work, the value systems, the needs, and the motivations of individuals" (p. 191). To justify not distinguishing among motivational constructs such as needs, values, and interests, some theorists have argued that these diverse motivational constructs are measured by a common pool of inventory items and behavioral events (e.g., Holland, 1976). The strongest empirical evidence supporting this assertion appeared in Thorndike, Weiss, and Dawis (1968), who, based on a canonical analysis of scales in the *Strong Vocational Interest Blank* and *Minnesota Importance Questionnaire* concluded that interests and needs belong to the same class of variables.

Holland (1976) proposed one solution to this problem of discriminating between interests and other motivational constructs when he urged researchers to regard as similar phenomena the concepts of "preferences for, choices of and characteristics of people in or seeking the same or similar occupations" (p. 521). Holland integrated knowledge about vocational interests, career choice, and occupational membership using six dimensions (i.e., RIASEC types). For example, Investigative types possess scientific interests, engage in scientific activities, and prefer scientific occupations. Holland (1976) presented extensive research to document that "the history of a person's vocational interests, choices, and work experiences have continuity and lawfulness rather than disjunctiveness and randomness" (p. 522). Holland's pivotal argument is that all three concepts (i.e., interests, preferences, and experiences) manifest or express a relatively stable, common personal disposition. Holland (1966) thus defined vocational interests as "the expression of personality in work, hobbies, recreational activities, and preferences" (p. 3). He cogently observed that psychologists have constructed personality theories around sexuality (e.g., Freud) or inferiority (e.g., Adler), so they should be able to center a personality theory around vocational life. And this Holland (1997) does masterfully.

Despite the attractiveness of Holland's approach, it is still important to attempt conceptual distinctions, if for no other reason than to explain what interests are not. Thus some researchers do discriminate among needs, values, and interests as separate and distinct domains (e.g., Katz, 1969, 1993; Super, 1973). Unfortunately, those who make such discriminations cannot yet agree about which behaviors distinguish among motivation variables. For example, after decades of research and reflection scholars still disagree about the relation of interests to needs and values. What follows is a brief survey of diverse conceptions about how interests relate to other motivational variables, particularly needs and values.

Needs. Several personality and vocational theorists assert, without much explication, that interests result from needs, lacks, or deficits. For example, Kitson (1925) maintained that "vocational choice offers opportunity for escape from inferiorities. . . . It is a matter of common observation that a lack of some sort acts as a spur to effort" (p. 153). Maslow (1954) asserted that interests arise from need gratification, or the "intrinsic requiredness, and the effects of gratification" (p. 117). Combs and Snygg (1959) believed that "we are interested in what serves to satisfy a need" (p. 111). Allport (1961, p. 225) defined interests as culturally learned ways of satisfying a drive, a contention similar to Murphy's view of interests as learned canalizations and conditionings. To illustrate his point Allport explained that the need for food becomes an interest in particular types of food. An interest in chocolate includes the need for food, yet it is not the need. Of course, an interest does not have to relate to a biological need; therefore, arguing that interests may arise from needs does not significantly advance our understanding of the origin and development of interests.

Bordin's (1990) psychoanalytic theory proposed that interests represent pathological fixations transformed into socially acceptable sublimations (or needs). Along with Segal and Nachman, Bordin devised a framework for mapping occupation based on id-psychology, especially libidinal and other basic motives, such as manipulation, sensuality, anality, genitality, exploration, exhibition, and rhythmic movement. Their characterization of occupations emphasized impulse gratification and anxiety reduction. From this perspective an interest in plumbing may sublimate an anal fixation, whereas an interest in dentistry may sublimate sadistic impulses. Subsequently Bordin revised his theory to reflect ego-psychology, thinking that it may be more useful to map occupations using lifestyles and character styles rather than psychic dimension and body zones. He replaced the id-based motives with ego-based character traits (and needs) such as curiosity, precision, power, and expressiveness. Bordin concluded that this ego-system complemented the systems that Darley and Hagenah (1955) and Holland (1966) devised to interpret score patterns on interest inventories from a clinical perspective. Bordin's revised theory accorded with the view of several prominent theorists who had defined the ego as a system of interests (Allport, 1946; Mowrer, 1946; Rice, 1946).

Values. Berdie, Layton, Swanson, and Hagenah (1963, p. 50) compared interests to values. Values, although closely related to interests, more directly reflect what individuals consider important, and come close to reflecting a philosophy of life. There is widespread agreement about the function of values (Dawis, 1991)—individuals use values as criteria by which to evaluate the relative importance of environmental objects and activities. Berdie and his colleagues concluded that values influence the style of enacting a chosen occupation, not the choice of an occupation. They illustrated this conclusion by comparing two individuals who were both interested in engineering. One may be attracted to engineering because it allows artistic expression, whereas the other may be attracted to engineering because it pays well. As the two pursue careers in engineering, one may choose positions that foster creativity, while the other may chose positions that maximize economic return. A choice to pursue creativity rather than wealth represents a behavioral manifestation of values in that it shows the relative importance of two goals.

The dimension of importance has been used to distinguish values from interests. For example, Carter (1944, p. 9) observed that "some things may be regarded as interesting but not important, and vice versa." Accordingly, Dawis (1991) resolved that values refer to evaluations of importance/unimportance and are scaled with items that represents *ends,* such as goals or standards, whereas interests refer to evaluations of liking/disliking and are scaled with items that represent *means* such as activities or instrumentalities. This view of interests as means to an end corresponds well with the etymology of the word *interest.*

Interests. Personality psychologists generally view vocational interests from the vantage point provided by the root meaning of the Latin *inter est:* "it is between." Dewey (1913, p. 17) and Kitson (1925, p. 20) were among the first to view interest as a sign of "organic union" between the person and environment. Personologists, especially those who adhere to a Gestalt psychology or Lewin's field theory, view interests as circuits between an individual and the environment, with interests themselves being different ways of interacting with the environment.

Andras Angyal (1941), a psychiatrist and personologist who advocated Gestalt psychology, explained that life occurs in the "biosphere" between the person and the environment, not within the person. Thus he argued that counselors should focus on "biospheric occurrences in their integral reality" (p. 101) rather than organismic processes or environmental influences. In a conception reminiscent of Dewey's (1896) "reflex arc," Angyal asserted that each biospheric occurrence includes three components: the subject, a goal, and the dynamic relationship between the subject and object. Angyal (1941) used the word *tension* to denote the relationship between the two poles of subject and object. If the individual symbolically elaborates this biospheric tensional state, then the resulting "psychological experience of biospheric tension could be called interests" (p. 126).

Gardner Murphy (1948), a personologist who advocated the biosocial-field perspective on personality, also asserted that interests develop through the dynamic relation between individuals and environment. Murphy contended that "there is organization within the organism and organization within the environment, but [it] is the cross organization of the two that is investigated in personality research" (p. 8). From this perspective, an individual possesses a pattern of needs, the environment displays a pattern of reinforcers, and interests cross-organize the two patterns. This cross organization, or connection between inner wants and outer reinforcers, is learned.

Consistent with the views of personologists such as Angyal and Murphy, Darley and Hagenah (1955, p. 191) claimed that "interests are, in effect, the end-product of individual development and the bridge by which a particular individual pattern of development crosses over to its major social role in our culture." Their metaphor of a bridge aptly portrays interests as a biosocial tensional state, a state both culturally elaborated and linguistically encoded.

The metaphor of interests as a biosocial bridge connecting subject to object evokes the idea that interests constitute a path toward a goal. Several theorists have thus conceptualized interests as means for achieving goals. For example, John Dewey (1913) connected interests to goals when he wrote that the goal is the main interest; the series of acts that are a means of getting to the goal are the temporary interests. Strong (1955) also linked interests to goals by stating, "Progress toward a goal brings satisfaction and the useful activity is liked . . . . Changes in our goals must lead to some reversals in our interests" (p. 139). Strong (1955) also believed that goals precede interests. Once goals are set, abilities determine the range of available means and "interests will point out which means are most appropriate in terms of liked/disliked activities" (p. 145). A few writers have addressed explicitly how the motives of need, value, and interest coalesce within a personality, that is, the matrix of motives.

Motivational Matrix. Katz (1963, 1969, 1993) has devoted sustained attention to arranging the motivational mix. Katz (1993) defined *needs* as "basic motivating forces (often unconscious), the inner psychological and physiological drives for which satisfaction is sought" (p. 105). These unconscious motives are best recognized in their outer expressions and cultural manifestation as values. According to Katz, "They are teleologically described in terms of the satisfying goal or desired state or reward that is sought" (p. 106). Similar to Lent, Brown, and Hackett (1994), Katz viewed values as "feelings and judgments about the satisfactions and rewards that may be expected as outcomes or results of a decision"

(p. 106), while he saw interests as "differentiated means by which the valued goal may be reached." For example, altruistic values can be expressed through different ways of helping people. Katz claimed that interests are "concerned with satisfactions inherent primarily in the process rather than in the outcome of an activity" (p. 106). This definition stresses that interests are intrinsically appealing. Based on this definition, Katz sagaciously observed that the importance that one places on doing interesting work is itself a value. One must value intrinsically pleasing activity to make interests a criterion in the choice of an occupation.

Super (1973) also reflected on the arrangement of needs, interests, and values, eventually concluding that they reside at different levels in a hierarchy of motivation. The deepest level of personality consists of needs. Super (1973), following the personological tradition, viewed a need as a state of deprivation, in contrast to Lofquist and Dawis (1969, 1991), who viewed a need as a preference for certain kinds of reinforcers or rewards. Super (1973) defined a need as "a lack of something which, if present, would contribute to the well-being of the individual and which is accompanied by a drive to do something about it" (p. 189). Personality traits and values arise from these needs. According to Super, "Traits are ways of acting to meet a need in a given situation. . . . Values are objectives that one seeks to attain to satisfy a need" (pp. 189–190). Super (1973) called values generic objectives and interests specific objectives by proclaiming, "Interests are the specific activities and objects through which values can be attained and needs met" (p. 190). Thus Super proposed a hierarchical structure of motivational constructs ranging from the deepest level of needs (which may be unconscious), through traits and values, to the surface level of conscious interests.

Savickas (1995, 1997) regarded motivation as a state that energizes and directs a person's movement to a goal. Needs, values, and interests are three modes of character expression. They point in the direction that individuals think they can move to become more complete. Needs first of all arise from a felt sense of incompleteness. They indicate qualities that people lack yet think they require to feel secure and become more whole. Values, the second mode of character expression, teleologically denote the objects or gratifications in the world that people seek to satisfy a need. Values are general goals that confirm who we are and what we wish to become; they are also rankings of usefulness and commitments to a way of life. The third mode, interests, symbolizes the relationship between an individual and the community. Interests state a preferred *how,* a proposed path that links needs to values. Stated another way, needs impel movement, values guide movement, and interests fashion movement. In the ordinary language of everyday life a need states *why,* a value states *what,* and an interest states *how.* Together needs, values, and interest characterize an individual's motives—that is, the why, what, and how of her or his movement in the world. How people satisfy their needs and strive toward their values through behavior—that is, interests—depends on society's opportunity structure and situational affordances. Consequently, interests are less stable and more difficult to assess than needs and values.

In this section we have concluded that the determinants that govern the origin and development of interest dispositions include genetic influence, experiential learning, ability self-perception, role-model identification, social-role accommodation, personality expression, and self-concept implementation. Compared to other motives, interests are closest to the surface of personality and they mediate person– environment interactions. Although quite stable in themselves, interests are less stable than needs and values.

CONCLUSIONS

It has become abundantly clear that *interest* signifies multiple meanings. Psychologists seem to find what they are looking for when they investigate the state of being interested. For example, to cognitive psychologists interest means attention, to existentialists interest means feeling, to purposivists interest means striving, to functionalists interest means action, and to psychometricians interest means verbal preferences. Given the empirical evidence produced by psychologists who examine interest from diverse vantage points and with multiple perspectives, it seems prudent to conclude that they are all partially correct. Thus at this point in time and based on the literature reviewed herein, I draw the following conclusions about interest as a state and interests as a trait.

The most cogent conceptualizations of interest portray the construct as a molar fact. For example, Dewey's (1913, p. 17) "organic union" in a reflex arc and Angyal's (1941, p. 101) "biospheric tension" both portray the fact of interest as a vital relationship among subject, object, and behavior. Although functionally irreducible to component parts, interest can be qualitatively characterized by its most prominent features. These attributes do indeed include cognitive meaning, felt worth, conative striving, and a course of action. Yet interest as a fact in itself is not identical to any of these attributes. What then is interest?

Interest denotes a complex, adaptive effort to use one's environment to satisfy needs and fulfill values. Interest can be described as a state of consciousness characterized by (a) a readiness to respond to particular environmental stimuli (including objects, activities, people, and experiences) or to thoughts about these stimuli. When activated, this attitude or outlook prompts (b) awareness of a stimulus leading to (c) selective attention that narrows the perceptual field to more clearly illuminate the attention-exciting stimulus. This attention is accompanied by (d) an affective state of pleasant feeling and (e) an evaluation of liking that may prompt (f) an impulse to do something regarding the stimulus (such as learn more about it) in (g) anticipation of future gratification or satisfaction. This anticipation passes into (h) volition that steers goal-directed striving toward the stimulus and maintains (i) a course of action that fulfills some personal desire, need, or value. If the individual identifies self with the activity, then the individual may incorporate it as a new interest into the existing self-concept system. The symbolic representation of an interest is usually signified by the stimulus that evokes attention and action (e.g., "I like books").

As a psychological state, interest describes an individual's *position* in relation to a single, specific stimulus. In contrast, a homogeneous group of specific interests constitutes a general *disposition*. Interests, being plural, are characterized by quantitative attributes. The shift from a singular interest to plural interests involves a move from verb to noun, from state to trait, from percept to concept, and from awareness to self-awareness.

As a trait, interests denote a homogeneous group of specific interest(s) that form a consistent, persistent, and stable dispositional response tendency, which increases one's readiness to attend to and act upon a particular group of environmental stimuli. This orientation shows habit (or absolute) strength in how much stimulation it requires to activate. Habit strength can be assessed by behavioral analyses and interest autobiographies that reveal the ease and frequency with which an interest is initiated as well as the duration for which it extends and the length of time for which it persists. A disposition shows relative strength in activity preferences—that is, competition with other interests for behavioral expression. Relative strength of interests can be measured with interest inventories. Self-awareness about an interest disposition may lead to linguistically encoding, in the vocabulary of the work world, the disposition in a new self-concept that elaborates the existing system of self-concepts and vocational identity. This self-conscious symbolic representation, in turn, fosters stability and continuity of the disposition and related personality traits.

Determinants that govern the origin and development of interests include genetic influence, experiential learning, ability self-perception, role-model identification, social role accommodation, personality expression, and self-concept implementation. Compared to needs and values, interests are closest to the surface of personality and are the least stable.

In sum, interests expedite person–environment interactions by uniting subject, object, and behavior into a vital relationship. This relation between person and environment is manifest in actions that satisfy needs, fulfill values, foster self-development, enhance contextual adaptation, and substantiate identity. Given all that they are and do, interests seem quite interesting.

REFERENCES

Allport, G. W. (1937). *Personality: A psychological interpretation.* New York: Henry Holt.

Allport, G. W. (1946). Effect: A secondary principle of learning. *Psychological Review, 53,* 335–347.

Allport, G. W. (1961). *Pattern and growth in personality.* Austin, TX: Holt, Rinehart and Winston.

Angyal, A. (1941). *Foundations for a science of personality.* New York: The Commonwealth Fund.

Arnold, F. (1906a). The psychology of interest (I). *Psychological Review, 13,* 221–238.

Arnold, F. (1906b). The psychology of interest (II). *Psychological Review, 13,* 291–315.

Arnold, M. (1960). *Emotion and personality: Volume 1, Psychological aspects.* New York: Columbia University Press.

Bandura, A. (1977). Self-efficacy: Toward a unifying theory of behavioral change. *Psychological Review, 84,* 191–215.

Bandura, A. (1997). *Self-efficacy: The exercise of control.* New York: Freeman.

Barak, A. (1981). Vocational interests: A cognitive view. *Journal of Vocational Behavior, 19,* 1–14.

Barber, B. (1957). *Social stratification.* Orlando: Harcourt Brace.

Bellido, J. M. (1922). *El fenomen psico-galvani en psicotecnica.* Paper presented at the Second International Conference of Psychotechnics Applied to Vocational Guidance and Scientific Management, Institut d'Orientacio Professional, Barcelona, Spain.

Berdie, R. F., Layton, W. L., Swanson, E. O., & Hagenah, T. (1963). *Testing in guidance and counseling.* New York: McGraw-Hill.

Berlyne, D. E. (1949). "Interest" as psychological concept. *British Journal of Psychology, 40,* 184–195.

Betsworth, D. G., Bourchard, T. J., Jr., Cooper, C. R., Grotevant, H. D., Hansen, J. C., Scarr, S., & Weinberg, R. A. (1994). Genetic and environmental influences on vocational interests assessed using biological and adoptive families and twins reared apart and together. *Journal of Vocational Behavior, 44,* 263–278.

Bingham, W. V. (1937). *Aptitudes and aptitude testing.* New York: Harper & Row.

Bordin, E. S. (1943). A theory of vocational interests as dynamic phenomena. *Educational and Psychological Measurement, 3,* 49–65.

Bordin, E. S. (1990). Psychodynamic model of career choice and satisfaction. In D. Brown, L. Brooks, & Associates. *Career choice and development* (2nd ed., pp. 102–144). San Francisco: Jossey-Bass.

Campbell, D. P., Borgen, F. H., Eastes, S. H., Johansson, C. B., & Peterson, R. A. (1968). A set of basic interest scales for the *Strong Vocational Interest Blank* for Men. *Applied Psychology Monographs, 52* (6, Whole No. 2), 1–54.

Carter, H. D. (1940). The development of vocational attitudes. *Journal of Consulting Psychology, 4,* 185–191.

Carter, H. D. (1944). Vocational interests and job orientation: A ten-year review. *Applied Psychology Monographs, 24* (Whole No. 2).

Claparede, E. (1930). Autobiography. In C. Murchinson (Ed.), *A history of psychology in autobiography* (Vol. 1, pp. 63-97). Worcester, MA: Clark University Press.

Combs, A. W., & Snygg, D. (1959). *Individual behavior: A perceptual approach to behavior* (Rev. ed.). New York: Harper & Row.

Crites, J. O. (1969). Interests. In R. L. Ebel (Ed.), *Encyclopedia of educational research* (4th ed., pp. 678-686). Old Tappan, NJ: Macmillan.

Darley, J. G. (1941). *Clinical aspects and interpretations of the Strong Vocational Interest Blank.* New York: The Psychological Corporation.

Darley, J. G. (1943). *Testing and counseling in the high-school guidance program.* Chicago: Science Research Associates.

Darley, J. G., & Hagenah, T. (1955). *Vocational interest measurement: Theory and practice.* Minneapolis: University of Minnesota Press.

Dawis, R. V. (1991). Vocational interests, values, and preferences. In M. D. Dunnette & L. M. Hough (Eds.), *Handbook of industrial and organizational psychology* (2nd ed., Vol. II, pp. 833–871). Palo Alto, CA: Consulting Psychologists Press.

Day, S. X, & Rounds, J. (1997). "A little more than kin, and less than kind": Basic interest in vocational research and career counseling. *Career Development Quarterly, 45,* 207–220.

Dewey, J. (1896). The reflex arc concept in psychology. *Psychological Review, 3,* 357–370.

Dewey, J. (1903). *Interest in relation to training of the will.* Yearbook of the National Herbart Society (1895) 2nd Supplement. Bloomington, IL: Public School Publishing. (Original work published 1896)

Dewey, J. (1913). *Interest and effort in education.* Boston: Houghton Mifflin.

English, H. B., & English, A. C. (1958). *A comprehensive dictionary of psychological and psychoanalytic terms.* London: Longmans, Green, and Co.

Fryer, D. (1930). The objective and subjective measurement of interests—an acceptance-rejection theory. *Journal of Applied Psychology, 14,* 549–556.

Fryer, D. (1931). *The measurement of interests.* New York: Henry Holt.

Glare, P.G.W. (1982). *Oxford Latin dictionary.* Oxford, England: Clarendon Press.

Gobetz, W. (1964). Suggested personality implications of the Kuder Preference Record (Vocational) scores. *Personnel and Guidance Journal, 43,* 159–166.

Goldberg, R., & Gechman, A. (1976). Psychodynamic inferences from the *Strong Vocational Interest Blank. Journal of Personality Assessment, 40,* 285–301.

Gottfredson, G. D., & Jones, E. M. (1993). Psychological meaning of profile elevation in the *Vocational Preference Inventory. Journal of Career Assessment, 1,* 35–49.

Gottfredson, L. S. (1996). Gottfredson's theory of circumscription and compromise. In D. Brown, L. Brooks, & Associates. *Career choice and development* (3rd ed., pp. 179–232). San Francisco: Jossey-Bass.

Grinder, R. E. (1989). Educational psychology: The master science. In M. C. Wittrock & F. Farley (Eds.), *The future of educational psychology* (pp. 3–18). Hillsdale, NJ: Erlbaum.

Hackett, G., & Betz, N. E. (1981). A self-efficacy approach to the career development of women. *Journal of Vocational Behavior, 18,* 326–339.

Harmon, L. W., Hansen, J. C., Borgen, F. H., & Hammer, A. L. (1994). *Strong Interest Inventory: Applications and technical guide.* Stanford, CA: Stanford University Press.

Herbart, J. F. (1891). *A text-book in psychology: An attempt to found the science of psychology on experience, metaphysics, and mathematics.* New York: D. Appleton. (Original work published 1816)

Herbermann, C. G., Pace, E. A., Pallen, C. B., Shahan, T. J., & Wynne, J. J. (Eds.). (1913). The psychology of interests. *The Catholic encyclopedia* (Vol. 8, pp. 75–76). New York: Gilmary Society.

Holland, J. L. (1966). *The psychology of vocational choice: A theory of personality type and model environments.* Waltham, MA: Blaisdell.

Holland, J. L. (1976). Vocational preferences. In M. Dunnette (Ed.), *Handbook of industrial and organizational psychology* (pp. 521–570). Skokie, IL: Rand McNally.

Holland, J. L. (1985). *Vocational Preference Inventory manual—1985 edition.* Odessa, FL: Psychological Assessment Resources.

Holland, J. L. (1997). *Making vocational choices: A theory of vocational personalities and work environments* (3rd ed.). Odessa, FL: Psychological Assessment Resources.

Holland, J. L., Powell, A. B., & Fristsche, B. A. (1994). *The Self-Directed Search professional user's guide.* Odessa, FL: Psychological Assessment Resources.

Jary, D., & Jary, J. (1991). *HarperCollins dictionary of sociology.* New York: HarperCollins.

Katz, M. R. (1963). *Decisions and values: A rationale for secondary school guidance.* New York: College Entrance Examination Board.

Katz, M. R. (1969). Interests and values. *Journal of Counseling Psychology, 16,* 460–462.

Katz, M. R. (1993). *Computer-assisted career decision making.* Hillsdale, NJ: Erlbaum.

Kitson, H. D. (1925). *The psychology of vocational adjustment.* Philadelphia: Lippincott.

Kuder, F., & Zytowski, D. G. (1991). *Kuder Occupational Interest Survey: General manual.* Monterey, CA: CTB/McGraw-Hill.

Lent, R. W., Brown, S. D., & Hackett, G. (1994). Toward a unifying social cognitive theory of career and academic interest, choice, and performance. *Journal of Vocational Behavior, 45,* 79–122.

Lofquist, L. H., & Dawis, R. V. (1969). *Adjustment to work: A psychological view of man's problems in a work-oriented society.* Englewood Cliffs, NJ: Appleton-Century-Crofts.

Lofquist, L. H., & Dawis, R. V. (1991). *Essentials of person-environment correspondence counseling.* Minneapolis: University of Minnesota Press.

MacIver, R. M. (1937). *Society: A textbook of sociology.* New York: Farrar & Rinehart.

McDougall, W. (1908). *Introduction to social psychology.* London: Methuen.

McDougall, W. (1929). *Outline of psychology.* New York: Scribner.

Maslow, A. H. (1954). *Motivation and personality.* New York: Harper & Row.

Mill, J. S. (1869). *Addendum to James Mill's Analysis of the phenomena of the human mind.* London: Longmans, Green, Reader, and Dyer.

Mowrer, O. H. (1946). The law of effect and ego-psychology. *Psychological Review, 53,* 321–334.

Murphy, G. (1948). *Personality: A biosocial approach to origins and structure.* New York: Harper & Row.

Onions, C. T. (1966). *Oxford dictionary of English etymology.* Oxford, England: Clarendon Press.

Paterson, D. G., & Darley, J. G. (1936). *Men, women and jobs: A study in human engineering.* Minneapolis: University of Minnesota Press.

Prediger, D. J. (1998). Is interest profile level relevant to career counseling? *Journal of Counseling Psychology, 45,* 204–211.

Rice, P. B. (1946). The ego and the law of effect. *Psychological Review, 53,* 307–320.

Roe, A. (1956). *The psychology of occupations.* New York: Wiley.

Roe, A., & Lunneborg, P. W. (1990). Personality development and career choice. In D. Brown, L. Brooks, & Associates. *Career choice and development* (2nd ed., pp. 68–101). San Francisco: Jossey-Bass.

Savickas, M. L. (1995). Examining the personal meaning of inventoried interests during career counseling. *Journal of Career Assessment, 3,* 188–201.

Savickas, M. L. (1997). The spirit in career counseling: Fostering self-completion through work. In D. P. Bloch & L. J. Richmond (Eds.), *Connections between spirit and work in career development: New approaches and practical perspectives* (pp. 3–25). Palo Alto, CA: Davies-Black.

Sears, S. (1982). A definition of career guidance terms: A National Vocational Guidance Association perspective. *Vocational Guidance Quarterly, 31,* 137–143.

Seligman, E.R.A. (Ed.). (1937). *Encyclopaedia of the Social Sciences* (Vols. 1–7). Old Tappan, NJ: Macmillan.

Small, A. W. (1905). *General sociology.* Chicago: University of Chicago Press.

Stout, G. F. (1896). *Analytic psychology.* Old Tappan, NJ: Macmillan.

Strong, E. K., Jr. (1943). *Vocational interests of men and women.* Stanford, CA: Stanford University Press.

Strong, E. K., Jr. (1955). *Vocational interests 18 years after college.* Minneapolis: University of Minnesota Press.

Stumpf, C. (1883). *Tonpsychologie: Volume I.* Leipzig, Germany: S. Hirzel-Verlag.

Stumpf, C. (1890). *Tonpsychologie: Volume II.* Leipzig, Germany: S. Hirzel-Verlag.

Super, D. E. (1949). *Appraising vocational fitness by means of psychological tests.* New York: Harper & Row.

Super, D. E. (1960). Interests. In C. W. Harris (Ed.), *Encyclopedia of educational research* (3rd ed.). Old Tappan, NJ: Macmillan.

Super, D. E. (1963). Self-concepts in vocational development. In D. E. Super, R. Starishevsky, N. Matlin, & J. P. Jordaan (Eds.), *Career development: Self-concept theory* (pp. 1–16). New York: College Entrance Examination Board.

Super, D. E. (1973). *The Work Values Inventory.* In D. Zytowski (Ed.), *Contemporary approaches to interest measurement* (pp. 189–205). Minneapolis: University of Minnesota Press.

Super, D. E., & Dunlap, J. W. (1951). Interest in work and play. In D. H. Fryer & E. R. Henry (Eds.), *Handbook of applied psychology* (pp. 100–108). Austin, TX: Holt, Rinehart & Winston.

Thorndike, E. L. (1915). The permanence of interests and their relation to abilities. In M. Bloomfield (Ed.), *Readings in vocational guidance* (pp. 386–395). Boston: Ginn and Company.

Thorndike, E. L. (1935a). *Adult interests.* Old Tappan, NJ: Macmillan.

Thorndike, E. L. (1935b). *The psychology of wants, interests, and attitudes.* Englewood Cliffs, NJ: Appleton-Century-Crofts.

Thorndike, R. M., Weiss, D. J., & Dawis, R. V. (1968). Canonical correlations of vocational interests and vocational needs. *Journal of Counseling Psychology, 15,* 101–106.

Titchener, E. B. (1898). The postulates of a structural psychology. *Philosophical Review, 7,* 449–465.

Titchener, E. B. (1899). *An outline of psychology.* Old Tappan, NJ: Macmillan.

Todt, E., Drewes, R., & Heils, S. (1994). The development of interests during adolescence: Social context, individual differences, and individual significance. In R. Silberheisen & E. Todt (Eds.), *Adolescence in context: The interplay of family, school, peers, and work in adjustment* (pp. 82–95). New York: Springer-Verlag.

Todt, E., & Schreiber, S. (1996, June). *Development of interests.* Paper presented at Seeon Conference on interest and gender, Germany.

Tyler, L. E. (1951). The relationship of interests to abilities and regulation among first-grade children. *Educational and Psychological Measurement, 11,* 255–264.

Tyler, L. E. (1955). The development of "vocational interests": I. The organization of likes and dislikes in ten-year-old children. *Journal of Genetic Psychology, 86* 33–44.

Tyler, L. E. (1964). Work and individual differences. In H. Borow (Ed.), *Man in a world at work* (pp. 174–195). Boston: Houghton Mifflin.

Tyler, L. E. (1978). *Individuality: Human possibilities and personal choice in the psychological development of men and women.* San Francisco: Jossey-Bass.

Wolman, B. B. (1973). *Dictionary of behavioral science.* New York: Van Nostrand Reinhold.

Woodworth, R. S. (1964). *Contemporary schools of psychology* (3rd ed.). New York: Ronald Press.

CHAPTER THREE

The Nature and Nurture of Vocational Interests

Linda S. Gottfredson

Vocational psychology is known for its interest measurement. Millions of people take a vocational interest inventory each year to learn more about themselves. The field's theories of career choice and development, however, actually say little about how interests develop. All the major psychological theories of careers (see Brown & Brooks, 1996) state that at least some career-relevant traits (e.g., abilities, interests) are genetic to some extent, but none ventures much opinion about the magnitude or relevance of that heritability. For the most part these theories take stable traits as their starting point and then focus on how various personal attributes and social influences affect career development. The theories differ considerably in how much importance they attach to vocational interests relative to other traits and circumstances that influence career choices (e.g., compare Holland [Spokane, 1996] with Gottfredson, 1996), but all seem equally silent when it comes to explaining how interests themselves originate.

This theoretical lacuna is understandable. Much less was known about the genetics of human behavior when most of today's vocational theories were formulated, and the one theory about the childhood experiential origins of interests (Roe, 1956) fared badly when tested. But the situation is different today. The last decade of behavioral genetic research has produced a torrent of relevant information, much of it counterintuitive. It turns out that even behavioral geneticists had been mistaken in their assumptions about how genes and environments influence human traits and behaviors. As a result the developmentalists among them (e.g., Scarr & McCartney, 1983) have begun to reconceptualize human development in exciting new ways—ones, moreover, that vocational psychologists should find very congenial. As I shall try to demonstrate here, behavioral genetics not only provides powerful new tools for answering old questions about vocational interests, but it also poses intriguing new questions about their origins and development.

WHAT IS BEHAVIORAL GENETICS?

Behavioral genetics is a method for studying *variability* among individuals. It asks, most simply, to what extent observed (phenotypic) differences among individuals can be traced to differences in genetic versus nongenetic sources. As such it is another tool in the long tradition of individual differences research. What is special is that it uses genetically sensitive research designs to trace the impact of both genetic and environmental sources of variation in complex human traits and behaviors. Behavioral geneticists use knowledge about the genetic relatedness of different family members, together with natural experiments in the relatedness of their environments, to disentangle genetic and nongenetic influences in development. As I will describe, some of the most dramatic findings in behavioral genetics concern the effects of environments.

Genetic relatedness among family members ranges from zero (adopted siblings and their adoptive parents) to 1.0 (identical twins). Individuals share exactly half of their segregating genes with each biological parent, an average of half with their biological siblings, one quarter with half-siblings and grandparents, an eighth with uncles, and so on. If a trait were entirely genetic in origin (and if we assume that all genetic influence is additive), then relatives would be phenotypically similar to each other in proportion to their genetic similarity. Thus identical twins would (absent measurement and sampling error) correlate 1.0, biological parents would correlate .5 with their children (as would fraternal twins with each other), and adoptive family members would be no more similar to each other than complete strangers. (When there are nonadditive genetic effects, only identical twins share them, which means, for example, that the phenotypic similarity of fraternal twins will be less than half that of identical twins.)

In most families, members share both genes and environments, so any similarity between parents and children or siblings may be due both to shared genes and shared environments. Behavioral genetics capitalizes on cases where genetic and environmental relatedness diverge markedly. Identical twins reared apart share 100% of their genes but little or none of their postnatal environment. (There is disagreement about whether prenatal environments tend to make twins more alike [Daniels, Devlin, & Roeder, 1997] or less alike [Jensen, 1997; see also Phelps, Davis, & Schartz, 1997].) The correlation between identical twins thus provides a direct estimate of an attribute's heritability. In contrast, adoptive siblings share none of their genetic heritage but they do experience the same family environments, that is, they are only "environmental relatives." Their correlation on an attribute therefore directly estimates the effect of shared rearing environments on that attribute. Indirect estimates of heritability can be obtained from other combinations of environmental and genetic relatedness—for example, by doubling the difference between the correlations for identical and for fraternal twins reared together. All heritability estimates, whether direct or indirect, rely on the truth of various assumptions (such as degree of assortative mating among parents, selective placement of adoptees, absence of nonadditive effects), all of which can be tested (e.g., Loehlin, 1992; Plomin, DeFries, McClearn, & Rutter, 1997, pp. 73–75).

These straightforward estimates of heritability and environmentality illustrate the logic behind behavioral genetic analyses, but quantitative behavioral genetics has actually advanced far beyond such simple analytical methods. Today structural equation modeling is used to combine data from different kinds of samples (adoptees, identical and fraternal twins reared apart, biological siblings and half-siblings, etc.) and to test different models of genetic and environmental influence (Loehlin, 1992; Plomin, DeFries et al., 1997). Such modeling can be used to test complex hypotheses, for example, about when in the life cycle genes and environments exert their effects to produce stability or change in various attributes.

The early research focused mostly on intelligence, cognitive disabilities, and psychopathology, but much evidence has now begun to accumulate on personality and, to a lesser extent, interests and attitudes. Heritabilities have been estimated for many such attributes, and I will briefly summarize the most pertinent, focusing in particular on evidence for adolescents and adults. The most illuminating research, however, moves far beyond estimating heritability, so I will concentrate here on new developments that seem particularly important for the study of vocational interests.

HERITABILITY: THE OLD NEWS

It was still big news a decade ago when behavioral geneticists periodically came forward with evidence that yet another human trait or behavior is heritable: for example, depression or schizophrenia. No longer. It would be news today if some trait were found to be *not* at all heritable.

Heritability, or h^2, is a proportion of variance and therefore can range anywhere between zero and 1.0. Specifically it is the proportion of variance among individuals in a phenotypic characteristic, such as IQ, that is due to genetic variance in the population in question. The square root of heritability, or h, is the correlation between genotypes and phenotypes on that attribute. To illustrate, many human traits have heritabilities around 0.5 (50% of observed differences are genetic), which means that the phenotypes for those characteristics correlate about 0.7 (the square root of .5 rounded off) with their genotypes.

General intelligence is highly heritable, with estimates generally ranging between 0.6 and 0.8 in adulthood (Bouchard, 1997b), meaning that 20% to 40% of adult IQ differences can be attributed to differences in environment (and measurement error). Recent studies of identical twins reared apart, for example, yield heritabilities around 0.8 in late adulthood (Plomin, Pedersen, Lichtenstein, & McClearn, 1994). Specific mental abilities (e.g., verbal, spatial) are somewhat less heritable (0.4–0.6; McGue & Bouchard, 1989; Pedersen, Plomin, Nesselroade, & McClearn, 1992), as are specific information-processing skills (e.g., acquisition speed, 0.3–0.6; McGue & Bouchard, 1989). Heritabilities for personality traits generally average 0.4–0.5 (Bouchard, 1997a), as is true also for vocational interests (Moloney, Bouchard, & Segal, 1991; Betsworth, Bouchard, Cooper, Grotevant, Hansen, Scarr, & Weinberg, 1994) and work values (Keller, Bouchard, Arvey, Segal, & Dawis, 1992). For comparison purposes, consider the heritabilities for various anthropometric and physiological variables from a study of identical twins reared apart: fingerprint ridge count (.97), height (.86), weight (.73), systolic blood pressure (.64), and heart rate (.49; Bouchard, Lykken, McGue, Segal, & Tellegen, 1990).

Even behaviors and personal circumstances that are often assumed to be entirely environmental in origin turn out to be somewhat heritable: specific social attitudes (up to 0.6; Tesser, 1993), job satisfaction (0.3; Arvey, Bouchard, Segal, & Abraham, 1989), quality of social support (0.3; Plomin & Bergeman, 1991), and life events (0.4 for controllable ones such as divorce, and 0.2 for uncontrollable ones such as death of a child or spouse; Plomin, Lichtenstein, Pedersen, McClearn, & Nesselroade, 1990, p. 29). Self-esteem (McGuire, Neiderhiser, Reiss, Hetherington, & Plomin, 1994; Neiderhiser & McGuire, 1994) and the nature of many of one's personal relationships are also somewhat heritable: for example, attachment (Ricciuti, 1993), empathy (Zahn-Waxler, Robinson, & Emde, 1992), parental warmth (Rowe, 1981, 1983), and sexual orientation (Bailey & Pillard, 1991; Bailey, Pillard, Neale, & Agyei, 1993), but not style of romantic love (Waller & Shaver, 1994).

Individuals obviously are not born predestined to divorce or with a gene to disfavor the death penalty, censorship, or nudist camps (heritabilities of 0.5, 0.4, and 0.3; Tesser, 1993, p. 130). Genes are only codes for building proteins. However, those proteins create hormones and neurotransmitters that can affect personality, interests, and aptitudes, which can in turn affect interpersonal relations, socioeconomic trajectory, and world view. Heritability alone obviously says nothing about the mechanisms by which genes influence behavior.

It is important to note several other things that heritabilities do not tell us. They do not say how much of any single person's intelligence, extraversion, life events, or the like is due to genetic versus environmental influence. Heritability concerns only variability in a population. Nor do heritabilities say anything absolute about genetic influence on variability. Phenotypic variability, the denominator in calculating heritability, is the sum of variance due to genes and variance due to nongenetic factors. Reducing variability in relevant environments (say, through equalizing nutrition or opportunity) shrinks the denominator and thus necessarily increases the ratio comprising the heritability estimate. If we all lived in identical environments, heritabilities would be 1.0 because all remaining phenotypic differences among us would be genetic in origin.

Heritabilities, in other words, must be interpreted in context. They are always relative to the environment in which they were ascertained, which makes it very important to keep in mind the demographics and historical era of the populations studied. Most studies have been carried out in the United States and Western Europe, and they have not sampled from the extremes of advantage or disadvantage in these settings. Heritabilities allow some inferences about the malleability of traits in the environments where they were ascertained, but they say little or nothing about the molding power of existing or potential environments that were not captured in the research—for example, extremely deprived conditions or novel interventions. To take another example, if a shared national culture led all its members to behave differently than they would in another society, but if that culture did not increase or decrease the *differences* among its members, then its influence (on the mean) would not register in behavioral genetic studies restricted to that culture. Constants do not affect variance.

In sum, a wide range of individual differences in psychological traits is moderately to highly heritable, including the major dimensions of mental ability, personality, and vocational interests. Even less trait-like attributes and behaviors are somewhat heritable too: for example, social attitudes and life events. Until proven otherwise, developmental studies must now presume that every personal attribute under study is at least somewhat genetically influenced. No inferences about the magnitude of environmental effects on development can be safely drawn without using either an experimental or genetically sensitive research design.

NEW SURPRISES

The surprises coming out of behavioral genetics challenge our most basic assumptions about human development. I review five sets of unexpected findings and the new conceptions of development to which they lead. The research on career-relevant traits has focused primarily on intelligence, less on personality, and little on vocational interests. However, the rethinking prompted by the behavioral genetic research on intelligence and personality has direct implications for vocational development. I outline only a few, but they show the promise that behavioral genetics holds for advancing our understanding of vocational interests.

Heritability of IQ Rises with Age

Social scientists have long assumed that the events and circumstances of one's life cumulate and compound in shaping traits and behaviors. The more advantages or disadvantages we experience, and the earlier we experience them, the more powerful they are presumed to be in shaping who we become. Hence the frequent call for more and earlier childhood interventions to enhance the cognitive development of children from disadvantaged homes.

Much to the surprise of behavioral geneticists themselves, the research on intelligence shows precisely the opposite trend for environmental effects on IQ. They *fade* with age. The many behavioral genetic studies of intelligence, both longitudinal and cross-sectional, reveal that heritabilities rise from 0.4 or less in childhood to 0.6 in adolescence to 0.8 late in life (Bouchard, 1997b; Plomin & Petrill, 1997). This means, astonishingly, that IQ phenotypes correlate 0.9 with genotypes by late adulthood. Plomin, Fulker, Corley, and DeFries (1997) have just documented the same process for specific cognitive abilities (verbal, spatial, speed of processing, and recognition memory): "Adopted children resemble their adoptive parents slightly in early childhood but not at all in middle childhood or adolescence. In contrast, during childhood and adolescence, adopted children become more like their biological parents, and to the same degree as children and parents in control families" (p. 442). It is possible, of course, that a childhood IQ or temperament could deflect a life in one direction rather than another by affecting events and opportunities at the time (e.g., admission to or expulsion from a good school). However, the traits themselves may move inexorably closer to their genetic substrate, at least in Western societies.

Evidence on age trends in the heritability of personality is less clear, partly because there are so many personality traits. However, the trends that are found involve increased heritability, both during childhood and adulthood (Plomin, DeFries et al., 1997, p. 202). I know of no data regarding age trends in heritability for vocational interests.

The theory that Scarr (Scarr & McCartney, 1983) has proposed to explain the counterintuitive trend in IQ heritabilities provides a conception of human development that should resonate well with vocational psychologists. She argues that as people become more autonomous with age, they take a more active role in shaping their lives. They are better able to choose experiences and modify their environments in line with their genetic proclivities. Scarr's is one of several theories (e.g., Bouchard, Lykken, Tellegen, & McGue, 1996) that explicate how genes drive experiences, which in turn influence development. Social scientists have long stressed that our experiences shape us, but they have missed the fact that our genetic propensities help to construct those very experiences and that those experiences augment, not negate, the expression of genotypes.

There are two general ways in which people's genes structure their experience: by influencing their *exposure* and their *sensitivity* to environments. These are referred to, respectively, as gene–environment (g–e) correlations and gene–environment interactions. Gene–environment correlation means that genetic propensities are correlated with individual differences in experience. Genotypes are not randomly distributed across environments. Stated another way, there are genetically induced risks of exposure to different experiences, some good (social support; Bergeman, Plomin, Pedersen, McClearn, & Nesselroade, 1990; Kessler, Kendler, Heath, Neale, & Eaves, 1992) and some bad (trauma or childhood accidents; Lyons, Goldberg, Eisen, True, Tsuang, Meyer, & Henderson, 1993; Phillips & Matheny, 1995).

There are three types of g–e correlation, commonly called passive, active, and evocative (or reactive). Passive exposure occurs when children passively inherit from their parents family environments that are correlated with their genotypic propensities. The child's environments and propensities are correlated because both flow from the parental genotypes. For example, musically or intellectually gifted parents are likely to provide their children with both environments and genes that are conducive to developing musical or intellectual talent.

Children are not simply passive, neutral figures within their environments, however. Far from it. Gregarious youngsters actively seek out different experiences than do shy ones, and bright students pursue different challenges than do athletic ones. These are examples of *active* g–e correlation. On the other hand, children with different traits evoke different reactions from their environments, creating *evocative* g–e correlations. For instance, aggressive children provoke hostility among peers, and smart children evoke different kinds of encouragement and opportunities than do their intellectually average or retarded siblings. Our gene-driven individuality prompts parents, peers, and others to treat us differently than they do other phenotypes. We evoke different developmental environments for ourselves. Any parent will recognize these processes upon reflection. Parents do not treat their children alike, oblivious to their differences in talent, taste, and temperament. Nor is parent–child interaction and influence a one-way affair. Many a parent (this one included) often feels that it is the child who shapes the parent's behavior.

G–e *interaction* is a different phenomenon. It simply means that the same environment has different effects on different genotypes. That is, people are differentially responsive, sensitive, or susceptible to the same circumstances, be they pharmacological, educational, or social. For example, stressful life events produce more depression among people who are genetically at risk for it (Kendler, Kessler, Walters, MacLean, Neale, Heath, & Eaves, 1995). Similarly some people are more susceptible to criminal environments. Mednick, Gabrielli, and Hutchings (1984) found that criminal behavior among adoptive parents did not lead to criminal behavior among their adopted children unless the adoptees were at genetic risk, that is, had *biological* parents with criminal convictions. Responsiveness to good environments can also differ. For instance, providing musical instruments, lessons, and encouragement to children will result in quite modest talent development among most (many of whom will resist the opportunity), creditable achievement by some, but prodigious feats for a handful.

Perhaps paradoxically, the finding that IQ heritability increases with age has led to developmental theories, such as Scarr's, which emphasize that development results from people interacting with their environments, much of that interaction in turn being driven by the individual's own genetic propensities. Such theory seems quite consistent with vocational psychology's emphasis on the importance of person–environment fit and congruence and on career choice as a process by which individuals implement their self-concepts in order to achieve that fit. In another parallel, vocational theories view the self-concept as incorporating or reflecting one's major personal traits. Neither set of theories presumes that the "self" is genetically fixed, but only that it is constructed in line with inner propensities that in turn help produce formative experiences.

In this sense, vocational psychology has anticipated the new thinking on human development. However, current career theories fall short in two key respects. First, none provides a good account of how career-relevant traits themselves develop. To take a specific example, my own theory of circumscription and compromise (Gottfredson, 1996), although focusing more than most on career development in childhood, fails to address the process by which people shape their experiences and in turn are shaped by them. As in some other theories, crucial personal traits just seem to appear on the scene already fully developed or to unfold unaided.

Second, the emphasis by many theories on "social learning" overstates or misstates the role of learning in development. It often reflects what Rowe (1997) has called "passive exposure theory," in which learning is thought to be primarily a function of exposure governed by families, schools, and other social agents. Change the nature and amount of exposure, and the learning changes accordingly for all those exposed. The new behavioral genetic perspective emphasizes, however, that much exposure and experience, and thus much learning and reinforcement, is self-directed. Even when environments are imposed, people tend to remake them in various and unexpected ways, thus redirecting learning more in line with their genotypes. As noted before, learning therefore tends to magnify, not muffle, the expression of genotypes.

As others have noted, it is crucial to understand the hyphen in nature-nurture—that is, the interplay of genes and environments via experience. This raises a new set of questions for vocational psychology. What *is* the gene-prompted process by which people select, avoid, and attach meaning to their experiences and in the process express, discover, and further develop their interests, abilities, and temperaments? What menus of experience and exploration do environments typically provide (e.g., relevant to Holland's [1997] RIASEC hexagon) for testing and developing interests and aptitudes? How do the menus offered differ by age, sex, or personality type of child (passive and evocative g–e correlation)? How do these youngsters pick and choose from their menus of experience or expand the menus they are offered (active g–e correlation), and how do the effects of experience, exploration, and interventions vary from child to child (g–e interaction)?

If traits develop only in transaction with environments, the opportunities for and the nature of those transactions are critical.

IQ-Relevant Environments Are Partly Genetic in Origin

Social scientists tend to think of family and social environments as powerful, outside forces impinging on individuals, much like the heavens raining down on annoyed picnickers or grateful farmers. Thus developmentalists have long used measures such as the *Home Observation for Measurement of the Environment* (HOME) to study the effects of family environments on infants and toddlers. In like fashion, psychologists and sociologists have sought to catalogue the impact of parental status, encouragement, attitudes, and interests on adolescent career development. The previous discussion of gene–environment correlations indicates, however, that environments do not exist just "out there" independent of the individuals presumably subject to them. Environments themselves are often heritable because their occupants make, remake, and interpret them (Plomin, 1994). Proximal environments are, in effect, people's "extended phenotypes" (Plomin & Bergeman, 1991, p. 374), and they can be studied with the same behavioral genetic techniques as are measures of intelligence and personality. This sort of genetic research "consistently shows that family environment, peer groups, social support, and life events often show as much genetic influence as do measures of personality" (Plomin, DeFries et al., 1997, pp. 203–204).

Consider the HOME, which measures aspects of the home environment such as parental responsivity, encouraging developmental advance, and provision of toys. HOME ratings of sibling-specific parental behavior at ages 1 and 2 were found to be more similar for nonadoptive (.58 and .57) than for adoptive siblings (.35 and .40), and model fitting confirmed a heritability of 40% for the HOME (Braungart, Fulker, & Plomin, 1992). The HOME, in turn, is correlated with cognitive development later in childhood. It turns out, in fact, that half of the HOME's ability to predict cognitive development can be accounted for by that measure's (child-generated) genetic component (Plomin, 1994, p. 122). In other words, effects of the rearing "environment" are due partly to the effects of the child's own genotype acting through the environment created by and for that unique individual.

Videotaped and observational studies also show that parental interaction with infants and adolescents is heritable, especially for child-initiated interaction (Dunn & Plomin, 1986; Lytton, 1977, 1980; O'Connor, Hetherington, Reiss, &

Plomin, 1995). Ratings of rearing environments obtained retrospectively via questionnaires are likewise routinely found to be heritable. For instance, adult identical twins raised apart (or together) rated their childhood environments more similarly than did fraternal twins raised apart (or together), yielding heritabilities of about 0.4 for parental warmth, 0.2 for emphasis on personal growth, and 0.1 for parental control (Plomin, McClearn, Pedersen, Nesselroade, & Bergeman, 1988).

It is easy to see how *perceived* environments might be partly genetic in origin, because individuals come to situations with different dispositions and capacities for interpreting the world around them. Some people may be more inclined to perceive warmth in others. But as just described, objectively ascertained environments can also originate partly in the genotypes of their presumed targets of socialization. It is likely, as in the case of the adult twins just mentioned, that phenotypic differences among children evoke different responses (more versus less warmth) from family members. Parental behavior, then, is partly the extended phenotype of the child. Nurture responds to nature, to genetically driven individuality.

An aspect of "environmental genetics," the foregoing results warn us that our measures of "environment" are not necessarily entirely nongenetic (for examples, see Baumeister & Bacharach, 1996; Longstreth, Davis, Carter, Flint, Owen, Rickert, & Taylor, 1981). A little reflection reveals that family environments, like classroom environments (Sizer, 1984), are often negotiated with charges rather than imposed upon them. We should also be warned that, as discussed above, even if the individuals subjected to an environment had no role in creating it, they will experience that environment only as they interpret it. Moreover, they may remake it in ways never intended. Such may be the fate of some vocational interventions that have had weak or spotty effects: The experience received was not the experience intended. The intervention checks that reveal this "experimental noise" can perhaps provide grist for the developmental study of person–environment interaction. Just how *do* children perceive, experience, and deflect attempts to influence their traits and behaviors?

Although the transmutation of intended environments by recipients can be frustrating to socialization agents, it may be the heart of the adjustment process throughout life, whether personal or vocational. Greater person–environment fit can be achieved by just moving to a more congenial environment, but that is not always an option. There is often leeway, however, to remake elements of home, school, and work settings for greater satisfaction (albeit sometimes to the consternation of other occupants). Many people have to compromise their goals, but they differ in the extent to which they can "make lemonade out of lemons" and in how they do so.

In sum, vocational psychology might benefit by rethinking how to measure rearing environments and by investigating individual differences in how people create and remake objectively measured environments, including vocational interventions.

Shared Family Effects on IQ Dissipate by Adolescence

Behavioral genetic evidence is clear in showing that not all environmental effects are genetically mediated. What does the research say, then, about environmental effects that are independent of genes? Behavioral geneticists expected the research to confirm what Rowe (1997) calls "family effects theory," namely, the widespread assumption that family circumstances (parental education, occupation, income, etc.) and child rearing styles (cold, authoritative, etc.) mold children permanently in fundamental ways. What the research actually shows, however, is that we have badly misunderstood how the environment works.

Behavioral genetics partitions environmental effects into two classes—shared and nonshared (also referred to as between- and within-family effects). *Shared* effects are those aspects of the rearing environment that siblings share in common and that make them more similar. As just noted, most developmental theories have assumed that shared features of the environment, such as parental education, social class, and parenting style, indelibly shape their children's personal traits. *Nonshared* effects are those events and circumstances that affect the development of one sibling but not another. These effects make siblings more different. They may include illness, parental favoritism, different peers, and the like. Environmental effects are parallel in this sense to the effects of genes on siblings— they can create both similarity and difference within families. The 50% of segregating genes that siblings share on the average makes them phenotypically similar, but the 50% they do not share ensures that siblings will differ among themselves (and from each of their parents, with whom they also share only 50% of their segregating genes).

There are several ways to estimate the proportion of phenotypic variation that is due to shared versus nonshared environments. The correlation between adopted siblings provides a direct estimate of shared effects, because the only family heritage they share is environmental. Shared effects can also be estimated by subtracting the correlation between identical (or fraternal) twins who were reared apart from the correlation for identical (or fraternal) twins reared together. Being 100% (or 50%) alike genetically, any additional similarity between the twins reared together must be due to the environments they shared. The remaining phenotypic variance (i.e., that which is not explained by either genetic or shared environmental effects) is due to nonshared environments and measurement error. Variance due to nonshared effects can be directly estimated by the phenotypic dissimilarity of identical twins reared together or apart (after subtracting measurement error), those reared together generating a smaller estimate if shared environments have made them more similar.

As already discussed, the "environmentality" of IQ drops with age. The question, then, is whether it is mostly the shared or the nonshared component of environmental effects that dissipates with age. The answer was entirely unexpected: Shared effects on IQ become nil by adolescence. Genetic factors, nonshared environment, and shared environment appear to account for, respectively, 40%, 25%, and 25% of phenotypic variance in childhood (10% measurement error) but for 60%, 35%, and 0% (with 5% for error) just after adolescence (Loehlin, Horn, & Willerman, 1989; Plomin, DeFries et al., 1997, p. 150). Longitudinal studies of adoptive families show that as adoptive children grow up they become less like their adoptive parents (the correlation drops to zero) and more like the biological parents and siblings they may never have seen (Loehlin, Horn, & Willerman, 1989; Scarr & Weinberg, 1978). By the same token, biological siblings who have grown up together become less alike as the effects of their shared environments dissipate.

These results are momentous because they indicate that the class of causes that most social scientists still assume to be most powerful in creating IQ differences in typical environments actually have no lasting impact on IQ. Conversely, the research has revealed a very important class of nongenetic effects hitherto ignored. Scarr's theory provides an explanation for why shared effects might dissipate by adulthood: Children become increasingly independent of their families with age. However, the discovery of substantial nonshared effects across the life span presents an enormous new puzzle: What do they consist of? What can it be that is so important in development but that affects the IQ of only one sibling in a home and creates no differences between families (no shared effects)? The most systematic treatment of the question for IQ (Jensen, 1997) suggests that nonshared influences may not be psychosocial or systematic but mostly biological and akin to random noise in development.

To what extent do the foregoing results on shared versus nonshared environments generalize to other career-relevant traits? Shared effects for personality, psychopathology, and social attitudes are negligible even in childhood, except for delinquency (Rowe, 1994), and shared effects on antisocial behavior mostly dissipate by adulthood (Lyons, 1996). Even weight and attitudes toward eating and weight turn out to be unaffected by shared family environments (Grilo & Pogue-Geile, 1991; Rutherford, McGuffin, Katz, & Murray, 1993). Nonshared effects on nonintellectual traits generally rival or exceed genetic effects. Plomin, DeFries et al. (1997, p. 257) conclude that nonshared influences are, in fact, the general mode by which environments affect psychological development. Counterintuitively, then, rearing environments end up making siblings less alike, not more similar. Siblings lead surprisingly separate lives, even in the same household (Dunn & Plomin, 1990).

But again, what are the nonshared factors that make siblings different? As did Jensen (1997) for IQ, Dunn and Plomin (1990) emphasize the importance of chance in the development of psychological traits (accidents, illness, etc., and the chance concatenation of events). However, they suggest that psychosocial environments may also constitute important sources of nonshared effects on development: for example, differential parent-child relationships, differential experiences within the sibling relationship, the impact of growing up with an individual very different from oneself, and influences beyond the family. However, efforts to identify those nonshared psychosocial effects have met with limited success, generally accounting for no more than 2% to 10% of the nonshared effect (McGue & Bouchard, 1998). In contrast, studies are beginning to indicate that pre- and perinatal factors, including obstetrical complications, may account for a significant portion of the nonshared effects on psychopathology (e.g., schizophrenia).

With regard to vocational interests, what little evidence there is tells much the same story: Environmental effects are mostly of the nonshared variety. Betsworth et al. (1994) modeled *Strong* vocational interest data for twins reared together, twins reared apart, adoptive families, and biological families. The results suggest that the variance in a wide range of vocational interests (*Strong* General Occupational Themes as well as Basic Interest Scales) can be attributed 36% to genetic variance, 9% to shared environment, and 55% to nonshared environmental effects and measurement error. The results were very similar for all six Holland themes of work.

By these estimates genetic effects are four times as large as shared family effects. The importance of shared effects relative to nonshared ones is less clear, however, because the 55% estimate for the latter includes measurement error, which may be a bit larger in this study than others. The great strength of the Betsworth et al. study is that it combined studies of interests from different family types, but this necessitated a tradeoff in reliability of measurement.

The constituent studies had used different forms of the *Strong Interest Inventory,* so the behavioral genetic modeling was based on only those interest items that were common across all studies. Longer, more reliable scales would have yielded higher heritabilities and shared environmental effects and reduced the nonshared plus error component of variance. To illustrate, Bouchard (1997b) showed that the heritabilities of the six general occupational themes (Realistic, Investigative, etc.) averaged .32 in a sample of about 50 adult twins reared apart when assessed with the brief scales in the Betsworth et al. study but that the heritabilities averaged .38 using the full SCII scales and .50 using factor scores derived from the SCII and a second interest inventory. Higher scale reliability would also be expected to increase the estimate of shared effects, but they would still be a relatively small proportion of total phenotypic variance. The bottom line is that, unlike for intelligence and personality, shared environments may have some lasting effects on adult vocational interests. Nonetheless, consistent with those other traits, vocational interests seem to stem primarily from genetic and *non*shared environmental factors.

Estimates such as those of Betsworth et al. are of the *total* effect that *all* shared (or nonshared), nongenetic influences exert in the population studied. However, behavioral genetic designs can incorporate measures of specific events or circumstances for individual children (e.g., each sibling's perceptions of parental warmth, divorce, or encouragement) in order to test hypotheses about whether they constitute either shared or nonshared influences. For example, Pike, McGuire, Hetherington, Reiss, and Plomin (1996b) confirmed that parental negativity may create nonshared effects on adolescent adjustment when they found a correlation between *differences* in parents' negativity toward their identical twins and *differences* in those twins' adjustment. In this case, environmental effects were small (Pike, McGuire, Hetherington, Reiss, & Plomin, 1996a), but the research illustrates how behavioral genetic research can help identify which specific elements of rearing environments may have affected development.

Vocational researchers might consider studying nonshared effects, but doing so requires studying more than one child per family and measuring environments specific to each child. It now appears that it is precisely the differences between siblings that hold greatest promise for understanding environmental effects on development. It is not that family environments are unimportant in creating individual differences in stable traits but rather that their effects tend to be specific to each child. Environments as well as genes enhance individuality.

Intelligence, Special Abilities, and School Achievement Have Common Genetic Roots

The structure or architecture of (phenotypic) aptitudes has been a major issue in the study of human intelligence. Factor analysis produces a hierarchical picture of aptitudes, with g (general intelligence) at the top (Carroll, 1993). The next level is comprised of more specific aptitudes such as verbal, spatial, mathematical reasoning, and speed of processing. Further down the hierarchy are the more elementary processes involved in processing cognitive input. Factor analyses suggest that tests of specific aptitudes measure g more than they do any specific aptitude, and behavioral genetic analyses show these aptitudes to be heritable in proportion to their correlation with g. Individual differences in scholastic achievement and grades are also moderately to highly correlated with g, as well as being moderately heritable (Plomin, DeFries et al., 1997, pp. 164–166). But to what extent does this overlap among traits arise from common genetic or environmental roots?

This is the realm of multivariate genetic analysis. It investigates the sources of covariance between two traits rather than of the variance in a single trait. For example, instead of correlating one twin's verbal score with the co-twin's verbal score, a twin's verbal score is correlated with the co-twin's *spatial* score. The same rules of inference apply as for the analyses of trait variance: If the cross-twin correlations are greater for identical than fraternal twins, they constitute evidence of genetic influence in the covariance.

To the surprise of many, the same genetic factors tend to influence different mental abilities. To the extent that special abilities phenotypically overlap each other and g, that overlap is mostly due to a common genetic source. Only a small portion of the heritability of the specific aptitudes is not related to g. The same general pattern is found for the correlation (about .5) between scholastic achievement and intelligence (Thompson, Detterman, & Plomin, 1991; Wadsworth, 1994). To the degree that achievement and IQ correlate, their similarity is almost entirely genetic in the populations studied (Jensen, 1998). Conversely, it appears that the divergence between the two is mostly environmental.

There are multivariate genetic analyses for personality but none that I know of for vocational interests. Those for personality highlight the sorts of questions that could be asked for interests. All could provide novel kinds of evidence for the construct validity of different interest measures, as is illustrated by the following three examples from the personality domain. Largely the same genetic factors are involved in twins' self-reports as in peers' ratings of their personality. Parents' ratings are odd by contrast, often being less genetic and more subject to contrast effects (i.e., exaggerating the differences between siblings; Plomin, DeFries et al., 1997, pp. 199–200). The second example is that the genetic variation in the personality trait of neuroticism largely accounts for genetic variation in symptoms of anxiety and depression (Eaves, Eysenck, & Martin, 1989). The three attributes thus have much the same genetic roots. (Their environmental roots are somewhat less similar.) Lastly, although not doing a multivariate analysis per se, Loehlin (1992, ch. 4) showed that subtraits (e.g., impulsivity) within the individual "Big Five" personality dimensions (extraversion) show unique genetic variance not shared with other subtraits (sociability) in the factor. As Plomin, DeFries et al. (1997, p. 198) suggest, multivariate genetic analyses can compare different ways to "slice" the personality domain.

Multivariate genetic analyses could be used to address some of the longest-running debates concerning vocational interests: What is the most accurate structural representation of interests (Rounds, 1995), and do personality and interests represent two domains or one (Waller, Lykken, & Tellegen, 1995)? Where psychometrics has its hierarchy, vocational psychology has its hexagon. In contrast to the broad dimensions of mental ability, all of which manifest generally the same moderate degree of relation with each other, broad-band interests (e.g., Realistic, Investigative) correlate more highly with some among them than others, but in a definite pattern, and one that produces Holland's famous RIASEC hexagon (Holland, 1997).

The question, then, is what accounts for the systematic patterns of similarity and difference around the hexagon. Holland (1997) describes his six interest types as "personality types," each with its distinctive cluster of attitudes, beliefs, preferences, and personal styles. The six types are not traits in the usual sense but are configurations of different personality traits (extraversion, traditionalism, sensation-seeking, etc.), for most of which there are heritability data. If the formulations of the types are correct, then multivariate genetic analyses should reveal a pattern of genetic overlap and nonoverlap around the hexagon, both overall and for particular personality traits, that is consistent with the formulation of the types.

For example, Conventional and Realistic types are described as being traditional and conforming, whereas Investigative and Artistic types are nonconforming. Because traditionalism (conservatism versus liberalism) is heritable (Bouchard, 1997b; Lykken, 1982), multivariate analyses could be expected to show not only that Conventional and Realistic interests share genetic variance with each other that they do not with the Investigative and Artistic interests but also that part of that shared genetic variance relates to traditionalism. On the other hand, Investigative types are cautious and retiring but Artistic types are impulsive and expressive, so there is genetic variance they could be expected to share with other types (respectively, Realistic and Enterprising) but not each other. Holland says little about the relation of the types to mental abilities, but there is probably some genetic overlap between particular interests and abilities too. Investigative work, for example, seems to require higher g than do the other interest categories. To take an example regarding specific aptitudes, spatial aptitude might share genetic variance with interests in mid- to high-level Realistic work. Some of these relations have already been observed at the phenotypic level (Ackerman & Heggestad, 1997). Genetically sensitive research could estimate to what extent such similarities around the hexagon are due to common environmental versus common genetic sources of variance, thus producing new evidence concerning the meaning and structure of vocational interests.

Such analysis would simultaneously inform the "how many domains?" debate. If the most general or broad-band interests reflect personality best, as Holland (this volume) states, then the multivariate genetic analyses just suggested should provide evidence relevant to his claim that interests are, in fact, measures of personality. Multivariate behavioral genetic analysis could also answer a question with a long-standing parallel in the study of mental abilities: What is the genetic overlap between general and specific measures of interests? And what is the overlap between self-ratings and behavioral measures of interests?

IQ Stability Is Mostly Genetic in Origin Whereas Age-to-Age Change Is Mostly Environmental in Origin

Some of a person's environments change considerably over the life cycle, but others may not. Some genes turn on or off during development and others have different effects at different ages, which means that heritability does not necessarily imply stability. Both environments and genes can produce stability and change.

The most informative research for studying the sources of stability and change are longitudinal, genetically sensitive designs that measure traits, behaviors, and environments at periodic intervals beginning in early childhood. Examples include the Colorado Adoption Project, the MacArthur Longitudinal Twin Study, the Twin Infant Project (see Fulker, Cherney, & Cardon, 1993, for these three), and the Texas Adoption Project (Loehlin, Horn, & Willerman, 1989). They have used model fitting to determine whether new environmental or genetic influences appear at successive ages.

Such studies for intelligence show that genes contribute primarily to stability rather than change in IQ relative to one's age peers. There is some evidence of genetic change, especially at certain transitions in childhood. One occurs soon after children enter school, suggesting a g–e interaction when children are introduced to this novel environment (i.e., some children are genetically more sensitive or responsive to schooling). Shared environmental factors apparently contribute only to IQ stability in childhood, but nonshared effects (which are the only environmental effects on IQ from adolescence on) are the major source of age-to-age change in IQ relative to age-mates. Moreover, nonshared effects contribute only to change in IQ (Fulker et al., 1993, p. 93). To keep the change data in perspective it should be noted that IQ is relatively stable. Research on elementary school children shows that most change in IQ is either negligible or due to measurement error. Where change is marked and real, it tends to be idiosyncratic and transient (Moffitt, Caspi, Harkness, & Silva, 1993).

There is less behavioral genetic evidence concerning the sources of stability and change in personality, but the findings are similar to those for cognitive ability. It appears that there is little genetic influence on change in personality, that most genetically induced change occurs during childhood, and that it is larger for some traits (reactivity) than others (shyness; Plomin, DeFries et al., 1997, pp. 202–203). Genes promote primarily stability of personality. Most change is due to nonshared environmental effects (Bouchard, 1995; Loehlin, 1992).

I am not aware of any pertinent evidence on the genetic versus environmental sources of stability and change in vocational interests. Considering that interests are fairly stable from adolescence on (Swanson, this volume), we might expect to find much the same picture for interests as for personality, especially if there is genetic overlap between the two realms. Clearly, however, most of the developmental action occurs prior to adolescence, and we do not have even the most basic knowledge about the development and nature of vocational interests in childhood.

Do interests even exist in early childhood in the same sense that personality does, and if so, how can we measure them? It takes time for specific abilities to differentiate, and it may be so with interests too. Do interests begin crystallizing—becoming "traited"—only after substantial and relevant interaction with environments? Some behavioral geneticists have begun to speculate that this is the case. Lykken, Bouchard, McGue, and Tellegen (1993) suggest that "precursor traits" closer to the genetic level, such as physique, aptitude, temperament, and personality, help determine which experiences an individual selects from a given "cafeteria of experience" as well as how the individual reacts to those experiences. Social convention affects what is in the cafeteria, and interests that are not experienced do not become well traited. As a result, those particular interests may be unstable as environments change or individuals move out of them.

Lykken et al. suggest, then, that stability comes with traitedness, the crystallization of which comes with relevant experiences initiated in large part by prior genetic dispositions. In contrast, theories in vocational psychology have generally attributed stability in interests largely to the environment. For example, although Holland's (1997) recent theorizing is sensitive to the interaction of genes and environments, he views personality dispositions as the result (not the cause) of accumulated learning and experience. Here, then, are two competing views about the early development of vocational personalities and interests that could help guide research on the origins and development of interests. Although Lykken et al.'s theory seems more consistent with the evidence on intelligence and personality, it is not clear yet that vocational interests are genetically comparable to those traits. Recall that Holland's six vocational personality types seem to be affected by shared family influence in adolescence but the former traits do not.

REFLECTIONS ON COUNSELING

The guidance that behavioral genetics provides counselors so far is of a general rather than specific nature. It cannot be specific because the research currently says more about what aspects of the environment do *not* seem to have much affect on psychological development (i.e., shared family influences) than what do (i.e., particular aspects of nonshared environments). What it says of a general nature, however, should reassure the counseling field, both by confirming its fundamental orientations and illuminating some of its challenges.

Human Agency and Individuality

Counseling psychology regards individuals as active agents in their own self-development. Behavioral genetics supports this perspective by showing that our fates in life are not "determined" or "fixed" by either our genes or our environments.

Hereditarians and environmentalists have both been mistaken. Rather, we become who we are through our *experiences,* which emerge from the complex interplay between our genes and our environments. That interplay is far from understood, but its very existence confirms that we are by nature active, seeking, self-creating beings, working incessantly to mold, remake, and exploit environments to our needs and tastes. Our genes do not predestine who we become, but they do assure that we will take an active hand in creating ourselves.

Genes assure not only that we help steer our own course of development but also that our inner gyroscopes differ from birth. Our genes do not predestine our paths, but they do attract us toward or repel us from different possibilities. The possibilities for us are constrained, of course, by the time, place, and circumstances of our birth. But, as behavioral genetics shows, the environments that we experience and that nudge our development this way and that may be as unique to us as are our genotypes and, indeed, partly because of them. Behavioral genetics thus supports another of counseling psychology's bedrock principles: respect for individuality.

Ethics and Feasibility of Fostering or Frustrating the Expression of Genotypes

People bring genetic individuality with them into the world. That individuality is expressed and enhanced through experience—experience that is increasingly but only partially self-directed over the life span. Much of life consists of seeking and building niches to suit that individuality. In essence, the function of counselors, like that of parents and teachers, is to facilitate this gene-influenced process when it is constructive and to redirect or suppress it when it is not. Therein lie the dilemmas as well as the opportunities of counseling.

Vocational counseling to a large degree involves helping people to develop vocational options that are congruent with their temperaments. To an extent, then, vocational psychology facilitates the phenotypic expression of genotypes, and it does so by helping people to explore, discover, develop, and implement their vocational interests and aptitudes in congruent environments. Deviations from this facilitative process are often thought to be unethical, as when women and minorities are channeled into certain directions on the basis of sex or race regardless of their interests and capabilities.

Deciding to foster person–environment fit is not as simple a matter when the traits in question range from better to worse (abilities) or may be disapproved by society at large (hostile aggressiveness). For instance, we think it perfectly appropriate to encourage bright students to pursue high-level jobs, but we do not approve of encouraging dull students to seek low-level work. So there are times when we refuse, at least openly, to facilitate person–job match. Often we prefer to try to alter the attribute involved (e.g., increase aptitudes). And there are times when we would actively interfere with person–environment match if we possibly could (e.g., the search for peers with whom to express antisocial tendencies). These are issues with which counselors are uncomfortable. Unlike parents and even teachers, they prefer not to deflect people into or off of certain paths when that seems contrary to the client's desires.

Behavioral genetics provides no guide to the *ethics* of intervening to frustrate or facilitate the expression of genotypes (even if we could discern individuals' genotypes, which we cannot). It does, however, provide some hints as to the *feasibility* of doing so. Facilitating or suppressing the development of certain phenotypes is no doubt easiest when the intervention works in tandem with—not contrary to—the underlying genotypes. "Educating" people into or out of trait-like behaviors is probably difficult to impossible when the genotype is not propitious. For instance, efforts to interest women in engineering will work better with the relatively few women who have Realistic propensities than with the many who have Social proclivities. Extensive exposure of girls with Social interests to Realistic developmental opportunities is unlikely to engender enduring Realistic interests in many, if any, such girls.

To take another example, efforts to prevent drug use, risky sex, and smoking by educating youngsters about the risks of such behavior will probably have the least effect on the individuals who need it most: those at greatest genetic risk. Such individuals may be better protected by closing off or closely monitoring opportunities to engage in such behavior, as some parents can attest, or by somehow diverting youngsters into more constructive activities. Stated another way, because some individuals are more sensitive to exposure (stress, temptation), it may be more feasible to protect them from exposure than to decrease their sensitivity to exposure. Nonetheless, just as increasing one's exposure to good developmental environments often may do little to enhance a valued trait, minimizing exposure to risk may have limited effect in suppressing problematic traits that are in part genetically propelled.

Responsibilities Regarding Individuality Versus Variability

The counseling profession is ambivalent, as are many others, about individuality itself. Individuality produces variability, and variability often means inequality. Variability is fine only when it involves no invidious distinctions. Differences in

interests are welcome, for instance, but differences in ability are not, often leading to confusion and inconsistency in the guidance that counselors get and give.
As shown above, differences in abilities as well as interests are both substantially heritable in the populations vocational counselors serve, although the dilemmas for counselors would be the same were stability to result from environments
rather than genes. There is nothing counselors or society can do to make all people equal in ability or any other valued trait, except perhaps to take the dubious
step of inducing negative ("compensatory") genotype–environment correlations
(i.e., providing the worst environments to the most favorable genotypes and the
best environments to the least favorable genotypes). Variability can be increased
or reduced somewhat, but it will always be substantial.

In any case, it is not the business of counselors to increase or decrease phenotypic variability, no matter how they feel about it. Their job is to enhance individual development, either by working with individuals or their environments
(families, schools, etc.). Valuing individuality means accepting that variability
will emanate from it; they are two sides of the same coin. If counselors seek to
overcome the limits of certain genetic as well as environmental constraints,
whether by behavioral, pharmacological, or other means, that effort should be
aimed at promoting the welfare of individual clients, not reducing variability
itself.

Opportunities for Enhancing Specific Versus General Attributes

Behavioral genetic research provides no guidance yet about how counselors
might manipulate environments to enhance vocational development, except, as
discussed earlier, to help assure broad menus of experience by which young people can discover and develop their talents and interests. It does counsel realism,
however, concerning which behaviors may be more versus less malleable under
typical circumstances. In particular the moderate to high heritabilities of various
general traits suggest that manipulating or redistributing current sociopsycho-
logical environments will do little to change the distribution of traits among the
vast majority of children in the West. To the extent that chronic debilitating traits
(such as depression or anxiety) are rooted in genetic risk rather than conditioned
by a lifetime of unfortunate circumstances, there may be nonpsychosocial interventions (e.g., medication) that can provide enough relief for behavioral interventions to have some salutary effect.

The genetically induced stability of highly general (mostly context-free) traits
does not mean, however, that important specific skills and behaviors further

from the genetic substrate cannot be substantially enhanced. They can, as we see happening everyday in homes, schools, and on the job. As long as environments are adequate for general trait development to proceed, our focus in dealing with individuals at this time (in addition to providing menus of experience) probably ought to be in providing specific opportunities to enhance specific skills. General traits affect the ease with which context-specific skills and behaviors can be trained, but there seems to be much more latitude in enhancing the specific (e.g., setting priorities in career exploration) than the general (vocational maturity).

Genetic Differences Between and Within Subgroups

Just as individuals differ genetically, so too may subgroups of the population. Subgroup diversity makes us even more uncomfortable than does individuality. Behavioral genetics has recently developed methods to investigate the extent to which a mean difference between two subpopulations (between-group variance) is environmental versus genetic in origin (Rowe, 1997). It seems probable, for example, that the worldwide male-female differences in preferences for dealing with things versus people (and thus in Realistic versus Social activities) will be found to have some genetic underpinning. Such genetically influenced subgroup differences would have two important implications for counselors. First, the menus of experience—the social environments—that cultures provide to the two sexes probably differ partly for genetic reasons. (Recall that people's rearing environments are to some extent their "extended phenotypes.") To the extent that gene–environment correlations involving gender generalize to create cultural norms for gender socialization, they are probably targeted to the modal genotypes or average tendencies of a sex. But males and females differ enormously among themselves, so gender-based menus of experience, while perhaps serving the majority of both sexes tolerably well, may stunt the development of the many less typical members of each sex. If anything, then, genetically driven average gender differences in interests and other traits make it even more imperative that young people be exposed to a wide variety of environments. The differences between the subgroups should be respected, but so too should the individual differences within them.

A second implication of genetically based sex differences in psychological traits is that we should not expect the same distributions of interests and occupations among free men and women who have had ample opportunity to explore and develop their individual interests and capabilities. The challenge for counseling, of course, would still be what it is today—to assure individuals the opportunity to develop. In this context it is important to point out that, although genes probably produce stability of interests, a genetic propensity cannot be inferred from an apparently stable interest. Restricted environments may have limited or stunted the expression of a genotype or imposed on people activities and beliefs that they will discard when given the opportunity. To repeat, optimal development depends on adequate opportunity for exploration and experience.

In summary, behavioral genetics engenders a realism that social science often lacks. Individual differences have genetic roots. So do "environments." Behavioral genetics thereby engenders a more profound respect for the inner forces that propel us forward, each in our particular directions, through the thickets and meadows of circumstance. Listening for the whispers of that genetic substrate as we engage life is part of what constitutes self-understanding. Vocational psychology has yet to know how our genetic inheritance speaks to us and with what effects on our most public of selves, our vocational lives. However, behavioral genetics can help us begin unraveling that mystery by illuminating better the etiology of vocational interests.

REFERENCES

Ackerman, P. L., & Heggestad, E. D. (1997). Intelligence, personality and interests: Evidence for overlapping traits. *Psychological Bulletin, 121,* 219–245.

Arvey, R. D., Bouchard, T. J., Jr., Segal, N. L., & Abraham, L. M. (1989). Job satisfaction: Environmental and genetic components. *Journal of Applied Psychology, 74,* 187–192.

Bailey, J. M., & Pillard, R. C. (1991). A genetic study of male sexual orientation. *Archives of General Psychiatry, 48,* 1089–1096.

Bailey, J. M., Pillard, R. C., Neale, M. C., & Agyei, Y. (1993). Heritable factors influence sexual orientation in women. *Archives of General Psychiatry, 50,* 217–223.

Baumeister, A. A., & Bacharach, V. R. (1996). A critical analysis of the Infant Health and Development Program. *Intelligence, 23,* 79–104.

Bergeman, C. S., Plomin, R., Pedersen, N. L., McClearn, G. E., & Nesselroade, J. R. (1990). Genetic and environmental influences on social support: The Swedish Adoption/Twin Study of Aging (SATSA). *Journals of Gerontology: Psychological Sciences, 45,* P101–P106.

Betsworth, D. G., Bouchard, T. J., Jr., Cooper, C. R., Grotevant, H. D., Hansen, J.-I.C., Scarr, S., & Weinberg, R. A. (1994). Genetic and environmental influences on vocational interests assessed using adoptive and biological families and twins reared apart and together. *Journal of Vocational Behavior, 44,* 263–278.

Bouchard, T. J., Jr. (1995). Longitudinal studies of personality and intelligence: A behavior genetic and evolutionary psychology perspective. In D. H. Saklofske & M. Zeidner (Eds.), International handbook of personality and intelligence. New York: Plenum.

Bouchard, T. J., Jr. (1997a). The genetics of personality. In K. Blum & E. P. Noble (Eds.), *Handbook of Psychiatric Genetics* (pp. 273–296). Boca Raton, FL: CRC Press.

Bouchard, T. J., Jr. (1997b). Twin studies of behavior: New and old findings. In A. Schmitt, K. Atzwanger, K. Grammar, & K. Schafer (Eds.), *New aspects of human ethology* (pp. 121–140). New York: Plenum.

Bouchard, T. J., Jr., Lykken, D. T., McGue, M., Segal, N. L., & Tellegen, A. (1990). Sources of human psychological differences: The Minnesota Study of Twins Reared Apart. *Science, 250,* 223–228.

Bouchard, T. J., Jr., Lykken, D. T., Tellegen, A. T., & McGue, M. (1996). Genes, drives, environment, and experience: EPD theory revised. In C. P. Benbow & D. Lubinski (Eds.), *Intellectual talent: Psychometric and social issues* (pp. 5–43). Baltimore: Johns Hopkins University Press.

Braungart, J. M., Fulker, D. W., & Plomin, R. (1992). Genetic mediation of the home environment during infancy: A sibling adoption study of the HOME. *Developmental Psychology, 28,* 1048–1055.

Brown, D., & Brooks, L. (Eds.) (1996). *Career choice and development* (3rd ed.). San Francisco: Jossey-Bass.

Carroll, J. B. (1993). *Human cognitive abilities: A survey of factor-analytic studies.* New York: Cambridge University Press.

Daniels, M., Devlin, B., & Roeder, K. (1997). Of genes and IQ. In B. Devlin, S. E. Fienberg, D. P. Resnick, & K. Roeder (Eds.), *Intelligence, genes, and success: Scientists respond to The Bell Curve* (pp. 45–70). New York: Springer-Verlag.

Dunn, J., & Plomin, R. (1986). Determinants of maternal behavior towards three-year-old siblings. *British Journal of Developmental Psychology, 4,* 127–137.

Dunn, J., & Plomin, R. (1990). *Separate lives: Why siblings are so different.* New York: Basic Books.

Eaves, L. J., Eysenck, H. J., & Martin, N. G. (1989). *Genes, culture and personality: An empirical approach.* London: Academic Press.

Fulker, D. W., Cherny, S. S., & Cardon, L. R. (1993). Continuity and change in cognitive development. In R. Plomin & G. E. McClearn (Eds.), *Nature, nurture, and psychology* (pp. 77–97). Washington, DC: American Psychological Association.

Gottfredson, L. S. (1996). Gottfredson's theory of circumscription and compromise. In D. Brown & L. Brooks (Eds.), *Career choice and development* (3rd ed., pp. 179–232). New York: Guilford Press.

Grilo, C. M., & Pogue-Geile, M. F. (1991). The nature of environmental influences on weight and obesity: A behavior genetic analysis. *Psychological Bulletin, 110,* 520–537.

Holland, J. L. (1997). *Making vocational choices: A theory of vocational personalities and work environments* (3rd ed.). Odessa, FL: Psychological Assessment Resources.

Jensen, A. R. (1997). The puzzle of nongenetic variance. In R. J. Sternberg & E. Grigorenko (Eds.), *Intelligence, heredity, and environment* (pp. 42–88). New York: Cambridge University Press.

Jensen, A. R. (1998). *The g factor: The science of mental ability.* New York: Praeger.

Keller, L. M., Bouchard, T. J., Jr., Arvey, R. D., Segal, N. L., & Dawis, R. V. (1992). Work values: Genetic and environmental influences. *Journal of Applied Psychology, 77,* 79–88.

Kendler, K. S., Kessler, R. C., Walters, E. E., MacLean, C., Neale, M. C., Heath, C., & Eaves, L. J. (1995). Stressful life events, genetic liability, and onset of an episode of major depression in women. *American Journal of Psychiatry, 152,* 833–842.

Kessler, R. C., Kendler, K. S., Heath, A., Neale, M. C., & Eaves, L. J. (1992). Social support, depressed mood, and adjustment to stress: A genetic epidemiologic investigation. *Journal of Personality and Social Psychology, 62,* 257–272.

Loehlin, J. C. (1992). *Genes and environment in personality development.* Thousand Oaks, CA: Sage.

Loehlin, J. C., Horn, J. M., & Willerman, L. (1989). Modeling IQ change: Evidence from the Texas Adoption Project. *Child Development, 60,* 993–1004.

Longstreth, L. E., Davis, B., Carter, L., Flint, D., Owen, J., Rickert, M., & Taylor, E. (1981). Separation of home intellectual environment and maternal IQ as determinants of child IQ. *Developmental Psychology, 17,* 532–541.

Lykken, D. T. (1982). Research with twins: The concept of emergenesis. *Psychophysiology, 19,* 361–373.

Lykken, D. T., Bouchard, T. J., Jr., McGue, M., & Tellegen, A. (1993). Heritability of interests: A twin study. *Journal of Applied Psychology, 78,* 649–661.

Lyons, M. J. (1996). A twin study of self-reported criminal behaviour. In G. R. Bock & J. A. Goode (Eds.), *Genetics of criminal and antisocial behaviour* (pp. 1-75). Chichester, UK: Wiley.

Lyons, M. J., Goldberg, J., Eisen, S. A., True, W., Tsuang, M. T., Meyer, J. M., & Henderson, W. G. (1993). Do genes influence exposure to trauma: A twin study of combat. *American Journal of Medical Genetics (Neuropsychiatric Genetics), 48,* 22–27.

Lytton, H. (1977). Do parents create or respond to differences in twins? *Developmental Psychology, 13,* 456–459.

Lytton, H. (1980). *Parent-child interaction: The socialization process observed in twin and singleton families.* New York: Plenum.

McGue, M., & Bouchard, T. J., Jr. (1989). Genetic and environmental determinants of information processing and special mental abilities: A twin analysis. In R. J. Sternberg (Ed.), *Advances in the psychology of human intelligence* (pp. 7–44). Hillsdale, NJ: Erlbaum.

McGue, M., & Bouchard, T. J., Jr. (1998). Genetic and environmental influences on human behavioral differences. *Annual Review of Neuroscience, 21,* 1–24.

McGuire, S., Neiderhiser, J. M., Reiss, D., Hetherington, E. M., & Plomin, R. (1994). Genetic and environmental influences on perceptions of self-worth and competence in adolescence: A study of twins, full siblings, and step siblings. *Child Development, 65,* 785–799.

Mednick, S. A., Gabrielli, W. F., & Hutchings, B. (1984). Genetic factors in criminal behavior: Evidence from an adoption cohort. *Science, 224,* 891–893.

Moffitt, T. E., Caspi, A., Harkness, A. R., & Silva, P. A. (1993). The natural history of change in intellectual performance: Who changes? How much? Is it meaningful? *Journal of Child Psychology and Psychiatry, 34,* 455–506.

Moloney, D. P., Bouchard, T. J., Jr., & Segal, N. L. (1991). A genetic and environmental analysis of the vocational interests of monozygotic and dizygotic twins reared apart. *Journal of Vocational Behavior, 39,* 76–109.

Neiderhiser, J. M., & McGuire, S. (1994). Competence during middle childhood. In J. C. DeFries, R. Plomin, & D. W. Fulker (Eds.), *Nature and nurture during middle childhood* (pp. 141–151). Cambridge, MA: Blackwell.

O'Connor, T. G., Hetherington, E. M., Reiss, D., & Plomin, R. (1995). A twin-sibling study of observed parent-adolescent interactions. *Child Development, 66,* 812–824.

Pedersen, N. L., Plomin, R., Nesselroade, J. R., & McClearn, G. E. (1992). A quantitative genetic analysis of cognitive abilities during the second half of the life span. *Psychological Science, 5,* 346–353.

Phelps, J. A., Davis, J. O., & Schartz, K. M. (1997). Nature, nurture, and twin research strategies. *Current Directions in Psychological Science, 6*(5), 117–121.

Phillips, K., & Matheny, A. P., Jr. (1995). Quantitative genetic analysis of injury liability in infants and toddlers. *American Journal of Medical Genetics (Neuropsychiatric Genetics), 60,* 64–71.

Pike, A., McGuire, S., Hetherington, E. M., Reiss, D., & Plomin, R. (1996a). Family environment and adolescent depressive symptoms and anti-social behavior: A multivariate genetic analysis. *Developmental Psychology, 32,* 590–603.

Pike, A., McGuire, S., Hetherington, E. M., Reiss, D., & Plomin, R. (1996b). Using MZ differences in the search for nonshared environmental effects. *Journal of Child Psychology and Psychiatry, 37,* 695–704.

Plomin, R. (1994). *Genetics and experience: The interplay between nature and nurture.* Thousand Oaks, CA: Sage.

Plomin, R., & Bergeman, C. S. (1991). The nature of nurture: Genetic influence on "environmental" measures. *Behavioral and Brain Sciences, 14,* 373–427.

Plomin, R., DeFries, J. C., McClearn, G. E., & Rutter, M. (1997). *Behavioral genetics* (3rd ed.). New York: Freeman.

Plomin, R., Fulker, D. W., Corley, R., & DeFries, J. C. (1997). Nature, nurture, and cognitive development from 1 to 16 years: A parent-offspring adoption study. *Psychological Science, 8,* 442–447.

Plomin, R., Lichtenstein, P., Pedersen, N. L., McClearn, G. E., & Nesselroade, J. R. (1990). Genetic influence on life events during the last half of the life span. *Psychology and Aging, 5,* 25–30.

Plomin, R., McClearn, G. E., Pedersen, N. L., Nesselroade, J. R., & Bergeman, C. S. (1988). Genetic influence on childhood family environment perceived retrospectively from the last half of the life span. *Developmental Psychology, 24,* 738–745.

Plomin, R., Pedersen, N. L., Lichtenstein, P., & McClearn, G. E. (1994). Variability and stability in cognitive abilities are largely genetic later in life. *Behavior Genetics, 24,* 207–215.

Plomin, R., & Petrill, S. A. (1997). Genetics and intelligence: What's new? *Intelligence, 24,* 53–77.

Ricciuti, A. E. (1993, March). *Child-mother attachment: A twin study.* Poster presented at the Sixteenth Anniversary Meeting of the Society for Research in Child Development, New Orleans.

Roe, A. (1956). *The psychology of occupations.* New York: Wiley.

Rounds, J. (1995). Vocational interests: Evaluating structural hypotheses. In D. Lubinski & R. V. Dawis (Eds.), *Assessing individual differences in human behavior: New concepts, methods, and findings* (pp. 177–232). Palo Alto, CA: Davies-Black.

Rowe, D. C. (1981). Environmental and genetic influences on dimensions of perceived parenting: A twin study. *Developmental Psychology, 17,* 203–208.

Rowe, D. C. (1983). A biometrical analysis of perceptions of family environment: A study of twin and singleton sibling kinships. *Child Development, 54,* 416–423.

Rowe, D. C. (1994). *The limits of family influence: Genes, experience, and behavior.* New York: Guilford Press.

Rowe, D. C. (1997). A place at the policy table? Behavior genetics and estimates of family environmental effects on IQ. *Intelligence, 24,* 133–158.

Rutherford, J., McGuffin, P., Katz, R. J., & Murray, R. M. (1993). Genetic influences on eating attitudes in a normal female twin population. *Psychological Medicine, 23,* 425–436.

Scarr, S., & McCartney, K. (1983). How people make their own environments: A theory of genotype → environment effects. *Child Development, 54,* 424–435.

Scarr, S., & Weinberg, R. A. (1978). The influence of "family background" on intellectual attainment. *American Sociological Review, 43,* 674–692.

Sizer, T. R. (1984). *Horace's compromise: The dilemma of the American high school.* Boston: Houghton Mifflin.

Spokane, A. R. (1996). Holland's theory. In D. Brown & L. Brooks (Eds.), *Career choice and development* (3rd ed., pp. 33–74). New York: Guilford Press.

Tesser, A. (1993). The importance of heritability in psychological research: The case of attitudes. *Psychological Review, 100,* 129–142.

Thompson, L. A., Detterman, D. K., & Plomin, R. (1991). Associations between cognitive abilities and scholastic achievement: Genetic overlap but environmental differences. *Psychological Science, 2,* 158–165.

Wadsworth, S. J. (1994). School achievement. In J. C. DeFries, R. Plomin, & D. W. Fulker (Eds.), *Nature and nurture during middle childhood* (pp. 86–101). Oxford, England: Blackwell.

Waller, N. G., Lykken, D. T., & Tellegen, A. (1995). Occupational interests, leisure time interests, and personality: Three domains or one? Findings from the Minnesota Twin Registry. In D. Lubinski & R. V. Dawis (Eds.), *Assessing individual differences in human behavior: New concepts, methods, and findings* (pp. 233–259). Palo Alto, CA: Davies-Black.

Waller, N. G., & Shaver, P. R. (1994). The importance of nongenetic influence on romantic love styles: A twin family study. *Psychological Science, 5,* 268–274.

Zahn-Waxler, C., Robinson, J., & Emde, R. N. (1992). The development of empathy in twins. *Developmental Psychology, 28,* 1038–1047.

CHAPTER FOUR

Why Interest Inventories Are Also Personality Inventories

John L. Holland

I USUALLY COMPLAIN THAT "I have had many difficulties in preparing this chapter." This time things are different. I had too much material to report and not enough pages in which to report it. I finally decided that a personal account of the experience and speculation that led to my belief that interest inventories are personality inventories would hold readers' interest. And such a chapter would be easy to organize. At the same time I could avoid a comprehensive textbook-like chapter that I would not enjoy preparing and you would not enjoy reading.

My chapter presents an incomplete, loosely organized tour of my education and work history. To satisfy dissenters who believe that interests and personality belong to different domains, I have also included three tables to illustrate some of the positive evidence. You will have to take my word for my qualitative information. On the other hand, thanks to constructivist speculation, qualitative data have recently acquired a sacred status because of their plausibility and sensitivity to the idiosyncracies of the person and the chaotic influences of the environment. I am delighted that some of my personal memories now have publishable merit. It is great to be free of that misguided empirical straitjacket of reliable and valid information.

I will start with my military experience from 1942 to 1946 and end with my retirement from 1980 to the present. Along the way I will report some interpretations that may be useful for practitioners and researchers.

MILITARY CAREER

I spent my military career in an exploratory stage. (Super was right about some things.) I served as a classification interviewer, bombsight maintenance mechanic, Wechsler administrator, paralegal clerk, and duty sergeant.

In retrospect this extended practicum led to some lifelong beliefs, such as the common person is not as infinitely complex as my undergraduate training suggested. Instead, military people appeared to fall into a few common characters or types, but I thought I was just imagining this. I also discovered that the average male was a decent, competent, and sensitive person. I rarely met a truly nasty or evil person. The base rate for bad guys in the military seems about the same as the base rate I experienced in academia.

GRADUATE SCHOOL

I entered graduate school at the University of Minnesota in the fall of 1946 and began work as a clinical fellow in the counseling center. Among other things I began to worry about a thesis topic. My advisor, John Darley (1938), just happened to have a pile of reprints for "A Preliminary Study of Relations Between Attitude Adjustment and Vocational Interest Tests." This old research for a sample of 383 men who had taken the old *Strong Vocational Interest Inventory,* the *Bell Adjustment Inventory,* and two attitude inventories implied that college males with different interests have different personalities. The analyses leading to this interpretation were weak but often plausible. Most of all they stimulated my thinking that a person's interests, attitudes, and personality may go together in meaningful ways.

Somewhat later I met an artist in the General College at Minnesota who claimed that he could tell what was going on in a student's life by looking at her paintings. Fully indoctrinated by the Minnesota push for evidence, I replied, "I find that hard to believe," while I said to myself, "Bull stuff." I visited his painting class to observe student painters and to hear his interpretations. I remained skeptical. However, I did join his Sunday painting group for recreation as an escape from graduate school. This experience led to a quasi-experimental thesis (Holland, 1952) in which the ratings of a person's free paintings were compared with his or her *Minnesota Multiphasic Personality Inventory* (MMPI) scores. Surprise! Some MMPI scores were correlated with ratings. For instance, the rating of "Painting is depressing" was related to high "Depression" results. The results were generally negative for most ratings, but the positive results left me believing that one's personality can be expressed in content or materials that personality inventories do not use. In addition, I began to doubt the conventional assumption that personality inventories provide the fundamental characterizations of a person and that interest inventories and other assessments provide only superficial assessments.

Later I speculated that this state of affairs would not have occurred if E. K. Strong had preceded Freud and his disciples. For instance, the analysis of early vocational memories would now be more popular than dream analysis.

WESTERN RESERVE UNIVERSITY

After graduate school, I began my career at Western Reserve, where I worked as an instructor and vocational counselor and gave talks that senior faculty thought would be good for my personal development. As it turned out, my experience at Reserve (1950–1953) was a helpful source of research ideas that persist to the present time. A key event was the death of a senior faculty member who had a large collection of reprints, vocational tests, and books. His widow donated these materials to our vocational center, probably something she had dreamed about for many years. This intellectual rubbish was available to anyone with the energy to wade through it.

I discovered an *Occupational Interest Blank* by Bruce LeSuer (undated) that was scored for the level of occupation rather than the kind of occupation. My reaction was that nearly everyone knows the level to which they aspire, but most people are interested in occupations that match their interests. Why not build an interest inventory that uses only occupational titles but organized by *kind* of occupation. LeSuer's inventory was the direct stimulus for the *Vocational Preference Inventory* (VPI; Holland, 1985).

I also discovered Forer's (1948) *Diagnostic Interest Blank*. Forer believed that his interest blank items could not be scaled but instead the individual items should be interpreted clinically. For me the key element in this journal article was that Forer gave inference lessons. For instance, if a person prefers "going to movies," then it implies x. His lessons appeared useful, because I also discovered a set of the old *Strong* scoring stencils for about 25 occupations as well as some group keys.

So, following Forer's training, I decided to interpret the *Strong* keys (1943), including the Vocational Maturity, Occupational Level, and Masculinity-Femininity keys. This task went on forever, or at least it seemed that way. I made notes about each scale, grouped items that seemed to imply the same thing, and so on. I was surprised that my grouping of the notes for each scale led to plausible sketches of people in different occupations. Later I reorganized my interpretations according to the six interest scales in the VPI. These interpretive summaries eventually became the formulations for the personality types (Holland, 1959).

I went to hear Forer's paper at the American Psychological Association (APA) in 1951. The differences he reported for different patient groups who took the Kuder are a mixed bag. They imply that interests and personality are related but like many or most of the early studies on this topic, how and why they are related is unclear.

VETERANS ADMINISTRATION HOSPITAL AT PERRY POINT

My next move was to the Perry Point Veterans Administration Hospital in Maryland (1953–1956). There I initiated a small vocational counseling service. We provided service to psychiatric patients and internships for graduate students. In retrospect Perry Point was one of my most gratifying jobs. I finally had some research assistants to do my dirty work, and my clinical colleagues became good friends and provided three years of informal training in projectives and therapy. This experience led to questioning patients about their responses (a clinical inquiry) to VPI items. After only four or five patients I discovered that they paid little or no attention to the directions to respond according to their interests. Years later I discovered that college students and adults also ignore similar directions in the *Self-Directed Search* (SDS; Holland, Fritzsche, & Powell, 1994). Instead, a person's abilities, values, concern with status, sex role, and almost any quality may affect item responses.

This was the heyday of blind analyses of projective techniques and tests. I got caught up in the spirit of the time and tried my hand. I remember being on an APA symposium where three or four of us did blind analyses of a *Strong* profile. I can't remember much about this experience, but I was the only panelist to correctly predict the client's age: 28. It was marked on the answer sheet.

My most dramatic interpretation came later. Two trainees brought me a VPI profile for a patient being considered for discharge; he had been hospitalized for more than 20 years for a sexual offense, among other things. One of the major questions at the case conference was, "Is he still a threat to others?" The trainees thought they had me stumped because the patient had said yes to almost everything in an experimental VPI form that had 457 occupational titles. I said, "Let's look at what he said no to." He said no to "chicken sexer" and "morals squad patrolman."

About this time I discovered that Garman and Uhr (1958) had developed a Manifest Anxiety scale for the *Strong* that had impressive evidence for its validity as assessed by the MMPI and the *16 Personality Factors Questionnaire*® (16PF®). This anxiety scale of 33 *Strong* items was most consistently correlated with artistic scales in the *Strong*—artist, architect, musician, author-journalist. At that time the Garman and Uhr (1958) study provided the most persuasive evidence that vocational interests and one facet of personality (anxiety) have a moderate, positive correlation with selected interest items.

NATIONAL MERIT SCHOLARSHIP CORPORATION (1957–1963)

I spent the next six years at the National Merit Scholarship Corporation, whose research mission was to study bright high school students. Most research was concerned with academic and nonacademic achievement, education, and college outcomes. We did discover that different vocational interests related to characteristic achievements, self-ratings, competencies, coping behaviors, originality scales, parental attitudes, and values (Holland, 1997).

Among other things, Artistic and Scientific interests most closely related to a wide range of originality measures, while Realistic and Conventional interests were most weakly related. This pattern of relations is very similar to the relation of the six interests in the SDS and the Openness scale of the *NEO Personality Inventory*™ (NEO-PI™; Costa & McCrae, 1992) discovered much later. The Openness scale is also positively correlated with many measures of originality (McCrae, 1994).

AMERICAN COLLEGE TESTING PROGRAM

In 1963 I moved to the American College Testing Program (ACT) in Iowa City, where I could have access to large samples of relatively normal college students. I was tired of studying gifted high school students. I continued a series of monographs (Holland, 1968) on my theory of vocational choice in which I learned that interests—as assessed by the VPI, major field, or expressed vocational choice—were related to a great range of personal characteristics. I also learned that editors were not keen on publishing monographs on the same topic by the same author. So I gave monographs Roman numerals and disguised many as journal articles.

My colleagues and I also engaged in a lot of scale building, usually oriented to achievement and competency. For example, Baird and I (Holland & Baird, 1968) developed an Interpersonal Competency scale modeled after Foote and Cottrell's (1955) rationale for that concept. We discovered that our scale was most closely related to Social and Enterprising interests as opposed to the four other kinds of interests. We also developed an originality scale modeled after Kubie's (1958) theory of the creative process. This scale was most closely related to Artistic interests in the VPI in 1958 and in the SDS in 1991 (Holland, Johnston, Hughey, & Asama, 1991).

JOHNS HOPKINS UNIVERSITY

In 1969 I left ACT for Johns Hopkins University. This career move was involuntary but advantageous in the long run. I put together the first form of the SDS in 1970. Later I realized that developing the SDS was an attempt to demonstrate that I was still a valuable person. After all, I had no self-efficacy training for getting fired. Most of my research and development effort at Hopkins was spent resolving the problems the SDS had created—writing manuals and dealing with critics—and with the engineering, testing, and revising of my theory of careers. Fortunately in 1973 I met Gary Gottfredson, who became my research partner. His creative and technical talents have extended or salvaged much of my work.

RETIREMENT YEARS

I retired in 1980 and bought a grand piano so I could live a more leisurely life. This didn't last long. My interest in the relation of vocational interests to personality was rekindled by Costa and McCrae, who initiated a study of the relation of the SDS to the NEO-PI (Costa, McCrae, & Holland, 1984) using an adult sample of men and women (see Table 4.1).

Table 4.1 is remarkable in several ways. For the first time, the correlations between interests and personality are often substantial and consistent with the formulations for the individual interest scales. For instance, Extraversion correlated .65 and .51 for men and women with Enterprising interests. In a similar fashion Openness goes with Artistic and Investigative interests; Neuroticism was not systematically related to any interest scale.

TABLE 4.1 Correlations of Self-Reported Neuroticism (N), Extraversion (E), and Openness (O) Scores with *Self-Directed Search* (SDS) Scales for Men and Women

SDS scale	Men (N = 217)			Women (N = 144)			Total (N = 394)	
	N	E	O	N	E	O	Age	Sex
Realistic								
Activities	−08	13	17*	12	00	11	−12*	-44**
Competencies	−03	10	12	10	00	19*	−02	-60**
Occupations	−06	12	03	11	06	17*	−08	-47**
Abilities	−11	12	09	00	09	08	−07	-38**
Total	−08	14*	12	09	05	17*	−08	-55**
Investigative								
Activities	−14*	-05	26**	−03	06	30**	00	-27**
Competencies	−17*	08	22*	−03	15	40**	−03	-45**
Occupations	−04	-01	37**	02	07	32**	01	-19**
Abilities	−12	-01	21*	−15	20*	28**	−04	-43**
Total	−13*	00	33**	−05	14	40**	−01	-38**
Artistic								
Activities	11	16*	50**	03	20*	50**	−24*	28**
Competencies	−03	18*	30**	11	24*	49**	−14*	15*
Occupations	23**	11	41**	−01	31**	39**	−20*	15*
Abilities	14*	15*	36**	00	30**	38**	−19*	20**
Total	16*	18*	49**	03	33**	53**	−24*	24**
Social								
Activities	-05	44**	07	-05	35**	14	-03	23**
Competencies	-10	52**	12	-26*	43**	24*	-12*	23**
Occupations	02	23**	14*	-06	25*	25*	-03	07
Abilities	-19*	42**	18*	-19*	40**	23*	-07	08
Total	-09	50**	17*	-17*	43**	28**	-08	18**
Enterprising								
Activities	-06	54**	16*	-04	41**	28**	-15*	-14*
Competencies	-22*	57**	16*	-17*	51**	20*	-03	-22**
Occupations	09	45**	11	05	30**	10	-19*	-19**
Abilities	02	54**	07	-09	42**	16	-16*	-13*
Total	-04	65**	16*	-08	51**	23*	-17*	-21**

Conceptualizing Vocational Interests

TABLE 4.1 Correlations of Self-Reported Neuroticism (N), Extraversion (E), and Openness
(O) Scores with *Self-Directed Search* (SDS) Scales for Men and Women *continued*

SDS scale	Men (N = 217)			Women (N = 144)			Total (N = 394)	
	N	E	O	N	E	O	Age	Sex
Conventional								
Activities	−05	07	−04	08	−23*	−24*	00	15*
Competencies	07	21*	13	07	−05	−04	−22*	11*
Occupations	04	12	00	01	−03	−07	−05	−08
Abilities	10	08	−07	-07	−02	−12	−07	21**
Total	05	15*	00	02	−10	−15	−10*	12*
Social								
Activities	−05	44**	07	−05	35**	14	−03	23**
Competencies	−10	52**	12	−26*	43**	24*	−12*	23**
Occupations	02	23**	14*	−06	25*	25*	−03	07
Abilities	−19*	42**	18*	−19*	40**	23*	−07	08
Total	−09	50**	17*	−17*	43**	28**	−08	18**
Enterprising								
Activities	−06	54**	16*	−04	41**	28**	−15*	−14*
Competencies	−22*	57**	16*	−17*	51**	20*	−03	−22**
Occupations	09	45**	11	05	30**	10	−19*	−19**
Abilities	02	54**	07	−09	42**	16	−16*	−13*
Total	−04	65**	16*	−08	51**	23*	−17*	−21**
Conventional								
Activities	−05	07	−04	08	−23*	−24*	00	15*
Competencies	07	21*	13	07	−05	−04	−22*	11*
Occupations	04	12	00	01	−03	−07	−05	-08
Abilities	10	08	−07	−07	−02	−12	−07	21**
Total	05	15*	00	02	−10	−15	−10*	12*

Note: *p < .05 **p < .001; Decimal points are omitted.

From Table 1 in "Personality and vocational interests in adulthood," by P. T. Costa, Jr., R. R. McCrae, and J. L.
Holland, 1984, *Journal of Applied Psychology, 69*, p. 395. Copyright 1984 by the American Psychological Association.
Reprinted by permission.

These results are impressive because there was a five-month interval between
the taking of the two inventories. Also notice that the SDS *subscales* usually contributed to the significant correlations with the NEO.

There are now seven investigations (Costa, McCrae & Holland, 1984; Tokar &
Swanson, 1995; Tokar, Vaux, & Swanson, 1995; Holland, Johnston, & Asama,
1994; Gottfredson, Jones, & Holland, 1993; De Fruyt & Mervielde, 1997; Holland

TABLE 4.2   Pearson Correlation Coefficients Between BZO95 Scale Scores (Activities/ Competencies/Occupational Preferences) and NEO-PI-R Domain Scores

	REA	INV	ART	SOC	ENT	CON
Neuroticism	**−.19**	−.10	.10	.04	**−.33**	**−.24**
Male	**−.13**	−.10	**.13**	.09	**−.24**	**−.23**
Female	−.05	−.03	−.05	**−.13**	**−.36**	**−.19**
Extraversion	.10	.00	.08	**.29**	**.48**	**.14**
Male	**.14**	.00	.01	**.29**	**.54**	**.25**
Female	**.13**	.03	**.15**	**.28**	**.46**	.00
Openness	−.05	.09	**.56**	**.30**	.07	**−.18**
Male	−.03	**.15**	**.56**	**.36**	.10	−.10
Female	**.18**	.09	**.50**	**.15**	.12	**−.22**
Agreeableness	−.07	.04	−.01	**.29**	**−.23**	−.03
Male	.07	.07	−.06	**.21**	**−.21**	−.02
Female	−.07	.06	−.05	**.30**	**−.20**	.03
Conscientiousness	.11	.05	**−.16**	.02	**.32**	**.42**
Male	**.17**	.05	**−.23**	−.01	**.32**	**.45**
Female	.01	.05	−.08	.07	**.31**	**.39**

Note: Total Sample $N = 934$, males $N = 498$, and females $N = 436$; Correlations > .13 for the total sample are significant at the $p < .001$ level and are printed bold. For males and females, correlations higher than .12 are significant at the $p < .01$ level and are printed bold.

From "The five factor model of personality and Holland's RIASEC interest types," by F. De Fruyt and I. Mervielde, *Personality and Individual Differences, 23*, p. 94. Copyright 1997 by Elsevier Science, Ltd., The Boulevard, Langford Lane, Kidlington OX51GB, UK. Reprinted by permission.

& Gottfredson, 1994) that have explored the SDS or VPI-NEO relations. Six studies have used the five-factor NEO that replaced the three-factor model. The new factors were Conscientiousness and Agreeableness. The Tokar and Swanson study (1995) replicates the pattern of correlations found earlier for N, E, and O, but the new factors of Conscientiousness and Agreeableness have only weak or insignificant correlations with the expected SDS scale.

Recent work (De Fruyt & Mervielde, 1997) in Belgium, where translations of the SDS and NEO were used, produced Table 4.2.

Table 4.2 summarizes the main findings in the NEO-SDS literature. The main findings are exactly what you would predict from a knowledge of the scales involved. The sex differences usually appear trivial.

In Table 4.3, the NEO *facet* scales appear to clarify some of the differences between adjacent types. For instance, compare the Social and Enterprising scales using the

TABLE 4.3 Pearson Correlations of NEO-PI-R Facet Scores with BZO95 Scale Scores (Activities/Competencies/Occupational Preferences)

	REA	INV	ART	SOC	ENT	CON
Neuroticism						
N1: Anxiety	**−.23**	−.12	.06	.07	**−.31**	**−.16**
N2: Angry hostility	−.10	−.08	.10	−.06	−.10	**−.14**
N3: Depression	**−.15**	−.07	.08	.03	**−.34**	**−.23**
N4: Self-consciousness	−.12	−.05	−.02	−.02	**−.34**	−.11
N5: Impulsiveness	−.05	−.05	**.18**	.07	−.01	**−.22**
N6: Vulnerability	**−.19**	−.08	.04	.01	**−.39**	**−.21**
Extraversion						
E1: Warmth	−.03	−.01	**.14**	**.38**	**.23**	.05
E2: Gregariousness	−.03	−.05	−.03	**.24**	**.30**	.10
E3: Assertiveness	**.13**	−.02	.07	**.14**	**.59**	.12
E4: Activity	.11	.06	.01	**.15**	**.34**	**.14**
E5: Excitement-seeking	**.18**	.01	−.01	.05	**.27**	.07
E6: Positive emotions	.03	.04	.12	**.24**	**.21**	.05
Openness						
O1: Fantasy	−.01	.02	**.35**	**.13**	−.07	**−.23**
O2: Aesthetics	−.11	.08	**.58**	**.27**	.00	**−.14**
O3: Feelings	**−.16**	−.06	**.33**	**.28**	−.01	**−.19**
O4: Actions	.02	.05	**.30**	**.22**	**.16**	−.09
O5: Ideas	**.14**	**.26**	**.32**	**.15**	**.18**	.05
O6: Values	−.08	−.02	**.28**	**.13**	−.03	**−.15**

NEO facets. The differences appear to support the formulations for the types as well as a few stereotypes about counselors versus administrators. You can also identify the facets in these comparisons that any pair of interests share. For instance, Es and Cs share Competence, Achievement Striving, and Self-Discipline but not Order, Dutifulness, and Deliberation. The latter qualities go with Conventional interests.

SO WHERE ARE WE NOW?

Now I will try to summarize where we are at this time.

First, we have substantial empirical evidence that interest inventories assess many of the factors entailed in a comprehensive personality inventory.

TABLE 4.3   Pearson Correlations of NEO-PI-R Facet Scores with BZO95 Scale Scores (Activities/Competencies/Occupational Preferences) *continued*

	REA	INV	ART	SOC	ENT	CON
Agreeableness						
A1: Trust	.04	.10	.02	**.25**	−.01	.03
A2: Straightforwardness	−.09	−.02	−.02	**.13**	**−.31**	−.08
A3: Altruism	−.03	.03	.04	**.31**	.04	.09
A4: Compliance	−.02	.02	**−.13**	.11	**−.16**	.07
A5: Modesty	−.05	.03	−.11	.08	**−.29**	−.01
A6: Tender-mindedness	**−.17**	−.01	**.20**	**.37**	**−.21**	**−.18**
Conscientiousness						
C1: Competence	.07	.05	−.05	.06	**.36**	**.32**
C2: Order	.07	.03	**−.14**	−.03	**.17**	**.36**
C3: Dutifulness	.05	.05	**−.16**	.09	.12	**.26**
C4: Achievement striving	**.14**	.05	−.08	.03	**.41**	**.35**
C5: Self-discipline	**.14**	.07	**−.13**	.03	**.28**	**.35**
C6: Deliberation	.03	.03	**−.18**	−.05	.09	**.30**

Note: *N* = 934, minimum pairwise *N* of cases = 910; Correlations > .12 are significant at the p < .001 level and are printed bold.

From "The five factor model of personality and Holland's RIASEC interest types," by F. De Fruyt and I. Mervielde, Personality and Individual Differences, 23, p. 95. Copyright 1997 by Elsevier Science, Ltd., The Boulevard, Langford Lane, Kidlington OX51GB, UK. Reprinted with permission.

Second, old and new clinical experience also implies that vocational interests can be interpreted as signs of personality.

Third, the assumption that interest inventories mimic personality inventories has been a useful scientific strategy. The belief that they are unrelated has not been a productive strategy.

The early work on this topic by Cottle (1950) and others may have failed because the old *Strong Vocational Interest Blank* was composed of multifactor scales and because the old personality scales and inventories assessed little slivers of pathology with obvious items. In contrast, the NEO-PI and SDS have broad-band scales with innocuous or subtle items. Likewise, recent work by Waller, Lykken, and Tellegen (1995) may have failed to show substantial correlations between interests and personality because they used narrow-band measures of interests (17) and personality (11).

SOME RESERVATIONS AND OMISSIONS

My interpretations should be tempered by several cautions.

I omitted any discussion of what constitutes an interest or personality inventory. Both kinds of inventories occasionally share a few items with similar content, and some scales with vocational item content appear to straddle the interest and personality domains.

For instance, the *Vocational Identity Scale* (Holland, Daiger, & Power, 1980) is composed only of vocational content, but it has moderate correlations with standard measures of Neuroticism or adjustment. Likewise, several self-efficacy measures in three studies (Betz, Harmon, & Borgen, 1996; Lenox & Subich, 1994; Tracey, 1997) appear to assess the peaks and valleys on a person's interest profile. Self-efficacy doesn't look like a new variable. Put another way, interest inventory profiles may be more efficacious than self-efficacy measures.

In addition the interest profile elevation or the sum of a person's scores in the SDS is positively but weakly correlated with the good NEO factors (E, O, A, C) and negatively with neuroticism in three replications (De Fruyt & Mervielde, 1997; Holland, Johnston, & Asama, 1994; Gottfredson, Jones, & Holland, 1993).

To be brief I have omitted a discussion of the VPI versus the personality inventory research. A rough summary (see Holland, 1985) of the VPI versus the 16PF, *California Psychological Inventory*™, *Edwards Personal Preference Scale, Guilford-Zimmerman Temperament Survey,* and *DF Opinion Survey* is that these inventories usually support the main findings in the NEO-SDS work. Those inventories having masculinity-femininity scales also rescue Realistic interests from oblivion by suggesting that these interests are sometimes moderately and positively correlated with masculinity scales. Or Realistic interests are related to personality. Unfortunately, masculinity was banished as an important psychological concept several years ago, so we now have some old evidence that Realistic interests are related to a nonexistent personal quality. When I think of the effort that went into that data collection, I could cry.

I have also omitted any discussion of the canonical or factor analyses in many investigations because they add little information beyond the more interpretable information in simple, zero-order correlations.

At any rate it seems reasonable to believe that personality can be assessed by inventories, scales, or ratings that use vocational *or* nonvocational content. Or people express their personality in multiple activities and situations, not just in a particular inventory.

UNFINISHED RESEARCH

I see some unfinished research business. A large American sample of adults ($N >$ 800) is needed to replicate the Belgium study of the NEO-SDS linkage and to learn if we have reached the limit on the overlap. A similar sample could be used to examine the relations between *subsamples* of SDS participants—classified according to their two-letter codes—and their characterization by NEO factor scales as well as the NEO facet scales. Earlier work (Holland, 1968) indicates that subtypes within a main type do differ on a variety of criteria.

In a recent review and meta-analysis Ackerman and Heggestad (1997) report that vocational interests, personality, *and* intelligence overlap and that this commonality provides support for the RIASEC model. The trait complexes (see Figure 1 in Ackerman & Heggestad, 1997) resemble the hexagonal model. This work includes both new and old research that might benefit from replication with well-established measures of personality, interests, and abilities, and with samples with more variance.

PRACTICAL APPLICATIONS

The practical implications of the interest-personality connection can be useful in individual assessment and counseling. Counselors and clinicians could improve the use of interest inventories with two simple strategies.

First, try your hand with a few simple inquiries. Ask clients for their explanations of the highs and lows in their interest profiles, how their successive vocational daydreams came and went. Ask about the origins of their high and low self-ratings of abilities; likewise ask about the origins of their competencies and incompetencies. These inquiries can often clarify or support other diagnostic information.

Second, read the manuals for the interest inventories you use. I know this is a distasteful activity. In the case of the SDS, we tried to make it easier by producing a user's guide (Holland, Powell, & Fritzsche, 1994) and a technical manual (Holland, Fritzsche, & Powell, 1994). We expected that most people would order the user's guide. Not so. Nearly everyone orders both manuals. Now there are two unread manuals instead of one. The editor and I have read both manuals, and I have read selected portions of the *Strong* manual (Harmon, Hansen, Borgen, & Hammer, 1994). It is beautifully written and very informative. This is an endorsement for the manual only. Seriously, these manuals contain a wealth of training ideas and technical information that could make the lives of practitioners and researchers easier and more productive.

Perhaps the most important implication of this chapter is to see interest and personality inventories as partners in the diagnostic and treatment process. They provide both similar and different information about personality. Together they provide more comprehensive information than either one alone. Put another way, neuroticism can be as relevant as congruence in understanding a dissatisfied worker, or congruence can be as relevant as neuroticism when a clinician meets an unhappy client.

REFERENCES

Ackerman, P. L., & Heggestad, E. D. (1997). Intelligence, personality, and interests: Evidence for overlapping traits. *Psychological Bulletin, 121,* 219–245.

Betz, N. E., Harmon, L. W., & Borgen, F. H. (1996). The relationships of self-efficacy for the Holland themes to gender, occupational group membership, and vocational interests. *Journal of Counseling Psychology, 43,* 90–98.

Costa, P. T., Jr., & McCrae, R. R. (1992). *NEO PI-R professional manual.* Odessa, FL: Psychological Assessment Resources.

Costa, P. T., Jr., McCrae, R. R., & Holland, J. L. (1984). Personality and vocational interests in adulthood. *Journal of Applied Psychology, 69,* 39–400.

Cottle, W. C. (1950). A factorial study of the Multiphasic, Strong, Kuder, and Bell inventories. *Psychometrica, 15,* 25–47.

Darley, J. G. (1938, September). A preliminary study of the relations between attitude, adjustment, and vocational interest tests. *Journal of Educational Psychology, 29* 467–473.

De Fruyt, F., & Mervielde, I. (1997). The five-factor model of personality and Holland's RIASEC interest types. *Personality and Individual Differences, 23,* 87–103.

Foote, N. N., & Cottrell, L. S. (1955). *Identity and interpersonal competence.* Chicago: University of Chicago Press.

Forer, B. R. (1948). A diagnostic interest blank. *Rorschach Research Exchange and Journal of Projective Techniques, 12,* 1–11.

Forer, B. R. (1951). Personality dynamics and occupational choices. Paper presented at APA Convention, Chicago, IL.

Garman, G. D., & Uhr, L. (1958). An anxiety scale for the *Strong Vocational Interest Inventory:* Cross-validation and subsequent tests of validity. *Applied Journal of Psychology, 42,* 241–246.

Gottfredson, G. D., Jones, E. M., & Holland, J. L. (1993). Personality and vocational interests: The relation of Holland's interest dimensions to five robust dimensions of personality. *Journal of Counseling Psychology, 40,* 518–524.

Harmon, L. W., Hansen, J. C., Borgen, F. H., & Hammer, A. L. (1994). *Strong Interest Inventory applications and technical guide.* Stanford, CA: Stanford University Press.

Holland, J. L. (1952). *A study of measured personality variables and their behavioral correlates as seen in oil paintings.* Unpublished doctoral dissertation, University of Minnesota, Minneapolis.

Holland, J. L. (1959). A theory of vocational choice. *Journal of Counseling Psychology, 6,* 35–45.

Holland, J. L. (1968, February). Explorations of a theory of vocational choice: VI. A longitudinal study using a sample of typical college students. *Journal of Applied Psychology, 52,* No. 1, Part 2.

Holland, J. L. (1985). *Manual for the Vocational Preference Inventory.* Odessa, FL: Psychological Assessment Resources.

Holland, J. L. (1997). *Making vocational choices.* Odessa, FL: Psychological Assessment Resources.

Holland, J. L., & Baird, L. L. (1968). An interpersonal competency scale. *Educational and Psychological Measurement, 28,* 503–510.

Holland, J. L., Daiger, D. C., & Power, P. G. (1980). Some diagnostic scales for research in decision-making and personality: Identity, information and barriers. *Journal of Personality and Social Psychology, 39,* 1191–1200.

Holland, J. L., Fritzsche, B. A., & Powell, A. B. (1994). *The Self-Directed Search technical manual.* Odessa, FL: Psychological Assessment Resources.

Holland, J. L., & Gottfredson, G. D. (1994). *Career Attitudes and Strategies Inventory.* Odessa, FL: Psychological Assessment Resources.

Holland, J. L., Johnston, J. A., & Asama, N. F. (1994). More evidence for the relationship between Holland's personality types and personality variables. *Journal of Career Development, 18,* 91–100.

Holland, J. L., Johnston, J. A., Hughey, K. F., & Asama, N. F. (1991). Some explorations of a theory of careers: VI. A replication and some possible extensions. *Journal of Career Development, 18,* 91–100.

Holland, J. L., Powell, A. B., & Fritzsche, B. A. (1994). *The Self-Directed Search professional user's guide.* Odessa, FL: Psychological Assessment Resources.

Kubie, L. S. (1958). *Neurotic distortion of the creative process.* Lawrence: University of Kansas Press.

Lenox, R. A., & Subich, L. M. (1994). The relationship between self-efficacy beliefs and inventoried vocational interests. *Career Development Quarterly, 42,* 302–313.

LeSuer, B. V. (undated). *Occupational Interest Blank.* New York: Psychological Corporation.

McCrae, R. R. (1994). Openness to experience as a basic dimension of personality. *Imagination, Cognition and Personality, 13,* 39–55.

Strong, E. K., Jr. (1943). *Vocational interests of men and women.* Stanford, CA: Stanford University Press.

Tokar, D. M., & Swanson, J. L. (1995). Evaluation of the correspondence between Holland's vocational personality typology and the five-factor model of personality. *Journal of Vocational Behavior, 46,* 89–108.

Tokar, D. M., Vaux, A., & Swanson, J. L. (1995). Dimensions relating Holland's vocational personality typology and the five-factor model. *Journal of Career Assessment, 3,* 57–74.

Tracey, T. J. (1997). The structure of interests and self-efficacy expectations: An expanded examination of the spherical model of interests. *Journal of Counseling Psychology, 44,* 32–43.

Waller, N. G., Lykken, D. T., & Tellegen, A. (1995). Occupational interests, leisure time interests, and personality. In D. Lubinski & R. V. Dawis (Eds.), *Assessing individual differences in human behavior: New concepts, methods, and findings* (pp. 233–259). Palo Alto, CA: Davies-Black.

CHAPTER FIVE

Describing, Evaluating, and Creating Vocational Interest Structures

James Rounds and Susan X Day

CIVIL RIGHTS ACTIVISTS become social workers. Social workers become psychologists. English teachers become lawyers. Women who have run households become real estate agents. Secretaries become office managers. When people change jobs like this, friends and even strangers are not surprised. When a bookkeeper joins a chorus line, or when a hair stylist becomes a systems analyst, eyebrows are raised. Why? Because we each have a theory of how different types of work hang together: which job changes are natural progressions and which changes of work constitute breaking away from the past. One aspect of vocational psychology involves the identification of interest categories and investigation of how (and whether) they relate to each other. This aspect concerns the structure of vocational interests.

WHY DO IT? AND WHO CARES?

Readers of this book probably already have some commitment to the subject, yet an overview of the import of structural study may be in order. The first use that comes to mind is scale development that accurately and parsimoniously portrays a person's vocational interests. It is best to have instruments that group activities or occupations in some coherent way. If we can be sure that someone who enjoys bookkeeping will also enjoy inventory control, for example, we can present the client with an array of job titles that are linked by basic similarity. Insight into this similarity will help the client see possibilities that may have been outside of awareness before. The World-of-Work Map (Prediger, 1976; Swaney, 1995a), a tool frequently presented to career counseling clients, is based on such thinking, and the fact that it is a map reflects the structural aspect of the system.

Beyond this practical use, structural studies are essential to person–environment fit theories. These theories claim that both people and work environments can be categorized in parallel ways and that a match between the person and the environment bodes well for job performance, stability, and satisfaction. A mismatch bodes ill. Such theories depend on veridical characterization of both personality types and work settings.

A pressing question today involves whether vocational interest measures and scales can be applied cross-culturally and multiculturally. If different groups consistently respond in different patterns to the same measures, one explanation is that the groups have differing mental representations of the world of work. This is a matter of structure: If it is not cross-cultural, scores on interest inventories cannot be interpreted the same way for all people. In other word, the construct validity of the measures is in doubt.

Structural studies allow us to understand the relations among preferences. Most interest inventories are based on people's reports of what they like and dislike. Theoretically these likes and dislikes associate with each other in a lawful way. For example, one of the most basic structural claims is that people who enjoy working with people will not enjoy occupations that involve working mostly with things. They would probably rather plan someone's vacation than assemble children's tricycles. From this type of fundamental structural thought come our stereotypes of the college professor who won't put up the screen windows, the auto mechanic who resists explaining your car problem in words, or the engineer who can't say "I love you."

These relations go to the heart of validity studies. How many highly articulate auto mechanics do we need to know before we question our understanding of the verbal/mechanical opposition? Even more threatening to the validity of a vocational structure would be the discovery of a geographical region where folk wisdom associates auto mechanics with playwriting.

Like all well-defined constructs, entities such as Holland types are characterized by a description of what they *are,* by contrast with what they are *not,* and by comparison with what is *similar* but not quite the same. The meaning of each type stands in a network of other concepts. Imagining this network is the job of vocational interest structure experts.

REPRESENTATION OF INTEREST DATA: MODELS

Vocational interest models come in three basic types: dimensional, classificatory, and spatial. Dimensional models are the oldest and most well known. They are usually presented as factor lists, such as the basic interests identified by Guilford, Christensen, Bond, and Sutton (1954) and more recently Jackson (1977, 1986); Kuder (1977); Droege and Hawk (1977); Rounds and Dawis (1979); and Day and Rounds (1997). Day and Rounds have summarized the major factor-analytic studies, creating a catalogue of basic interests. Such lists are often derived from factor-analytic studies of correlations among responses to inventory items. Independent, underlying dimensions are sought, defined, and labeled. An individual's interest in each factor is assumed to be a spot located on a continuum. This type of model suggests, in most cases, that the factors are independent entities, so a high score in one direction does not imply a low score in another. This approach dominates research on interest scale construction. The basic interest level of vocational structure, lying between the general Holland types and the specific job titles (Occupational Scales), has lain neglected since the 1970s, in good part due to historical accident (see Day & Rounds, 1997).

Prediger (1982) used the dimensional approach to identify a remarkably sturdy two-factor structure that underlies Holland's spatial model. The two continua of People/Things and Data/Ideas furnish labels for the first two dimensions of more complex spatial models. Independent verification of Prediger's dimension labels is slender but generally strong in support for the People/Things concept and weaker for Data/Ideas (Rounds, 1995; Rounds & Tracey, 1993). The Data/Ideas dimension is reliably present, but the label may not accurately capture its substance. Even People/Things may more exactly denote a desire to be with people versus a desire to avoid people (Goh & Leong, 1993; Schneider, Ryan, Tracey, & Rounds, 1996).

Classificatory models go a step further in model complexity by suggesting some relationships among the categories usually drawn from dimensional models. Classificatory methods are rarely used for scale development purposes, though they could be. The best known of these is Gati's (1979, 1991) three-group partition of RIASEC categories (Fig. 5. 1), the most revolutionary post-Holland blueprint. This partition proposes that in the choice process the first decision is made among three paths: the Realistic/Investigative path, the Artistic/Social path, and the Enterprising/Conventional path. Obviously the model suggests a close relationship between the elements of these three pairs and a more distant relationship between elements not paired together. It does not specify relationships further than these discrete clusters. Rounds and Tracey (1996) have also proposed a successful partition model to account for cross-cultural data (see Fig. 5.1).

Gati (1979, 1991) also has devised a multistage classification of Roe's (1956) eight occupational fields (shown in Fig. 5.1), again advancing a process of vocational choice in which each path leads to a decision point precluding certain destinations. Gati's ideas of representing vocational interests in a discrete fashion breaks with the dimensional and spatial traditions and offers new potential for understanding the vocational choice process. Nevertheless, his work has not picked up adherents, being widely ignored among interest researchers.

Holland's (1973, 1985a, 1997) circular RIASEC model exemplifies spatial models of vocational interests (Fig. 5.2). These models are multidimensional, specifying interconnections among all the elements. An interest scale item can have weight on more than one dimension. The structure suggests a dynamic: A push in one direction implies a pull in another. Consistent with Holland's theory of personality and work environments, the model allows us to map people and occupations in the same interest space. Both persons and work settings can be described with RIASEC codes. Two images of the RIASEC model are customarily considered (Rounds, 1995; Rounds, Tracey, & Hubert, 1992): The looser, circular model postulates only the RIASEC ordering of types, while the more stringent, circumplex model postulates that the distances between opposite, adjacent, and alternate types are correspondent. Fig. 5.2 represents the circumplex model.

Circular models provide a significant link with circumplex models in personality, such as Kiesler's (1983) or Wiggins' (Wiggins & Broughton, 1985) interpersonal circle, which share the structural qualities and perhaps also the underlying network of meaning. Holland (1973, 1997) has attributed an interpersonal component to his types, and his theory of types and environments is based on the idea that people are the environment. The Schneider, Ryan, Tracey, and Rounds (1996) paper that investigated the two broad interpersonal dimensions of Affiliation and Power and their relations to Holland's circular model is an example.

Before Holland's conceptualization, Roe (1956) divided occupations into eight fields—Technical, Science, Outdoors, Arts and Entertainment, Service, General

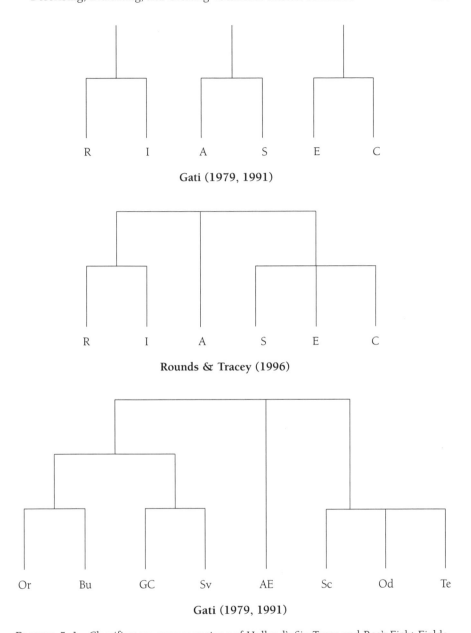

Gati (1979, 1991)

Rounds & Tracey (1996)

Gati (1979, 1991)

FIGURE 5.1   Classificatory representations of Holland's Six Types and Roe's Eight Fields

Note: R = Realistic, I = Investigative, A = Artistic, S = Social, E = Enterprising, C = Conventional; Te = Technical, Od = outdoors, Sc = science, GC = general culture, AE = arts & entertainment, Sv = service, Bu = business, Or = organization.

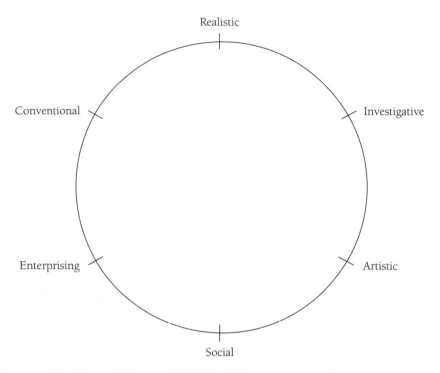

FIGURE 5.2   Holland's Circular RIASEC Model Represented as a Circumplex
Note: R = Realistic, I = Investigative, A = Artistic, S = Social, E = Enterprising, C = Conventional

Culture, Organization, and Business Contact. As shown in Fig. 5.3, several different circular arrangements of Roe's fields have been proposed (Roe & Klos,
1969; Meir, 1970, 1973; Knapp, Knapp, & Knapp-Lee, 1990).

There is no reason why the ideal vocational interest structure would have only
two dimensions, and a third dimension is often identified, such as level of
responsibility, prestige, occupational level, or status. A third dimension, for
example, is implicit in the interpretation of the *Self-Directed Search,* when consideration of a general educational requirement is overlaid on Holland type.
Gottfredson and Holland (1996) have proposed complexity as a third dimension
for both people and environments. For example, occupations vary according to
the cognitive demands made on workers, and people vary according to their abilities. Similarly Dawis and Lofquist (1984) propose in their theory of work adjustment that satisfactoriness results from a good fit between an individual's abilities
and the occupation's ability requirements. Roe and Klos (1969) defined six levels of responsibility as a third dimension, depending on how many, how difficult,

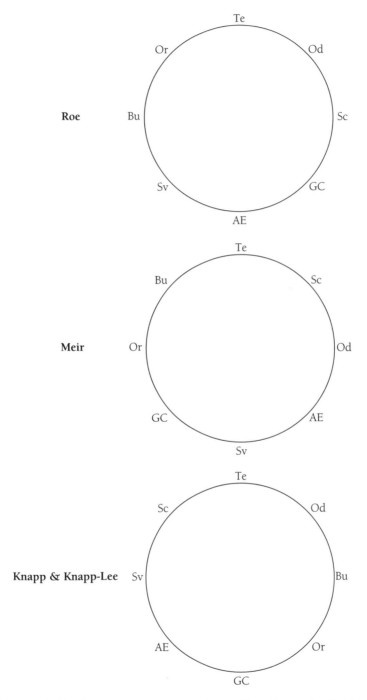

FIGURE 5.3   Three Circular Representations of Roe's Occupational Fields

Note: Te = technical, Od = outdoors, Sc = science, GC = general culture, AE = arts & entertainment, Sv = service, Bu = business, Or = organization

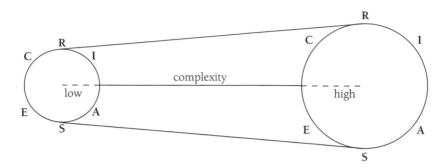

Gottfredson & Holland (1996)

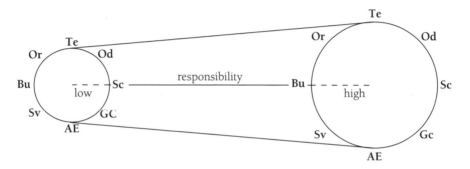

Roe & Klos (1969)

FIGURE 5.4   Roe and Klos (1969) and Gottfredson and Holland's (1996)
              Conical Representation of Vocational Interests

Note: Te = technical, Od = outdoors, Sc = science, GC = general culture, AE = Arts & entertainment, Sv = service, Bu = business, Or = organization; R = Realistic, I = Investigative, A = Artistic, S = Social, E = Enterprising, C = Conventional. Copyright 1997 by Rounds and Day.

and how many kinds of decisions had to be made at each level. Roe and Klos (1969) and Gottfredson and Holland (1996) visualized the third dimension as a conical link between two vocational circles (Fig. 5.4), while Tracey and Rounds (1996) suggested that the third dimension of prestige lies orthogonal to the other two dimensions, creating a spherical representation of vocational interests (also see Tracey, 1997). Fig. 5.5 displays three planes from this sphere, showing how the idea of prestige relates to the People/Things and Data/Ideas dimensions.

What about current interest inventories? Can a third dimension be located? Einarsdóttir (1996) found that for men taking the *Strong Interest Inventory*, the third dimension of prestige correlated with sex type, while for women it did not,

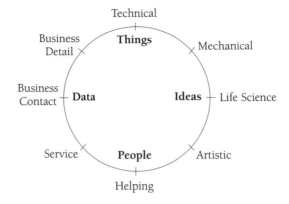

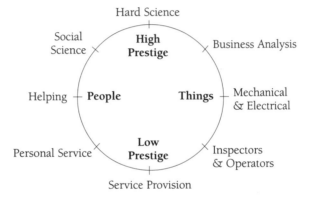

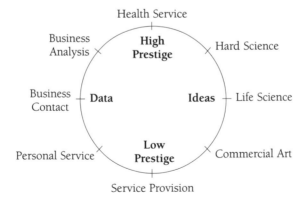

FIGURE 5.5 Three Planes from Tracey and Rounds' (1996) Spherical Representation

although the prestige dimension also appears in their pattern of responses. Day (1997), examining the *Unisex Edition of the American College Testing Interest Inventory* (UNIACT), found a third dimension that could be interpreted as an accommodation to activities that share qualities opposite on the Holland hexagon. So far the third dimension has accounted for a small portion of response variation (Einarsdóttir, 1996; Tracey & Rounds, 1996; Day, 1997), typically 5%, and like any interest dimension it is defined by the kinds of items used in the inventory. For instance, consciously varying the levels of prestige in the list of items will produce a third dimension of prestige in the analysis.

Much earlier Strong (1943) had based his classification of Occupational Scales on a three-dimensional factor analysis and had graphically displayed 34 Occupational Scales on a spherical model. Fig. 5.6 shows a slice of his spherical model. In his 1945 manual he even furnished his Interest Globe Chart to counselors, urging them to give the globe to their clients as an aid to understanding their interest scores. Thus the idea of a third dimension has persisted over 50 years but has remained a background hum. Modern statistical techniques, in concert with computers' ability to present three-dimensional schemes easily and accessibly, may provide the tune that makes everyone want to dance.

More than two factors have also been found through factor analysis (e.g., Jackson, 1977; Prediger, 1982). The People/Things and Data/Ideas factors are actually the second and third, while the first factor extracted is usually labeled a "general factor" accounting for a good deal of variance, perhaps up to 40% (Prediger, 1982). As its label indicates, there is no concert on what the factor really means—Prediger (1982) and Jackson (1977, 1986) assert that it is a form of acquiescence (the subjects' general tendency to respond "Like" or "Dislike" no matter what items are presented), and some interpret it as reflecting personality. Berdie (1943) and Stewart (1960) reported that people with a high number of likes tend to be enthusiastic, dominant, sociable, and cheerful, whereas those with many dislikes are seen as cautious, cynical, depressive, and moody. The meaning of this general factor still eludes researchers.

BRIEF HISTORY: EVALUATION OF STRUCTURAL MODELS

Keep in mind that whereas personality theory has a long tradition of dueling structures, with the latest contender in the ring the "Big Five" factors (Digman, 1990; Goldberg, 1993; McCrae & Costa, 1997), vocational theory has never endeavored to pin down the fundamental dimensions or factors of vocational interests. This lacuna

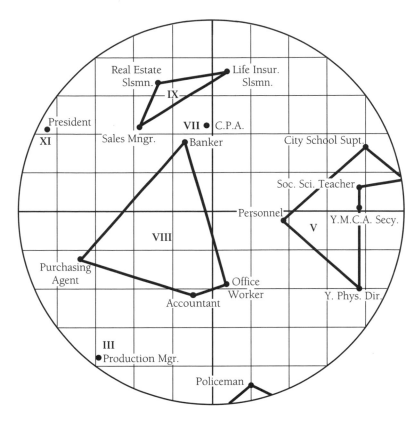

FIGURE 5.6   A Slice of Strong's (1943) Spherical Model

may be due to a preoccupation with specific measures and their efficacy. The *Strong* and its progeny have dominated the area of career counseling and have probably drawn boundaries around the ways people conceptualize the field. By analogy, the concept of intelligence for a very long time was bounded by what intelligence tests measured. Vocational interest experts may yet discover still-unfathomed ways to look at their subject matter. To date, model comparison studies have often focused on defending one model over another rather than enhancing exactness of representation.

Beginning with Thurstone (1931) and until the late 1970s dimensional models were the focus of inquiry. The typical study involved application of factor analysis to a pool of items usually drawn from an existing interest inventory. The main questions involved the number and kinds of factors (that is, factor interpretation, relying on the investigators' intuition and prowess in comparing factors across studies, an approach frequently criticized [Meehl, Lykken, Schofield, & Tellegen, 1971]). Factor-analytic interest research has not been programmatic. The investigators tended to study their own inventories for construct validity purposes or for the purpose of scale construction. Unlike personality assessment research and researchers, the field of interest measurement has not had a concerted effort over time to identify the fundamental dimensions.

With some exceptions (e.g., Guilford et al., 1954), explicit tests of vocational interest models did not begin until the 1970s. Explicit tests involve an a priori model and a method to evaluate model-data fit. The explicit evaluation of interest models coincided with the shift of focus from dimensional models to spatial models and the advent of multidimensional scaling (Rounds & Zevon, 1983), a method ideally suited to testing spatial models. Meir (1970, 1973; Gati & Meir, 1982; Meir & Ben-Yehuda, 1976) conducted the first explicit evaluations of interest models. He and Gati (1982, 1991) did extensive analyses of Roe's structural hypothesis, failing to support Roe's circular ordering of occupational fields as shown in Fig. 5.3. Rounds and Zevon (1983) reviewed Meir's and Gati's studies and reported that none of 10 spatial representations yielded by these studies reproduced Roe's hypothesized circular order of occupational fields. A meta-structural analysis (Tracey & Rounds, 1994) using 24 correlation matrices of Roe's fields came to the same conclusion: Roe's circular model does not fit the data. Strikingly, these studies are some of the few instances in which a vocational interest model has failed to receive support, and an alternative model, Meir's hypothesized circular order (see Fig. 5.3), shows clearly a better model-data fit.

Explicit evaluation of Holland's model also began in the 1970s (Rounds, Davison, & Dawis, 1979). Unfortunately, much of this early research evaluating Holland's model was based on Wakefield and Doughtie's (1973) and Gati's (1979, 1982) hypothesis-testing procedure. Both procedures—Wakefield and Doughtie's and Gati's—were later found to be incorrect and without statistical legitimacy (Hubert & Arabie, 1987; Rounds, Tracey, & Hubert, 1992), necessitating a reanalysis of these and other studies. That reanalysis (Rounds, 1995; Tracey & Rounds, 1993) yielded the unsurprising conclusion that Holland's circular order model showed a reasonable fit to RIASEC correlation matrices. In fact, it is rare, as Dawis (1992) notes, to find a RIASEC matrix that does not display the circular ordering.

(Unfortunately, history seems to repeat itself with Myors' [1996] proposed use of the Spearman measure of rank correlation to evaluate Holland's structural hypotheses. The Spearman index can be used legitimately for descriptively assessing the degree of correspondence between two matrices but not as a statistical test of Holland's order relations.)

Comparing two or more models against each other rather than testing whether or not a single model fits the data is a relatively new pursuit. After Gati (1982) introduced his three-group partition model, he began a series of studies (Gati, 1991) comparing his classificatory models (Fig. 5.1) with Holland's and Roe's spatial models (see Figs. 5.2 and 5.3). Gati's model-comparison studies culminated in his *Psychological Bulletin* review, where he concluded that his three-group partition model was superior to Holland's model and Roe's model.

Shortly afterwards Tracey and Rounds (1993, 1994), in part responding to Gati's review, conducted a series of structural meta-analyses aimed at evaluating various structural assertions. In the case of Gati versus Holland, Tracey and Rounds concluded that Holland's order and circumplex model were better representations of the structure of RIASEC types than Gati's hierarchical model. In an arresting conclusion they found little difference in goodness-of-fit between these dueling models. Taking other concerns than fit into account, Holland appeared superior to Gati in a specific way: Holland's spatial model captures the blending and the mutuality among the types, compared to Gati's discrete representation, which is overreductive. Holland's circular model is designed to portray how the RIASEC types relate to each other, focusing on the overlap and continuous nature of types. Similarly, in the case of Gati's hierarchical model versus Meir's circular order model, both representations fit Roe's eight fields equally well, again leaving the decision of what model is better to criteria other than goodness of fit.

A problem with model comparisons arises when commentators unwittingly reify visual RIASEC representations in two-dimensional space, which results from multidimensional scaling or similar operations. Holland (1997; Holland & Gottfredson, 1992), for example, is fond of labeling the results of spatial analyses of real-world data *misshapen polygons*. What Holland and Gottfredson fail to understand is that these structures, in most cases, fit a variety of circumplex models (see Fouad, Cudeck, & Hansen, 1984; Rounds, Tracey, & Hubert, 1992; Rounds & Tracey, 1993; Tracey & Rounds, 1993).

Reification leads people to overinterpret uneven distances among the six plotted points or between solutions for different groups, an overinterpretation that leads to mistaken and embarrassing conclusions about structural differences. For example, researchers would never eyeball two mean scores and conclude that they differ because they are not identical. The same holds for model-data comparisons. The viewer of two-dimensional plots must keep in mind, first, that samples are not perfect population estimators; second, that each point theoretically includes other points surrounding it in an undefined confidence region; third, that no one has defined how much statistical variability represents meaningful diversity in this area; and fourth, that it is inconceivable that human categorization processes really reproduce Euclidean geometrical operations. Researchers would be less willing to rule out a circumplex if confidence regions—for example, ellipses around the scale points (Heiser & Meulman, 1983)—were made available for the RIASEC solutions.

Almost all of the model-data fit comparisons have involved spatial versus discrete representations. An exception is the comparison of Prediger's (1982) bipolar factor representation (People/Things and Data/Ideas) to Hogan's (1983) unidimensional factor (sociability and conformity) representation of Holland's RIASEC circumplex (Rounds & Tracey, 1993). It was found that the orientation of the People/Things and Data/Ideas factors fit neither better nor worse than did the sociability and conformity dimensions. Both factor models received support when predictions from these models conform to predictions from the circumplex. Simply put, if you have a circumplex there is no preferred orientation of dimensions.

Because the outcomes of the Holland-Gati model-data fit wars are a draw when based strictly on model-data fit indexes with U.S. samples, often suggesting that models complement each other, nest within each other, or simply find graphical expression of the same ideas in different forms, it may behoove us to use other criteria to judge the usefulness of a vocational interest structure. The characteristics of the model itself, rather than its veridicality, may be of import. For example, what can we do with one model that can't be done with another? What opportunities and possibilities do spatial and classificatory representations afford us? One model may be more heuristic in producing important research questions, while another may be better for use with career counseling clients.

INDIVIDUAL DIFFERENCES: RIASEC MEASURES

When Holland's RIASEC structure is accepted, as it commonly is, the question arises of which inventory best represents this structure. A counselor would hope to choose an inventory that elicits responses most interpretable using the RIASEC model. Rounds and Tracey (1993) evaluated the model-data fit of six major measures, the *Vocational Preference Inventory* (VPI; Holland, 1985b), the *Self-Directed Search* (SDS; Holland, Fritzsche, & Powell, 1994), the *Unisex Edition of the American College Testing Interest Inventory* (UNIACT; Swaney, 1995a), the *Career Decision-Making Interest Inventory* (CDM; Harrington & O'Shea, 1993), the *Career Assessment Inventory* (CAI;

Johansson, 1986), and the *Strong Interest Inventory* (SII; Harmon, Hansen, Borgen, & Hammer, 1994). Fig. 5.7 shows the results of the scaling analysis: a graph of the salience ratio and the variance accounted for (VAF) by the RIASEC measures. The VAF, in the present case, indicates the goodness of fit of the Holland circumplex to the RIASEC data. The relative salience indicates the importance of the two dimensions (People/Things and Data/Ideas) in the overall goodness of fit: Salience ratio values greater than zero indicate that Data/Ideas was accounting for more data variation than People/Things, negative values indicate that People/Things was accounting for more data variation than Data/Ideas, and values of zero indicate an equal balance.

The location of the inventories on Fig. 5.7 provides information about their structural properties. It is apparent that the best fit is with the UNIACT, SII, and VPI and the worst with the SDS, CDM, and CAI. The salience ratio indicates that SII and UNIACT are much better at differentiating individuals on the Data/Ideas dimension than the People/Things dimension. The opposite was found for the SDS, CDM, and CAI: They do a better job differentiating individuals on the People/Things dimension. But the VPI nicely differentiates individuals on both dimensions. Given these findings, it appears that the SDS, CDM, and CAI RIASEC types have different structural properties than the UNIACT, SII, and VPI RIASEC types. We would expect that the UNIACT, SII, and VPI would yield more accurate RIASEC scores for an equilateral hexagon—a circumplex.

INDIVIDUAL DIFFERENCES
IN MODEL-DATA FIT: GROUPS

Holland (1985a) baldly stated that "[t]he [RIASEC] ordering of types or occupational categories is similar even when the data, sexes, and cultures vary" (p. 119). Such generalizations are born to strife, especially in an individual-differences-rapt zeitgeist like today's. As though Holland had thrown down the glove, researchers sprang to the ready.

With clearly differing tradition, socialization, and opportunity, men and women seem obvious candidates to differ in their responses to the world of work. However, this does not seem to hold true, according to a meta-analysis by Rounds and Tracey (1993). When they evaluated Holland model-data fit, they found that the model accounted for 76% of the variance among 31 samples of women and for 76% of the variance among 31 samples of men. Anderson, Tracey, and Rounds (1997) concurred when they found no difference between matched male and female groups

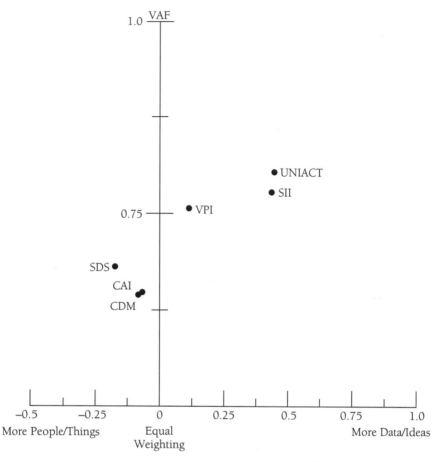

FIGURE 5.7   Graph of the Salience Ratio and Model-Data Fit
(Variance Accounted For, or VAF) by RIASEC Inventory

Note: CAI = *Career Assessment Inventory;* CDM = *Career Decision-Making Interest Inventory;* SDS = *Self-Directed Search;* SII = *Strong Interest Inventory;* UNIACT = *Unisex Edition of the ACT Interest Inventory;* VPI = *Vocational Interest Inventory.*

From "Prediger's dimensional representation of Holland's RIASEC circumplex," by J. Rounds and T. J. Tracey, 1993, *Journal of Applied Psychology, 78,* p. 886. Copyright 1993 by the American Psychological Association. Adapted with permission of the authors.

in the ordering of General Occupational Themes from the *Strong Interest Inventory*. These findings of structural similarity of Holland types for men and women should not be extrapolated to mean that there are no differences at all. They only apply to Holland types. Factor-analytic studies (see Kuder, 1977; Rounds, 1995), possibly on a larger domain of vocational interests, have come to mixed conclusions concerning the similarity of the structure for men and women.

Other subgroups who might be expected to hold different worldviews from the White majority are ethnic and racial minorities within the United States. Rounds and Tracey (1996) analyzed model-data fit for male and female samples of African Americans, American Indians, Hispanics, and Asian Americans. They used a metastructural analysis, finding a better fit with data from 73 U.S. White majority samples than with data from 20 U.S. ethnic samples. They concluded that both Holland's and Gati's models were inadequate representations of the structure of interests for ethnic citizens.

In the same meta-analysis Rounds and Tracey (1996) analyzed 76 samples from 18 countries outside the United States. Compared to the fit to Holland's model displayed by U.S. White majority benchmark samples, the fit of the foreign samples was significantly lower. In fact, 94% of the U.S. benchmark samples evidenced a better fit than the international samples did. Fifteen of the eighteen countries failed to fit the model, and potential moderators such as per capita gross national product and cultural values of individualism-collectivism and masculinity-femininity did not explain model-fit differences among countries.

Rounds and Tracey (1996) also investigated the fit of Gati's three-group partition and of an alternative three-group partition that isolates A as a category and includes S with the E and C group (see Fig. 5.1). Fig. 5.8 portrays the success levels of the three models in explaining the structure of 18 countries' samples by depicting the correspondence indexes of three models (dots stand for the Gati model, squares for the alternative model, and triangles for the Holland model). The correspondence index is a ratio of order predictions met minus unmet to total predictions made for each model; it is a mark of model-data fit, with 1 indicating a perfect fit. Gati's model and the alternative model make many fewer predictions than Holland's; Rounds and Tracey suggest that the weaker set of conditions better generalizes across nations, indicating some level of structural similarity across countries. Small numbers of samples and small sample sizes for several countries, the researchers note, may compromise these findings in undefined ways.

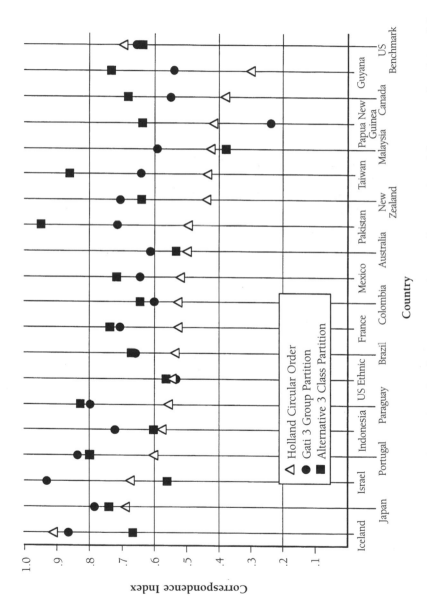

FIGURE 5.8   Mean Correspondence Index Values for 18 Countries, the U.S. Ethnic Sample, and the U.S. Benchmark Sample by RIASEC Model

From "Cross-cultural structural equivalence of RIASEC models and measures," by J. Rounds and T. J. Tracey, 1996, *Journal of Counseling Psychology, 43*, p. 321. Copyright 1996 by the American Psychological Association. Reprinted with permission of the author.

RETHINKING U.S. ETHNIC
DIFFERENCES IN STRUCTURE

Recently we have considered the question, "How much difference makes a difference?" A group's deviation from a model may not mean much in terms of the group's conceptions of the world of work. In something as basic as everyday human activities our networks of meaning could easily be similar enough to be sufficient for interest measurement. So far we have seen no concrete example of a single group's meaningful departure from the way other groups conceptualize their activities. For example, all groups probably see sorting, counting, and classifying as related to each other and furthermore as related to certain personality characteristics and associated with certain job preferences and other activities, which anyone would agree do not include frenzied dancing under the full moon with strangers. Proof to the contrary would require testing this tapestry of relations, not merely relations within a structure of vocational interests. In other words we would have to find cultures or biological groups who do not think of bookkeepers, in general, as cautious people with quiet, solitary habits. No matter what statistical deviations are found within and among models of measured vocational interests, it could be that deeper claims of similarity hold true.

These deeper claims have been considered by researchers into ethnic and racial issues. For example, Walsh and Holland (1992) reviewed eight studies of adult workers' RIASEC occupational codes. They found that workers in the same field, Black or White, men or women, generate similar occupational codes, agreeing with Holland's typology and other data. Researchers at ACT (Swaney, 1995a) checked the question prospectively by identifying students from five racial/ethnic groups who were "very sure" of their occupational choices. They obtained these students' Holland profiles, plotted them on a two-dimensional plane, and statistically evaluated the agreement between pairs. They found that students who chose the same occupations landed in similar hexagon locations, no matter what their racial or ethnic group.

Recently Fouad, Harmon, and Borgen (1997) studied adult workers from African American ($N = 805$), Hispanic/Latino/a ($N = 686$), Asian American ($N = 795$), and White American groups ($N = 36,632$) and found no differences in Holland model-data fit. Taking a different approach, Day, Rounds, and Swaney (1998) studied a sample of college-bound students who completed the revised UNIACT (Swaney, 1995a), as well as a comparison group of 10th-graders. Among African Americans ($N = 2,745$), Mexican Americans ($N = 1,809$), Native

Americans (N = 2,643), Asian Americans (N = 1,959), and White Americans (N = 2,454) no differences in Holland model-data fit were apparent. This study also found no differences in fit for the African American, Hispanic, and Caucasian 10th-grade students, ruling out the possibility that the college bound students' good fit stemmed from their shared status as good students. That is, the 10th-grade sample included students who were not bound for college or even, in some cases, for 11th grade, and this inclusion made no difference in fit. Finally no fit differences were found between males and females within or between ethnic/racial groups. Day and colleagues (1998) found in three-way multidimensional scaling analyses a plot reflecting the placement of the RIASEC types when all ethnic groups are scaled simultaneously. This melting-pot plot is shown in Fig. 5.9 and is overlaid on a plot derived from a three-way multidimensional scaling of 77 U.S. RIASEC matrices (Rounds & Tracey, 1993) representing all published and unpublished RIASEC data sets from 1969 to 1989. These matrices were used as benchmarks to evaluate the structural equivalence of RIASEC models across cultures (Rounds & Tracey, 1996). The similarity of the melting-pot plot, which equally represents the five ethnic groups, to the U.S. benchmark plot is uncanny. Both plots show the gap between the Conventional and the Realistic types, which may invite further exploration of the categories' functional equivalence.

Using larger samples (N = 49,450) and a more stringent analysis, Day and Rounds (1998) reproduced the finding: no differences among ethnic/racial groups nor between sexes. These findings call into doubt Rounds and Tracey's generalization that Holland's model does not fit U.S. minority samples.

The conflicting results from the Rounds and Tracey (1996) meta-analysis, we think, may be traced to sampling problems in the 20 U.S. ethnic/racial studies available to them. Obtaining large, representative samples of minority populations is a perennial problem in group differences research, and there are several ways in which samples may not behave as the whole population would (Day & Rounds, 1998).

The difficulty of obtaining sizable general samples of ethnically and racially diverse groups is frequently discussed in ethics and multicultural literature (e.g., Blanck, Bellack, Rosnow, Rotheram-Borus, & Schooler, 1992; Dana, 1993). Methods of acquiring participants from an identifiable group may unintentionally select for other qualities than racial or ethnic category: Examples might be recruitment of participants from Black church rosters or university ethnic study centers.

Furthermore, unmotivated and suspicious respondents may resist providing accurate information, in what Ogbu (1990) labels *cultural inversion,* an identity-preserving strategy that endorses opposition to White-majority expectations.

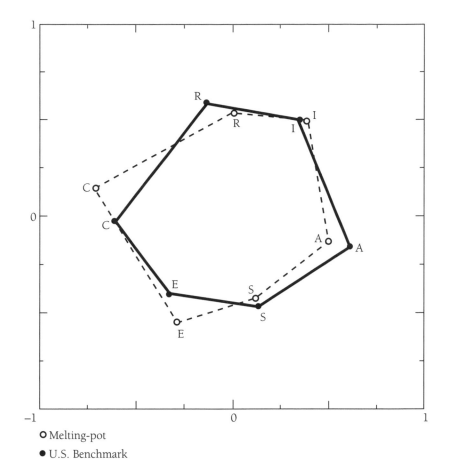

O Melting-pot

● U.S. Benchmark

FIGURE 5.9   Melting Pot Plot (Day, Rounds, & Swaney, 1998) and U.S. Benchmark Plot

Note: R = Realistic, I = Investigative, A = Artistic, S = Social, E = Enterprising, C = Conventional

From "Prediger's dimensional representation of Holland's RIASEC circumplex," by J. Rounds and T. J. Tracey, 1993, *Journal of Applied Psychology, 78,* p. 882. Copyright 1993 by the American Psychological Association. Also from "The structure of vocational interests for diverse racial ethnic groups," by S. X Day, J. Rounds, and K. Swaney, 1998, *Psychological Science, 9,* p. 44. Copyright 1998 by the American Psychological Society. Adapted with permission of the authors.

Many White samples have completed vocational interest measures for career counseling purposes (giving them a motivation to be accurate), while minority samples have been asked to fill out measures simply because of their minority status. Wholehearted devotion to accurate response among such samples cannot reasonably be anticipated. Valid responses to inventories require a satisfactory degree of cooperation and commitment, which we may not be able to count upon.

Finally race and ethnicity are not firm categories, and both biological and cultural underpinnings are inexact (Zuckerman, 1990). A mere self-report of group membership does not provide a clue to a person's acculturation into that group or any other (Dana, 1993; Betz & Fitzgerald, 1995); yet such self-reports are used to undergird broad statements about cultural differences. For these reasons a cautious course is most wise in reviewing research that claims significant group differences.

VOCATIONAL INTEREST CIRCLE

The circular structure of vocational interests seems singularly robust and stable across groups, and Tracey and Rounds (1995) suggest that the circle, not the number of categories carved from it, is the key structure. They suspect, as others (e.g., Dawis, 1992; Trapnell, 1989) have acknowledged, that broad-band interests around the circle's circumference could number four (Prediger), six (Holland), eight (Roe and Jackson), or twelve (Guilford) depending on the uses to be made of it. When they looked at items on the next level of generality, basic interests, they found that the items spread themselves between categories on the circle rather than gathering in clusters. Gottfredson and Holland (1996) concur that the categories are not separate and distinct: "It is more accurate to think of the main categories in the Holland classification as bands or rings that blend into each other than to view the categories as six separate bins" (p. 13). Fig. 5.10 shows an example of how the sciences spread between Realistic and Artistic sites along a Hard Science to Soft Science continuum. Along the same lines as Zytowski's (1986) interconnection of Roe and Holland's categories, Tracey and Rounds used concentric circles within the larger circumplex to represent various levels of complexity. Rounds has extended the concentric circle representation to map the catalogue of basic interests, forming the Vocational Interest Circle (Fig. 5.11; Rounds, 1997), a highly integrated interpretive framework that could be adapted for many research purposes and testing situations. The framework can accommodate many theoretical concentrations.

The idea that one framework might encompass most systems of classification is not surprising from a cognitive categorization point of view. Basic interests are distributed around the circle because the broad-based types are fuzzy sets, probabilistic rather than discrete. Following Medin's (1989) idea that concepts are organized around theories, we might say that the structure lies not merely in similarity of occupations but rather in a theory of what people do: create, teach, persuade, trade, build, think, plan, keep track, communicate, nurture, protect, entertain. "What people do" may lend itself to a naturalistic approach to categorization, in which the principles of reasoning have evolved since the early

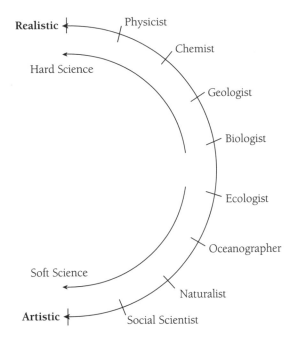

FIGURE 5.10   Slice of the Vocational Interest Circle: A Hard Sciences to Soft Sciences Continuum Between Realistic and Artistic Types

Copyright 1997 by Rounds and Day.

hominids (who did these same basic things) and are thus the same the world over, like categorizations of colors and animals (Gardner, 1987).

DEVELOPMENTAL QUESTIONS

Like the adult studies, the early structural studies of children's interests began with a factor-analytic approach to model development. Tyler (1955, 1956) set the precedent for the study of the structure of children's vocational interests. In a paper considered a classic, Tyler (1955) reported that analyses of fourth-grade student responses to an interest inventory yielded a factor for both boys and girls that represented the rejection of stereotypic opposite-gender activities, suggesting the early influence of sex roles on interest activities. Since Tyler there has been an on-and-off trickle of factor-analytic and scale development studies (e.g., Freeberg & Rock, 1973; Zbaracki, Clark, & Wolins, 1985).

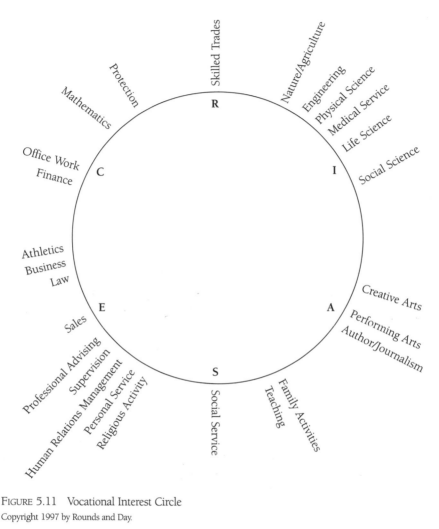

FIGURE 5.11   Vocational Interest Circle
Copyright 1997 by Rounds and Day.

Once Holland discovered the hexagon among high school respondents, the obvious next questions have to do with generalizability to other populations. Currently the RIASEC categories and structure are firmly set among high school and college students and adult workers. But the question remains: When do children acquire the structure we see steadily established among adults? The lower bound for successful replications of the RIASEC circular order structure is the eighth grade (Swaney, 1995a). Attempts to identify a RIASEC structure at an earlier age have yielded mixed results. For example, Edwards, Nafziger, and Holland

(1974), studying elementary school students in grades four through six, discerned the RIASEC structure using a simplified version of the *Vocational Preference Inventory*. Swaney (1995b), using the grade six through seven version of the UNIACT, has also reported finding a circular RIASEC structure with sixth-grade students. Nevertheless, recent studies at the University of Illinois with children in elementary and middle school failed to show that they differentiate among occupations and activities in the same way grownups do (Mueller, 1995; Tracey & Ward, 1998; Ward, 1997). We believe that the differences among these studies are probably due to how researchers are assessing model-data fit.

Assessing children's interests presents daunting problems, especially when we have relied on methods, like paper-and-pencil instruments, that have been used to assess the interests of adults. Lengthy lists with scaled responses (for example, from 1 for "Dislike" to 5 for "Like") may tax children's attention and concentration. Items describing activities that most parents discourage, such as "Telling others what to do" (being bossy) and "Trying to talk your parents into doing something you want" (whining), may elicit "Dislike" responses from children for reasons other than dislike, such as social pressure. Ultimately we may have to forgo the convenience of handing out questionnaires and find other ways to assess children's interests. Alternatively, we may want to forgo vocational interests and study aspirations (Gottfredson, 1981; Holland, Gottfredson, & Baker, 1990). So far Trice's programmatic research (Trice, 1991a, 1991b; Trice, Hughes, Odom, Woods, & McClellan, 1995) on children's career aspirations has much wider applicability to understanding the development of vocational preferences than do the structural studies. Although there has not been a concerted effort (as there has been with adults), research on children has tentatively pointed to four conclusions:

1. Factor-analytic studies have identified several factors similar to factors reported for adults. For example, Zbaracki, Clark, and Wolins (1985) assessed the interests of boys and girls in grades four through six and identified factors such as Athletic, Mechanical, Religion, Science, Social, and Verbal (cf. Day & Rounds, 1997).

2. The general factor, sometimes called a response bias (yea-saying or naysaying) factor, is much larger for younger respondents (Mueller, 1995; Tyler, 1955). Prediger (1997) has summarized the contribution of the general factor for five age groups (percentage of variance in parenthesis): adults (37%), grade 12 students (44%), grade 10 students (49%), grade 8 students (54%), and grade 6 students (56%). Prediger's UNIACT data nicely show how the general factor increases with decreasing age.

3. The first substantive interest factor to emerge from studies evaluating Holland's model seems to be a variation on the People/Things dimension (Mueller, 1995; Ward, 1997). The People/Things dimension is probably the most replicated interest factor, first reported by Strong (1943).
4. The structure of interests may vary for boys and girls. With the notable exception of Freeberg and Rock (1973), most studies have reported sex differences. But we caution readers, these results are far from etched in stone.

CONCLUDING THOUGHTS

After this review one might ask is there anything new since Roe's three-dimensional model, Holland's six types rather than eight fields, or Strong's attempt to classify the Occupational Scales on a globe. Recent proposals have been in the shadow of these pioneers. What's new is a realization that an absolute, consistent, and veridical representation of vocational interest structure may not exist at all. For a specific purpose one of these representations may be right as far as being efficient and meaningful in context. For example, a cognitive psychologist might find our most whiz-bang, fully articulated models the most interesting for a study of the network of meaning. However, models with few dimensions, like Prediger's People/Things, Data/Ideas representation, may be most appropriate for helping a career counseling client who has never before considered how to approach work choices. A more sophisticated client may have a good idea of the general area of interest, and this client needs more detailed ways to look at choices within this area, calling for a model with more complexity.

The best next questions in the field concern this new type of goodness of fit. A structure's power lies in its ability to explain the world of work usefully in specific contexts. In this sense, models make meaning.

Many of the ideas that we express in this chapter come from arguments and discussions with Larry Hubert, Terry Tracey, Rene Dawis, and Mark Davison. Let us especially thank Larry Hubert, who has been a patient tutor on quantitative methods.

REFERENCES

Anderson, M. Z., Tracey, T.G.T., & Rounds, J. (1997). Examining the invariance of Holland's vocational interest model across gender. *Journal of Vocational Behavior, 50,* 349–364.

Berdie, R. F. (1943). Likes, dislikes, and vocational interests. *Journal of Applied Psychology, 27,* 180–189.

Betz, N. E., & Fitzgerald, L. F. (1995). Career assessment and intervention with racial and ethnic minorities. In F.T.L. Leong (Ed.), *Career development and vocational behavior of racial and ethnic minorities* (pp. 263–279). Hillsdale, NJ: Erlbaum.

Blanck, P. D., Bellack, A. S., Rosnow, R. L., Rotheram-Borus, M. J., & Schooler, N. R. (1992). Scientific rewards and conflicts of ethical choices in human subjects research. *American Psychologist, 47,* 959–965.

Dana, R. H. (1993). *Multicultural assessment perspectives for professional psychology.* Needham Heights, MA: Allyn & Bacon.

Dawis, R. V. (1992). The structure(s) of occupations: Beyond RIASEC. *Journal of Vocational Behavior, 40,*171–178.

Dawis, R. V., & Lofquist, L. H. (1984). *A psychological theory of work adjustment.* Minneapolis: University of Minnesota Press.

Day, S. X, & Rounds, J. (1997). "A little more than kin, and less than kind": Basic interests in vocational research and career counseling. *Career Development Quarterly, 45,* 207–220.

Day, S. X, & Rounds, J. (1998). Universality of vocational interest structure among racial and ethnic minorities. *American Psychologist, 53,* 728–736.

Day, S. X, Rounds, J., & Swaney, K. (1998). The structure of vocational interest for diverse racial/ethnic groups. *Psychological Science, 9,* 40–44.

Digman, J. M. (1990). Personality structure: Emergence of the five-factor model. *Annual Review of Psychology, 41,* 417–440.

Droege, R. C., & Hawk, J. (1977). Development of a U.S. Employment Service interest inventory. *Journal of Employment Counseling, 14,* 65–71.

Edwards, K. J., Nafziger, D. H., & Holland, J. L. (1974). Differentiation of occupational perceptions among different age groups. *Journal of Vocational Behavior, 4,* 311–318.

Einarsdóttir, S. (1996). *Application of a three dimensional model of vocational interests to the Strong Interest Inventory.* Unpublished master's thesis, University of Illinois at Urbana-Champaign.

Fouad, N. A., Cudeck, R., & Hansen, J. C. (1984). Convergent validity of the Spanish and English forms of the *Strong-Campbell Interest Inventory* for bilingual Hispanic high school students. *Journal of Counseling Psychology, 31,* 339–348.

Fouad, N. A., Harmon, L. W., & Borgen, F. H. (1997). The structure of interests in employed male and female members of U.S. racial/ethnic minority and non-minority groups. *Journal of Counseling Psychology, 44,* 339–345.

Freeberg, N. E., & Rock, D. A. (1973). Dimensional continuity of interests and activities during adolescence. *Human Development, 16,* 304–316.

Gardner, H. (1987). *The mind's new science.* New York: Basic Books.

Gati, I. (1979). A hierarchical model for the structure of vocational interests. *Journal of Vocational Behavior, 15,* 90–106.

Gati, I. (1982). Testing models for the structure of vocational interests. *Journal of Vocational Behavior, 21,* 164–182.

Gati, I. (1991). The structure of vocational interests. *Psychological Bulletin, 109,* 309–324.

Gati, I., & Meir, E. I. (1982). Congruence and consistency derived from the circular and the hierarchical models as predictors of occupational choice satisfaction. *Journal of Vocational Psychology, 20,* 354–365.

Goh, D. S., & Leong, F.T.L. (1993). The relationship between Holland's theory of vocational interests and Eysenck's model of personality. *Personality and Individual Differences, 15,* 555–562.

Goldberg, L. R. (1993). The structure of phenotypic personality traits. *American Psychologist, 48,* 26–34.

Gottfredson, G. D., & Holland, J. L. (1996). *Dictionary of Holland occupational codes* (3rd ed.). Odessa, FL: Psychological Assessment Resources.

Gottfredson, L. S. (1981). Circumscription and compromise: A developmental theory of occupational aspirations. *Journal of Counseling Psychology, 28,* 545–579.

Guilford, J. P., Christensen, R. R., Bond, N. A., & Sutton, M. A. (1954). A factor analytic study of human interests. *Psychological Monographs, 68* (4, Whole No. 375).

Harmon, L. W., Hansen, J. C., Borgen, F. H., & Hammer, A. L. (1994). *Strong Interest Inventory: Applications and technical guide.* Stanford, CA: Stanford University Press.

Harrington, T. F., & O'Shea, A. T. (1993). *The Harrington-O'Shea Career Decision-Making System revised manual.* Circle Pines, MN: American Guidance Service.

Heiser, W. J., & Meulman, J. (1983). Constrained multidimensional scaling, including confirmation. *Applied Psychological Measurement, 7,* 381–404.

Hogan, R. (1983). A socioanalytic theory of personality. In M. M. Page (ed.), *Nebraska symposium on motivation 1982. Personality: Current theory and research* (pp. 55–89). Lincoln: University of Nebraska Press.

Holland, J. L. (1973). *Making vocational choices: A theory of careers.* Englewood Cliffs, NJ: Prentice Hall.

Holland, J. L. (1985a). *Making vocational choices: A theory of vocational personalities and work environments* (2nd ed.). Englewood Cliffs, NJ: Prentice Hall.

Holland, J. L. (1985b). *Manual for the Vocational Preference Inventory.* Odessa, FL: Psychological Assessment Resources.

Holland, J. L. (1997). *Making vocational choices: A theory of vocational personalities and work environments* (3rd ed.). Odessa, FL: Psychological Assessment Resources.

Holland, J. L., Fritzsche, B. A., & Powell, A. B. (1994). *The Self-Directed Search technical manual.* Odessa, FL: Psychological Assessment Resources.

Holland, J. L., & Gottfredson, G. D. (1992). Studies of the hexagon model: An evaluation (or, the perils of stalking the perfect hexagon). *Journal of Vocational Behavior, 40,* 158–170.

Holland, J. L., Gottfredson, G. D., & Baker, H. G. (1990). Validity of vocational aspirations and interest inventories: Extended, replicated, and reinterpreted. *Journal of Counseling Psychology, 37,* 337–342.

Hubert, L., & Arabie, P. (1987). Evaluating order hypotheses within proximity matrices. *Psychological Bulletin, 102,* 172–178.

Jackson, D. N. (1977). *Manual for the Jackson Vocational Interest Survey.* Port Huron, MI: Research Psychologists Press.

Jackson, D. N. (1986). *Career Directions Inventory manual.* Port Huron, MI: Research Psychologists Press.

Johansson, C. B. (1986). *Career Assessment Inventory: The enhanced version.* Minneapolis: National Computer Systems.

Kiesler, D. J. (1983). The 1982 interpersonal circle: A taxonomy for complementarity in human transactions. *Psychology Review, 90,* 185–214.

Kuder, F. (1977). *Activity interests and occupational choice.* Chicago: Science Research Associates.

Knapp, R. R., & Knapp-Lee, L. (1990). *The COPES Interest Inventory, technical manual.* San Diego, CA: EdITS.

McCrae, R. R., & Costa, P. T. (1997). Personality trait structure as a human universal. *American Psychologist, 52,* 509–516.

Medin, D. L. (1989). Concepts and conceptual structure. *American Psychologist, 44,* 1469–1481.

Meehl, P. E., Lykken, D. T., Schofield, W., & Tellegen, A. (1971). Recaptured-item technique (RIT): A method for reducing somewhat the subjective element in factor-naming. *Journal of Experimental Research in Personality, 5,* 171–190.

Meir, E. I. (1970). Empirical test of Roe's structure of occupations and an alternative structure. *Journal of Counseling Psychology, 17,* 41–48.

Meir, E. I. (1973). The structure of occupations by interests—a smallest space analysis. *Journal of Vocational Behavior, 3,* 21–31.

Meir, E. I., & Ben-Yehuda, A. (1976). Inventories based on Roe and Holland yield similar results. *Journal of Vocational Behavior, 8,* 269–274.

Mueller, D. (1995). *The structure of vocational interests of elementary school children.* Unpublished master's thesis, University of Illinois at Urbana-Champaign.

Myors, B. (1996). A simple, exact test for the Holland hexagon. *Journal of Vocational Behavior, 48,* 339–351.

Ogbu, J. U. (1990). Minority status and literacy in comparative perspective. *Daedalus, 119,* 141–168.

Prediger, D. J. (1976). A world-of-work map for career exploration. *Vocational Guidance Quarterly, 24,* 198–208.

Prediger, D. J. (1982). Dimensions underlying Holland's hexagon: Missing link between interests and occupations? *Journal of Vocational Behavior, 21,* 259–287.

Prediger, D. J. (1997, May). *Integrating interests with abilities.* Paper presented at the conference on Vocational Interests: Their Meaning, Measurement, and Use in Counseling, Lehigh University, Bethlehem, PA.

Roe, A. (1956). *The psychology of occupations.* New York: Wiley.

Roe, A., & Klos, D. (1969). Occupational classification. *Counseling Psychologist, 1,* 84–89.

Rounds, J. B. (1995). Vocational interests: Evaluating structural hypotheses. In D. Lubinski & R. V. Dawis (Eds.), *Assessing individual differences in human behavior: New concepts, methods, and findings* (pp. 177–232). Palo Alto, CA: Davies-Black.

Rounds, J. B. (1997, August). Basic interest structure. In J. Rounds (Chair), Mapping vocational interest structures. Symposium conducted at the meeting of the American Psychological Association, Chicago.

Rounds, J. B., Davison, M. L., & Dawis, R. V. (1979). The fit between Strong-Campbell Interest Inventory General Occupational Themes and Holland's hexagonal model. *Journal of Vocational Behavior, 15,* 303–315.

Rounds, J. B., & Dawis, R. V. (1979). Factor analysis of *Strong Vocational Interest Blank* items. *Journal of Applied Psychology, 64,* 132–143.

Rounds, J. B., & Tracey, T.J.G. (1993). Prediger's dimensional representation of Holland's RIASEC circumplex. *Journal of Applied Psychology, 78,* 875–890.

Rounds, J. B., & Tracey, T.J.G. (1996). Cross-cultural structural equivalence of RIASEC models and measures. *Journal of Counseling Psychology, 43,* 310–329.

Rounds, J. B., Tracey, T.J.G., & Hubert, L. (1992). Methods for evaluating vocational interest structural hypotheses. *Journal of Vocational Behavior, 40,* 239–259.

Rounds, J. B., & Zevon, M. A. (1983). Multidimensional scaling research in vocational psychology. *Applied Psychological Measurement, 7,* 491-510.

Schneider, P. L., Ryan, J. M., Tracey, T.J.G., & Rounds, J. (1996). Examining the relation between Holland's RIASEC model and the interpersonal circle. *Measurement and Evaluation in Counseling and Development, 29,* 123–133.

Stewart, L. H. (1960). Modes of response on the Strong Blank and selected personality variables. *Journal of Counseling Psychology, 7,* 127–131.

Strong, E. K., Jr. (1943). *Vocational interests of men and women.* Stanford, CA: Stanford University Press.

Strong, E. K., Jr. (1945). *Manual for Strong Vocational Interest Blank for men.* Stanford, CA: Stanford University Press.

Swaney, K. B. (1995a). *Technical manual: Revised Unisex Edition of the ACT Interest Inventory (UNIACT).* Iowa City, IA: American College Testing.

Swaney, K. B. (1995b). *Supplement to the UNIACT technical manual: Development of a grade 6–7 version of UNIACT.* Iowa City, IA: American College Testing.

Thurstone, L. L. (1931). A multiple factor study of vocational interests. *Personnel Journal, 3,* 198–205.

Tracey, T.J.G. (1997). The structure of interests and self-efficacy expectations: An expanded examination of the spherical model of interest. *Journal of Counseling Psychology, 44,* 32–43.

Tracey, T.J.G., & Rounds, J. (1993). Evaluating Holland's and Gati's vocational interest models: A structural meta-analysis. *Psychological Bulletin, 113,* 229–246.

Tracey, T.J.G., & Rounds, J. (1994). An examination of the structure of Roe's eight interest fields. *Journal of Vocational Behavior, 44,* 279–296.

Tracey, T.J.G., & Rounds, J. (1995). The arbitrary nature of Holland's RIASEC types: A concentric-circles structure. *Journal of Counseling Psychology, 42,* 431–439.

Tracey, T.J.G., & Rounds, J. (1996). The spherical representation of vocational interests. *Journal of Vocational Behavior, 48,* 3–41.

Tracey, T.J.G., & Ward, C.C. (1998). The structure of children's interest and competence perceptions. *Journal of Counseling Psychology, 45,* 290–303.

Trapnell, P. D. (1989). *Structural validity in the measurement of Holland's vocational typology: A measure of Holland's types scaled to an explicit circumplex model.* Unpublished master's thesis, University of British Columbia, Vancouver.

Trice, A. D. (1991a). Stability of children's career aspirations. *Journal of Genetic Psychology, 152,* 137–139.

Trice, A. D. (1991b). A retrospective study of career development: I. Relationship among first aspirations, parental occupations, and current occupations. *Psychological Reports, 68,* 287–290.

Trice, A. D., Hughes, M. A., Odom, C., Woods, K., & McClellan, N. C. (1995). The origins of children's career aspirations: IV. Testing hypotheses from four theories. *Career Development Quarterly, 43,* 307–322.

Tyler, L. E. (1955). The development of "vocational interests": I. The organization of likes and dislikes in ten-year-old children. *Journal of Genetic Psychology, 86,* 33–44.

Tyler, L. E. (1956). A comparison of the interests of English and American school children. *Journal of Genetic Psychology, 88,* 175–181.

Wakefield, J. A., & Doughtie, E. B. (1973). The geometric relationship between Holland's personality typology and the Vocational Preference Inventory. *Journal of Counseling Psychology, 20,* 513–518.

Walsh, W. B., & Holland, J. L. (1992). A theory of personality types and environments. In W. B. Walsh, K. H. Craik, & R. H. Price (Eds.), *Person-environment psychology: Models and perspectives* (pp. 35–70). Hillsdale, NJ: Erlbaum.

Ward, C. C. (1997). *The structure of career interests in children.* Unpublished master's thesis, University of Illinois at Urbana-Champaign.

Wiggins, J. S., & Broughton, R. (1985). The interpersonal circle: A structural model for the integration of personality research. In R. Hogan & W. H. Jones (Eds.), *Perspectives in personality: Vol. 1* (pp. 1–47). Greenwich, CN: JAI Press.

Zbaracki, J. U., Clark, S. G., & Wolins, L. (1985). Children's Interests Inventory, grades 4–6. *Educational and Psychological Measurement, 45,* 517–521.

Zuckerman, M. (1990). Some dubious premises in research and theory on racial differences. *American Psychologist, 45,* 1297–1303.

Zytowski, D. G. (1986). Comparison of Roe's and Holland's occupational classifications: Diverse ways of knowing. *Journal of Counseling Psychology, 33,* 479–481.

CHAPTER SIX

Stability and Change in Vocational Interests

Jane L. Swanson

CONCERN ABOUT the "permanence" of interests began as early as the 1930s, not long after the birth of interest measurement. The earliest writers (Fryer, 1931; Strong, 1931) realized the crucial role that stability of vocational interests would play in acceptance of the new technology of interest measurement by the public and scholarly community. E. K. Strong, Jr., captured the fundamental dilemma regarding stability versus change in interests:

> If interests change from year to year, they are not trustworthy guides to the choice of a career. If they do not change greatly, then they may be safely so employed. The popular notion, supported by many psychologists, is that interests fluctuate from day to day, and are so unstable that little or no reliance can be placed upon them. It seems to most people impossible that present interests can be utilized as a basis for directing future behavior. (Strong, 1931, p. 3)

These early writers outlined important conceptual issues that defined the way in which interest stability was conceptualized and empirically examined, issues that continue to challenge researchers today. The topic of interest stability occupies a central role in all aspects of consideration of vocational interests, and questions regarding interest stability are at the very heart of the subjects addressed in this volume. Knowledge about the degree of stability and change has profound implications for theories of interests, for psychometric concerns in developing measures of interests, and for using interest inventories to help clients make career decisions.

The traditional ways in which psychologists conceptualize validity and reliability assume that the trait measured by an instrument is stable. Individual differences in stability of interests can therefore serve as a confounding factor in studies designed to assess predictive validity. If an individual's interests change dramatically, then predictive validity as a psychometric characteristic of the instrument itself is not accurately determined. Herzberg, Bouton, and Steiner (1954) commented on the confounding of stability and validity:

> In the sense in which interest measures are being utilized in vocational guidance a measure of stability of such interests over a period of time becomes a measure of validity . . . Extreme fluctuations in interest areas of young persons over a period of time would defeat any predictions based on them. (p. 90)

As an empirical illustration of this confound, Hansen and Swanson (1983) reported that substantially higher predictive validity hit rates were observed for college students with stable interest profiles versus those with unstable profiles.

"Stability" of interests often has been confused with test-retest reliability of an instrument, or what at times is called its "temporal stability" (Hansen, 1984). This too is an important distinction. This chapter focuses on stability of interests as a trait and as a characteristic of the person possessing the trait, not on reliability of scale scores as a characteristic of an instrument. Nevertheless, stability, validity, and reliability all affect one another, and a discussion of one topic necessarily requires an acknowledgment of the others.

This chapter reviews the literature regarding stability and change in vocational interests over the life span. I begin with a brief discussion of methods used to examine interest stability, followed by a summary of the empirical evidence about interest stability. In the subsequent section I raise several questions regarding stability and change that need additional attention, as well as offer some speculations drawn from literature relevant to structure of interests, personality psychology, and behavior genetics. Throughout the chapter, implications for theoreticians and practitioners are discussed.

THE STUDY OF INTEREST STABILITY

Empirical attention to stability of interests has waxed and waned several times since the early 1900s. Each reappearance has brought a new focus and a greater specificity of questions. Early research focused on documenting the *general stability* or permanence of interests within the framework of theoretical questions regarding the development of interests and in the context of then-current concerns about the utility of interest measurement. Later research turned to examining *individual differences* in stability of interests, with an increasing concentration on predictors and correlates of interest stability.

Without a doubt, E. K. Strong, Jr., was the most prolific contributor to the literature regarding stability of interests (Strong, 1931, 1935, 1943, 1951, 1952a, 1952b; Strong & Tucker, 1952). One of his contributions was a clarification of the methodology for determining interest stability (Strong, 1943). He suggested four primary methods, each of which rely on a slightly different use of longitudinal test-retest data. The first method computes test-retest correlations of interest scale scores, as is typically done to indicate reliability of an instrument over time, and yields one correlation per scale. These correlations indicate how consistently individuals have maintained their relative position in a group, on specific scales. The second method compares mean scale scores across time. This comparison furnishes evidence as to whether there has been increase or decrease in specific interests for a group and thus emphasizes amount of change in the strength of interests expressed in scale-score metric. The third method uses letter grades assigned to scores on *Strong Vocational Interest Blank* (SVIB) profiles to suggest how much reliance can be placed upon different ratings or classifications of individuals' interests in predicting their future behavior. The fourth method compares total profiles for an individual between two test administrations, via an intraindividual correlation. This method allows description of how much one person's profile is like another profile he or she produces at a later date, thus yielding one correlation coefficient per person. In this case the correlation coefficient reflects the relative ordering of scales for the same person at two different times.

The first three methods consider similarity of test and retest scores of a single scale within a *group* of people. Method 1 indicates the consistency of an individual's relative position within a group. Methods 2 and 3 indicate the amount and direction of change in a particular interest area, again for the group as a whole. Only Method 4 estimates the stability of interests for an individual. These four methods provide slightly different views; and the four methods in tandem allow a comprehensive view of interest stability and change. Fortunately they all point to the same basic conclusion.

In addition to the quantitative data underlying the methods outlined by Strong (1943), researchers also have relied on case study information to examine interest stability. Case studies offer the richness of context that is generally unavailable in other types of studies. For example, Helwig and Myrin (1997) examined stability of Holland typology codes for 20 members of an extended family over a 10-year interval, and knowledge of family history and intervening events allowed a complex interpretation of stability and change. Zytowski (1996) provided an interpretation of four of his own interest profiles obtained over a 30-year span, suggesting themes that were consistent throughout his career. Again, case study methodology provides a different perspective on interest stability yet supports the same basic conclusion.

EMPIRICAL EVIDENCE REGARDING INTEREST STABILITY

Since the 1930s approximately 30 studies have directly addressed the long-term stability of vocational interests. Table 6.1 contains those studies corresponding to the first method outlined by Strong (1943)—that is, computing test-retest correlations of interest scale scores. Table 6.2 contains studies that specifically address intraindividual stability using Strong's (1943) fourth method, through computation of a rank-order or Pearson product-moment correlation between two profiles obtained for a single individual. Based on the studies summarized in Tables 6.1 and 6.2, five conclusions can be drawn about stability of vocational interests.

1. *Interests are remarkably stable over long time intervals.*

This is by far the most fundamental and far-reaching conclusion. Hansen (1984) concluded that it was "the most well-documented knowledge in the entire field of interest measurement" (p. 114). This conclusion was articulated in the earliest studies conducted in the 1930s and continues to be confirmed in virtually every study since that time, using different statistical methods, different populations, and different measures of interests. For example, Johansson and Campbell (1971) summarized SVIB data from 66 groups of men. Test-retest correlation coefficients ranged from .54 to .84, over intervals ranging from 1 year to 23 years. Both age and length of time interval affected these coefficients. When interval was held constant, stability increased with subjects' age at first testing. With age held constant, stability was lower the longer the time interval between test and retest.

The same conclusion can be reached from the alternate viewpoint of examining intraindividual correlation coefficients. The median coefficients indicated in Table 6.2 (ranging from .57 to .92) suggest that 50% of individuals have an interest profile that shows substantial similarity to a second interest profile obtained

TABLE 6.1 Studies Examining Interest Stability via Strong's (1943) Method 1: Test-Retest Correlations of Scale Scores

Study	Scales	Sample	Time of First Testing	Interval	Coefficients	
					Range	Median
Strong (1935)	23 SVIB Occupational Scales	223 men	College seniors	5 years	.59 to .84	.76
Van Dusen (1940)	5 SVIB Occupational Scales	76 men	College freshmen	3 years	.50 to .85	.59
Canning, Taylor, & Carter (1941)	7 SVIB Occupational Scales	64 boys	10th grade	3 years	.48 to .65	.57
Fox (1947)	9 Kuder Interest Scales	58 boys	9th grade	8 weeks	.42 to .85	.71
		76 girls			.54 to .85	.81
Strong (1952a)[a]	SVIB Engineer Occupational Scale	247 men	College freshmen	1 year	Not reported	.91
		185 men	College freshmen	9 years		.77
		203 men	College freshmen	19 years		.76
		223 men	College seniors	5 years		.84
		168 men	College seniors	10 years		.83
Rosenberg (1953)	9 Kuder Interest Scales	91 boys	9th grade	3 years	.47 to .75	.61
		86 girls			.50 to .69	.61
Herzberg, Bouton, & Steiner (1954)	10 Kuder Interest Scales	101 college-bound boys	High school	23–42 mos.	.59 to .75	.67
		48 college-bound girls			.59 to .82	.70
		49 work-bound boys		15–49 mos.	.51 to .86	.70
		74 work-bound girls			.65 to .83	.74

TABLE 6.1 Studies Examining Interest Stability via Strong's (1943) Method 1: Test-Retest Correlations of Scale Scores *continued*

Study	Scales	Sample	Time of First Testing	Interval	Coefficients Range	Median
Herzberg & Bouton (1954)	10 Kuder Interest Scales	62 college-bound boys 68 college-bound girls	High school	4 years	.51 to .84 .61 to .79	.63 .68
Stordahl (1954b)	44 SVIB Occupational Scales	111 urban boys 70 rural boys	12th grade	2 years	.54 to .85 .45 to .81	.72 .67
Campbell (1966a)	SVIB Banker Occupational Scale	48 bankers	Various	30 years	Not reported	.56
Johansson & Campbell (1971)[a]	59 SVIB Scales	1,306 men	Age 19	5 years 10 years 20 years	Not reported	.75 .61 .54
			Age 25	5 years 18 years 23 years		.82 .75 .75
			Age 33	12 years		.80

[a]Coefficients reported in the table are selected samples of more extensive data reported in the study.

Note: SVIB = *Strong Vocational Interest Blank*

TABLE 6.2 Studies Examining Interest Stability via Strong's (1943) Method 4: Intraindividual Stability Coefficients

Study	Coefficient	Scales	Sample	Time of First Testing	Interval	Coefficients	
						Range	Median
Finch (1935)	rho	20 SVIB Occupational Scales	112 high school students	11th & 12th grade	3 weeks to 3 years	Not reported	Not reported
Taylor & Carter (1942)	rho	12 SVIB Occupational Scales	58 girls	11th grade	1 year	-.65 to .99	.74
Strong (1951, 1951, 1955)[a]	rho	34 SVIB Occupational Scales	50 men	College freshmen	1 year / 9 years / 19 years	Not reported	.88 / .67 / .72
			50 men	College seniors	5 years / 10 years / 22 years		.84 / .82 / .75
Powers (1954)	rho	44 SVIB Occupational Scales	Unemployed men	Age 16 to 63	10 years	-.38 to .96	.80
Stordahl (1954a)	Kendall's W	44 SVIB Occupational Scales	181 men	12th grade	2 years	.42 to .98	.74
King (1956)	rho	44 SVIB Occupational Scales	242 men	College freshmen	6 months	.26 to .95	.85
Hoyt, Smith, & Levy (1957)	rho	SVIB Occupational Scales	116 boys and girls	12th grade	2 years	Not reported	Not reported
Hoyt (1960)	rho	SVIB Occupational Scales	121 men	12th grade	4 years	-.48 to .95	Not reported
Dunkleberger & Tyler (1961)	rho	SVIB Occupational Scales	141 boys and girls	11th grade	1 year	Not reported	Not reported
Sprinkle (1961)	Pearson	44 SVIB Occupational Scales	143 men	College freshmen & sophomores	1–11 years	.11 to .92	.69

TABLE 6.2   Studies Examining Interest Stability via Strong's (1943) Method 4: Intraindividual Stability Coefficients *continued*

Study	Coefficient	Scales	Sample	Time of First Testing	Interval	Coefficients Range	Coefficients Median
Joselyn (1968)	Pearson	SVIB Occupational Scales	923 boys, 918 girls	11th grade	5 months	.20 to .99	.92
Zytowski (1976)	rho	Kuder Male Occupational Scales	729 students (5 samples)	Age 13	12 years	Not reported	.58
				Age 15	12 years		.70
				Age 15	18 years		.58
				Age 17	12 years		.69
				Age 20	12 years		.76
Hansen & Stocco (1980)	Pearson	124 SCII Occupational Scales	31 boys, 39 girls	9th grade	3 years	-.31 to .96	.72
			262 men, 353 women	College freshmen	3 ½ years	.17 to .97	.80
Hansen & Swanson (1983)	Pearson	162 SCII Occupational Scales	261 men	College freshmen	3 ½ years	-.23 to .96	.77
			354 women			-.23 to .97	.79
Swanson & Hansen (1988)[a]	Pearson	207 SCII Occupational Scales	79 men, 125 women	College freshmen	4 years	.23 to .98	.81
			167 men, 242 women	College seniors	8 years	.25 to .98	.83
				College freshmen	12 years	-.11 to .96	.72
Lubinski, Benbow & Ryan (1995)	Pearson	6 SCII GOT	Mathematically gifted (114 boys, 48 girls)	Age 13	15 years	-.71 to .99	.57
		23 SCII BIS				-.02 to .91	.51

[a]Coefficients reported in the table are selected samples of more extensive data reported in the study.

Note: SVIB = *Strong Vocational Interest Blank*, SCII = *Strong-Campbell Interest Inventory*, GOT = General Occupational Themes, BIS = Basic Interest Scales

after considerable numbers of intervening years. For example, high median coefficients have been reported for ninth-graders over a 3-year interval (Hansen &
Stocco, 1980), unemployed men over a 10-year interval (Powers, 1954), college
freshmen over a 12-year interval (Swanson & Hansen, 1988), and college seniors
over a 22-year interval (Strong, 1951). Moreover, for many individuals their two
profiles at different times are virtually identical in the relative ordering of scale
scores, as evidenced by correlations in the high .90s over time intervals ranging
from 3 to 15 years (Hansen & Stocco, 1980; Hansen & Swanson, 1983; Hoyt,
1960; Lubinski, Benbow, & Ryan, 1995; Powers, 1954; Swanson & Hansen,
1988; Zytowski, 1976). For these individuals there has been essentially *no*
change in their interests over long periods of time.

2. *However, some individuals' interests change substantially over time.*

There are considerable individual differences in stability of interests. Although
the majority of individuals do exhibit stable interests, some people show large
changes in their interest patterns. For some individuals stability coefficients are
zero, and for other individuals they are moderately negative, suggesting that two
interest profiles for the same person bear no resemblance to one another (Hansen
& Stocco, 1980; Hansen & Swanson, 1983; Hoyt, 1960; Lubinsky, Benbow, &
Ryan, 1995; Powers, 1954; Swanson & Hansen, 1988). This also is a consistent
finding throughout the literature (Table 6.2). Psychologists clearly need to know
more about individual differences in stability. They do not yet know what precipitating factors lead to such drastic changes, nor do they fully understand the
outcomes of interest instability.

3. *Degree of stability may be related to a number of variables.*

A number of researchers have examined the correlates of interest stability.
Unfortunately, most studies of stability have been post hoc in design, with little
prospective information available to researchers. Despite this limitation, previous
studies do suggest several categories of variables that may prove fruitful in determining predictors of degree of interest stability.

(a) Stability appears to increase with age, at least during the period of time
most frequently studied, from adolescence through young adulthood. Strong
(1951) summarized SVIB data from several samples tested up to three times, concluding that interests become "better established with increasing age" (p. 91).
Johansson and Campbell (1971) reached a similar conclusion in their summary
of SVIB data from 66 groups of men, cited earlier, and other studies support this

conclusion (Hansen & Stocco, 1980; Zytowski, 1976).

(b) Stability may relate to the specific types of interests that individuals possess, as characterized in a number of ways. First, early studies examining specific scales frequently reported higher test-retest coefficients for scales reflecting mechanical or scientific interests for men, and for scales reflecting artistic interests for women, than for other scales (Herzberg & Bouton, 1954; Herzberg, Bouton, & Steiner, 1954; Rosenberg, 1953; Strong, 1935; Strong, 1955; Van Dusen, 1940). Second, there is some evidence that sex-typical interests are more stable or, put another way, that interests are more likely to change toward those that receive societal support (Hoyt, Smith, & Levy, 1957; Swanson, 1984). Parenthetically a similar finding has been reported relative to personality traits: That is, traits exhibiting stability tended to be those congruent with sex-typed behavior (Stein, Newcomb, & Bentler, 1986). Third, "lukewarm" or indifferent interests may be most susceptible to change, whereas strong likes and strong dislikes are more likely to remain stable (Stordahl, 1954b; Trinkaus, 1954).

(c) Interest profiles that are well differentiated and that reflect consistency in terms of Holland's (1997) RIASEC hexagon may show more stability (Joselyn, 1968; Swanson, 1986). Well-differentiated and consistent interests may be more "mature" or firmly established and therefore less likely to fluctuate.

(d) Instability of interests may be associated with difficulty in career decision making and with more changes in jobs and careers (Swanson, 1986), possibly reflecting a willingness to consider a wider variety of career options (Joselyn, 1968).

(e) Finally, personality variables may be related to interest stability. One study concluded that high school juniors whose interest profiles had changed one year later tended to be more well adjusted, leading the researchers to conclude that interest change during adolescence should be considered an index of development rather than of instability (Dunkleberger & Tyler, 1961).

4. *Attempts to predict stability have not yet been particularly successful.*

Although individual differences in interest stability have been easy to document, it has proven more difficult to predict stability for a given individual. One result of Strong's early attention to the permanence of interests was the Interest Maturity (IM) scale (Strong, 1931, 1933, 1943). He reasoned that if there were consistent age-related changes in interests, then these changes could be used as a marker of an individual's development. Strong (1935, 1943) reported substantial relations between the IM scale and interest stability; however, later investigators cast doubt on the strength and utility of that relationship (King, 1956; Sprinkle, 1961; Stordahl, 1954a).

Other researchers have attempted to predict stability by identifying profile characteristics that might be empirically related to stability. Hoyt, Smith, and Levy (1957), for example, developed indexes of "interest integration" based upon the consistency of an individual's responses to a group of related SVIB items and the consistency of an individual's scores on a group of related SVIB Occupational Scales. Although the indexes were significantly related to interest stability as operationally defined by rank-order correlations, the magnitude of the relationship was not large enough to offer practical significance in terms of predicting the likely degree of stability of any given individual's profile.

A number of authors (Hoyt, 1960; Stordahl, 1954a) have suggested the possibility of constructing a scale to predict stability, using the same logic that underlies the empirically keyed Occupational Scales of the *Strong*. That is, one could identify two groups of individuals, one with stable and one with unstable interests, select items that differentiate the two groups, and combine these items into a scale. Several researchers have attempted to construct such scales (Hoyt, 1960; Swanson, 1984). Items were identified that clearly distinguished the two groups from one another, and the scales functioned well within the initial validation samples. However, these scales did not survive cross-validation with new groups of individuals, suggesting idiosyncratic characteristics of the initial development samples.

5. *There are few documented age-related changes in interests.*

It is important to recognize the possibility both of stability *and* of change; further, it is important to define the differences between these two processes. Developmental psychologists have observed that there is "no contradiction in describing both consistency and change within a particular group over time" (Stein, Newcomb, & Bentler, 1986). Moreover, the focus on *change* versus a focus on *stability* implies different philosophical perspectives. Discussions of *change* typically entail normative, developmental shifts over the life span. To examine change psychologists frequently examine differences in mean scores *for groups* over time and across cohorts (see Strong, 1931, 1935). Important questions might include the following: Are there predictable changes in vocational interests that occur as women and men age? How do interests during early adulthood compare to interests at retirement? In contrast, when discussing *stability* (or rather *instability*), psychologists attend to what are probably nonnormative, nondevelopmental shifts that occur for individuals over the life span. To examine stability they investigate the similarity of interest patterns *for individuals* to determine the constancy of their interests over time. Important questions thus are as follows: How stable are interests? Do individuals vary in the amount of interest stability they evince? What factors relate to degree of interest stability?

This fifth conclusion, then, is related to life-span changes that are normative, developmental, and predictable. There are few systematic changes in interests over time, particularly after age 30 (Hansen, 1978, 1984; Strong, 1931, 1943). Moreover, any documented cross-sectional differences between age groups seem to be less than differences observed between occupational groups. The minor changes that do occur seem to be of the sort that indicate that interests become better defined over time.

Summary of Empirical Evidence

Overall, interests show a substantial amount of permanence over long periods of time. It is equally important, however, to recognize that individuals vary widely in degree of stability. Stability seems to increase with age and also may relate to other characteristics of interest patterns. Finally, there are few documented developmental changes in interest patterns over time.

THEORETICAL ISSUES AND UNANSWERED QUESTIONS

Given these general conclusions about the stability of interests, this final section presents conceptual and theoretical issues about stability and change over the life span, including some questions that are yet unanswered.

1. *How much stability is desirable? How much is necessary to use interests as a guide?*

In early writings regarding stability there was a clear negative connotation attached to "unstable" interest patterns, perhaps as a result of the common belief at that time that interests in general were not a worthy base for one's life decisions (Strong, 1931). However, several writers have suggested that "unstable" interests actually may be accompanied by positive characteristics, such as openness to experience or flexibility, whereas "stable" interests may even reflect foreclosure and unimaginative plodding through life (Dunkleberger & Tyler, 1961; Joselyn, 1968). As noted earlier, we do not know what the outcomes are of stability or instability of interests. "Instability" may actually represent an adaptive response to an environment that is characterized by economic and technological changes. This is a question that clearly needs more attention.

The second question certainly relates to the first. If instability is not necessarily a negative characteristic or outcome, then how much should be tolerated, theoretically speaking? Fryer captured this dilemma in his writing in 1931:

> To hold that human interests are stable, that interests are permanent, necessarily denies any great amount of variability in the life of the individual. But, on the other hand, to hold that interests are unstable, absolutely lacking in permanence, denies any possibility of the genetic development of interests, of the formation of habits of being interested. (Fryer, 1931, pp. 143–144)

In addition to theoretical ramifications, the amount of instability we can "tolerate" also has implications for the measurement of interests and for the use of interest inventories in counseling. Substantial change in the trait being measured influences psychometric characteristics of an instrument in ways that may render it useless to a counselor or test-taker. The questions therefore of what constitutes "substantial" change, and how to predict who is likely to exhibit "substantial change," must remain in the forefront of continued research.

2. *What precipitating factors lead to a shift in interest patterns? Is it possible to predict an individual's level of interest stability?*

Psychologists know that, for the majority of people, interests remain quite stable over long time periods. However, what about those individuals who do demonstrate substantial change in their interests? What leads individuals to change their interest patterns? The question about the precipitating factors has theoretical implications for how researchers view the nature and development of interests. The second question about predicting stability addresses practical implications. Is it possible to predict which clients' interest profiles are likely to remain constant versus those that are more transitory in nature? What kind of statements should we be making to clients about the likelihood of stability of their interests?

Several options exist as potential predictors of interest stability. First, as attempted by previous researchers, item responses may be used to construct empirically keyed scales. Second, researchers could use profile pattern characteristics, such as differentiation and consistency. Third, stability may be predictable from collateral sources such as personality measures. For example, individuals who exhibit a great degree of openness to experience may be more susceptible to environmental influences that foster a change in interests.

An alternate view suggests that instability of interests *is by its very nature unpredictable*. Environmental influences may simply be too serendipitous to predict in any useful way. This view may seem pessimistic to scholars and frustrating to practitioners; as Dunkleberger and Tyler (1961) noted, "We may thus assume a fairly high degree of stability of high and low scores in the majority of cases. But a counselor never knows whether an individual with whom he [sic] is working belongs to the stable majority or the unstable minority" (p. 70). However, even if counselors cannot make predictions about which specific individuals will dramatically change their interest patterns, they can make probabilistic statements about the likelihood that an individual's interests will change, based on the high median coefficients reported in Table 6.2. For example, "the majority of people have interests that remain relatively stable over time" is a fair and empirically supported statement that counselors can offer to clients.

3. What is the degree of stability throughout the life span?

As mentioned earlier, the majority of evidence regarding interest stability pertains to adolescence and the college years. In addition, several studies have focused on individuals in specific occupations in middle to late adulthood (Campbell, 1966a & b), and case study information suggests stability of interests throughout the life span. Zytowski's (1996) analysis suggested thematic consistency in his Kuder interest profiles ranging from early career (age in mid-30s) to postretirement (age in mid-60s). Likewise, the 20 family members in Helwig and Myrin's (1997) study ranged in age from 29 to 72 at the first administration of the *Self-Directed Search* (SDS), and age did not seem to be related to stability of their SDS codes.

Evidence from these and other sources suggests that the amount of interest stability should increase with age. However, that awaits empirical verification, particularly beyond the period of early adulthood. Another issue is the general lengthening of the life span, offering individuals many more years past traditional retirement age to pursue career and leisure interests. Examining stability throughout the life span thus becomes an issue with theoretical and practical relevance.

A word about research methodology is in order. Research attention to interest stability obviously requires longitudinal designs, with all of their attendant problems. One of the major problems in a longitudinal study is mortality, or attrition from the study. "Mortality" occurs for a number of reasons, including the death of participants, but also for many other more mundane reasons related to difficulty in locating participants for follow-up, such as geographic relocation, name changes, and general unwillingness to participate. Mortality is a problem in any longitudinal research design. However, mortality is a particular problem in research regarding interest stability because of its direct relationship to the variable under study. Mortality thus uniquely threatens the validity of conclusions that psychologists can make regarding stability.

Consider two hypothetical participants in a longitudinal study, each of whom took an interest inventory as part of freshman orientation at the University of Minnesota. The task is now to conduct a follow-up study 24 years later, or 20 years after college graduation (Swanson, 1997). Participant A lived with her parents in a suburb of Minneapolis while she attended college. Upon graduation she took a job in the same city, married her high school boyfriend, and eventually bought a home within 10 miles of where she was raised. She has remained at the same work organization, in which she has advanced through a series of positions with increasing responsibility. When the follow-up research materials are mailed to her parents, they give them to her during their scheduled weekly visit with their grandchildren.

Participant B, in contrast, lived in a series of apartments, with a series of roommates, while in college. After graduating, he hitchhiked to New Mexico because he was not yet ready to settle down to a job. In the following year he took a job in San Francisco and has since lived in Seattle, Montana, and Utah. He recently moved to Boston to pursue a job promotion. His parents no longer live at their original address because they have retired to a warmer climate.

Participant B clearly presents a greater challenge to a researcher interested in locating him after 20 years. Even more importantly, who is more likely to have stable interests, Participant A or Participant B? Unfortunately, we cannot yet answer this question empirically. However, intuitively Participant A would seem to be a better candidate for a stable pattern of interests in early adulthood. If a follow-up sample is predominated by participants who are the easiest to locate, the researcher may get an inaccurate picture of the degree of interest stability in this population.

This inaccurate picture of stability may be further exacerbated by the fact that most studies focus on samples that are generally easier to reach—that is, adolescents and college students. Psychologists know very little about individual differences in interest stability after the college years and throughout the remainder of the life span. Moreover, they know little about stability for members of racial-ethnic minority groups and for individuals who do not attend college.

4. *What are the implications of evidence of interest stability for a theoretical under-standing of interests?*

The answers to questions regarding stability of interests may have far-reaching implications for theories of interests. Moreover, an interactive, reciprocal relation-ship exists between theoretical perspectives on interests and evidence regarding stability of interests: How psychologists view stability of interests affects their view of interests, and their view of interests affects expectations regarding stability.

Several concepts from fields of study outside of interest measurement provide a context for this discussion: (a) the link between models of personality and models of interests, (b) life-span stability and change in personality dimensions, and (c) heritability of interests and of personality. These three bodies of literature may help frame the next set of questions that are asked regarding life-span sta-bility and change in interests.

Link Between Structural Models of Personality and Interests

The first body of literature focuses on the structural links between personality and interests (see Holland, this volume). The search for theoretical and empiri-cal correspondence between the domains of personality and of vocational inter-ests has recently accelerated. As Borgen (1986) described it, "Personality and vocational psychologists have sliced up the world of individual differences with their unique concepts, but they are often looking at the same world" (p. 108).

Within the realm of vocational interests several theoretical models have been proposed over the years to provide a parsimonious, heuristic summary of the structure of vocational interests (see Rounds & Day, this volume). By far the most enduring and thoroughly researched has been the typology proposed by John Holland (1959, 1997), and virtually all of the research examining the intersec-tion of personality and of interests has used Holland's model to describe the domain of interests.

In the domain of personality, the five-factor model represents a widely recog-nized system for describing at a global level the basic dimensions of personality: Neuroticism, Extraversion, Openness to Experience, Agreeableness, and Conscientiousness (Digman, 1990). These five dimensions are recovered repeat-edly in factor analyses of peer- and self-ratings of personality traits involving diverse methodologies and populations, and a large body of research has demon-strated that the five-factor model provides an appropriate structure in which other personality systems may be interpreted and organized. On the other hand,

Holland's theory assumes that vocational interests are an important expression of personality. Holland's model explicitly recognizes the role of personality; in fact, Holland's taxonomy is a personality taxonomy (Holland, 1997). Therefore, in content, Holland's model and the five-factor model should correspond meaningfully.

The association between Holland's typology and personality variables has generally been supported in empirical studies relating scores on measures of Holland types to a wide range of personality inventories, such as Cattell's *16 Personality Factor Questionnaire* (Bolton, 1985; Peraino & Willerman, 1983), the *Myers-Briggs Type Indicator* (Dillon & Weissman, 1987; Martin & Bartol, 1986), and the *Eysenck Personality Questionnaire* (Goh & Leong, 1993), among others. Recent investigators have proposed that it may be more parsimonious and heuristically useful to describe the structural overlap of the basic dimensions underlying personality and interests (Rounds, 1995; Tokar & Swanson, 1995).

Research directly examining the overlap between models of interests and models of personality suggests points of convergence as well as areas in which the models offer unique perspectives. There are consistent results connecting aspects of the five-factor model of personality to portions of Holland's (1997) model: Investigative and Artistic interests are related to Openness to Experience or Intellect, and Social and Enterprising interests are strongly related to Extraversion (Costa, Fozard, & McCrae, 1977; Costa, McCrae, & Holland, 1984; De Fruyt & Mervielde, 1997; Gottfredson, Jones, & Holland, 1993). Even more compelling is evidence that suggests that scores on measures of the five-factor model could predict concurrent membership in Holland's vocational interest categories: Openness to Experience and Extraversion, plus the addition of Agreeableness for females, reproduced the Holland hexagon in two-dimensional space (Tokar & Swanson, 1995).

In spite of these points of convergence, there also are demonstrated points of divergence between the two models: Neuroticism and Conscientiousness, as well as Agreeableness, have not been well represented in the interest domain (Gottfredson, Jones, & Holland, 1993), even though these constructs have clear implications for work-related behavior (Barrick & Mount, 1991). There also is consistent evidence that the correspondence of interest and personality domains appears to be moderated by gender, with somewhat different relationships existing for men and for women (Gottfredson, Jones, & Holland, 1993; Tokar & Swanson, 1995; Tokar, Vaux, & Swanson, 1995).

Another personality model receiving attention is Wiggins' Interpersonal Circle (Kiesler, 1983; Wiggins, 1979). The Interpersonal Circle rests upon the two underlying dimensions of power and affiliation, with the power dimension defined by two types, Dominant on one end and Submissive on the other, and the affiliation dimension defined by two types, Hostile and Friendly. Some evidence suggests that the affiliation dimension links the Interpersonal Circle and Holland's schema, as translated through Prediger's (1982) People/Things dimension (Schneider, Ryan, Tracey, & Rounds, 1996).

Thus these comparisons reveal two general conclusions: (1) Personality and interests do have common dimensions, yet (2) they do not map onto one another in any exhaustive or comprehensive way. The importance of the continued attention to the relationship between personality and interests is evidenced by the attempts of scholars in each field, respectively, to describe the intersection from their own vantage points. Studying the link between personality and interests may inform the theoretical understanding in each of the two domains, as well as further describe the links of each domain to other important variables.

Life-Span Stability and Change in Personality Variables

Personality psychology offers a body of literature with clear parallels to a discussion of interest stability. Issues related to stability and change of personality dimensions over the life span have received prominent attention by researchers. There is growing consensus that personality stabilizes in adulthood and that change throughout the life span is relatively minimal (McCrae & Costa, 1990; McGue, Bacon, & Lykken, 1993). Average levels of personality traits change with childhood and adolescent development but stabilize at about age 30. After age 30, changes in personality are considered to be "few and subtle" (McCrae & Costa, 1994, p. 173). The most consistently reported change is a small decline in activity level with advancing age. Moreover, stability of traits is evident across the major domains of personality (Neuroticism, Extraversion, Openness to Experience, Agreeableness, and Conscientiousness), and also seems to hold regardless of sex, race, and health status (McCrae & Costa, 1994).

Heritability of Personality and Interests

The third relevant body of literature includes studies related to behavior genetics, which provide estimates of the relative influence of genetic and environmental factors on psychological characteristics. There is consistent evidence to suggest that genetic factors strongly influence personality. Moreover, another line of research indicates that the "*stable* core of personality is strongly associated with genetic factors but that personality *change* largely reflects environmental factors"

(McGue, Bacon, & Lykken, 1993). In contrast, literature regarding heritability of vocational interests suggests that environmental influences, particularly non-shared environmental effects, exert more influence than do genetic effects (Betsworth, Bouchard, Cooper, Grotevant, Hansen, Scarr, & Weinberg, 1994; Moloney, Bouchard, & Segal, 1991). Taken together, these studies suggest that personality has greater genetic roots than do interests. Heritability also has been documented for other career-related variables, such as job satisfaction (Arvey, Bouchard, Segal, & Abraham, 1989) and work values (Keller, Bouchard, Arvey, Segal, & Dawis, 1992), variables that may have stronger links to personality dimensions than do interests.

Costa (1994) described vocational interests as one category of what he called *characteristic adaptations:* that is, acquired skills or attitudes that result from the interaction of the individual and the environment. Essentially, then, interests could be viewed as concrete manifestations of latent personality traits. If so, then the lower heritability of interests as compared to personality makes sense, as does the speculation that stability of personality is more heritable than stability of interests.

Application to Stability of Interests

So what do these bodies of literature offer to a consideration of vocational interest stability? I suggest three possible implications. First, it may be useful to propose that types of interests are *differentially heritable,* a notion that has been applied to personality traits (McCartney, Harris, & Bernieri, 1990). It may not make sense to talk about heritability of "interests" as a broad construct but rather of the specific type of interests. There is enough variation in heritability rates by interest scales and measures to warrant further consideration of differential heritability.

Second, researchers need to consider the possibility of *differential stability.* Current methodology examines stability by looking for *consistency in patterns within profiles.* If researchers presume that interests are differentially stable, so that artistic interests, for example, are more stable than enterprising interests, then an individual's relative pattern of interests is likely to change although his or her core interests may be quite durable. The notion of differential stability suggests that we need to continue to examine stability from a number of different perspectives. A test-retest coefficient for groups of people tells us about the stability of a specific type of interests, whereas a correlation coefficient between a person's profiles at two different times tells us about individual differences in stability. Or, alternatively, we need to develop some indexes that will account for both constancy of interests and change in patterns *for individuals.*

Finally, *differential heritability* and *differential stability* may be connected within the domain of interests. Interests and personality do appear to have some common dimensions, as indicated by the earlier discussion. It is plausible that stability may be most evident for the types of interests that are most closely linked to personality structure, perhaps through the mechanism of heritability. For example, two personality traits that are likely to be well established in early childhood are extraversion and achievement motivation (Emmerich, 1964). We might then expect greater stability in interests linked to these two traits. There is some evidence to support this speculation: Moloney, Bouchard, and Segal (1991) and Betsworth and her colleagues (1994) both reported higher relative heritability estimates for interest scales or factors with direct parallels to these two personality traits, namely, *Strong Interest Inventory* scales measuring Introversion–Extraversion and academic comfort.

Another way to state this speculation is that it is the overlapping portions of models of personality and models of interests that have the strongest genetic components. This suggests that the more genetic component there is to a dimension of interests, the more stability that should be observed over time. In a similar vein, Waller, Lykken, and Tellegen (1995) speculated that some interests are less stable because "they are, in fact, less traited" (p. 253).

Another possible link exists between personality variables and stability of interests. Interest stability may be greatest for people with certain personality traits, regardless of the exact nature of their pattern of interests. The most likely candidate, again, is Openness to Experience, which is probably associated with fluctuation in interest patterns. Individuals high in Openness may be more likely to seek situations in which they are exposed to new and varied activities, which in turn could influence the strength and pattern of their interests.

SUMMARY

In summary, psychologists know a great deal about the extent to which interests, as a construct, are stable throughout people's lives. They also know a great deal about the extent to which individuals' interests may vary in degree of stability. These conclusions have held up to over 60 years of study, yet researchers need to move ahead to address some of the unanswered questions such as those outlined herein. The unanswered questions hold the key to understanding how individuals' interests develop and change, with corresponding implications for theoretical development and practical applications.

REFERENCES

Arvey, R. D., Bouchard, T. J., Jr., Segal, N. L., & Abraham, L. M. (1989). Job satisfaction: Environmental and genetic components. *Journal of Applied Psychology, 74,* 187–192.

Barrick, M. R., & Mount, M. K. (1991). The Big Five personality dimensions and job performance: A meta-analysis. *Personnel Psychology, 44,* 1–26.

Betsworth, D. G., Bouchard, T. J., Jr., Cooper, C. R., Grotevant, H. D., Hansen, J. C., Scarr, S., & Weinberg, R. (1994). Genetic and environmental influences on vocational interests assessed using adoptive and biological families and twins reared apart and together. *Journal of Vocational Behavior, 44,* 263–278.

Bolton, B. (1985). Discriminant analysis of Holland's occupational types using the Sixteen Personality Factor Questionnaire. *Journal of Vocational Behavior, 27,* 210–217.

Borgen, F. H. (1986). New approaches to the assessment of interests. In W. B. Walsh & S. H. Osipow (Eds.), *Advances in vocational psychology: Vol. 1 The assessment of interests* (pp. 31–54). Hillsdale, NJ: Erlbaum.

Campbell, D. P. (1966a). Stability of interests within an occupation over thirty years. *Journal of Applied Psychology, 50,* 51–56.

Campbell, D. P. (1966b). The stability of vocational interests within occupations over long time spans. *Personnel and Guidance Journal, 44,* 1012–1019.

Canning, L., Taylor, K., & Carter, H. D. (1941). Permanence of vocational interests of high-school boys. *Journal of Educational Psychology, 32,* 481–494.

Costa, P. T., Jr. (1994, August). *Traits through time, or the stability of personality: Observations, evaluations, and a model.* Invited address presented at the annual meeting of the American Psychological Association, Los Angeles.

Costa, P. T., Fozard, J. L., & McCrae, R. R. (1977). Personological interpretation of factors from the *Strong Vocational Interest Blank* scales. *Journal of Vocational Behavior, 10,* 231–243.

Costa, P. T., Jr., McCrae, R. R., & Holland, J. L. (1984). Personality and vocational interests in an adult sample. *Journal of Applied Psychology, 69,* 390–400.

De Fruyt, F., & Mervielde, I. (1997). The five-factor model of personality and Holland's RIASEC interest types. *Personality and Individual Differences, 23,* 87–103.

Digman, J. M. (1990). Personality structure: Emergence of the five-factor model. In M. R. Rosenzweig & L. W. Porter (Eds.), *Annual review of psychology* (Vol. 41, pp. 417–440). Palo Alto, CA: Annual Reviews.

Dillon, M., & Weissman, S. (1987). Relationship between personality types on the Strong-Campbell and Myers-Briggs instruments. *Measurement and Evaluation in Counseling and Development, 20,* 68–79.

Dunkleberger, C. J., & Tyler, L. E. (1961). Interest stability and personality traits. *Journal of Counseling Psychology, 8,* 70–74.

Emmerich, W. (1964). Continuity and stability in early social development. *Child Development, 35,* 311–332.

Finch, F. H. (1935). The permanence of vocational interests. *Psychological Bulletin, 32,* 682.

Fox, W. H. (1947). The stability of measured interests. *Journal of Educational Research, 41,* 305–310.

Fryer, D. (1931). *The measurement of interests.* New York: Henry Holt.

Goh, D. S., & Leong, F.T.L. (1993). The relationship between Holland's theory of vocational interests and Eysenck's model of personality. *Personality and Individual Differences, 15,* 555–562.

Gottfredson, G. D., Jones, E. M., & Holland, J. L. (1993). Personality and vocational interests: The relation of Holland's six interest dimensions to five robust dimensions of personality. *Journal of Counseling Psychology, 40,* 518–524.

Hansen, J. C. (1978). Age differences and empirical scale construction. *Measurement and Evaluation in Guidance, 11,* 78–87.

Hansen, J. C. (1984). The measurement of vocational interests. In S. D. Brown & R. W. Lent (Eds.), *Handbook of counseling psychology* (pp. 99–136). New York: Wiley.

Hansen, J. C., & Stocco, J. L. (1980). Stability of vocational interests of adolescents and young adults. *Measurement and Evaluation in Guidance, 13,* 173–178.

Hansen, J. C., & Swanson, J. L. (1983). Stability of interests and the predictive and concurrent validity of the 1981 Strong-Campbell Interest Inventory for college majors. *Journal of Counseling Psychology, 30*(2), 194–201.

Helwig, A. A., & Myrin, M. D. (1997). Ten-year stability of Holland codes within one family. *Career Development Quarterly, 46,* 62–71.

Herzberg, F., & Bouton, A. (1954). A further study of the stability of the Kuder Preference Record. *Educational and Psychological Measurement, 14,* 326–331.

Herzberg, F., Bouton, A., & Steiner, B. J. (1954). Studies of the stability of the Kuder Preference Record. *Educational and Psychological Measurement, 14,* 90–100.

Holland, J. L. (1959). A theory of vocational choice. *Journal of Counseling Psychology, 6,* 35–45.

Holland, J. L. (1997). *Making vocational choices: A theory of vocational personalities and work environments* (3rd ed.). Odessa, FL: Psychological Assessment Resources.

Hoyt, D. P. (1960). Measurement and prediction of the permanence of interests. In W. Layton (Ed.), *The Strong Vocational Interest Blank: Research and uses.* Minneapolis: University of Minnesota Press.

Hoyt, D. P., Smith, J. L., Jr., & Levy, S. (1957). A further study in the prediction of interest stability. *Journal of Counseling Psychology, 4,* 228–233.

Johansson, C. B., & Campbell, D. P. (1971). Stability of the SVIB for men. *Journal of Applied Psychology, 55,* 34–36.

Joselyn, E. G. (1968). *The relationship of selected variables to the stability of measured vocational interests of high school seniors.* Unpublished doctoral dissertation, University of Minnesota.

Keller, L. M., Bouchard, T. J., Jr., Arvey, R. D., Segal, N. L., & Dawis, R. V. (1992). Work values: Genetic and environmental influences. *Journal of Applied Psychology, 77,* 79–88.

Kiesler, D. J. (1983). The 1982 interpersonal circle: A taxonomy for complementarity in human transactions. *Psychological Review, 90,* 185–214.

King, L. A. (1956). *Factors associated with the stability of vocational interests of General College freshmen.* Unpublished doctoral dissertation, University of Minnesota.

Lubinski, D., Benbow, C. P., & Ryan, J. (1995). Stability of vocational interests among the intellectually gifted from adolescence to adulthood: A 15-year longitudinal study. *Journal of Applied Psychology, 80*(1), 196–200.

Martin, D. C., & Bartol, K. M. (1986). Holland's Vocational Preference Inventory and the Myers-Briggs Type Indicator as predictors of vocational choice among master's of business administration. *Journal of Vocational Behavior, 29,* 51–65.

McCartney, K., Harris, M. J., & Bernieri, F. (1990). Growing up and growing apart: A developmental meta-analysis of twin studies. *Psychological Bulletin, 107,* 226–237.

McCrae, R. R., & Costa, P. T., Jr. (1990). *Personality in adulthood.* New York: Guilford Press.

McCrae, R. R., & Costa, P. T., Jr. (1994). The stability of personality: Observations and evaluations. *Current Directions in Psychological Science, 3*(6), 173–175.

McGue, M., Bacon, S., & Lykken, D. T. (1993). Personality stability and change in early adulthood: A behavioral genetic analysis. *Developmental Psychology, 29,* 96–109.

Moloney, D. P., Bouchard, T. J., Jr., & Segal, N. L. (1991). A genetic and environmental analysis of the vocational interests of monozygotic and dizygotic twins reared apart. *Journal of Vocational Behavior, 39,* 76–109.

Peraino, J. M., & Willerman, L. (1983). Personality correlates of occupational status according to Holland types. *Journal of Vocational Behavior, 22,* 268–277.

Powers, M. K. (1954). *A longitudinal study of vocational interests during the Depression years.* Unpublished doctoral dissertation, University of Minnesota.

Prediger, D. J. (1982). Dimensions underlying Holland's hexagon: Missing link between interests and occupations? *Journal of Vocational Behavior, 40,* 259–287.

Rosenberg, N. (1953). Stability and maturation of Kuder interest patterns during high school. *Educational and Psychological Measurement, 13,* 449–458.

Rounds, J. B. (1995). Vocational interests: Evaluating structural hypotheses. In D. Lubinski and R. V. Dawis (Eds.), *Assessing individual differences in human behavior: New concepts, methods, and findings* (pp. 177–232). Palo Alto, CA: Davies-Black.

Schneider, P. L., Ryan, J., Tracey, T. J., & Rounds, J. (1996). Examining the relation between Holland's RIASEC types and the Interpersonal Circle. *Measurement and Evaluation in Counseling and Development, 24,* 123–133.

Sprinkle, R. L. (1961). *Permanence of measured vocational interests and socio-economic background.* Unpublished doctoral dissertation, University of Minnesota.

Stein, J. A., Newcomb, M. D., & Bentler, P. M. (1986). Stability and change in personality: A longitudinal study from early adolescence to young adulthood. *Journal of Research in Personality, 20,* 276–291.

Stordahl, K. E. (1954a). Permanence of interests and interest maturity. *Journal of Applied Psychology, 38,* 339–341.

Stordahl, K. E. (1954b). Permanence of *Strong Vocational Interest Blank* scores. *Journal of Applied Psychology, 38,* 423–427.

Strong, E. K., Jr. (1931). *Change of interests with age.* Stanford, CA: Stanford University Press.

Strong, E. K., Jr. (1933). Interest maturity. *Personnel Journal, 12,* 77–90.

Strong, E. K., Jr. (1935). Permanence of vocational interests. *Journal of Educational Psychology, 25,* 336–344.

Strong, E. K., Jr. (1943). *Vocational interests of men and women.* Stanford, CA: Stanford University Press.

Strong, E. K., Jr. (1951). Permanence of interest scores over 22 years. *Journal of Applied Psychology, 35,* 89–91.

Strong, E. K., Jr. (1952a). Nineteen-year follow-up of engineer interests. *Journal of Applied Psychology, 36,* 65–74.

Strong, E. K., Jr. (1952b). Twenty-year follow-up of medical interests. In L. L. Thurstone (Ed.), *Applications of psychology.* New York: HarperCollins.

Strong, E. K., Jr. (1955). *Vocational interests 18 years after college.* Minneapolis: University of Minnesota Press.

Strong, E. K., Jr., & Tucker, A. C. (1952). The use of vocational interest scales in planning a medical career. *Psychological Monographs, 66,* 9.

Swanson, J. L. (1984, August). Can stability of interests be empirically predicted? In J. C. Hansen (Chair), *New Directions in Interest Measurement.* Symposium presented at the annual meeting of the American Psychological Association, Toronto, Canada.

Swanson, J. L. (1986). Predictors and correlates of 12-year stability of vocational interests. (Doctoral dissertation, University of Minnesota, 1986). *Dissertation Abstracts International, 48*(02), 55518. (University Microfilms No. 87-06, 965)

Swanson, J. L. (1997). *Intersection of personality and interests in adulthood.* Unpublished manuscript, Southern Illinois University.

Swanson, J. L., & Hansen, J. C. (1988). Stability of vocational interests over four-year, eight-year, and twelve-year intervals. *Journal of Vocational Behavior, 33,* 185–202.

Taylor, K. von F., & Carter, H. D. (1942). Retest consistency of vocational interest patterns of high school girls. *Journal of Consulting Psychology, 6,* 95–101.

Tokar, D. M., & Swanson, J. L. (1995). Evaluation of the correspondence between Holland's vocational personality typology and the five-factor model. *Journal of Vocational Behavior, 46,* 89–108.

Tokar, D. M., Vaux, A., & Swanson, J. L. (1995). Dimensions relating Holland's vocational personality typology and the five-factor model. *Journal of Career Assessment, 3,* 57–74.

Trinkaus, W. K. (1954). The permanence of vocational interests of college freshmen. *Educational and Psychological Measurement, 14,* 641–647.

Van Dusen, A. C. (1940). Permanence of vocational interests. *Journal of Educational Psychology, 31,* 401–424.

Waller, N. G., Lykken, D. T., & Tellegen, A. (1995). Occupational interests, leisure time interests, and personality: Three domains or one? Findings from the Minnesota Twin Registry. In D. Lubinski & R. V. Dawis (Eds.), *Assessing individual differences in human behavior: New concepts, methods, and findings* (pp. 233–259). Palo Alto, CA: Davies-Black.

Wiggins, J. S. (1979). A psychological taxonomy of trait descriptive terms: The interpersonal domain. *Journal of Personality and Social Psychology, 37,* 395–412.

Zytowski, D. G. (1976). Long-term profile stability of the Kuder Occupational Interest Survey. *Educational and Psychological Measurement, 36,* 689–692.

Zytowski, D. G. (1996). Three decades of interest inventory results. *Career Development Quarterly, 41,* 141–148.

MEASURING VOCATIONAL INTERESTS

T HE OPENING SECTION OF THIS BOOK dealt with conceptual definitions and the theory of vocational interests. In contrast, Section 2 concentrates on operational definitions of vocational interests. In the opening chapter Crites deals with operational definitions of vocational interests. He starts by distinguishing interests from aptitudes, abilities, skills, and personality. Next he reviews a widely recognized conceptual definition of vocational interests and offers one of his own. He then explains that conceptual—that is, linguistic—definitions of vocational interests can be operationally defined in five different ways and proceeds to compare and contrast the empirical measurement of vocational interests by verbal expressions, manifest behavior, cognitive tests, attitudinal inventories, and physiological reactions. After articulating the importance of each of these five operational definitions, Crites notes that the vast majority of research on vocational interests has been conducted using the operational definition provided by attitudinal inventories, the topic of the next two chapters.

In a superb primer detailing the essentials of how vocational interests can be operationally defined with inventories, Harmon illuminates the divergent approaches used in constructing different scales to measure the same constructs. She compares two basic approaches to interest measurement in explaining critical concepts such as homogeneous versus heterogeneous item groups, rational versus empirical criteria for item selection, content and format issues, and the questions involved in using norms. The measurement issues related to reliability and validity are addressed next. Harmon persuasively argues that while there may be cultural and social changes, scales constructed long ago may still retain their validity for use. After examining measurement issues, Harmon discusses how individual differences in sex, race, and socioeconomic status relate to concerns about the reliability and validity of interest inventories. Harmon uses this information to show that widely utilized interest inventories are constructed in different ways, resulting in distinct advantages and disadvantages for particular applications. In the end she asserts that it is incumbent on counselors who use an interest inventory to know the type of scales contained in that inventory, how the inventory was developed, and for whom and when the inventory is most useful.

The complementary chapter on interest inventories offers a comprehensive summary of their validity evidence. Fouad organizes this fund of knowledge by using Messick's conceptual framework for validity and its six facets. She explains each facet of validity and then summarizes the available evidence for that facet as it pertains to interest inventories. In turn she reports on the content, substantive, structural, general, external, and consequential validity of interest inventories. Fouad closes the chapter by drawing four major conclusions based on the accumulated validity evidence and by identifying six key issues for future research on interest inventories.

As noted by Crites, in addition to attitudinal inventories, the only other operational definition of vocational interests to attract much attention from researchers and practitioners involves expressed interests. Accordingly, the final two chapters in Section 2 address the topic of expressed interests. The first of these complementary chapters, written by Spokane and Decker, explains differences between measured and expressed interests and then questions the validity of counselors' preference for inventorying rather than inquiring about client interests. Spokane and Decker review empirical evidence that shows expressed interests are highly predictive of eventual occupational choice and at least equal to inventories in predictive accuracy. Of course counselors do not have to choose between assessment by inventory or expressed preferences; the best practice is to assess a client's measured and expressed interests. When those interests concur, then counselors can expect the most predictive accuracy. Spokane and Decker elaborate this conclusion with seven cases that show varying degrees of agreement between direct and indirect measures of vocational interests. They conclude the chapter by offering suggestions for interpreting the meaning of a client's interests when expressed and measured data disagree.

In the next chapter Hartung explains how counselors can assess expressed interests with a technique called vocational card sorts. Hartung asserts that vocational card sorts offer practitioners and researchers an alternative or supplement to inventorying interests as well as a general intervention strategy. He then explains how vocational card sorts implement a phenomenological perspective for operationally defining vocational interests, one that places the personal meaning of vocational interests at the center of the process. Next Hartung discusses the evolution of card sorts as a structured yet flexible interview technique assessing interests. Hartung closes the chapter by describing how counselors can use eight different vocational card sorts to elicit a client's expressed interests and their personal meaning.

As a group, the five chapters in Section 2 provide a comprehensive summary of research on the operational definition of vocational interests by inventories and verbal expressions. This information about the technical problems involved in measuring interests provides a crucial background for Section 3, using inventory results in counseling.

CHAPTER SEVEN

Operational Definitions of Vocational Interests

John O. Crites

W HAT ARE VOCATIONAL INTERESTS? How can they be defined? But first, what is a definition? There are several different ways to define a definition. One is literary. According to *Webster's Third International Dictionary,* a definition is "2. A word or phrase expressing the essential nature of a person or thing or class of persons or of things: an answer to the question 'what is x?' or 'what is an x?'" Another definition of *definition* is from logic and the philosophy of science. Cohen and Nagel (1934) write, "A phenomenon or variable is defined by specifying what it is and what it is not." Best expressed by Venn diagrams, what is and what is not distinguishes vocational interests from other variables, such as aptitudes, personality characteristics, and skills. All A's are B's but not all B's are A's. Vocational interests are neither aptitudes, nor personality characteristics, nor skills. They are defined separately. Aptitude, achievement, and skills tests have right and wrong answers. Vocational interest inventories do not. Personality inventories do not have right or wrong answers, but the item content is different and the response formats are different. One more differentium of vocational interests is the distinction between career choice process and career choice content (Crites, 1978). The former is exemplified by career development measures such as the Revised Career Maturity Inventory (Crites, 1995), whereas vocational interest inventories are content laden, with a response format for eliciting preferences. Accordingly, vocational interests can be defined as not aptitudes, not achievement, not skills, not personality, not career maturity—but *preferences for different life activities.*

True to the question of what are vocational interests, and how they can be defined from other variables, there is even now a controversy. Are they personality variables, as Holland (this volume) has proclaimed, on minimal evidence from Darley and Hagenah's (1955) interpretation of Cottle (1950) study, or are they also related to aptitude variables, the highest correlation between the two being in the range of .20 to .30. What is the definition of vocational interests? They are neither aptitudes nor personality variables. Vocational interests are vocational interests. They are uniquely defined.

Probably the most widely recognized linguistic definition of vocational interests is Strong's (1943), who compared them to "tropisms":

> activities for which we have liking or disliking and which we go towards or away from, or concerning which we at least continue or discontinue the status quo; furthermore, they may or may not be preferred to other interests and they may continue over varying intervals of time.

From this we can conclude that vocational interests are individual difference variables that express preferences—liking, indifference, disliking—but that can be measured in several ways. In contrast to linguistic definitions, the measurement of vocational interests provides operational definitions.

Super and Crites (1962) enumerated four different methods for operationally defining and assessing vocational interests: expressed, manifest, tested, and inventoried. To these Harry Dexter Kitson (1925) added the "interest machine" and Crites (1969) the "preference machine," an experimental set-up that assessed response time to preference statements. Unfortunately, there are no diagrams or pictures of these machines, but there are materials available on expressed, manifest, tested, and inventoried interests.

EXPRESSED INTERESTS

Super and Crites (1962) have defined *expressed* interests as "the verbal profession of interest in an object, activity, task, or occupation." The typical question used to elicit an expressed interest is, "Which occupation do you intend to enter when you leave school?" Similar questions can be framed for other stimuli. Super and Crites (1962, p. 378) have pointed out that

> The importance which may be attached to expressions of specific interests clearly varies with the maturity of the individual. . . . it also depends upon the phrasing of the question, for some questions concerning vocational preferences are so put as to elicit information concerning expectations, some so as to ascertain preferences and some to evoke fantasies. The degree of realism of preferences varies with the question asked.

Expressed interest in an occupation is more than a statement of liking. It involves a complex, conscious evaluation of many additional factors beyond simple liking. Thus in some ways expressed interest is even more predictive of future behavior than a simple reaction of affective liking when presented with an environmental stimuli.

MANIFEST INTERESTS

In contrast to the verbal nature of expressed interests, *manifest* interests denote active participation in an activity or occupation. The rationale for this definition of manifest vocational interests is that if individuals do not have an interest in an activity or occupation, they would not participate in that activity or occupation. Obviously a person may engage in an activity or occupation for reasons other than manifest interest. Super and Crites (1962, pp. 378–379) observe that

> it is assumed that the high school youth, who was active in the dramatic club, has artistic or literary interests and that the accountant, who devotes two evenings per week to building and operating a model railroad system, is interested in mechanics or engineering. It is generally appreciated that such manifest interests are sometimes the result of interest in the concomitants or byproducts of the activity rather than in the activity itself.

In other words, many factors can influence and determine manifest interests. Bingham (1937), who wrote about "interests manifest," imagined observing the behavior of individuals walking around a specially arranged museum, watching how much time they spent with each exhibit. He realized that this was inconvenient yet concluded that "instead of relying solely on what a person says are his interests, observe, if possible, that in which he actually takes interest" (p. 67). Bingham (1937) also offered a practical method for assessing manifest interests. He urged the use of an interest diary in which individuals would record, over time, their activities. He believed that these "notes of doings" would clearly indicate manifest interests and with analysis by a counselor could produce an interest "behaviorgram."

Fryer (1931) also emphasized the importance of manifest interest He urged counselors to take an interest history of their clients' manifest behavior as a means for diagnosing interests to provide vocational guidance. Fryer would help his clients construct an "interest autobiography" by focusing on different developmental eras: (1) earliest recollections, (2) entering school, (3) last years of elementary school, (4) last years of high school, (5) entering college, (6) graduation from college, (7) time of going to work, and (8) after several years of occupational activity (p. 370). Clearly analysis of behaviorgrams or interest histories secured by the autobiographical method reveals a continuity. As Fryer (1931) noted, "when the pattern is completed it is not so difficult to follow the design" (p. 412). Fryer did note, however, that the pattern may not be easy to forecast from early interests alone. Like Bingham, Fryer wished that an interest autobiography did not have to be retrospective. He strongly encouraged parents and teachers to help their children and students prospectively write and frequently revise an interest autobiography.

TESTED INTERESTS

Again, a definition from Super and Crites (1962, p. 379): Tested interests

> refer to interest as measured by objective tests, as differentiated from inventories which are based on subjective self-estimates. It is assumed that, since interest in a vocation is likely to manifest itself in action, it should also result in an accumulation of relevant information.

The first interest test was reported by Kelley (1914), who developed a battery of questions that both asked people to estimate their interests and then tested some factual information. This pioneering study did not seem to influence the field. The exemplar of the testing approach to defining vocational interests was Greene's (1940) *Michigan Vocabulary Profile Test*, which was predicated on the assumption that if one knew the vocabulary of an occupation, therefore he or she had an interest in it.

During World War II Super and his colleagues in the Aviation Psychology Program used the concept of tested interests with great success (Super & Roper, 1941; Super & Haddad, 1943; Older, 1944). For example, they developed a *General Information Test,* which gave differential scores for pilots, navigators, and bombardiers and which proved to be the most valid single test in the Air Force's selection and classification battery. They also constructed an interest test for nursing consisting of 30 slides depicting nurses on the job. Each slide was shown for 15 seconds. After viewing the slides, the participants responded to a four-part test: two dealing with information given in the film (retention of facts) and two dealing with recall for images in the pictures (recognition of pictures). The participants' scores were unrelated to IQ test scores or previous information about nursing. The scores for 35 nurses and for 111 high school seniors correlate -.01 and .001 to their scores on the *Strong* nurses' scale. However, both the *Strong* and the interest test differentiated between nurse and non-nurses quite effectively, with the test doing a little better. Although unrelated to each, Super concluded that both the inventory and the test seemed valid. He interpreted this to mean that the *Strong* measured similarity to those employed as nurses and the interest test measured interest in nursing. Although psychometricians such as Greene and Super did have an intriguing idea about how to measure vocational interests, subsequent use of tested interests, including those developed during World War II, have not proved to be useful for either criterion-relevant or predictive validity. Again, as with manifest interests, extraneous factors such as economic conditions, familial and social pressures, and individual idiosyncrasies confounded the measurement of tested interests.

INVENTORIED INTERESTS

Inventoried interests, the fourth type of operational definition of vocational interests described by Super and Crites, denote responses of like, dislike, and indifference to verbal presentations of activities, objects, and types of people. These responses can be summed to produce scaled scores on standardized profiles that depict an individual's vocational interests in reference to some normative group. Miner (1918) appears to be one of the first to use an interest inventory. He developed one at Carnegie Institute of Technology and in 1918 administered it to 10,000 high school students in Pittsburgh (Bingham, 1937; Cleeton, 1940). Miner's (1922) inventory was published in 1922 under the title *Analysis of Work Interests*. Miner's inventory divided occupational activities into four categories: making useful things, dealing with people, producing artistic results, thinking out problems. He recommended that teachers use the inventory to orient high school students to their work interests.

A graduate student seminar group led by Clarence S. Yoakum at Carnegie Institute of Technology in 1919–1920 conducted the first systematic work to construct a numerically ranked interest inventory. They started in 1919 by developing a list of 1,000 items. Various items from this list were used to form several inventories. The first of these inventories was developed by Moore (1921), who used 10 mechanical and 10 social items (agreed upon by 14 judges) to distinguish between sales engineers and design engineers who worked at Westinghouse. The items correctly placed 82% of the design engineers and 78%

of the sales engineers. When the inventory was later given to engineers in training, it showed on follow-up that 85% were correctly placed. Subsequently others used items from the list to distinguish successful and unsuccessful salesmen (Ream, 1924) and to extend Moore's study of engineering specialties (Freyd, 1922). In 1921 Yoakum's group produced the first standardized interest inventory, the *Carnegie Interest Analysis Form;* the first edition of this form, prepared by Ream and Freyd, can be found in an article by Freyd (1922). This inventory was adapted and modified by at least half a dozen researchers, who each gave a different name to their inventory. For example, Cowdery, Strong's graduate student at Stanford, revised the Carnegie in 1924, calling it the *Interest Report Blank.* After using it for some time, Strong eventually revised and extended Cowdery's inventory from 263 to 420 items, thinking that more items would increase its validity.

Of course Strong's (1943) book based his work with his inventory stands as the outstanding treatise on vocational interests. Then his follow-up 18 years later of his college students at Stanford University validated his initial work (Strong, 1955). His design for the initial *Strong Vocational Interest Blank* (1938), as it was called then, was a "Like-Indifference-Dislike" response format, in which each response was weighed 4 to -4 to optimize the differentiation among occupations. In subsequent research by the Center for Interest Measurement at the University of Minnesota it was found that unit weight for responses to the *Strong* were as differentiating as the original ones.

EXPERIMENTAL INTERESTS

Experimental interests denote measures of interests defined by behavioral responses to objects that represent various occupations, and the voluntary or involuntary responses are measured by experimental techniques such as reaction time and galvanic skin response. To explain the difference between objective and subjective interests psychologists sometimes enjoy describing the first objective—but unscientific—measure of vocational interests. The measure was administered to infants on their first birthday by placing them on the floor in front of an apple, a bible, and a dollar. If the infant grabbed the apple, then an interest in agriculture was recorded. If the infant played with the bible, then ministry seemed to be the occupational preference. Of course the dollar represented interest in business. A few versatile infants ended up sitting on the bible while holding the apple in one hand and the dollar in the other; they were to be politicians!

The initial scientific attempts to measure objective interests experimented with reaction time techniques and the galvanometer (Bellido, 1922). Later experimental techniques to measure interests objectively were devised by Kitson (1925) and Crites (1969). Harry Dextor Kitson, Donald Super's mentor at Columbia University, called his experimental apparatus an "interest machine." It was made of wood and had many different joints and appurtenances, each of which defined a different interest. A second example of an objective measure of experimental interests was Crites' "experimental" set-up at the University of Iowa, which had verbal stimuli, but the scoring system was response time. A 3 x 5 card, which had a vocational preference printed on it, was flashed in a shutter box and the subject pushed a button to indicate either liking or disliking for the stimulus. The measure of preference was reaction time. Neither Kitson's nor Crites' attempts to assess vocational interests with experimental paradigms had any known reliability or validity. Nevertheless, these objective measures are novel and worth including in a review of the definition of vocational interests.

CONCLUSION

Of the five operational definitions of vocational interests discussed herein, only one has been extensively studied: inventoried interests. There is an embryonic literature on expressed interests (Spokane, this volume), yet, overall, research on expressed, tested, manifested, and experimental interests has lagged considerably behind operational definitions of inventoried interests. There has been even less effort devoted to research that compares and contrasts the five operational definitions to one another. Further advances in the field's understanding of vocational interests requires a concerted effort to integrate these disparate definitions into a comprehensive theory of vocational interests. Let us build on the great success of empirical research on inventoried interests by constructing a theory of vocational interests, one informed by multiple linguistic and operational definitions of interest.

REFERENCES

Bellido, J. M. (1922). *El fenomen psico-galvani en psicotecnica.* Paper presented at the Second International Conference of Psychotechnics Applied to Vocational Guidance and Scientific Management, Institut d'Orientacio Professional, Barcelona, Spain.
Bingham, W. V. (1937). *Aptitudes and aptitude testing.* New York: HarperCollins.

Cleeton, G. U. (1940). *Studies in the psychology of vocational adjustment.* Pittsburgh: Carnegie Institute of Technology.

Cohen, M. R., & Nagel, E. (1934). *An introduction to logic and scientific method.* Orlando, FL: Harcourt Brace.

Cottle, W. C. (1950). A factorial study of the Multiphasic, Strong, Kuder, and Bell inventories using a population of adult males. *Psychometrika, 15,* 25–47.

Crites, J. O. (1969). *Vocational psychology.* New York: McGraw-Hill.

Crites, J. O. (1978). *The Career Maturity Inventory.* Monterey, CA: CTB/McGraw-Hill.

Crites, J. O. (1995). *The Revised Career Maturity Inventory.* Clayton, NY: Careerware.

Darley, J. G., & Hagenah, T. (1955). *Vocational interest measurement: Theory and practice.* Minneapolis: University of Minnesota Press.

Freyd, M. (1922). The measurement of interests in vocational selection. *Journal of Personnel Research, 1,* 319–328.

Fryer, D. (1931). *The measurement of interests.* New York: Henry Holt.

Greene, E. B. (1940). The Michigan Vocabulary Profile Test after ten years. *Educational and Psychological Measurement, 11,* 208–211.

Kelley, T. L. (1914). Educational guidance: An experimental study in the analysis and prediction of ability of high school pupils. *Contributions to Education,71.*

Kitson, H. D. (1925). *The psychology of vocational adjustment.* Philadelphia: Lippincott.

Miner, J. B. (1918). *Analysis of work interests blank.* Chicago: Stoelting.

Miner, J. B. (1922). An aid to the analysis of vocational interests. *Journal of Educational Research, 5,* 311–323.

Moore, B. V. (1921). Personnel selection of graduate engineers. *Psychological Monographs, 30* (Whole No. 138).

Older, H. J. (1944). An objective test of vocational interests. *Journal of Applied Psychology, 28,* 99–108.

Ream, M. J. (1924). *Ability to sell: Its relation to certain aspects of personality and experience.* Baltimore: Williams & Wilkins.

Strong, E. K., Jr. (1938). *Vocational Interest Blank for Men* (Revised). Stanford, CA: Stanford University Press.

Strong, E. K., Jr. (1943). *Vocational interests of men and women.* Stanford, CA: Stanford University Press.

Strong, E. K., Jr. (1955). *Vocational interests 18 years after college.* Minneapolis: University of Minnesota Press.

Super, D. E., & Crites, J. O. (1962). *Appraising vocational fitness* (Rev. ed.). New York: HarperCollins.

Super, D. E., & Haddad, W. C. (1943). The effect of familiarity with an occupational field on a recognition test of vocational interest. *Journal of Educational Psychology,* 103–109.

Super, D. E., & Roper, S. A. (1941). An objective technique for testing vocational interests. *Journal of Applied Psychology, 25,* 487–498.

Webster's Third International Dictionary. (1967). Springfield, MA: Merriam-Webster.

CHAPTER EIGHT

Measuring Interests
Approaches and Issues

Lenore W. Harmon

I_N THIS CHAPTER I describe and discuss interest scales, items, and norms to illustrate how different types of interest inventories may measure the same interest construct very differently. Then I discuss theoretical and measurement issues, and I review their relationship to attempts to analyze the structure of interests. The choice of one type of interest inventory over another is shown to be related to the purpose for measuring interests.

TWO TYPES OF INTEREST SCALES

Historically the first interest scales were empirically derived, heterogeneous scales composed of items that separated workers in specific occupational groups from other workers. Later, as part of an attempt to find more basic interest dimensions, homogeneous scales were devised.

Empirical Interest Scales

The first popular measure of interests, the *Strong Vocational Interest Blank,* utilized this type of scale exclusively. It is still used today in the *Strong Interest Inventory* (SII; Harmon, Hansen, Borgen, & Hammer, 1994) and the *Kuder Occupational Interest Scales* (KOIS; Kuder & Zytowski, 1991), although both utilize other types of scales as well. The basic data are the responses of a group of people of one sex who are employed in a specific occupation. In the SII these item responses are compared with the responses of another group of people of the same sex who are termed General Reference Samples. Campbell (1971, p. 351) cited evidence that this idea was first proposed by J. B. Miner. Items that differentiate between the two groups are gathered into a scale and weighted according to the direction of the differences. Table 8.1 shows how this works with some fictitious items and occupational groups. People in Occupation A like "Eating broccoli" much more than the typical worker in the General Reference Sample. The result is that the "Like" response to the item is awarded +1 and the "Dislike" response is awarded −1 on the scale for Occupation A. Since workers in Occupation B like "Eating broccoli" much less than the typical worker represented by the General Reference Sample, the "Like" response is awarded −1 on the scale for Occupation B and the "Dislike" response is awarded +1. Note that "Eating broccoli" may have nothing to do with the duties of workers in either Occupation A or Occupation B. This illustrates the generally atheoretical nature of empirical scales. They include whatever items work to differentiate the interests of individuals in specific occupations. In the KOIS there is no General Reference Sample, so the procedure is somewhat different. An individual's item responses are compared directly with the responses of workers of the same sex in a given occupation. A pattern of answers that is similar to those of the occupational group earns a higher score. Note that in Table 8.1, Individual Y will score more like members of Occupation A on the item illustrated because the pattern of his or her responses is more similar to the typical member of Occupation A.

In addition to the SII, the *Campbell Interest and Skill Survey* (CISS; Campbell, Hyne, & Nilsen, 1992) and the *Career Assessment Inventory* (CAI; Johansson, 1985) use the technique of comparing item responses from an occupational group with a larger reference group. The composition of these groups is quite important. If Occupational Group A is named Psychologist and includes only members of the APA Divisions of Clinical and Private Practice, some of us might argue that it is unlikely to represent the broader interests of all psychologists. If Occupational Group B is called Financial Analysts but contains only people under 30 years of age, we might question its representativeness. Although the problems are obvious, every occupational sample is biased in some ways by the availability of members of the occupation for sampling. To be contacted efficiently they must be members of an occupational organization, or employees of a certain company, or on a list of licensed or certified practitioners. Because the General Reference Samples are made up of representatives of the occupational groups, any biases that occurred in selecting the occupational group members are passed on to the General Reference Samples. Fig. 8.1 shows how the occupational groups are combined to make a larger sample of workers from many occupations.

TABLE 8.1   Item Selection and/or Weighting in Empirical Interest Scales

Scales Using General Reference Samples

Item	L%	I%	D%
Eating broccoli			
Occupation A	90	8	2
Occupation B	31	10	59
General Reference Sample	50	8	42
Difference A vs. GRS	40	0	–40
Difference B vs. GRS	–19	2	17

Scales Without Reference Samples

Choose the most and least preferred from the following:	Eating broccoli	Eating apples	Eating cake

Percent Most Preferring/or Individual Response

Occupation A	*75%*	*20%*	*5%*
Individual X	Least		Most
Individual Y	Most		Least

Note: All comparisons are between or among individuals of the same sex. L = Like, I = Indifferent, D = Dislike, GRS = General Reference Sample

Homogeneous Interest Scales

These scales are all formed by using some sort of clustering technique. The technique may be a rational procedure in which items that seem to go together rationally are gathered into a scale, or a statistical clustering technique (such as factor analysis), or a combination of the two. The scales are characterized by homogeneity of content and by the fact that scoring is usually based on endorsements only. Table 8.2 shows how a set of item responses, each with a different level of endorsement, might be separated into two scales by a factor analysis with Factor I representing a liking for fruits and vegetables and Factor II representing a liking for desserts. Homogeneous scales usually come in sets distinguished by how many scales are in the set of scales presented to cover the interest domain. Perhaps the most popular early set of scales of this type was on the *Kuder Preference Record* (Kuder, 1964), which ultimately contained ten scales.

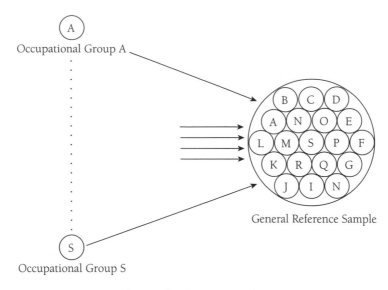

FIGURE 8.1   Composition of General Reference Samples

More common today are six or eight scales sometimes called Themes or Orientations. They are most often developed to measure the six Holland types or similar constructs. Before the popularity of Holland's theory, a set of Basic Interest Scales (BISs) was developed for the *Strong* (Campbell, Borgen, Eastes, Johansson, & Peterson, 1968), and several inventories continue to use this level of abstraction to measure a set of constructs, usually 20 or more, with names such as Science, Writing, Teaching, and Computer Activities. These constructs are often presented as subdivisions of the more general theme or orientation. The techniques used to develop them are the same as those used for smaller sets of homogeneous scales; the difference is in the level of generality.

Other Scales

The examples above illustrate that the techniques can be used whether or not the content is related to vocational interests. Other types of scales have been developed using interest inventory items. They include scales for college majors, scales to determine whether the responses of individuals suggest that their scores on the other scales are valid, and scales to measure personal characteristics.

TABLE 8.2 Homogeneous Scale Building

Items	% Like Responses	Factor Loadings	
		I	II
Eating broccoli	45	.50	.10
Eating spinach	60	.63	.24
Eating cake	56	.10	.61
Eating carrots	71	.65	.12
Eating ice cream	61	.17	.56
Eating apples	80	.70	.20
Eating pie	44	.23	.40

SCALES ARE BUILT FROM ITEMS

Interest scales all rest on items that may differ in content or format. The scope of the content covered by a set of items may be broad or narrow.

Item Content

The content of empirical or heterogeneous scales may be somewhat of a mystery because they use items that differentiate—regardless of theoretical elegance. Empirical scales use whatever items work, but authors and developers may be biased toward item content that seems related to scales they hope to develop, the socioeconomic class of people they expect to inventory, or simply their own view of what is interesting. Of course some items tried out for use in empirical scales may ultimately be dropped because they do not work well or are used on only a few scales. However, whole areas of content can be ignored because they were never considered for inclusion. Homogeneous scales usually have content that is easily related to the type of interest that is being measured. Especially in homogeneous scales that were constructed to reflect a theory, such as those rationally developed to reflect Holland's typology of interests, the items are rather equally distributed. In the *Self-Directed Search* (SDS; Holland, Fritzsche, & Powell, 1994) this distribution is across six areas: Realistic, Investigative, Artistic, Social, Enterprising, and Conventional.

Some interest inventories use items with only one type of content, while others use several. The KOIS, for instance, uses only activities items, whereas the SII uses occupational names, names of school subjects, activities, leisure activities, types of people, personal characteristics, and world-of-work preferences. The SDS uses activities, competencies, occupations, and self-estimates. The CISS includes some items that combine occupational names with illustrative activities.

Note that some types of interest inventories such as the SDS include items about competency within the interest scales. Others, such as the SII and the CISS, include separate items and scales for skills or self-efficacy. Theoretically self-efficacy or estimates of skills would seem to be conceptually different although not unrelated to interests.

In summary, item content is very important in defining the concepts we call interests. Yet the inventory user may know very little about the content of some scales because the actual items on the more complex scales are not easily accessed. The scoring is often done by computer and considered proprietary information by the test publisher.

Item Format

There are essentially two formats for interest items. The first asks how much the respondent likes the occupation, activity, or characteristic (of jobs or people) contained in the item. He or she may be given a choice of "Yes" or "No," "Like," "Indifferent," or "Dislike," or asked to use a Likert type scale to indicate level of endorsement. The second format is the forced choice format in which the respondent is asked to select one of two choices or record highest and lowest preferences from a group of three. Some inventories use one format consistently, others use two, often in reference to different types of item content. Because interest inventories tend to continue to use the same format over revisions, it is difficult to study the effect of these different formats on scores because they do not vary independently from item content and scale development techniques.

Summary

Overall, the items that go into any scale, whether empirical or homogeneous, are not guaranteed to cover the intended domain of interests very well, although most developers have tried out innumerable items that do not appear on scales because they do not work as well as the ones that are retained. Neither do the items on any scale represent equal amounts of interest in specific occupations or interest domains. That is to say, no interest inventories are scaled as carefully as attitude measures where matters of social desirability and equal intervals between the response options are taken into account. Given these limitations, it is surprising that the measurement of interests works at all. But it does, and it usually works far better on a number of criteria than the measurement of other psychological constructs.

NORMS

Norms differ depending on the types of scales being utilized. Some inventories do not really use norms at all. SDS scales yield raw scores, and the summary code is based on those raw scores. For other homogeneous scales the score that is reported is based on a comparison of individuals' responses and a norm group. For instance, for the SII General Occupational Themes (GOTs) and Basic Interest Scales (BISs) standard scores reported are based on a distribution of scores for about 18,000 employed men and women that make up the General Reference Sample of the 1994 revision. The mean and standard deviation are set at 50 and 10 respectively for each scale. Scores do not reflect sex differences, although interpretive comments on the report form do. The CISS utilizes similar values (50 and 10) that were achieved in a somewhat different manner. Males and females were combined in one reference group. Although there were 3,400 males and only 1,800 females, they are equally represented in the General Reference Sample. (The median standard deviations among a group of 65 occupations were used to establish the standard deviation for each scale.)

Among empirically developed occupational scales, some inventories use norms and others do not. The SII uses the occupational group as the basis for the standard scores provided (separately by sex); the CISS uses the General Reference Sample to establish the mean (50) and the occupational sample to establish the standard deviation (10) combining the sexes in each case; and the KOIS uses the occupational group responses for males and females separately as the basis for computing the lambda coefficient, which has no normative meaning across individuals.

What all of these methods have in common is that they do provide a way to communicate to individuals about how they compare with others in terms of their interests in specific domains or occupations. However, only occupational scales provide for a direct comparison with people in an occupation. It is possible to get scores that suggest very different levels of interest from same-named scales on two inventories. Norming, sampling, and scale construction may all contribute to this phenomenon.

NOT ALL INTEREST MEASURES
ARE CREATED EQUAL

Looking at all of the differences in interest scales, we see that the methods of construction, including the item pools, the item selection procedures, the individuals included in both occupational and general comparison groups, and the scoring and norming procedures may differ markedly. Accordingly, a number of constructs that have the same names have been operationally defined in very different ways. That the resulting scales are not more diverse than they are gives strong testimony to the validity of the overarching construct of vocational interests. Nevertheless, I think that our willingness to assume constancy of constructs leads to some interesting issues.

ISSUES

Theoretical Issues

In general, empirically derived scales are not very satisfying to Investigative types—those most likely to be reading these words and using interest inventories. If instead Realistic types dominated our counseling practice, one would expect empirical scales to be more readily accepted. Homogeneous scales can be developed to explore or confirm theory. Empirically developed scores are usually atheoretical. Put another way, the items that appear on empirical scales or carry the most weight in such scales may not conform to a general theory of interests in any sense, although they may provide a lot of information (within the limits of the item pool) about the preferences of people who enter specific occupations. The use of negative scoring, the fact that some occupational groups have more clearly differentiated interests in theoretically derived interest areas than other groups, and the choice of occupations to study make it difficult to develop theory using occupational or empirical scales. That is not to say that it cannot be done. Some of John Holland's original impetus for developing his theory came from observing how occupational (empirical) scales work in practice. However, empirically derived scales are more conceptually complex than homogeneous scales. While an occupational group's scores on the Investigative GOT scale may indicate that it is an Investigative occupation, not all Investigative people will score high on that occupational scale. The occupational scale will contain items to which occupational group members respond negatively in ways not shared by

TABLE 8.3 Sample Items Appearing on Male and Female Scales
for Psychologist with Direction of Scoring

Item	Appears on Scales		
	Both	Female	Male
Scientific research work	+		
Perform scientific experiments	+		
Flight attendant	−		
Opera singer		+	
Symphony concerts			+
Checking printed material		−	
Bookkeeping			−

all investigative people. The members of the occupation may also score high on some other GOTs. Let's take psychologists as an example. Table 8.3 shows some items that are highly endorsed by psychologists that would certainly fit the Investigative GOT. However, the psychologists also dislike some items that help define their interests. These would not show up on the Investigative GOT scale.

Although the Psychologist scale is positioned with the Investigative scales on the SII, the manual (Harmon et al., 1994, Table 7.3) shows that for both male and female psychologists the Artistic theme is either tied or a close second. In fact, only 41% of female psychologists and 30% of male psychologists have Investigative as their highest GOT score. Of course not all occupational groups have such diverse patterns on the GOTs. The Musician scale is positioned with the Artistic scales, and, in fact, over 50% of both the male and female samples of musicians have Artistic as their highest GOT. These data suggest that the occupational scales and perhaps the people in occupations are so complex that they sometimes defy classification in a simple system that highlights only one or two components of interests. Such diversity of interests within members of occupational groups makes empirically developed occupational scales more closely related to occupations than the more general homogeneous scales. However, that specificity raises a question about whether this is the most efficient way to measure interests. If it is, how many occupational scales do we need? This question is related to the issue of how much we can generalize from one occupational scale to a similar occupation. It also raises the question of whether we have adequately covered the world of work in developing occupational scales. If we do need more, do we need more specificity or more generality? If interests can be adequately mapped using a few dimensions, why use empirically derived occupational scales at all? The key to answering this question is in deciding what is "adequate" for the purpose for which one intends to use an interest inventory. This leads to a consideration of validity.

Measurement Issues

Traditional measurement issues are less problematic than sex, race, socioeconomic status, and age. They will be discussed in a subsequent section, but first we should consider reliability and validity.

Reliability. Reliability for all interest scales is quite high. For homogeneous scales, measures of internal consistency are appropriate. For example, the SII GOTs have alpha coefficients ranging from .90 to .94; the BISs have alpha coefficients ranging from .74 to .94 with a median of .87. These scales also have adequate test-retest reliability, ranging from .84 to .92 for GOTs and from .80 to .94 for the BISs over three to six months among employed adults. For Occupational Scales (which are empirical scales) the test-retest coefficients are also high, ranging from .80 to .95 with a median of .90 for employed adults over three to six months. Test-retest correlations over longer periods of time have also been demonstrated (Swanson & Hansen, 1988). A few interest inventories have reliability coefficients in a range that is only marginally acceptable. High reliability is clearly desirable no matter what the use of an interest inventory.

Validity. Fouad (this volume) addresses issues of validity at length, so I do not want to discuss it comprehensively here except to note that the most important question is, "Validity for what group, for what purpose?" This question is relevant to determining whether we need a few scales that relate to an elegant and parsimonious structure of interests or many empirical although less theoretical scales. Empirical scales based on occupational groups have built-in concurrent validity. The items on the scales do distinguish the preferences of people in the occupations. The older versions of the *Strong* (Strong, 1955) and the *Kuder* (Zytowski, 1976) have also demonstrated rather impressive predictive validity over time. Many homogeneous scales have demonstrated concurrent validity in that they differentiate occupational groups appropriately (Harmon et al., 1994, Chapters 5 and 6; see especially Figs. 5.4–5.9 and 6.1–6.25). In a few cases predictive validity has been demonstrated for homogeneous scales (Lapan,

Shaughnessy, & Boggs, 1996). As in the case of reliability it seems clear that using the most valid scales is indicated.

Many people assume that cultural or social change (an example is our current technological revolution) invalidates interest scales constructed in the past. I am not sure that is so. Campbell did several ingenious studies during the 1960s in which he asked bankers, corporation presidents, ministers, and school superintendents, all of whom were in the same positions as those in the original occupational groups that responded to the SVIB, to take the *Strong*. The profiles for the groups tested in the 1930s and 1960s were remarkably similar (Campbell, 1971, Chapter 9, Figs. 9.1–9.4). Another way to examine this question is to look at the items that differentiate a group of people in an occupation that has changed considerably over time cross-sectionally before and after the change. For example, on the Business Education Teacher scale about half the items endorsed by both male and female business education teachers (collected in 1993) are occupations or activities that have been influenced by the electronic revolution, but only one of them (word processor) represents a totally new activity since the last time the occupation was sampled. Comparison with the items on the 1969 Occupation Scale for women business education teachers shows that all these items were scored in the same way as in 1994 even though the way the work is done is quite different. An example of such an item is "Operating office machines." The machines that are found in a typical office have changed considerably in the 25 years from 1969 to 1994, yet the way business education teachers respond to this item has not. They responded "Like" on both occasions.

The way items cluster on homogeneous scales seems constant over time as well. In 1994 a new analysis resulted in deleting some items from the GOTs and adding others (without changing the construct measured) in an attempt to increase internal reliability while maintaining the theoretical relationships among the six RIASEC scales. The 1985 and 1994 versions of the GOTs correlated very highly from .93 to .98 when a group of 18,000 adults tested in the early 1990s responded. Likewise the BISs, which were originally developed in 1968, were also revised to increase internal consistency. The item content remained quite stable with scales that had been changed correlating from .96 to .99 when a group of 18,000 adults tested in the early 1990s responded.

Issues Related to Individual Differences

Individual differences in sex, race, and socioeconomic status raise as many measurement issues as reliability and validity do, perhaps more.

Sex Differences. The issue of how the differing interests of men and women should be handled has been around from the very beginning. Strong developed separate sex versions of the SVIB in 1927 and 1933 (for males and females respectively) (Campbell, 1971). They contained very different items and scales. The female form from the early 1960s has scales for Elementary School Teacher, Housewife, Nurse, Secretary, and Social Worker. The men's form had scales for Engineer and President of a Manufacturing Concern. When the combined form of the *Strong* (SCII, Campbell, 1974) was published, the argument for retaining separate sex scales was based on data that showed that men and women, and boys and girls, responded very differently to some items.

Not until the 1994 revision of the SII did anyone examine that argument for its application to actual scales. In doing so, we found that the items that differentiated most highly between men and women seldom appeared on Occupational Scales (Harmon et al., 1994). Campbell and his colleagues (1992) used combined samples of men and women in the occupational samples for the CISS and compared them with a combined General Reference Sample. They developed three types of scales for eight occupations and found few important differences between scales for men, for women, or for combined sexes. We have found similar results in looking at the scales of the 1994 SII. There is a considerable amount of overlap between the items on the male and female scales for the same occupation, and the items that overlap are more valid (or stronger) than those that do not. Looking back at Table 8.3 suggests that although the actual items may differ across scales, they seem to reflect similar interests. While both men and women psychologists endorse items that involve science, women psychologists like opera more than the General Reference Sample of women, and men psychologists like symphony concerts more than the General Reference Sample of men. Although the items are different, they are similar in that they refer to classical music in the broadest sense. Women psychologists dislike checking printed material, men psychologists dislike bookkeeping. Again the "flavor" of the items is similar even though they are not the same. (It is possible that the item selection is based more on differences in the responses of the General Reference Samples than members of the occupation.)

Among homogeneous scales, items and scales are almost always developed from combined sex samples, although they may be normed separately for males and females.

Racial and Ethnic Differences. The issue of racial differences has been a question in interest measurement since the 1960s. Although there are some differences, recent research has convinced me that these differences are not as large as previously supposed. The most recent SDS manual (Holland, Fritzsche, & Powell, 1994) addresses ethnic differences by gender (Table 18), showing that gender differences are far greater than ethnic differences. The 1994 revision of the SII also examined racial differences (Fouad, Harmon, & Hansen, 1994). The most interesting data there show that among ethnic groups in specific occupations there are very few differences in occupational profiles between ethnic group members and other members of an occupational group. Again, while there are racial differences in response rates to some items, these do not have much effect at the level of occupational scales. These data are most informative because studying individuals in the same occupation holds socioeconomic status constant to a certain extent.

Socioeconomic Differences. Socioeconomic status is often confounded with sex and race in the world of work, with women and minority group members usually most highly represented in less prestigious occupations. When Linda Gottfredson suggested a theory of compromise in career selection in 1981, studying her proposal was difficult because it called for disentangling sex and socioeconomic status, which proved nearly impossible (Hesketh, Elmslie, & Kaldor, 1990; Holt, 1989; Leung & Harmon, 1990). Most interest inventories that use empirical scales do not cover the socioeconomic spectrum very well, based on the implicit assumption that no one would take an interest inventory to choose between becoming a ditch digger and a janitor. Roe's theory (Roe & Klos, 1969) eventually postulated that her circle of interests had a smaller radius as occupational level decreased (picture her inverted cone). It implied that there is less differentiation in interests at lower socioeconomic levels. Some early research of my own suggested that women could be placed in more satisfactory entry-level jobs requiring little training if interest measurement was used (Harmon, 1970). In another study (Campbell & Harmon, 1968) comparing the interests of women sewing machine operators and department store "salesladies" showed that there was a fundamental difference in their orientations toward people. I'm not sure that we need interest scales for occupations whose eventual incumbents rarely use interest inventories, but I do think that homogeneous scales are very likely to find some fundamental differences that might be helpful if one is trying to decide between becoming a mail carrier or a short order cook. Our failure to realize this, along with Roe, may be an indication that we are inappropriately socioeconomically chauvinistic. The Personal Styles scales on the SII may be a step in the direction of looking at some basic interest dimensions that may help even those choosing among occupations of low socioeconomic level to maximize their satisfaction on the job.

Age Differences. Another individual difference variable that may be of importance in understanding interest measurement is age. While there is evidence of a hereditary factor in interest development (Gottfredson, this volume), it is certainly shaped by experience. It seems equally clear that the theorists who suggest that interests develop over time in response to experiences must be correct. And I would add, the conceptual abilities of individuals at various ages and stages must be related to their ability to describe and experience their preferences differentially. Most measures are developed using late adolescents or adults and applied to groups somewhat younger than the groups used in development. Because of the difficulties of equivalent measurement across different age groups at different conceptual levels we have not been able to look at the structure of interests across developmental stages very effectively. We must recognize that there is a high probability that if we could do so, we would find structural differences related to simpler and more complex cognitive functions.

Issues Related to Structural Analyses

The structure of interests is a topic that has gained increasing attention in the last 10 years or so, although the first attention was given to the topic shortly after the advent of interest measurement. E. K. Strong gave a table of intercorrelations among the existing *Strong Vocational Interest Blank* (SVIB) scales to L. L. Thurstone, who used them in the first application of his factor analytic methods in 1929 (Campbell, 1971). Strong reviewed the results of six factor analyses of SVIB scales in his 1943 book and devoted two chapters to discussing the groupings obtained. He questioned whether factors are

> really functional units or are they merely mathematical co-ordinates in terms of which the occupations may be located in space? If the former, then they should be identified and interest tests developed to measure them directly. Not that such tests would necessarily enable us to measure occupations any better or to identify the occupation to which a man [sic] belongs any better, but that such tests should lead to a better understanding of the nature of interest and so to the development of better interest tests. (p. 315)

Strong developed scales to identify interests for specific occupations, yet he visualized the possibility of measuring more basic "functional units" that were more than just "mathematical coordinates" so that we could understand the nature of interests better. One can look at Holland's theory and associated measures (Holland, 1992) as an attempt to realize what Strong visualized. The recent interest in using Holland's theoretical dimensions to study the structure of interests can indeed be seen as an attempt to better understand the nature of interests.

Recent structural analyses use homogeneous scales measuring interests in Holland's six areas. Thurstone's analysis was actually based on the correlations of occupational scales that were developed using empirical techniques, so occupational scales can be used. However, homogeneous scales are conceptually clearer because they do not include negatively weighted items or empirically selected items that do not make theoretical sense. It seems important to consider carefully how the basic data might affect the results of these analyses. Clearly choosing scales with the best psychometric characteristics should provide the best basis for structural analysis. Both internal consistency and consistency over time should be high. Evidence that the scales are valid indicators of interests should be available as well.

Various researchers have attempted to explore the structure of interests across age, gender, and racial-ethnic groups. Because the conceptual organization of interests may depend on the age of the individuals studied, structural analyses should be identified by the age or developmental level of the people in the analyses. It is also important to be aware of how the underlying scales treat sex differences and exactly what numbers are used in structural analyses. If a scale has available a raw score, a combined sex standard score, and a separate sex percentile score, which numbers have been used in structural analyses? I have seen a lot of structural studies that present separate structures by sex but none that specify the nature of the scores on which the analyses were based. Usually one must look to the source of the original data or correlation matrix to find this information. It seems to me that the very reasons that suggest separate sex norms suggest that the underlying structure of interests—that is, how scores vary in relationship to each other—might be different for the two genders. Whether the type of score utilized in the analysis influences the structure that is found is an important question. If one uses scores that reflect combined sex norms but analyzes them separately by sex, what does the resulting structure represent? This does not seem to be a simple case where a mathematical transformation is applied to a whole group and thus need not be considered. The main thing to remember is that if normed scores of some type are used to study the structure of interests, it is important to know what method of norming was used and to recognize that different methods may produce different results.

Some research on the structure of interests has suggested that structure varies across culture and ethnic group—especially, but not always, when the samples are relatively small (Day, Rounds, Tracey, & Swaney, 1996; Fouad, Harmon, & Borgen, 1997; Rounds & Tracey, 1996). Different ethnic groups may have similar scores on relevant scales, but those scales may cluster differently for different ethnic groups in a structural analysis. Interpreting these differences may depend on knowing how ethnicity was treated in the original scale development.

One of the most promising pieces of work on the structure of interests is the work of Tracey and Rounds (1996), which adds a third dimension, prestige level, to the area of structural analysis. To do the work at all they had to devise a measure that allowed for differentiation on the prestige (or socioeconomic) level. Clearly socioeconomic status has a great deal to do with the development of interests, self-efficacy for various occupations, and career choice. At the very least, in studying the structure or interests we need to be clear about the assumptions the underlying measure makes about socioeconomic status and interests.

In summary, work on the structure of interests must take account of individual and group differences as they were treated in the original construction of the scales analyzed and as they are represented in the groups used in the structural analyses.

It is not clear in many instances whether studies of the structure of interests are attempts to test Holland's theory under differing conditions or to test the instruments used in the analysis. It is often not clear how the underlying measures treat issues of sex, race, or socioeconomic status. Assuming that the basic attempt is to confirm Holland's theory for various sex, ethnic, and socioeconomic groups, how can the results be used to inform theory? It seems to me that we are back to Strong's original question. Are the findings of structural analyses simply "mathematical coordinates," or do they allow us to understand how the sexes, races, and socioeconomic groups differ in the way that they perceive occupational characteristics? These questions must be answered before we can make use of the results of structural analyses.

Using Interest Inventory Scales

It is incumbent upon the user of an inventory to understand the types of scales it contains and the particular aspects of the scale's development that might make it especially fit or unfit for certain uses. The needs of the population to be served should guide the selection of an interest inventory. If you are dealing with a group of individuals who need only to differentiate among the choices that involve dealing with people or things, or those who require only preliminary direction to guide their initial exploration, you clearly do not need an inventory with a large number of empirically derived occupational scales. In fact, such scales might be more confusing than helpful to early adolescents or persons who cannot envision themselves in any professional level job. On the other hand, in dealing with clients who are differentiating between various occupations that are all in the same interest domain (for example, all Investigative, or all Conventional), empirically derived occupational scales may be indicated.

Of some concern is the fact that a number of homogeneous scales are used to provide a summary code that corresponds to Holland's typology, and this code is often treated as data. If the inventory is self-scored as Holland's is, the respondent can get some sense of when two scales are tied or very close together. However, in other cases where the summary code is provided by computer, it is often accepted with little question both by the counselor and the respondent even thought it may contain codes that are tied or very similar in strength and even though codes that are nearly as strong may be left off the summary code altogether. This problem translates to the classic question of how meaningful differences are communicated, and in this form it applies equally to homogeneous scales and to empirical scales. For homogeneous scales the standard error of measurement can be indicated in some way on the report form, although it is rarely done. For empirically developed scales where a General Reference Sample has been used, the standard error of measurement does not tell the whole story. Because the scale is based on differences between two groups, some method is needed to show how different each occupational group is from the General Reference Sample. The SII provides measures of overlap between the occupational groups and the reference groups in the form of Tilton's overlap, which is essentially a difference score. The best occupational scales are differentiated from the in-general groups by nearly three standard deviations and the worst by only one standard deviation. The CISS uses a method of showing differences between empirical scales and the General Reference Sample that is commendably also transparent to the inventory respondent, because the profile report locates the mean of the GRS for all occupations at 50 and profiles the middle 50% of the occupational group on which the scale is based at the appropriate level. It is very easy to pick out by visual inspection the occupations that are most and least like the General Reference Sample.

CONCLUSIONS

There are two questions we might want to answer about interest measurement. First, is interest measurement worth the effort? Second, what do the two types of interest measurement do best?

Developing interest measures is certainly a costly business. The more care that is taken in development by sampling better, larger, and more diverse (occupationally, ethnically, and socioeconomically) groups of respondents, the more expensive it is. Clearly developers are not able to make this investment without some hope of a return that at least covers their costs and ideally realizes a profit. Yet all of them are able to make their inventories available at a cost that meets the Harmon pizza criterion. That criterion is the cost of a typical pizza. Most people will admit to buying a pizza occasionally. I believe that anything that costs less, if it has the potential to make life better, is worth the cost. All the interest inventories I know of (perhaps without such frills as computerized interpretation) can be acquired for less than the cost of a pizza. Compared to the pizza, an interest inventory can have a profound impact. Interest inventories may change the way individuals look at themselves, at the world of work, and at the relationship between the two.

What are the important strengths of the two types of interest scales? Table 8.4 suggests some of them. In developing this table, I was aware that it is subjective in its choice of strengths and weaknesses. I also realize that like a profile of occupational scales, some items could go elsewhere in the table.

I think that the subtlety of the empirically derived scales is important. Homogeneous scales are a bit like expressed interests. One can tell which items go together in answering homogeneous scales. In fact, the SDS booklet even neatly categorizes the items for the respondent. While expressed interests have been shown to be predictive, especially when they match inventoried interests (Dolliver, 1969; Whitney, 1969), expressed interests have the potential to carry a great deal of excess baggage such as parental expectations, unrealistic aspirations, and glamorized illusions about what an occupation actually involves. While homogeneous scales have the advantage over expressed interests of multiple items and thus greater reliability, there is the possibility of the same kind of excess baggage that expressed interests carry, just because of this relative transparency.

Empirical scales also have built-in concurrent validity. For the kind of clients that I am most likely to work with, college students or adults, the connection to the world of work is desirable and the complexity of multiple scales is not daunting.

TABLE 8.4   Strengths and Weaknesses of Empirical and Homogeneous Scales

Strengths	Empirical Scales	Homogeneous Scales
Effective item pool	yes	yes
Diverse item content & format	yes	no
Subtle, use positives and negatives	yes	no
Utilize occupational groups; concurrent validity built in	yes	no
Theory based	no	yes
Easily scored	no	yes
Minimize sex and race differences	yes, potentially	race but not sex
Reliable	yes	yes
Valid	yes	yes
Easily explained to clients	no	yes

Weaknesses		
Sampling difficult	yes	less than empirical
Costly	yes	less than empirical
Items obvious	some but not all	yes
Require General Reference Sample	some do	no
Scoring errors	no	yes, due to hand scoring

Homogeneous scales may be best used when their purpose is to stimulate exploration without overloading the respondent with detailed results that are beyond their range of concern or comprehension. The use of larger sets of homogeneous scales has been found, on one hand, not to represent Holland's circular structure very well and, on the other, to be predictive of occupation for large groups of employed adults. Day and Rounds (1997) reported that two-dimension scaling of sets of Basic Interest Scales on the 1985 version of the SII (Hansen & Campbell, 1985) and the *Jackson Vocational Interest Survey* (Jackson, 1977) did not represent the hypothesized circular order of Holland types very well. However, using multidimensional scaling, Donnay and Borgen (1996) determined that the BISs of the 1994 revision of the SII (Harmon et al.) contributed significantly to the correct classification of employed adults. They concluded that the BISs "were found to deal most effectively with the multivariate complexity of vocational interests" (p. 275) among the homogeneous scales they studied.

Asking the question, "What type of scales are best?" demands the answer, "For what purpose?"

REFERENCES

Campbell, D. P. (1971). *Handbook for the Strong Vocational Interest Blank.* Stanford, CA: Stanford University Press.

Campbell, D. P. (1974). *Manual for the SVIB-SCII: Strong-Campbell Interest Inventory.* Stanford, CA: Stanford University Press.

Campbell, D. P., Borgen, F. H., Eastes, S., Johansson, C. B., & Peterson, R. A. (1968). A set of Basic Interest Scales for the *Strong Vocational Interest Blank* for men. *Journal of Applied Psychology Monographs, 52* (6, Part 2).

Campbell, D. P., & Harmon, L. W. (1968, December). *The vocational interests of non-professional women* (Final Report of Project No. 6-1820 Grant OEG 3-6-061820-0755 U.S. Department of HEW, Office of Education, Bureau of Research).

Campbell, D. P., Hyne, S. A., & Nilsen, D. L. (1992). *Manual for the Campbell Interest and Skill Survey: CISS.* Minneapolis: National Computer Systems.

Day, S. X, & Rounds, J. (1997). "A little more than kin, and less than kind": Basic interests in vocational research and career counseling. *Career Development Quarterly, 45,* 207–220.

Day, S. X, Rounds, J., Tracey, T. G., & Swaney, K. (1996). *The structure of vocational interests for diverse groups in the United States.* Paper presented at the annual meeting of the American Psychological Association, Toronto, Ontario, Canada.

Dolliver, R. H. (1969). *Strong Vocational Interest Blank* versus expressed vocational interests: A review. *Psychological Bulletin, 72,* 95–107.

Donnay, D.A.C., & Borgen, F. H. (1996). Validity, structure, and content of the 1994 SII. *Journal of Counseling Psychology, 43,* 275–291.

Fouad, N. A., Harmon, L. W., & Borgen, F. H. (1997). The structure of interests in employed male and female members of U.S. racial/ethnic minority and non-minority groups. *Journal of Counseling Psychology, 44,* 339–345.

Fouad, N. A., Harmon, L. W., & Hansen, J. C. (1994). Cross-cultural use of the *Strong.* In L. W. Harmon, J. C. Hansen, F. H. Borgen, & A. L. Hammer, *Strong applications and technical guide* (pp. 255–280). Palo Alto, CA: Consulting Psychologists Press.

Gottfredson, L. L. (1981). Circumscription and compromise: A developmental theory of occupational aspirations. *Journal of Counseling Psychology, 28,* 69–84.

Hansen, J. C., & Campbell, D. P. (1985). *Manual for the SVIB-SCII* (4th ed.). Palo Alto, CA: Consulting Psychologists Press.

Harmon, L. W. (1970). SVIB profiles of disadvantaged women. *Journal of Counseling Psychology, 17,* 519–521.

Harmon, L. W., Hansen, J. C., Borgen, F. H., & Hammer, A. L. (1994). *Strong applications and technical guide.* Palo Alto, CA: Consulting Psychologists Press.

Hesketh, B., Elmslie, S., & Kaldor, W. (1990). Career compromise: An alternative account to Gottfredson's theory. *Journal of Counseling Psychology, 37,* 49–56.

Holland, J. L. (1992). *Making vocational choices: A theory of vocational personalities and work environments.* Odessa, FL: Psychological Assessment Resources.

Holland, J. L., Fritzsche, B. A., & Powell, A. B. (1994). *Self-Directed Search technical manual.* Odessa, FL: Psychological Assessment Resources.

Holt, P. A. (1989). Differential effect of status and interest in the process of compromise. *Journal of Counseling Psychology, 36,* 42–47.

Jackson, D. N. (1977). *Manual for the Jackson Vocational Interest Survey.* Port Huron, MI: Research Psychologists Press.

Johannsson, C. B. (1985). *Career Assessment Inventory: Enhanced Version.* Minneapolis: National Computer Systems.

Kuder, F. (1964). *Manual: Kuder General Interest Survey.* Chicago: Science Research Associates.

Kuder, F., & Zytowski, D. G. (1991). *Kuder Occupational Interest Survey Form DD: General manual* (3rd ed.). Monterey, CA: CTB/McGraw-Hill.

Lapan, R. T., Shaughnessy, P., & Boggs, K. (1996). Efficacy expectations and vocational interests as mediators between sex and choice of math/science college majors: A longitudinal study. *Journal of Vocational Behavior, 49,* 277–291.

Leung, S. A., & Harmon, L. W. (1990). Individual & sex differences in the zone of acceptable alternatives. *Journal of Counseling Psychology, 37,* 153–159.

Roe, A., & Klos, D. (1969). Occupational classification. *The Counseling Psychologist, 1,* 84–92.

Rounds, J. B., & Tracey, T.J.G. (1996). Cross-cultural structural equivalence of RIASEC models and measures. *Journal of Counseling Psychology, 43,* 310–329.

Strong, E. K., Jr. (1955). *Vocational interests 18 years after college.* Minneapolis: University of Minnesota Press.

Swanson, J. L., & Hansen, J. C. (1988). Stability of interests over four year, eight year, and twelve year intervals. *Journal of Vocational Behavior, 33,* 185–202.

Tracey, T.J.G., & Rounds, J. B. (1996). The spherical representation of vocational interests. *Journal of Vocational Behavior, 48,* 3–41.

Whitney, D. R. (1969). Predicting from expressed choice: A review. *Personnel and Guidance Journal, 48,* 279–286.

Zytowski, D. G. (1976). Predictive validity of the Kuder Occupational Interest Survey: A 12- to 19-year follow-up. *Journal of Counseling Psychology, 23,* 221–233.

CHAPTER NINE

Validity Evidence for Interest Inventories

Nadya A. Fouad

THIS CHAPTER DISCUSSES evidence for the validity of vocational interest inventories. Evidence for score validity must show that a test result assesses the construct it purports to measure and that results relate in some meaningful way to predicted behaviors. With interest inventories, for example, knowledge about their validity tells us that the inventory does indeed measure an individual's interests related to the world of work and that those interests predict eventual occupational choice and job satisfaction.

Counselors cannot merely look up the validity coefficients of an inventory in a test manual. Validating an inventory does not involve arriving at a definitive score but rather is a process of accumulating evidence about that inventory. Counselors need to know what evidence is available about the validity of an instrument for particular populations, for particular settings, and at a particular time. Messick (1989) noted, "Validity is an integrated evaluative judgment of the degree to which empirical evidence and theoretical rationales support the adequacy and appropriateness of inferences and actions based on test scores" (p. 13). The test itself is not considered valid, but uses of test results, inferences made from test results, and the consequences of those inferences must be validated. Researchers collect evidence of the inferences made from inventory scores within specific contexts, as well as consequences of actions taken as a result of those inferences. For example, a score of 60 on a scale that measures Artistic interests is meaningless without some inference made about that score. Inferences about results depend on a variety of factors such as information about the test-taker (sex, race, educational level, age) and the form of the inventory (e.g., raw scores on the *Self-Directed Search* or scaled scores on the *Strong Interest Inventory*).

Validation of the inventory that included the Artistic scale would also include some examination of consequences for people who scored high on that scale. The latter includes the social consequences of testing as a facet of the overall validity of an instrument. This goes beyond the traditional view, which divides validity into four areas: content, predictive, concurrent, and construct validity. While Cronbach and Meehl (1955) noted that "One does not validate a test, but only a principle for making inferences" (p. 297), they did not incorporate the social consequences of testing as an aspect of validity. Messick (1995), however, asserted that because the outcomes of testing (both intended and unintended) become part of the meaning of the test score, the consequences of testing must be considered to be part of construct validity.

Messick (1995) outlined six facets of validity evidence, all of which are integrated together in an evaluation of a test. These are content, substantive, internal structure, generalizability, external, and consequential validity. Evidence of content validity assures that test items sample the domain adequately, neither overrepresenting some areas nor tapping irrelevant factors or behaviors. The substantive facet investigates responses to items, or the process of test-taking behavior. Internal structure validity examines whether the internal structure of an instrument adheres to hypothesized structures. The generalizability facet of validity checks that test results are equally applicable across populations, time, and settings. External validity is commonly thought of as concurrent and predictive validity; that is, expected relationships between test results and both current and future behaviors are found. Finally, as noted earlier, the consequential facet of validity provides evidence about the consequences of using the test.

This chapter examines the evidence collected on the validity of interest inventories over their 70-year history. It starts with specifying the constructs assessed in interest inventories, then examines interest inventory items as well evidence covering the process of using interest inventory information. Next the chapter will consider whether interest inventory results adhere to the proposed structure underlying interests, especially Holland's (1997) hexagonal theory. Then it will evaluate whether interest inventory results are generalizable across time, populations, and settings as well as how results on interest inventories relate in predicted ways to current and future behaviors. The chapter concludes with an examination of the utility of interest inventories, the implications of their use in facilitating career exploration, and the social consequences of using—or not using—them.

CONSTRUCT SPECIFICATION

To examine the validity evidence of interest inventories it is important to begin with specifying the construct. Interest inventories typically classify interests and/or compare an individual's interests to those of professionals engaged in a particular occupation.

E. K. Strong, Jr. (1943), a pioneer in the field of interest measurement, delineated three ways of viewing interests or inferences about interests from an individual's responses. The first is a response to a specific item (e.g., "I like arithmetic"), the second "a general tendency toward a constellation of items" (p. 19) (e.g., having scientific interests), and the third the total score on an interest inventory (e.g., an individual's score on the Engineer Occupational scale). Strong (1943) viewed summary scores on an interest inventory as an expression of interests, noting they are fairly permanent and stable and "indicate what the person wants to do" (p. 24). The 1994 revision of the *Strong Interest Inventory* (Harmon, Hansen, Borgen, & Hammer, 1994) goes slightly beyond this description, explaining that vocational interests may help individuals make career decisions and that the *Strong* describes common interests of people in the same occupation.

The *Strong Vocational Interest Blank* and its successors compare individuals' patterns of interests to the interests that differentiate that professional group from the population in general. It is the use of the general reference group (variously called, in different forms of *Strong* revisions, the General Reference Sample, or Men-in-General, Women-in-General) that distinguishes the *Strong* from other interest inventories. Strong (1943) advocated differentiating the interests of a professional group from a general group because "the interests which are significant for men [and women] in a given occupation are the interests which set that occupation apart from the general run of men [and women]" (p. 45). The 1994 revision of the *Strong Interest Inventory* (Harmon et al., 1994) continues the tradition of a General Reference Sample to differentiate interests of professionals; an individual is compared to professionals' differentiated interests. Recent revisions of the *Strong*, however, also have expanded to include scales that summarize general interests and others that classify individual's interests based on Holland's RIASEC themes.

Kuder (1977) began construction of his *Occupational Interest Survey* with the premise that "the purpose of interest inventories is to help young people discover the occupations they will find most satisfying" (p. 7). He noted that the inventory must validly predict job satisfaction and be useable with individuals who have limited work experience. Similar to the *Strong Interest Inventory*, the *Kuder*

Occupational Interest Survey also was designed to discriminate among occupational groups on the basis of the interest items, although Kuder's inventories did not use the intermediate step of comparing occupational groups to a General Reference Sample. Kuder believed strongly that the use of a general reference group obscured the real comparisons among occupations.

Other interest inventories are designed to assess and classify individuals' interests. Holland, Fritzsche, and Powell's (1994) revision of the *Self Directed Search* assesses an individual's aspirations, interests, self-rated competencies, preferences for activities and occupations, and self-estimates and categorizes the individual into one or more of Holland's (1997) vocational types. Holland et al. (1994) note that the *Self-Directed Search* relies on Holland's theory of vocational types to structure the instrument. They later comment that interest inventories are used "to stimulate a greater range of options, to reassure a person about a particular option, to increase self-understanding, to teach a career structure . . ." (p. 53).

The *Campbell Interest and Skill Survey* (Campbell, Hyne, & Nilsen, 1992) assesses interest in various academic and occupational areas, as well as the skills in occupational tasks. Individuals' results indicate their interest and confidence in each area assessed. The *Revised Unisex Edition of the ACT Interest Inventory* (UNIACT-R) (Swaney, 1995) was designed to assess Holland's (1997) basic interests in such a way that career options for males and females would be similar. Swaney suggests its use for career planning and to stimulate career exploration.

In summary, interest inventories assess an individual's vocational interests, often measuring Holland's (1997) types. Some inventories also compare an individual's interests to the common interests of an occupational group; this is intended to help individuals make satisfying career and educational decisions. For the last 70 years interest measurement researchers have accumulated evidence concerning the validity of interest inventories to assess whether result interpretations and uses have been adequate and appropriate. The remainder of this chapter addresses what we know about the accumulated validity evidence and areas in which we need to collect more evidence.

FACETS OF VALIDITY

Content

The first facet of validity deals with the content of interest inventories. Since this facet concentrates on inventory items rather than on inferences made about scores, inventory content is not technically considered part of validity. However, we will briefly discuss interest inventory items because their content relates to test scores.

Traditionally content validity concerns how adequately the domain under consideration was sampled. Cronbach and Meehl (1955) noted that content validity "is established by showing that the inventory items are a sample of a universe in which the investigator is interested" (p. 282). More recently concern with the content of a test specifies the boundaries of the construct to be assessed, and that "assessment should assemble tasks that are representative of the domain in some sense" (Messick, 1995, p. 745).

In sampling the domain of vocational interests, researchers must first determine the areas to be sampled, making sure they include all functional interest areas. This is particularly critical in interest inventories that span 70 years, ensuring that the inventory contains items that accurately reflect the domain of interests as they have changed over time and that the items accurately reflect contemporary demography and tasks of occupations.

Assessment of content validity is typically conducted through expert appraisal. The first avenue of investigation, beyond examining the items themselves, is review of the process used to choose and cull items from the list of possible items. Information about this process is usually provided in test manuals.

Item list descriptions have increased in detail. For example, Strong, in 1943, provided a paragraph on which types of items were in the original 400 *Strong Vocational Interest Blank.* He also made a brief reference to different items for men and women. By 1955, Strong referred to the issue of domain sampling by explaining that he had chosen items that differentiated groups of individuals without trying to use items that sampled trait differences. He also noted that the items should be as simple as possible to guard against some irrelevant variables that may contaminate an individual's response.

Kuder (1977) was quite interested in item selection. He outlined 12 principles that should be followed in constructing and using an interest inventory, including constructing items that are free from response bias, sampling widely from the domain of interests, avoiding the use of occupational titles, and using items that are not affected (or affected minimally) by contextual changes. He also recommended that items be well understood by subjects.

More recently concern about item selection has led test developers to be very specific about item construction and selection and to work diligently to eliminate or revise outdated or sexist items. For example, Swaney (1995) described item selection for the UNIACT-R in detail; he chose items that created scales in which men and women have similar distributions. The manual for 1994 revision of the SII (Harmon et al., 1994) indicates that 282 items had been retained from the 1985 revision, and the 35 new items were shown in a table. A chapter on items was provided in the *Applications and Technical Guide,* including the decision rules for which items were eliminated, chosen, or revised.

Examination of the items in the current versions of the most widely used interest inventories shows that content sampling has attempted to representatively sample among the Holland (1997) types. In addition, inventory constructors have clearly made efforts to sample from tasks considered representative of domains traditionally dominated by women and by men and to present items that are not overtly biased toward one group or another.

What is less clear from an examination of interest inventory content is whether the inventories adequately represent the occupational domain as it has evolved during the last decade. It is possible that the domain of interest inventories may be too narrowly constructed and that the items do not capture the changing nature of the world of work or the interests of professionals within those occupations. It is also possible that as the context of occupations change not only in terms of demographic characteristics but also in tasks and settings, new items will be needed to represent new work contexts.

Substantive

The second facet of validity involves the substantive area, or validity evidence based on response processes. Substantive validity examines whether respondents actually use interest inventory information to make career decisions, and if so, how that occurs. Messick (1995) notes that this facet provides "empirical evidence that the theoretical processes are actually engaged by respondents" (p. 745).

Researchers have produced surprisingly little evidence of this area of validity. Holland (1975) concluded that "the evidence about the actual effects of interest inventories is sparse" (p. 27). Little work has been done over the 20 subsequent years to change that assessment. Holland et al. (1994) report on 22 studies that examined the influence of the *Self-Directed Search* on various populations. They note that "Although the general effects studies demonstrate that the SDS has a desirable influence they do not show how its effects are achieved." (p. 56). Research has linked interest inventories to "exploration validity" (Randahl, Hansen, & Haverkamp, 1993). However, no studies have investigated whether, in fact, clients or students use interest inventory information in subsequent vocational decisions and if they do, how they use that information.

Structural

The third facet of validity involves the structural area: that is, the degree to which the internal structures of the test conform to the hypothesized construct. In the case of interest inventories, the hypothesized structure is typically Holland's hexagon. Rounds and Day (this volume) discuss the research on structural models of interests in detail, so it will not be repeated here. However, evidence on structural validity of interest inventories indicates that a perfect equilateral hexagon does not fit the data for any populations studied but that the circular ordering of Realistic, Investigative, Artistic, Social, Enterprising, and Conventional is found for men and women and for most ethnic groups studied. However, researchers also have reported that while the circular order has been found, groups are not similar in the perceived similarity among Holland types (Fouad, Harmon, & Borgen, 1997; Rounds & Tracey, 1996). In other words, the structures are not identical across cultural groups. After evaluating the fit of Holland's RIASEC model to data from 20 U.S. ethnic minority groups, Rounds and Tracey (1996) concluded that "the cross-cultural structural equivalence of Holland's circular order model was not supported" (p. 324). However Day and Rounds (1998), in a study with large samples of racial/ethnic groups, concluded that "people of different ethnicities and sexes hold the same cognitive map of the world of work" (p. 734).

Generalizability

The generalizability facet of validity concerns whether test scores may be generalized across populations and settings as well as across time. This facet of validity addresses whether inferences made about interest inventory results are similar across different demographic groups (e.g., men and women, racial/ethnic groups, people with disabilities), across time periods, and across measures.

Fouad, Harmon, and Hansen (1994) examined differences across racial/ethnic groups who participated in the 1994 *Strong* revision (Harmon et al., 1994). They reported few racial/ethnic differences at the item level and even fewer differences at the scale or profile level. Holland and his colleagues (1994) noted no substantial differences in distribution of high-point codes across ethnic groups on the revised *Self-Directed Search*. Swaney (1995) concluded that their research supported the use of the UNIACT-R with the racial/ethnic minority populations in the norming group.

These data would indicate that interest inventory results are generalizable across racial/ethnic groups. However, no studies have directly investigated whether interpretations are generalizable across cultures. In fact, a study by Fouad, Harmon, and Borgen (1997) also using the 1994 *Strong* revision sample concludes that there were differences among the groups in relationships among the Holland themes. Some themes (e.g., Realistic and Investigative) were closer than predicted, while other themes (e.g., Artistic and Conventional) were less similar than expected, and these relationships differed across groups. In other words, while few item or scale differences were found, racial/ethnic groups differed in the way they viewed the similarity of Holland themes to each other, suggesting that interpretations may not be generalizable.

Interest inventory results do appear to be generalizable across populations with and without disabilities. For example, studies have found that vocational interests are similar between adults with disabilities and those without (Brookings & Bolton, 1986; Rohe & Athelstan, 1985).

Validity evidence is less clear about the generalizability of interest results across men and women. There continue to be sex differences in interests on inventories, unless the inventory is explicitly constructed to reduce differences, such as is the case with the UNIACT-R (Swaney, 1995). This difference has been observed for several decades despite social changes that have increased women's participation in the workforce and the concomitant pressure to change interest inventories to be more sex-fair (e.g., Diamond, 1975; Tittle & Zytowski, 1978).

Sex differences appear at the item level as well as at the scale level. For example, endorsement rate differences for men and women on the *Self-Directed Search* ranged from 5.6% to 24.6%, with the largest differences on the Realistic and Social scales. The latest revision of the *Strong* (Harmon et al., 1994) also showed substantial differences between males and females, with a quarter of the items on the 1994 revision showing at least 16% endorsement rate differences between sexes. However, while men and women do differ in the items they endorse, there is substantial overlap between their interests. For example, Diamond and Raju (1977; reported in Diamond, 1990) found that men and women ranked similarly on the Kuder Occupational Interest Survey male- and female-normed occupations. Harmon and her colleagues (1994) reported that the items on which men and women differed substantially often did not appear on the Occupational Scales. Nonetheless, while evidence is mixed on the overlap between men's and women's interests, inferences made about those interests differ and thus are not considered to be generalizable.

All major interest inventories report relatively high correlations between revisions of the instrument, indicating generalizability across time within an instrument. This is not the same as evidence about stability of interests within an individual, which is discussed by Swanson (this volume). Rather, this evidence indicates that inferences made about inventory results given in previous revisions of the instrument are generalizable to the current interest inventory.

The final area of generalizability looks across types of interest inventories. In other words, how similar is a Realistic theme score measured by different inventories? Swaney (1995) reports high to moderate correlations between same scales measured by the UNIACT-R and the *Self-Directed Search,* the *Vocational Preference Inventory,* and the *Strong Vocational Interest Blank,* with lower correlations found between dissimilar scales. Harmon and her colleagues (1994) reported a median correlation of .77 between same scales (General Occupational Themes) on the *Strong* and the *Vocational Preference Inventory.*

In conclusion, validity evidence indicates that we can generalize inferences from interest inventories across time and types of measures, and we appear to be able to generalize to individuals with disabilities and possibly to individuals of diverse racial/ethnic groups. We do not have as much evidence of generalizability across men and women. More evidence is needed on the generalizability of interpretation across populations.

External Evidence of Validity

The fifth facet of validity involves external evidence. This is the area traditionally known as criterion-related validity, which is typically divided temporally into concurrent and predictive validity. Concurrent validity refers to assessment of external behavior measured at the same time, whereas predictive validity refers to criterion measures at some point in the future.

Concurrent Validity. Traditional methods to assess the concurrent validity of interest inventories examine how well occupations are differentiated from each other and whether group profiles correlate with the expected scale (e.g., whether science majors score highest on the Investigative scale). Evidence of concurrent validity also includes expected convergence among similar scales and discrimination from dissimilar scales.

Occupational differentiation was a critical aspect of validity for both Strong (1943) and Kuder (1977). Occupational differentiation is a fundamental premise to interest inventories that assert that interests of individuals in one occupation differ from those of persons in another occupation. It must be possible to differentiate among occupations on the basis of interests. This assumes that a reasonable amount of homogeneity exists within the occupation to identify a pattern of interests and that the pattern characteristic of the occupation differs from another occupation. In other words, accountants have similar interests, and those interests can be differentiated sufficiently from engineers and lawyers and physicians, who differ from each other enough to construct scales for each occupation.

While some questions have been raised about heterogeneity within an occupation, researchers for the most part have found that this has not seriously called the assumption into question (Benton, 1975; Betz & Taylor, 1982; Diamond, 1990; Dunnette, Wernimont, & Abrahams, 1964; Hill & Roselle, 1985; Nolting & Taylor, 1976; Smith & Hutto, 1975). Similarly, occupations continue to be found to differ substantially whether a general reference group is used or not (Campbell, 1971; Harmon et al., 1994; Kuder, 1977; Strong, 1943).

Another way to evaluate concurrent validity is to assess the similarity of group profiles to predicted interest code(s). Hansen and Tan (1992) showed that 66% of college majors scored highest in their declared major area. Holland and his colleagues (1994) showed that the relationship between *Self-Directed Search* scores and college major, field of study, or occupation ranged from 48% to 76%, with higher rates associated with older, employed workers.

The final area of research in concurrent validity involves convergent and discriminant validity. Some evidence of convergent and discriminant validity was presented in discussing generalizability across measures. Holland and his colleagues (1994) reported that *Self-Directed Search* scales correlated with each other (i.e., interests with competencies) show the expected relationship. Swaney (1995) reported that scales on the UNIACT-R also converged as expected with other instruments, and discriminated from scales measuring other interest types.

Predictive Validity. Validity evidence has shown that somewhere between 40% and 60% of individuals are in occupations that may be predicted from their interest inventory results. Moderators of a perfect relationship have been found to include whether interests are well defined (Campbell, 1966), the age at which individuals took an interest inventory and their educational level (Holland et al., 1994), and presence of emotional disturbance (Brandt & Hood, 1968). McArthur (1954) found that family expectations and social influences played a role for high socioeconomic Harvard students who entered family-expected occupations.

Zytowski (1976) and Zytowski and Laing (1978) followed over 200 individuals who had taken the *Kuder Occupational Interest Inventory*, finding that about 43% were in one of the their interest inventory's top five–rated occupations. Holland and his colleagues (1994) noted that including information about aspirations (expressed preferences) with SDS results increased predictive value of the SDS. Spokane (1979) reported predictive validity for 59% of females and 71% of males on the 1974 revision of the *Strong Vocational Interest Blank* over a $3\frac{1}{2}$-year period.

Strong (1943) outlined four propositions for evidence that should indicate predictive validity of an interest inventory:

1. Those continuing in an occupation should have higher interest results in that occupation than any other (e.g., accountants score highest on Accountant scale).
2. Those continuing in an occupation should have higher results in that occupation than other people entering other occupations (e.g., accountants higher on Accountant scale than engineers on Accountant Scale).
3. Those continuing in an occupation should have higher interest results in that occupation than those changing from that occupation to another (e.g., accountants continuing in accounting should be higher on Accountant scale than those changing from accounting to engineering).
4. Those changing from one occupation to another score higher in the second occupation prior to the change (e.g., those changing from accounting to engineering scored higher on Engineer scale prior to the change).

Strong (1943, 1955) reported support for the first three propositions and only partial support for the fourth. Laing, Lamb, and Prediger (1982), using the American College Testing Interest Inventory, also found support for the first three propositions but not the last one.

Consequential

Consequential validity is the newest area of validity evidence. This validity evidence requires an appraisal and evaluation of the consequences of interest inventory use. In the case of interest inventories, positive consequences may include greater exploration of options by inventory users, whereas negative consequences may include restriction of options for a particular group. The most critical notion is that negative consequences do not result from threats to validity.

Two potential threats to validity are that the content is not representative across the domains and that irrelevant factors are somehow incorporated into the items or the inventory. An example of possible lack of representativeness of the domain of interest items was an area of concern in the 1970s. Objections were raised about interest inventories that had separate item pools for women and men. Harmon (1975) noted that the items in the men's form of the SVIB had high-level technical and business activities, while the women's form had domestic and clerical activities. In this case an argument could be made that the domain was not adequately represented for both sexes. The consequences of such exclusion of items may have been that women were not considering the same occupations as men or that women were being systematically encouraged to enter a restricted range of occupations. Two volumes were dedicated to sex-fair interest testing (Diamond, 1975; Tittle & Zytowski, 1978), and counselors began to show a greater concern for increasing options for women. These consequences and the social policies that resulted from the concern about different items are considered to be part of consequential validity.

Counselors also need to know that irrelevant factors do not affect inventory results. For example, Prediger and Swaney (1986) reported that high interest results accompanied by relevant experiences were more predictive of occupational area than were high interest results for which there were few relevant experiences. As another example, Kuder (1977) and Swaney (1995) argued against the use of occupational titles as items, because they may introduce an irrelevant variable of familiarity in responding to interest inventory items.

Consequential validity includes both the intended and unintended consequences of test interpretation and test use. Messick (1995) delineated four facets of validity as a progressive matrix. The matrix is reprinted in Table 9.1, which shows a fourfold table with evidential basis for test interpretation and use, and consequential basis for test interpretation and use.

The evidential basis of test interpretation is the accumulation of the evidence presented in this chapter to this point—that is, evidence of validity supportive of result meaning. This subsumes evidence of content, substantive, structural, generalizability, external validity under construct validity. Counselors have a fair amount of evidence of the construct validity of test interpretation of interest inventories.

The evidential basis of test use needs to include evidence of the relevance and utility of that use in addition to evidence of construct validity. In the case of interest inventories, utility to applied settings would be evaluated. For example, counselors have evidence of appropriateness for interest inventories used in college counseling centers (e.g., Holland & Rayman, 1986). However, it is not

TABLE 9.1   Facets of Validity as a Progressive Matrix

	Test Interpretation	Test Use
Evidential Basis	Construct Validity (CV)	CV + Relevance/Utility (R/U)
Consequential Basis	CV + Value Implications (VI)	CV + R/U + VI + Social Consequences

From "Validity of psychological assessment: Validation of references from persons' responses and performances on scientific inquiry into score meaning," by S. Messick, 1995, *American Psychologist, 50*, pp. 741–749. Copyright 1995 by the American Psychological Association. Reprinted with permission of the author.

appropriate to use interest inventories, which are not an assessment of abilities, as a selection tool. As another example, interest inventories are increasingly being used in high schools. We have evidence for the use of interest inventories to stimulate exploration in high school students (e.g., Holland et al., 1994), yet we have no evidence that specific occupational scale results (e.g., on the *Strong* or the *Kuder*) assessed in high school predict later choice. Thus we have little evidence of the validity for use of interest inventories to predict specific choices (and occupational satisfaction) for high school students.

The consequential basis of test interpretation includes value implications. Counselors currently operate under the value implication that increasing occupational alternatives for both men and women is good, and inventory developers exhort counselors to use interest inventories to expand those options and reduce restrictions to career choices. Gottfredson (1986), however, advocated a different approach when she suggested simply viewing interest inventories as treatments rather than as instruments of social change. Messick (1995) notes that "value implications of score interpretation . . . often [trigger] score-based actions" (p. 748) and suggests that those actions linked to social policy be explicitly evaluated. This is an area in which we need more research. For example, as noted earlier, we have little evidence concerning how individuals use interest inventories to make career decisions, and we do not know if increasing options for women and men lead to greater consideration, or choice, of nontraditional occupations. Clearly evidence about the consequences of such policies would help counselors be most effective with clients.

The final area in the table, consequential basis of test use, includes all of the above—construct validity, relevance, utility, values—and includes the social consequences of using interest inventories. Consequences may be intended and unintended. For example, an intended consequence of using interest inventories with traditional Hispanic women may be to increase the career options they explore. However, this practice may have an additional unintended consequence of alienating women from their husbands, for whom being the sole provider is an important role. The consequences should be explicitly evaluated as a facet of validity of test use.

An illustration of the consequences of not using interest inventories may be occurring in many states that are currently initiating policies to move individuals from welfare subsistence to work. In many cases counselors helping individuals to make the transition are not given the tools to help fully assess an individual's abilities, interests, and needs. Often the decision as to area of employment is made on the basis of availability, geographic location, or reading ability. These clearly should be factors included in the placement of an individual into an occupational area, yet the consequence of not assessing interests may be that individuals are not considering all factors in making career decisions, which may eventually lead to unsuccessful placement and an unnecessarily higher turnover rate. Harmon (1970), writing about interest results of disadvantaged women, noted that the penalty for not using interest assessment results "might be equated to ignoring their individuality just to get them off the welfare rolls" (p. 520). She went on to suggest that such a policy may deny individuals on welfare "the dignity of making the best possible choice about what they will be trained to do" (p. 520). This social policy should be evaluated as part of consequential validity.

CONCLUSION

Based on the research and validity evidence examined in this chapter, counselors can draw four general conclusions:

1. Vocational interest inventories have sampled a domain of interests in a systematic manner, representative of domains traditionally encountered by women and by men, and efforts have been made to keep the content up to date and current.
2. Interest inventories appear to be generalizable across time and across measures.
3. Evidence of external validity appears to be appropriate and adequate, both concurrently and predictively. In other words, occupations may be differentiated on the basis of professionals' interests, group profiles are related to interest scales in expected ways, and between 50% and 70% of individuals who have high interests in an area are found to be in that occupation several years later.

4. Consequential validity has been most examined with regard to evidential basis for test use, and some evidence is available for test interpretation as a tool for career exploration.

The same review of validity evidence should also make counselors demand more information about:

1. Content representativeness for new occupations in a changing world of work, particularly with new populations
2. Possible content irrelevance across populations, examined for example, through differential item functioning
3. Substantive validity, examining whether interest inventory interpretations are used by test-takers in expected ways, and how that process occurs
4. Validity of test interpretation as test use changes, such as in high school settings and other new contexts
5. Consequential basis for inventory interpretation
6. Consequential basis for not using interest inventories

Having considered the strengths and weaknesses of the accumulated validity evidence for interest inventories, practitioners and researchers can be justifiably impressed with the rich knowledge base generated in 70 years of inventory development. This long tradition of sound, programmatic empirical research provides a strong foundation for improving the validity of interest inventories as the field enters the next millennium.

REFERENCES

Benton, A. L. (1975). Inventoried vocational interests of cartographers. *Journal of Applied Psychology, 60*, 150–153.

Betz, N. E., & Taylor, K. M. (1982). Concurrent validity of the *Strong-Campbell Interest Inventory* for graduate students in counseling. *Journal of Counseling Psychology, 29*, 626-635.

Brandt, J. E., & Hood, A. B. (1968). Effect of personality adjustment on the predictive validity of the *Strong Vocational Interest Blank. Journal of Counseling Psychology, 15*, 547–551.

Brookings, J. B., & Bolton, B. (1986). Vocational interest dimensions of adult handicapped persons. *Measurement and Evaluation in Counseling and Development, 18*, 168–175.

Campbell, D. P. (1966). Occupations ten years later of high school seniors with high scores on the SVIB life insurance salesman scale. *Journal of Applied Psychology, 50*, 369–372.

Campbell, D. P. (1971). *Handbook for the Strong Vocational Interest Blank*. Stanford, CA: Stanford University Press.

Campbell, D. P., Hyne, S. A., & Nilsen, D. L. (1992). *Manual for the Campbell Interest and Skill Survey*. Minneapolis: National Computer Systems.

Cronbach, L. J., & Meehl, P. E. (1955). Construct validity in psychological tests. *Psychological Bulletin, 52,* 281–302.

Day, S. X, & Rounds, J. (1998). Universality of vocational interest structure among racial and ethnic minorities. *American Psychologist, 53,* 728–736.

Diamond, E. E. (Ed.). (1975). *Issues of sex bias and sex fairness in career interest measurement*. Washington, DC: National Institute of Education.

Diamond, E. E. (1990). The *Kuder Occupational Interest Survey*. In C. E. Watkins, Jr., & V. L. Campbell (Eds.), *Testing in counseling practice* (pp. 211–278). Hillsdale, NJ: Erlbaum.

Diamond, E. E., & Raju, N. S. (1977). *Technical supplement, career development inventory* (Rev. ed.). Chicago: Science Research Associates.

Dunnette, M. D., Wernimont, P., & Abrahams, N. (1964). Further research and vocational interests differences among several types of engineers. *Personnel and Guidance Journal, 42,* 484–493.

Fouad, N. A., Harmon, L. W., & Borgen, F. H. (1997). The structure of interests in employed male and female members of U.S. racial/ethnic minority and nonminority groups. *Journal of Counseling Psychology, 44,* 339–345.

Fouad, N. A., Harmon, L. W., & Hansen, J. C. (1994). Cross-cultural use of the *Strong*. In L. W. Harmon, J. C. Hansen, F. W. Borgen, & A. L. Hammer, *Strong Interest Inventory: Applications and technical guide* (pp. 255–280). Stanford, CA: Stanford University Press.

Gottfredson, L. S. (1986). Special groups and the beneficial use of vocational interest inventories. In W. B. Walsh & S. H. Osipow (Eds.), *Advances in vocational psychology, Vol. 1: The assessment of interests* (pp. 127–198). Hillsdale, NJ: Erlbaum.

Hansen, J. C., & Tan, R. N. (1992). Concurrent validity of the 1985 *Strong Interest Inventory* for college majors selection. *Measurement and Evaluation in Counseling and Development, 19,* 53–57.

Harmon, L. W. (1970). *Strong Vocational Interest Blank* profiles of disadvantaged women. *Journal of Counseling Psychology, 17,* 519–521.

Harmon, L. W. (1975). Technical aspects: Problems of scale development, norms, item differences by sex, and the rate of change in occupational group characteristics. In E. E. Diamond (Ed.), *Issues of sex bias and sex fairness in career interest measurement* (pp. 45–64). Washington, DC: National Institute of Education.

Harmon, L. W., Hansen, J. C., Borgen, F. H., & Hammer, A. L. (1994). *Strong Interest Inventory: Applications and technical guide*. Stanford, CA: Stanford University Press.

Hill, R. E., & Roselle, P. F. (1985). The differences in the vocational interests of research and development managers vs. technical specialists. *Journal of Vocational Behavior, 26,* 92–105.

Holland, J. L. (1975). The use and evaluation of interest inventories and simulations. In E. E. Diamond (Ed.), *Issues of sex bias and sex fairness in career interest measurement* (pp. 19–44). Washington, DC: National Institute of Education.

Holland, J. L. (1997). *Making vocational choices: A theory of vocational personalities and work environments* (3rd ed.). Odessa, FL: Psychological Assessment Resources.

Holland, J. L., Fritzsche, B. A., & Powell, A. B. (1994). *The Self-Directed Search (SDS): Technical manual* (Rev. ed.). Odessa, FL: Psychological Assessment Resources.

Holland, J. L., & Rayman, J. R. (1986). *The Self-Directed Search.* In W. B. Walsh & S. H. Osipow (Eds.), Advances in vocational psychology, Vol. 1: The assessment of interests (pp. 55–82). Hillsdale, NJ: Erlbaum.

Kuder, F. (1977). *Activity interests and occupational choice.* Chicago: Science Research.

Laing, J., Lamb, R. R., & Prediger, D. J. (1982). An application of Strong's validity criteria to basic interest scales. *Journal of Vocational Behavior, 25,* 304–315.

McArthur, C. (1954). Long-term validity of the *Strong Interest Test* in two subcultures. *Journal of Applied Psychology, 38,* 346–354.

Messick, S. (1989). Validity. In R. L. Linn (Ed.), *Educational Measurement* (3rd ed., pp. 13–104). Old Tappan, NJ: Macmillan.

Messick, S. (1995). Validity of psychological assessment: Validation of references from persons' responses and performances on scientific inquiry into score meaning. *American Psychologist, 50,* 741–749.

Nolting, E., & Taylor, R. G. (1976). Vocational interests of engineering students. *Measurement and Evaluation in Guidance, 8,* 245–251.

Prediger, D. J., & Swaney, K. (1986). Role of counselee experiences in the interpretation of vocational interest scores. *Journal of Counseling and Development, 64,* 440–444.

Randahl, G. J., Hansen, J. C., & Haverkamp, B. E. (1993). Instrumental behaviors following test administration and interpretation: Exploration validity of the *Strong Interest Inventory. Journal of Counseling and Development, 71,* 435–439.

Rohe, D. E., & Athelstan, G. P. (1985). Change in vocational interests after spinal cord injury. *Rehabilitation Psychology, 30,* 131–143.

Rounds, J., & Tracey, T. J. (1996). Cross-cultural equivalence of RIASEC models and measures. *Journal of Counseling Psychology, 43,* 310–329.

Smith, R. C., & Hutto, G. L. (1975) Vocational interests of air traffic control personnel. *Aviation, Space, and Environmental Medicine, 46,* 871–877.

Spokane, A. R. (1979). Occupational preference and the validity of the Strong-Campbell Interest Inventory for college women and men. *Journal of Counseling Psychology, 26,* 312–318.

Strong, E. K., Jr. (1943). *Vocational interests of men and women.* Stanford, CA: Stanford University Press.

Strong, E. K., Jr. (1955). *Vocational interests 18 years after college.* Minneapolis: University of Minnesota Press.

Swaney, K. (1995). *Technical manual: Revised Unisex Edition of the ACT Interest Inventory.* Iowa City, IA: American College Testing.

Tittle, C. K., & Zytowski, D. G. (Eds.). (1978). *Sex-fair interest measurement: Research and implications.* Washington, DC: National Institute on Education.

Zytowski, D. G. (1976). Predictive validity of the Kuder Occupational Interest Survey. *Journal of Counseling Psychology, 23,* 221–233.

Zytowski, D. G., & Laing, L. (1978). Validity of other-gender-normed scales on the KOIS. *Journal of Counseling Psychology, 25,* 205–209.

CHAPTER TEN

Expressed and Measured Interests

Arnold R. Spokane and Alysia R. Decker

THE INDIRECT MEASUREMENT of social attitudes—that is, their assessment by methods that do not destroy their natural form (Campbell, 1950, 1996)—is one critical contribution of modern applied psychology to the understanding and prediction of human behavior. Indirect measurement permits the description and analysis of psychological phenomena while minimizing the alteration of their essential properties and interrelationships. Nowhere was the introduction of indirect measurement of attitudes more important than when Freyd (1923) suggested, and E. K. Strong (1927) successfully used, indirect three-position ("Like," "Indifferent," "Dislike"; Berdie, 1943) items of seemingly unrelated content (e.g., "Climbing along the edge of a precipice"; "Looking at a collection of rare laces") to empirically differentiate the inhabitants of 39 occupations. Rather than making direct inquiries of respondents (e.g., "What occupation are you interested in?"), Strong operationally defined occupational interests as an individual's pattern of responses to this indirect-item technology. He then compared this pattern of item responses to a normative or criterion sample of individuals successfully engaged in an occupation to make predictions about which occupation an individual might inhabit in the future. The change from direct measurement of expressed occupational attitudes to indirect measurement of these same attitudes augured a paradigm of interest measurement that would become a model of sophistication and cutting-edge technology, one widely emulated by other specialties in applied psychology.

FROM DIRECT TO INDIRECT
MEASUREMENT AND BACK AGAIN

Before Strong, "interests" had widespread although diffuse connotations for the lay public as well as for scientific psychologists. Interest was a universal concept that was discussed with respect to theory and embedded in the mainstream of motivation and behavior theory—a context that Savickas (1995) has recently reasserted by examining the personal meaning of interests to the test-taker. Although early discussions of the nature of interests were closely tied to theoretical psychology, the new technology in interest measurement would change that situation, perhaps permanently. Strong understood the departure he was proposing and the labyrinthine nature of the indirect measurement he was undertaking. Even a cursory reading of Strong's (1943) extensive analysis of the nature of interests reveals his penchant for a complex definition of the constructs that he was attempting to measure. According to Strong, *interests* refer to "what man [sic] wants to do, his drives, aspirations, daydreams, ambitions; his pleasures and satisfactions" (Strong, 1943, p. 4). Strong could not have anticipated how completely his particular operational definition of interests would alter our thinking about what an interest actually was.

This fundamental shift from direct to indirect measurement of occupational interests ensured the future of interest measurement by paving the way for our present (and superb) generation of interest inventories, but the widespread acceptance of indirect measurement hardened our definition of interests in very specialized ways. Following Strong's invention, interests had little meaning for vocational psychologists beyond that inferred from their operational definition by an interest inventory (Darley, 1938, 1941; Darley & Hagenah, 1955). Interests were simply the scores on an interest inventory (Darley, 1938). Direct measures of interest were thought to be affected by a host of irrational influences and biases (Dolliver, 1969) and therefore less worthy of scientific attention. When psychologists accepted Jack Darley's definition (he used a long, tortoise-shell cigarette holder with an "intellectual razor blade" on the end and was hard to argue with), they stripped interests of their motivational component. An interest was nothing more and nothing less than what an indirect occupational interest scale measured—namely the similarity between the respondent's pattern of item responses and the pattern of the norm group.

In spite of the clarity it provided, a restrictive definition of interests was not without its problems. As Tyler (1984) warned, a pattern of likes and dislikes can only indicate the direction of interests in comparison to a reference sample, not necessarily how much or how strong those interests are. According to Tyler (1984) it was possible to receive a high score on some occupational scales without ever having displayed any talent or motivation to enter that field. The example she used was the Author scale, indicating that one could receive a high score on "Author" even if one never wrote or planned to write. Thus, although the new technology was specific and operational, it was atheoretical, and therefore it became difficult to understand the true meaning of a high score on an indirect interest scale.

Despite the insistence upon defining interests empirically as the similarity of item response patterns between a respondent and an identified norm group, an occasional scale with obvious theoretical meaning slipped through. One example comes to mind in which validation data revealed that a scale was tapping a complex psychoneurotic tendency, and rather than incorporate this idiosyncrasy the test developer decided to delete the scale. We conveniently ignored the repeated observation that high scorers on this Musician-Performer scale were usually a little "flaky," thus ignoring or perhaps forgetting that interests reflect motivation, self-confidence, behavioral style, and personality.

Although the public still viewed interests as broad self-expressions, social scientists now regarded interests as specific, empirically defined variables that were more or less unconnected to the broader array of personality and attitudes. If there was a downside to E. K. Strong's enormous contribution, it was that agreement between the public and vocational psychology about the nature of interests was lost for nearly 50 years. This overly specific, indirect, operational definition of interests began to weaken in the 1970s, as psychologists and test developers became increasingly reluctant to accept the restricted operation definition of interests as the scores on an interest inventory. The theorists would eventually prevail in redefining the nature of interests.

The first assault on this narrow definition of interests came with the invention of Basic Interest Scales by Ken Clark and the Minnesotans; then came Occupational Theme Scales by Holland; skill estimates by David Campbell; self-efficacy estimates by Nancy Betz and her colleagues; and Workstyle Scales led by Fred Borgen, Lenore Harmon, and the new Minnesotans. These novel measures blend direct and indirect item technologies and appear within the boundaries of traditional interest inventories. These new hybrid scales challenge Strong's strictly empirical definition of interests as indirect measures of the similarity of response patterns between an individual respondent and a normative sample or samples. New measurement methods offered both the possibility of broadening the study and explanatory power of interests with regard to the nature of vocational choices, and the peril of a return to a primitive (pre-1930s) level of confusion about the meaning and definition of interests. Interest inventories now almost always combine criterion-based and homogeneous scaling methods to produce a comprehensive set of theoretical and empirically keyed scales.

The specific definition of interests as what is measured by an interest inventory now is being strained to its limits by renewed questions about the nature and structure of interests (Spokane & Jacob, 1996)—an aim of this volume. As we reopen unanswered questions about the nature of interests and the degree of overlap between interests and the newer scales such as self-estimates of ability and confidence, we will disagree about what an interest is and what it is not. This will be a healthy debate to the extent to which we relate our work to mainstream work in social and personality psychology, and to the extent that we engage in data collection and analysis as opposed to wishful thinking and speculation. This chapter differentiates between expressed and measured interests, reviews recent research on the topic of expressed and measured interests, provides several profile illustrations, and outlines a research agenda.

EXPRESSED VERSUS MEASURED INTERESTS

Stated simply, the term *measured interests* refers to the empirically keyed scores generated by a reliable and valid criterion-based inventory as compared with *expressed interests,* which refer to non-criterion-based inquiries such as direct questions. Expressed interests are most often self-reports concerning the individual's present or desired occupation. Homogeneous or theoretical basic interest and Holland type scales are also considered to be expressed interests, though more accurately expressed and measured interests lie on a continuum from most direct to least direct.

As Fig. 10.1 illustrates, interest inventory scales can be ordered according to the directness of the items used to construct the scales. Direct or expressed interests include daydream items and direct questions. At the indirect end of the measurement scales are Occupational Scales composed largely of subtle items. Because most contemporary inventories contain multiple subtypes of items that differ in directness, one is often faced with inconsistencies among those scales. The next section of this chapter offers several illustrative profiles in which multiple scale types disagree.

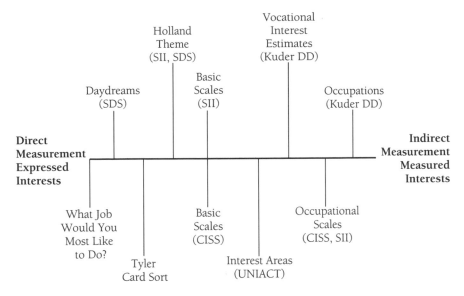

FIGURE 10.1   Scale Types on the Big Five Interest Inventories
              by Directness of Scaling Method

As Borgen (1986) noted, because interest inventories were so widely used and so technologically sophisticated, when there was disagreement between the results of a direct inquiry and the results of an interest inventory, counselors usually assumed the self-report to be inferior and less reliable. The publication of Dolliver's (1969) watershed review of expressed and measured interests raised fundamental questions not only about whether measured interests were actually more valid than self-expressions as predictors of eventual occupation (Borgen, 1986) but also about the wisdom of overreliance upon measured interests in counseling and career interventions.

Dolliver's (1969) Seminal Review

On occasion a single scholarly contribution generates a coherent area of research inquiry. Previous to Dolliver's uncompromising review of research on expressed and measured interests reviewers had simply examined the overall predictive validity of interest inventory scales without reference to expressed versus measured interests. Beginning with Fryer's (1931) book on interest measurement Dolliver reviewed dozens of studies on the relationship and differential validity of direct and indirect interest measures. Dolliver concluded that (a) direct and inventoried interests are only moderately related; (b) expressed interests are highly predictive but less reliable than measured interests; (c) expressed interests are at least as predictive of eventual choices as measured interests; and (d) there is no evidence to sustain the conclusion that the *Strong Vocational Interest Blank* (SVIB) is superior to expressed interests. Dolliver also operationally defined three types of agreement between expressed and measured interests:

> *Full Agreement*—"the two methods give the same result and identify the same occupations as being of interest" (Dolliver, 1969, p. 96).
>
> *Exclusion*—occupations with high scores on the *Strong* are excluded from consideration in expressed interests.
>
> *Inclusion*—occupations included in expressed interests do not receive high scores on the *Strong*.

Of course, it is the second category of disagreement, exclusion, upon which the clinical utility of the *Strong* is based. When the *Strong* suggests occupations that the respondent has not considered, new options are generated for consideration by the client.

Dolliver's conclusions about the validity of expressed interests caused a marked shift in researchers' attitudes toward the validity of expressed choices at the same time that the Holland *Self-Directed Search* (SDS) was emerging as a third dominant inventory for vocational counselors (Holland, 1963; Holland & Lutz, 1968).

Borgen and Seling's (1978) Study

Framing as a question who do we trust when the client and an interest inventory disagree, Borgen and Seling (1978) compared the expressed and measured interests of male National Merit scholars from 16 college major fields across four years of college. Twenty-two Occupational Scales from the SVIB were used to ascertain measured interests, and expressed choice was taken directly from the students' choice of majors and fields. Thirty percent of these respondents had congruent expressed and measured interests. More importantly, the SVIB correctly predicted college major four years later only 30.8% of the time and career choice only 40% of the time, whereas choices expressed by the respondents themselves were predictive of final major choice 52% of the time and career choice 50% of the time. When the inventory and the expressed choice coincided, predictive accuracy jumped to 70%. In contrast, when expressed and measured interests disagreed, the SVIB was an accurate predictor of college major only 15% of the time and career choice only 22% of the time. Expressed choice was still quite predictive (40%) even when expressed and measured interests disagreed. Borgen and Seling note the "superior predictive validity of expressed choices" in spite of the brief follow-up span and the limits of a National Merit sample and argue for a reweighting of expressed choice in counseling.

Studies Since Dolliver (1969) and Borgen and Seling (1978)

Although the number of studies is small, several recent studies examined the agreement of expressed and measured interests. Apostal (1985), for example, documented that only a small fraction of respondents will show substantial disagreement between expressed and measured interests, a finding that some may consider surprising. Similarly Laing, Swaney, and Prediger (1984) calculated the degree of congruence between expressed and measured interests for 603 male and 769 female employed adults using the ACT Interest Inventory. As expected, persistence in college or work was related significantly to congruence between expressed and measured interests. Noeth (1983) followed more than 2,000 high school juniors who were working full time after completing high school. Expressed choice consisted of the answer to "Print the name of the job that you are thinking about most." Interests were not used, but two measures of career development were: Career Planning Knowledge and Career Planning Involvement. Expressed choice predicted actual choice 38% of the time. Adding the career development scales to expressed choice did not significantly improve the predictability of choices.

In a series of studies Robert Slaney and his colleagues investigated the relationship between expressed and measured occupational choices (Slaney, 1980; Slaney & Russell, 1981; Slaney & Slaney, 1981). Slaney and Russell (1981) examined the career decisional status of 175 college students distributed evenly across seven levels of congruence between expressed and measured interests. In general, participants whose expressed and measured interests agreed tended to be in majors that coincided with their interests to a significant degree more than their incongruent counterparts. Although the distribution of Holland (RIASEC) types was highly skewed toward Social, this study lends some support to the improved predictability of individuals for whom expressed and measured interests agree. In a related study Slaney (1984) compared three groups of college women: those with stable expressed interests over a two-year period, those whose expressed interests had changed, and undecided students. The stable group appeared more decided about career goals, whereas the changed group was more undecided.

In an 11-year follow up of 408 college students Bartling and Hood (1981) found good "hit rates" using expressed choices of 50% to 60% for women using expressed choices, and 40% to 50% for men. Measured interests had hit rates only in the 30% range. In a replication of Borgen and Seling (1978), Bartling and Hood (1981) found slightly lower hit rates than did Borgen and Seling (60% as opposed to 70%) when expressed and measured interests agreed. The longer time span used by Bartling and Hood (11 years as opposed to 4 in Borgen and Seling) is probably responsible for the lower hit rate. Similarly to Borgen and Seling (1978), however, when expressed and measured interests disagreed, hit rates for expressed choices were more than four times higher than those for measured interests.

Gade and Soliah (1977) followed 151 undergraduates who had completed the *Vocational Preference Inventory* (VPI) through their senior year. Expressed choices were significantly more predictive of senior choices than were VPI codes in every case except Conventional. Only 10% to 15% of respondents had exact matches between expressed and measured interests in this study. A more relaxed index of agreement, however, revealed a moderate (45%) level of agreement, a figure consistent with previous findings.

Finally, Malett, Spokane, and Vance (1978) used an informational treatment to examine the effects of a brief intervention on the expressed and measured interests of a small sample of college freshmen. Increases in congruence were noted, and the authors concluded that any evidenced increases resulted from participants altering their measured interests to coincide with their expressed interests rather than the reverse.

More recent evidence, then, tends to confirm the findings of Dolliver (1969) and Borgen and Seling (1978) with respect both to the superiority of direct expressions of choices over more indirect measurements, as well as the higher "hit rates" that occur when expressed and measured interests are congruent.

PROFILES ILLUSTRATING AGREEMENT AND DISAGREEMENT BETWEEN EXPRESSED AND MEASURED INTERESTS

A complete understanding of the nature of expressed and measured interests requires some examination of interest inventory profiles. Fortunately archival data are easily presented to illustrate agreements or disagreements between expressed and measured interest on an interest profile. Although no direct

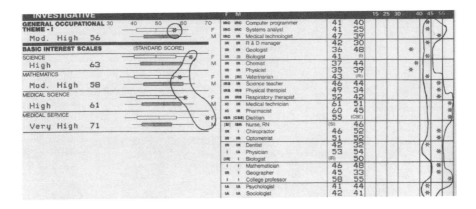

PROFILE 1   Partial (Investigative) scale group from the SCII Form T325

expressions of occupational preference have been elicited from these clients, we do have most of the continuum of direct and measured interest scales (Fig. 10.1) embedded in these inventory illustrations. It is worth noting that less than 10% of the profiles studied evidenced visible disagreements between Basic Interest and Occupational Scales. Thus we should be careful not to overestimate the prevalence of such scalar disagreements.

The first illustration (Profile 1) is the Investigative scale grouping taken from Form T325 of the SCII. In each profile relevant scales are circled. As is evident in this partial profile, all three scale types agree. The Holland Investigative Theme Scale is moderately high (56), the scatter on the Basic Interest Scales is very high, and 13 of 24 Occupational Scales fall in the similar or very similar range. Borgen and Seling (1978) presented compelling evidence that the predictive validity of this scale group will be high, perhaps as high as 70% hit rate with respect to eventual occupation chosen—i.e., the individual in question will wind up in an occupation consistent with this scale grouping 70% of the time.

In the second partial profile (Profile 2) taken from the *Campbell Interest and Skill Survey* (CISS; Campbell, 1994), once again there is substantial agreement across the three scale types (Orientation Scale, Basic Interest and Skill Scale, Occupational Scale). This partial profile is complicated by some disagreement between self-rated skills and interests in five of the eight subscales. We do not yet

CAMPBELL INTEREST AND SKILL SURVEY INDIVIDUAL PROFILE REPORT

aNalyzing Orientation

Orientation Scale		Occupational Scales	
	Standard Scores 30 35 40 45 50 55 60 65 70 Interest/Skill Pattern		Orien-tation Code Standard Scores 25 30 35 40 45 50 55 60 65 70 75 Interest/Skill Pattern
aNalyzing	I 60 / S 63 Pursue	Physician N	I 80 / S 75 Pursue
		Chemist NP	I 72 / S 61 Pursue
Basic Interest and Skill Scales		Medical Researcher NP	I 81 / S 78 Pursue
	Standard Scores 30 35 40 45 50 55 60 65 70 Interest/Skill Pattern	Engineer NP	I 65 / S 56 Pursue
Mathematics	I 53 / S 54	Math/Science Teacher NPH	I 74 / S 50 Develop
Science	I 63 / S 73 Pursue	Computer Programmer NO	I 59 / S 42 Develop
		Statistician NO	I 67 / S 54 Develop
		Systems Analyst NOP	I 64 / S 45 Develop

PROFILE 2   Partial (Analyzing) scale group from the CISS

know whether disagreements between self-rated ability scales and various forms of interest scales would affect their concurrent or predictive validity, though such research would certainly be useful.

Finally, Profile 3, from the SCII Form T325 shows nearly perfect concordance among Artistic scales of very different types. Profile 3 is not only concordant, it is highly differentiated, showing a clear and unimodal pattern of artistic interests. The predictive validity of this particular profile should be substantial, and this profile illustrates Dolliver's Full Agreement category.

Although agreement on scale types appears to be the norm for most respondents, a modest proportion of respondents show cross-scale inconsistencies or disagreements between expressed and measured interest scales. A review of 100 archival profiles showed that only 10% of profiles showed any visible disagreement between Basic Interests and Occupational Scales. The following profiles illustrate such inconsistencies.

Partial Profile 4 (Conventional) illustrates sharp disagreements between Holland Theme Scales, Basic Interest Scales, and Occupational Scales in the Conventional group. Even more common is the presence of high scores on the Holland Themes and on the Basic Interest Scales without collateral support on the Occupational Scales as illustrated in Profile 5 (SCII Form T325). This situation is what we called Inclusion in Dolliver's definitions and illustrates when the client expresses interests that are not reflected in the indirect measured interests.

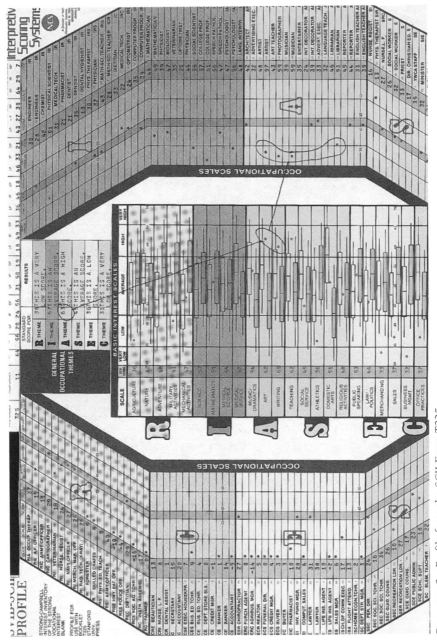

PROFILE 3 Profile from the SCII Form T325

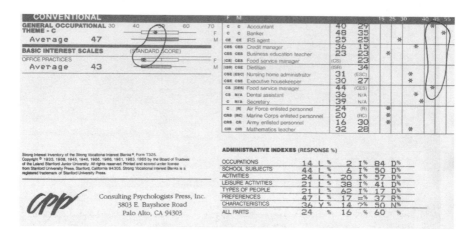

PROFILE 4   Partial (Conventional) scale group from the SCII Form T325

A somewhat more unusual profile is represented in Profile 6 (SVIB-SCII Form T325). Profile 6 indicates a high Holland Artistic Theme, only modest Artistic Basic Interests, and a clear and strong pattern of similar or very similar Occupational Scales in the Artistic group. This last example illustrates Dolliver's Exclusion situation, in which the expressed interests exclude patent high scores on the criterion-based scales.

This same pattern of disagreement between Holland Theme (high), Basic Interest (low), and Occupational Scales (high) can be seen in Profile 7 (SCII Form T325). Although the meaning of patterns in which scale disagreements are complex rather than straightforward is unclear, we discuss some general guidelines for interpreting inventories as well as some specific recommendations for interpreting scale disagreements in counseling in the next section of this chapter.

INTERPRETING PROFILES IN CAREER INTERVENTIONS

Although we attempt to summarize several sources regarding interest inventory interpretation, we can think of no better single source than Tinsley and Bradley (1986) as a resource for counselors. We will briefly review previous suggestions

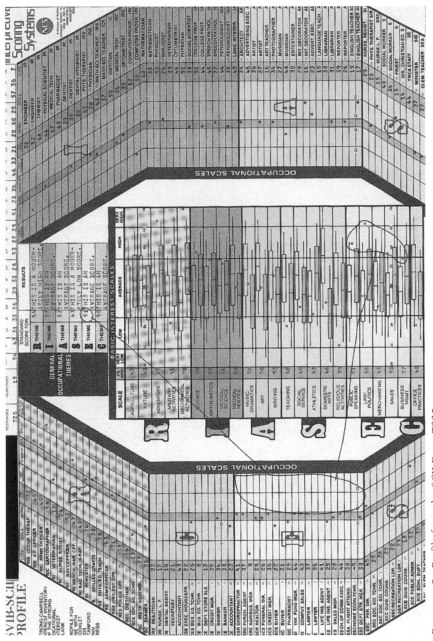

PROFILE 5   Profile from the SCII Form T325

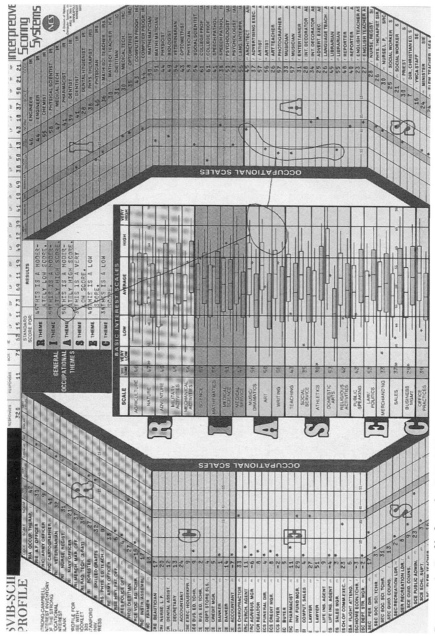

PROFILE 6 Profile from the SVIB-SCII Form T325

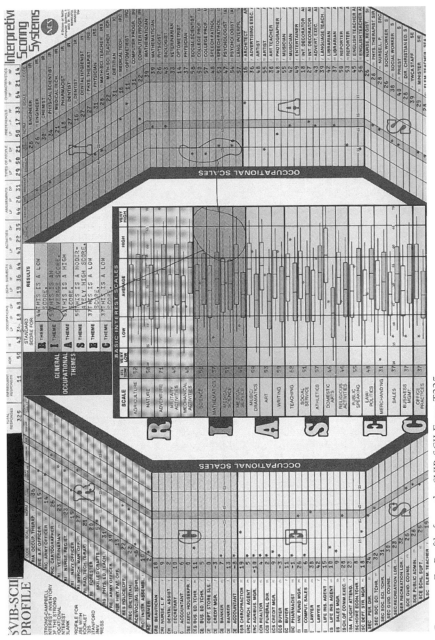

PROFILE 7 Profile from the SVIB-SCII Form T325

for interpreting inventories and focus instead on research on expressed and measured interests for indicators of how to interpret agreements and disagreements among scale types. The following suggestions, which are drawn from Anastasi (1985), Betz, (1992), Prediger and Garfield (1988), Spokane (1991), Tinsley and Bradley (1986), and Tyler (1984), are general rather than specific to the question of expressed versus measured interests:

- Interest inventories and their various scalar outputs are best thought of as "starting points for discussion" (Tyler, 1984) rather than as measurements of discrete traits.

- Test interpretation should be part of an ongoing process with social and therapeutic support provided.

- Every attempt should be made to ensure that the client understands the nature of the scores being discussed.

- Information from inventories should be placed in the context of other life information.

- The cultural and social biases and limits of the scores being presented must be clarified (Betz, 1992).

Research and reviews on expressed versus measured interests (Apostal, 1985; Bartling & Hood, 1981; Borgen & Seling, 1978; Dolliver, 1969; Savickas, 1995) adds the following suggestions of a specific nature to the general suggestions stated above:

- Examine the personal meaning of the scores to the client; this may include conflicts among specific scale types or scores as well as the general meaning of the scores. We cannot overemphasize the importance of this step in working across cultures and subcultures. A lack of parsimony across scores could, for example, be interpreted with alarm rather than as a source of useful information by some individuals.

- Expressed or direct interests contain a motivational component and thereby guide and direct actions and behavior (Savickas, 1995). An increasing evidential base underscores the superior predictive validity of direct expressions of interest over measured interests (Borgen & Seling, 1978; Dolliver, 1969). Interpretations with clients, then, must rely at least as heavily on direct expressions (see Fig. 10.1) as on indirect scales. Darley and Hagenah's (1955) conclusion—"claimed choices point to where he wants to go in this hierarchy.

His measured interests give a closer approximation of the type of work in which he will find intrinsic satisfaction" (p. 11)—still has some merit if we view claimed or expressed choices as a reflection of the clients' motivation level. But their conclusion no longer seems consonant with the evidence on the predictive validity of expressed and measured interests. This apparent contradiction cannot be understood without further attention to the nature and meaning of various measures of vocational interest.

■ When expressed and measured interests agree, which will be the majority of the time (Apostal, 1985), the predictive validity of the combined expressed and measured interests will be as high as 60% (Bartling & Hood, 1981; Borgen & Seling, 1978).

■ When expressed and measured interests disagree, expressed interests will be two to four times more predictive of eventual career choice when compared with measured or indirect interests (Bartling & Hood, 1981). What this appears to mean is that the understructure of interests in comparison with employed occupational groups will be less crucial in career decisions than will be the motivational nature of personal preferences and expressions. Indirect or Occupational Scales may suggest options not previously considered, but it would be a mistake to conclude that the client will automatically pursue such novel options when presented.

■ Expressed choices may be more predictive for women than for men, due in large measure to their endorsement of Social type options (Bartling & Hood, 1981) and to some degree to their selection of part-time employment to accommodate child rearing (Harmon, 1981). Likewise other moderator variables such as personal adjustment may alter the guidelines detailed here (Brandt & Hood, 1968).

■ When a complex combination of high and low scale types exists, it is probably wise to rely upon the more direct expressions (see Fig. 10.1) as the most likely directions the client will pursue.

■ Clients often present in counseling without clearly stated expressed choices. Although measured interests may be quite useful in such cases, they may also appear in flat or undifferentiated profiles or seem odd or unworkable to clients (Bartling & Hood, 1981; Borgen & Seling, 1978). Thus, even in cases where clients can state no expressed choices, there should be alternate attempts to elicit and clarify direct expressions (e.g., card sorts, fantasy exercises).

RECONSIDERING THE NATURE OF EXPRESSED AND MEASURED INTERESTS

We know more about the comparative predictive validity and counseling utility of expressed and measured interests than we do about the conceptual and theoretical nature of these constructs. Campbell (1950, 1996) underscored the importance of indirect measurement to modern psychology and correctly predicted over 35 years ago that contrary to prevailing opinions, direct measures of social attitudes would be as good as predictors of behavior as indirect ones: "Most efforts to develop indirect attitude tests are predicated upon the assumption that indirect tests will under certain conditions have higher validity than direct tests. It is worthy to note that none of the studies reviewed here offers any evidence that this is the case" (Campbell, 1950, pp. 30–31).

This prescient assertion has been supported repeatedly since (Dolliver, 1969; Borgen & Seling, 1978). Campbell (1950) also noted, however, that what he called the "face validity" of the indirect measures may actually be better than the direct ones. Stated another way, respondents may be more inclined to attribute credibility to the indirect measures than to the direct measures in spite of their predictive similarity.

An even greater problem lies in our failure to relate constructs such as expressed and measured interests, which derive from increasingly sophisticated measurement techniques, to theory and models of social and cognitive psychology. The result is that although we can observe what happens when expressed and measured interests disagree, we cannot explain why the resulting behavior should be the case. Thus we have measurement procedures for which no theoretical explanations exist.

How then do we know whether expressed and measured interests are tapping the same cognitive structures? How do we know that asking individuals what their preferred occupation is, examining their Holland Theme Scales, which are based upon a list of occupational titles, comparing their Basic Interest Scales and their criterion-based Occupational Scales represent measures of the same construct (Campbell & Fiske, 1959) rather than different constructs entirely? We do know that the internal consistency of these several measures and their reliabilities (even over long time periods) are substantial for expressed and for measured interests (higher generally for the *Strong*) (Dolliver, 1969: Lubinski, Benbow, & Ryan, 1995). Further, the correlations among these measures are sizeable, often in the .40 to .50 range (Berdie, 1950; Fabry & Poggio, 1977). Dolliver (1969) concluded that the overlap between expressed and measured interests, given the methodological problems in the studies, was moderate. What we do not yet know is what disagreements mean, even if we assume that expressed and measured interests are estimates of the same internal structures. Stated another way, if expressed and measured interests are truly measures of the same underlying construct, what is occurring in the individual when those two measures are unrelated? Dolliver noted that although expressed interests were valid, they were less reliable than measured interests—a conclusion that he did not place in any theoretical context.

We find some clues to the meaning of disagreements between expressed and measured interests in a scattered few early articles. Berdie (1946), for example, reasoned that as an individual becomes more and more ego centered—and reactive to other than immediate stimuli, a situation generally associated with neuroticism—there will be an associated restriction of range in interests. We must presume here that Berdie was referring to expressed interests rather than to measured interests as he did in an earlier paper (Berdie, 1943, 1944). The implication of this argument is that the more neurotic the individual, the more likely there would be a restriction of expressed interests that would result in Dolliver's inclusion condition, in which the disagreement resulted from occupations on which high scores were obtained not being considered by the respondent in expressed interests. Such an interpretation is supported by Spokane and Jacob (1996), who reviewed evidence for the neurotic component in career indecision and found it larger than expected.

Darley and Hagenah (1955) reasoned that expressed or direct interests were subject to pressures from the labor market and the economy and reflected, as well, individual aspirations. Tyler (1984) likewise noted that interest inventories were the only personality tests that had external or criterion references. Thus we could expect that both expressed (direct) and measured (indirect) interests would to different degrees reflect external criteria. Tyler (1984) further observed that interest inventories reflected only the similarity in response patterns between the individual and some criterion groups, and could not indicate how much interest an individual had in a given occupation. Although directly stated or claimed interests could reflect powerful motivational levels, indirectly measured interests could not. Thus, when expressed and measured interests disagree, though they may draw upon the same underlying construct, the direct inquiry will simply reflect a motivational component that the indirect measurement will not. This additional motivational component probably accounts for the superiority of expressed interests over measured interests in some individuals and some fields.

A FUTURE AGENDA ON EXPRESSED
AND MEASURED INTERESTS

Conceptual dead ends are not uncommon in career development. Whether the debate over expressed versus measured interests results in another dead end remains to be seen. We do know now that expressed interests are more valid even if less reliable than we once thought and that a balance of expressed and measured scale types should be employed in counseling. If this research tradition is to remain viable, new research will have to struggle with the meaning of disagreements between different levels of directness of expression and their meaning for the respondent's personality, behavior, and presence or absence of external barriers posed by minority status, socioeconomic status, etc. In addition to exploring the correlates of disagreements between expressed and measured interests, we should examine how and whether such agreements are ever resolved by clients and the extent to which they can be influenced by interventions (Malett, Spokane, & Vance, 1978). This will require intensive study of the processes by which individuals make and alter career choices, along the lines of Gati and Tikotzki (1989), and continued studies of how we can best interpret profiles of various types to the client's benefit. We should not automatically assume that clients desire new options rather than the elimination of options.

It is increasingly apparent that interests, personality, self-efficacy, and other variants of personality and vocational self-concept may be facets of a unified set of complex underlying traits (see Ackerman & Heggestad, 1997). If this is true, then different measures of interests and personality will tap these underlying traits in slightly different ways. Differences between expressed and measured interests then become something along the lines of genotypic and phenotypic estimates of these composite traits. How we measure these traits and how they influence behavior remains to be understood.

Finally, individuals may experience changes in expressed or measured interests at different points in the career life cycle. These changes could be incremental or developmental, or they could be initiated by external influences or events. Longitudinal studies of shifts in disagreement between expressed and measured interests would be fruitful. For the present we have a modest body of research support that can be used to direct interventions employing expressed and measured interests, and we have numerous inventories of very high quality with which to measure these constructs. What is needed now is clever application of previous findings to further our understanding and improve the potency of our intervention attempts.

REFERENCES

Ackerman, P. L., & Heggestad, E. D. (1997). Intelligence, personality and interests: Evidence for overlapping traits. *Psychological Bulletin, 121,* 219–245.

Anastasi, A. (1985). Mental measurement: Some emerging trends. In J. V. Mitchell, Jr., *Mental Measurements Yearbook* (9th ed., pp. xxiii–xxix) Lincoln: University of Nebraska Press.

Apostal, R. A. (1985). Expressed-inventoried interest agreement and type of *Strong-Campbell Interest Inventory Scale. Journal of Counseling Psychology, 32,* 634–336.

Bartling, H. C., & Hood, A. B. (1981). An 11-year follow-up of measured interest and vocational choice. *Journal of Counseling Psychology, 28,* 27–35.

Berdie, R. F. (1943). Likes, dislikes, and vocational interests. *Journal of Applied Psychology, 27,* 180–189.

Berdie, R. F. (1944). Factors related to vocational interests. *Psychological Bulletin, 41,* 137–157.

Berdie, R. F. (1946). Range of interests and psychopathologies. *Journal of Clinical Psychology, 2,* 161–166.

Berdie, R. F. (1950). Scores on the *Strong Vocational Interest Blank* and the *Kuder Preference Record* in relation to self ratings. *Journal of Applied Psychology, 34,* 42–49.

Betz, N. E. (1992). Career assessment: A review of critical issues. In S. D. Brown & R. W. Lent (Eds.), *Handbook of Counseling Psychology* (2nd ed., pp. 453–484). New York: Wiley.

Borgen, F. H. (1986). New approaches to the assessment of interests. In W. B. Walsh & S. H. Osipow (Eds.), *Advances in Vocational Psychology, Vol. I: The assessment of interests* (pp. 83–125). Hillsdale, NJ: Erlbaum.

Borgen, F. H., & Seling, M. J. (1978). Expressed and inventoried interests revisited: perspicacity in the person. *Journal of Counseling Psychology, 25,* 536–543.

Brandt, J. E., & Hood, A. B. (1968). Effects of personality adjustment on the predictive validity of the Strong Vocational Interest Blank. *Journal of Counseling Psychology, 15,* 547–551.

Campbell, D. P. (1994). *The Campbell Interests and Skills Survey.* Minneapolis: National Computer Systems.

Campbell, D. T. (1950). The indirect assessment of social attitudes. *Psychological Bulletin, 47,* 15–38.

Campbell, D. T. (1996). Unresolved issues in measurement validity: An autobiographical overview. *Psychological Assessment, 8,* 363–368.

Campbell, D. T., & Fiske, D. W. (1959). Convergent and discriminant validation by the multitrait-multimethod matrix. *Psychological Bulletin, 56,* 81–105.

Darley, J. G. (1938). A preliminary study of relations between attitude, adjustment, and vocational interest tests. *Journal of Educational Psychology, 29,* 467–473.

Darley, J. G. (1941). *Clinical Aspects and Interpretation of the Strong Vocational Interest Blank.* New York: The Psychological Corporation.

Darley, J., & Hagenah, T. (1955). *Vocational interest measurement: Theory and practice.* Minneapolis: University of Minnesota Press.

Dolliver, R. H. (1969). *Strong Vocational Interest Blank* versus expressed vocational interests: A review. *Psychological Bulletin, 72,* 95–107.

Fabry, J., & Poggio, J. P. (1977). The factor compatibility and communality of coded-expressed and inventoried interests. *Measurement and Evaluation in Guidance, 10,* 90–97.

Freyd, M. (1923). *Occupational interests.* Chicago: C. H. Stoelting.

Fryer, D. (1931). *The measurement of interests.* New York: Henry Holt.

Gade, E. M., & Soliah, D. (1977). Vocational Preference Inventory high point codes versus expressed choices as predictors of college major and career entry. *Journal of Counseling Psychology, 22,* 117–121.

Gati, I., & Tikotzki, Y. (1989). Strategies for collection and processing of occupational information in making career decisions. *Journal of Counseling Psychology, 36,* 430–439.

Harmon, L. W. (1981). The life and career plans of young college women: A followup study. *Journal of Counseling Psychology, 28,* 416–427.

Holland, J. L. (1963). Explorations of a theory of vocational choice and achievement: II A four-year prediction study. *Psychological Reports, 12,* 537–594.

Holland, J. L., & Lutz, S. W. (1968). The predictive value of a student's choice of an occupation. *Personnel and Guidance Journal, 46,* 428–434.

Laing, J., Swaney, K., & Prediger, D. J. (1984). Integrating vocational interest inventory results and expressed choices. *Journal of Vocational Behavior, 25,* 304–315.

Lubinski, D., Benbow, C. P., & Ryan, J. (1995). Stability of vocational interests among the intellectually gifted from adolescence to adulthood: A 15-year longitudinal study. *Journal of Applied Psychology, 80,* 196–200.

Malett, S. D., Spokane, A. R., & Vance, F. L. (1978). Effects of vocationally relevant information on the expressed and measured interests of freshman males. *Journal of Counseling Psychology, 25,* 292–298.

Noeth, R. J. (1983). The effects of enhancing expressed vocational choice with career development measures to predict occupational field. *Journal of Vocational Behavior, 22,* 365–375.

Prediger, D. J., & Garfield, N. J. (1988). Testing competencies and responsibilities: A checklist for counselors. In J. T. Kapes & M. M. Mastie (Eds.), *A counselor's guide to career assessment instruments* (2nd ed., pp. 45–59), Alexandria, VA: National Career Development Association.

Savickas, M. L. (1995). Examining the personal meaning of inventoried interests during career counseling. *Journal of Career Assessment, 3,* 188–201.

Slaney, R. B. (1980). Expressed vocational choice and vocational indecision. *Journal of Counseling Psychology, 27,* 122–129.

Slaney, R. B. (1984). Relation of career indecision to changes in expressed vocational interests. *Journal of Counseling Psychology, 31,* 349–355.

Slaney, R. B., & Russell, J.E.A. (1981). An investigation of different levels of agreement between expressed and inventoried vocational interests among college women. *Journal of Counseling Psychology, 28,* 221–228.

Slaney, R. B., & Slaney, F. M. (1981). A comparison of measures of expressed and inventoried vocational interests among counseling center clients. *Journal of Counseling Psychology, 28,* 515–518.

Spokane, A. R. (1991). *Career intervention.* Englewood Cliffs, NJ: Prentice Hall.

Spokane, A. R., & Jacob, E. (1996). Career and vocational assessment 1993–1994: A biennial review. *Journal of Career Assessment, 4,* 1–32.

Spokane, A. R., Malett, S. D., & Vance, F. L. (1978). Effects of vocationally relevant information on the expressed and measured interests of freshman males. *Journal of Counseling Psychology, 25,* 292–298.

Strong, E. K., Jr. (1927). *Vocational Interest Blank.* Stanford, CA: Stanford University Press.

Strong, E. K., Jr. (1943). *Vocational interests of men and women.* Stanford, CA: Stanford University Press.

Tinsley, H.E.A., & Bradley, R. W. (1986). Testing the test: Test interpretation. *Journal of Counseling and Development, 64,* 462–466.

Tyler, L. (1984). Testing the test: What tests don't measure. *Journal of Counseling and Development, 63,* 48–50.

CHAPTER ELEVEN

Interest Assessment Using Card Sorts

Paul J. Hartung

W HEN PEOPLE ENCOUNTER career decision-making diffi-
culties, they may turn to a career counselor for help. The career counselor may,
as a means of clarifying the client's career options and direction, administer a
standardized vocational interest inventory to assess the client's occupational preferences, likes and dislikes, and personality style. As evidenced in the chapters of
this volume, use of standardized interest measures such as the *Strong Interest
Inventory* (SII; Strong, Hansen, & Campbell, 1994) and the *Self-Directed Search*
(SDS; Holland, 1994) reflects the central role of interest measurement in career
counseling practice and vocational psychology research as they have evolved as
professional disciplines since the turn of the 20th century. For many clients and
counselors the practice of career counseling has indeed come to mean, at least in
part and for better or worse, interest assessment. For the science of vocational
psychology, interest measurement has been and remains a vital area of basic and
applied research.

Standardized interest inventories such as the SII and SDS certainly contribute
greatly as career assessment tools and interventions and will undoubtedly continue to do so for years to come. In an applied sense their use may become problematic, however, when clients or counselors view them as instruments capable
of providing definitive and authoritative "answers" to presenting or prospective
career problems. The present chapter considers an approach to assessment and
counseling for clarifying interests that can help to avoid this potential problem.

This chapter examines the *Vocational Card Sort* (VCS) as a structured interview
technique that emerged from basic research by Leona Tyler (1961) on individual

differences and evolved into a career intervention strategy aimed at helping people explore career paths and work-role alternatives to resolve their career decision-making difficulties. In so doing, the chapter advances the view that the VCS offers to practitioners and researchers alike both a general intervention strategy for career counseling and a specific alternative or supplement to traditional interest assessment.

Following this brief introduction, the chapter discusses the philosophical underpinnings of card sorts within the context of career assessment and traces the historical roots and development of the VCS as a career counseling technique in general and as a tool for assessing vocational interests in particular. It then describes and reviews existing card sorts available for use in career assessment, career counseling, and vocational psychology research. Some conclusions about vocational card sorts as a career intervention strategy close the chapter.

VOCATIONAL CARD SORTS: PHILOSOPHY AND HISTORY

Philosophical Perspectives on Career Assessment

Approaches to career assessment derive from two fundamental branches of philosophy, namely logical positivism and phenomenology (Savickas, 1992). In using criterion-referenced interest measures to help clients resolve their decisional dilemmas, counselors take an approach to career assessment grounded in the philosophical perspective of logical positivism. The positivist perspective on career assessment, most clearly embodied in the differential tradition in vocational psychology, asserts that vocational interests, as well as other individual traits such as aptitudes and values, can be observed, quantified, and objectively and normatively categorized. Taking this approach, counselors assist clients to answer the question "What do I possess?" (Savickas, 1992). Career assessment within a positivist framework thus centers on counting or inventorying interests as well as measuring aptitudes, values, abilities, personality traits, and skills.

Most career assessment tools, including interest measures, have their roots in a positivist philosophical perspective, which, to be sure, has both greatly influenced and significantly advanced career theory, practice, and research. By operating on the assumption that individuals can be understood apart from their environments, however, logical positivism decontextualizes and can depersonalize career assessment and counseling (Brown & Brooks, 1996). This potentiality, coupled with a disregard for individually construed meanings and subjective experiences in favor of normative behavioral standards and objective, verifiable realities, can limit the career assessment process when approached from a strictly positivist perspective. Some career theorists, researchers, and practitioners have therefore augmented positivist-based career assessment and counseling approaches with phenomenologically grounded philosophical perspectives on career that emphasize context (Collin, 1996; Young & Valach, 1996; Young, Valach, & Collin, 1996), personally construed meaning (Savickas, 1995a, 1995b; Super, 1954), and narrative (Cochran, 1997; Jepsen, 1990, 1994).

The phenomenological perspective on career assessment emphasizes exploring each client's subjective, qualitative, and personal career reality. From this position, vocational interests, as well as other traits, are best assessed using primarily idiographic rather than nomothetic strategies. This means working to understand each client's interests and the reasons for and personal intent or significance of those interests. By eliciting narratives (Cochran, 1997; Jepsen, 1990, 1994), reviewing early recollections (Savickas, 1997), and situating work in the context of people's lives (Richardson, 1991, 1996), counselors who take a phenomenologically based career assessment and counseling approach assist clients to answer questions such as "How do I use what I possess?" or "What meaning do I give to what I possess?" (Savickas, 1992). Career assessment within a phenomenological framework thus involves client and counselor in a collaborative endeavor to imbue the client's interests and other traits with personal meaning.

Because the VCS entails "a counselor-client active searching process" (Goldman, 1995, p. 385) whereby the client constructs her or his own interest categories and explores the meaning of those categories and their contents, it fundamentally reflects a phenomenological career assessment approach. Additionally, as Slaney and Croteau (1995) point out, the VCS does contain some "inventory-like aspects that need to be and have been investigated from a psychometric perspective" (p. 387). These "inventory-like aspects" refer to the use in most card sorts of occupational titles derived directly from or very similar to scales such as those occurring on standardized instruments, most notably the SII. This parallel, combined with the use in card sorts of elaborate tallying methods such as described by Gysbers and Moore (1987), reflects a more positivist approach and may account for Slaney and MacKinnon-Slaney's (1990) reference to the procedure as an "instrument" (p. 340). On balance, a historical look at the VCS should reveal that the original intent and use of the technique clearly derives from and promotes phenomenological perspectives on career assessment and counseling while recognizing the value and incorporating aspects of fundamentally positivist approaches.

A "Card Sort" of History

By most accounts (Goldman, 1995; Slaney, Moran, & Wade, 1994; Slaney & MacKinnon-Slaney, 1990) two individuals, Leona Tyler and Robert Dolliver, emerge as instrumental in originating, developing, and refining the VCS technique. Leo Goldman credits a third person, Cindy Rice Dewey, with presenting the card sort technique in its most detailed form, although this claim seems arguable. Goldman himself as well has done much to advance and advocate for the use of card sorts in career counseling. In coauthoring two chapters on the technique, developing his own card sort, and conducting programmatic research in the area, Robert Slaney additionally merits much credit for advancing the VCS as a counseling intervention, assessment tool, and research method. It is Tyler's groundbreaking work followed by Dolliver's revisions that figure most prominently, however, in the history of vocational card sorts.

Origins: Tyler's Work on Individual Differences. Interest inventories were not originally designed to assess individuals' unique reasons for their occupational preferences or choices. Early researchers and inventory developers such as Bingham (1937) and Strong (1938) had their roots in personnel selection, and this organizational perspective certainly influenced their decision to concentrate on how well interests fit an occupation rather than what those interests mean to an individual. In fact, Strong's inventory did not really measure a person's interests directly. Instead, it measured the similarity of individual interest patterns to the pattern for selected occupational groups. Early on, researchers such as Fryer (1931) and Carter (1940) feared that the inventory approach would cause counselors to lose sight of the insights and intuition available from assessing interests with case-history data.

This early history thus reveals that interest inventory developers did not devise these instruments to tap how individuals organize their vocational preferences. The aim and strength of traditional interest measures rather has always rested in their utility for identifying preferences common between and among individuals. Consequently, the problem arose for some researchers in the history of interest measurement as to how best to capture and retain individuality when using assessment methods that focus on commonality.

Recognizing this basic issue in individual differences research over 35 years ago, Tyler (1961) proposed the VCS as an alternative method to traditional interest assessment. She designed the VCS as a research method to uncover individual preferences as well as the specific reasons for and manner in which the individual organizes those preferences. Her work led to the development of the first card sort, aptly named after its author as the *Tyler Vocational Card Sort* (TVCS).

Tyler (1961) included in what emerged as the prototype VCS an assessment of occupations, leisure activities, first names, and community organizations. She also delineated as part of her research on individuality the core procedures for implementing the technique, which remain central in the counseling and research use of most card sorts today. As described by Slaney and MacKinnon-Slaney (1990), these procedures consisted of three basic steps.

In step one Tyler began the process by engaging the participant in a preliminary sorting activity wherein the participant grouped 100 cards containing either an occupational title, leisure activity, first name, or community organization into three columns marked "Would Choose," "Would Not Choose," and "No Opinion." As E. K. Strong and Frederic Kuder had done with their interest inventories of the day, Tyler felt it crucial to include the latter two response categories because she believed, and later found evidence to suggest, that interests depend "as much on [an individual's] *dislikes* or *rejections* as they do on his [sic] positive attitudes toward things" (Tyler, 1964, pp. 186–187). Tyler also noted that she "deliberately refrain[ed] from using the words 'Like' and 'Dislike' because [she] wish[ed] to leave [the individual] free to use other bases for choice and rejection" (1961, p. 195). In step two Tyler eliminated the "No Opinion" column and asked the participant to sort the items in the other two columns into smaller groups of items. These smaller groups reflected individuals' reasons for choosing or not choosing those items. This process allowed participants to construct their own subcategories of items that reflected their reasons for choosing or not choosing a particular occupation or other item. The process then moved to the third step, in which Tyler interviewed participants to discuss and ascertain their reasoning processes, rationales for, and perspectives on their choices. Tyler's initial research findings using this three-step procedure supported the VCS "as a reliable method for capturing some of the uniqueness of individual[s] that could be an important addition to more traditional approaches to measurement" (Slaney & MacKinnon-Slaney, 1990, p. 325).

Advances: Dolliver's Refinement of the TVCS. With Tyler's work as a starting point, Dolliver launched efforts of his own that did much to advance the VCS as a structured interview technique (Slaney & MacKinnon-Slaney, 1990). These efforts began with his dissertation in 1966 and a subsequently published article in 1967 that described changes to the TVCS. Dolliver specifically refined the TVCS in three important ways.

First, Dolliver revised the preliminary response categories to read "Would Not Choose," "Might Choose," and "In Question." He also adopted the 51 occupations from the *Strong Vocational Interest Blank* (men's form) for presentation on 3 x 5 cards. Using items from various versions of the *Strong* has proven a common characteristic of later card sorts in part because it permits comparing card sort and inventory results.

Second, Dolliver modified Tyler's three-step procedural outline and expanded it by having individuals select and rank order their ten most preferred occupations. This refinement incorporated Rosenberg's (1957) Requirements for an Ideal Job checklist, which prompted clients to select and rank order their criteria or motives for an ideal job. As part of this latter task Dolliver included an opportunity for individuals to include any occupations they wished to consider but that were excluded from the cards presented at the outset.

Finally, Dolliver adapted George Kelly's (1955) personal construct theory as a means of organizing and interpreting the results obtained from the TVCS. Kelly described decision making as a tripartite process of circumspection (taking different perspectives on the situation), preemption (reducing its number of personal meanings), and choice (selecting the most personally relevant alternative). Circumspection, involving "loose" or expansive thought, parallels Dolliver's step one in which clients first overview a broad range of potentially satisfying occupations. Preemption, involving "tight" or narrow thought, characterizes step two of Dolliver's modified TVCS process, in which clients weigh or give meaning to their various occupational preferences toward reducing their number of potential choices. Dolliver noted that the inability to preempt, or narrow one's decisional alternatives, represents a key factor in career indecision. Dolliver argued that the TVCS can more quickly identify individuals with an inability to move from loose to tight thought, from circumspection to preemption. Choice reflects the outcome of the two previous steps and involves the selection of an occupation based on the personally constructed meaning of and rationale behind the choice.

Elaborating the procedures in these ways and researching the technique led Dolliver to conclude that the TVCS represents a structured interview method that addresses clients' reasons for their choices. This conclusion reflected a departure from Tyler's view of the technique as an assessment method or "test" subject to concerns about validity and reliability of the choices made. Instead, Dolliver pointed out, validity and reliability mean something quite different vis a vis an interview. To determine the validity of the modified TVCS, "one would ask whether its use led more quickly than would a test or a straight interview to the identification of important vocational counseling topics for discussion" (Dolliver, 1967, p. 920). Reliability relative to the TVCS would be negatively valued because one would expect that clients' reasons and choices would change in the course of the counseling process. Relatedly Dolliver noted that the TVCS retains particular validity for evoking *expressed* interests. This proves significant because a later review of the research literature has shown expressed interests to be equivalent or superior to inventoried interests in terms of predictive validity (Slaney & MacKinnon-Slaney, 1990).

Evolutions: Beyond the TVCS. By originating and developing the VCS as first an assessment method and then a structured interview technique, Tyler and Dolliver collectively innovated a counseling and assessment approach as well as a research method others would soon adapt in their own work. In 1974, concerned with problems of sex-role bias inherent in vocational interest measures such as the *Strong,* Kuder, and including the TVCS, Dewey reported on her development of the *Non-Sexist Vocational Card Sort* (NSVCS) as "a process oriented tool that gives a greater range of vocational choices to both sexes" (p. 311).

Dewey derived the NSVCS directly from Tyler's and Dolliver's earlier work and promoted it as less sexist than traditional vocational counseling and interest assessment approaches. To support her claim Dewey noted that the NSVCS presents identical vocational alternatives to women and men, uses gender-neutral occupational titles, and permits counselor and client to address sex-role biases that emerge during counseling. Slaney and MacKinnon-Slaney (1990) aptly commented some years later, however, that revisions of leading standardized interest measures since 1974 weaken Dewey's first two arguments. Regarding Dewey's third point, Slaney and MacKinnon-Slaney noted that addressing sex-role bias in counseling relies "on the sensitivity and perceptiveness of the counselor and does not appear to be inherent in . . . the NSVCS" (p. 329).

Overall, the NSVCS represents an important contribution and perhaps a turning point in the history of card sorts specifically and career assessment generally. In constructing the NSVCS, Dewey raised key issues pertaining to women's career development and brought attention to larger issues of sex-role stereotyping that continue to hold relevance today in discussions of neglected areas in career theory, assessment, and counseling for both women *and* men (Harmon, 1997). Moreover, many card sort developers producing their materials after Dewey's would directly attend to occupational sex bias by using occupational titles intended to circumvent, if not eliminate, such problems.

Following Dewey, various other individuals have developed their own card sorts derived fundamentally from Tyler's pioneering work and Dolliver's refinements of the technique. The next section identifies several of these individuals and describes the card sorts they created.

ON DECK: EIGHT CARD SORTS TO ASSESS INTERESTS

Perusing the work of Slaney and his colleagues (1990, 1994) reveals a variety of specific card sorts presently available for use in career counseling practice and vocational psychology research. Some of these card sorts focus exclusively on either values, skills, or interests, whereas others focus on all or combinations of these variables. All but two of the card sorts Slaney et al. (1994) identified, namely the *Motivated Skills Card Sort* (Knowdell, 1991b) and the *Career Values Card Sort Kit* (Knowdell, 1991a), deal directly with interests. Only card sorts that specifically involve vocational interest assessment are outlined below beginning with the three most popular card sorts recognized by Spokane (1991). The reader interested in more detailed reviews of these card sorts may wish to consult an article by Dolliver (1981), chapters by Slaney et al. (1994) and Slaney and MacKinnon-Slaney (1990), and specific test critique resources such as the *Mental Measurements Yearbook*.

Common to the eight card sorts reviewed herein is the use to varying degrees of (a) Holland's RIASEC model, (b) occupational titles from established interest inventories, most notably the Strong (Strong, Hansen, & Campbell, 1994), and (c) varying educational levels required of occupations included on the cards. These card sorts and the VCS procedure in general additionally often require clients to be fairly articulate, verbal, and motivated. A final commonality underlying each card sort pertains to the fundamental use of the initial procedures first outlined by Tyler and later refined by Dolliver. Readers looking for a more complete description of these procedures and a sample case may wish to read Spokane (1991, pp. 130–133).

Non-Sexist Vocational Card Sort

Dewey (1974) included in the *Non-Sexist Vocational Card Sort* (NSVCS) 76 occupations derived from the female and male forms of the *Strong Vocational Interest Blank* and the *Kuder Occupational Interest Survey*. Each occupational title appears on a 3 x 5 card coded by primary Holland type (i.e., Realistic, Investigative, Artistic, Social, Enterprising, or Conventional) and worded in gender-neutral language (e.g., *police officer* rather than *policeman*). The extent of the actual changes Dewey had to make in these 76 occupational titles seems rather minimal, however. Dewey chose to use Holland's model for its parsimony, grounding in personality theory, and grouping of occupations by personality type rather than by occupational status or educational requirements. Interestingly, 65% of the occupations Dewey included in the NSVCS require at least a college degree. Attention to issues of sex-role stereotyping seems to have outweighed concerns of social status issues and educational access limitations.

Social occupations constitute the majority of cards (N = 21), and Conventional occupations constitute the minority (N = 9). This yields an uneven distribution of interests across the six Holland types. Given the fluid nature of the card sort method generally, however, counselors and researchers could certainly add more or delete some cards to balance the distribution. The reverse side of each card contains a *Dictionary of Occupational Titles* summary of the occupation's main duties and responsibilities. Three separate 4 x 6 cards contain the phrases used by Dolliver: "Would Not Choose," "In Question," and "Might Choose." These cards serve as the larger response category markers that clients use in the sorting process.

Reviews of the NSVCS point out several shortcomings of the method. These include the fact that Dewey gave no clear descriptions of how the included occupations were chosen, how to use Holland codes in sorting or in counseling in general, or how the method is "non-sexist" (Slaney & MacKinnon-Slaney, 1990; Slaney et al., 1994). One research study reviewed by Slaney et al. (1994) did indicate that the NSVCS suggested a broader range of career choices and more nontraditional career choices to women undergraduate students than did the *Self-Directed Search* (Holland, 1994). A study by Cooper (1976) found the NSVCS more effective than the *Strong-Campbell Interest Inventory* (Campbell & Hansen, 1981) in fostering women's career exploration.

Vocational Exploration and Insight Kit

Holland and Associates (1980) merged an interest inventory (namely the *Self-Directed Search;* SDS) with a vocational card sort to create the *Vocational Exploration and Insight Kit* (VEIK). The VEIK contains 84 occupational titles that directly parallel those found on the SDS and the *Vocational Preference Inventory*

(Holland, 1985). These occupations are evenly distributed among the six RIASEC types with approximately 50% requiring a college degree, 25% requiring a postgraduate degree, and 25% requiring a high school education or less. In the spirit of Dolliver's elaborated TVCS procedures counselors using the VEIK encourage clients to add any occupational titles not represented on the VEIK cards as they wish. A Holland code can be computed from the resulting sort. Similar to Dewey's work with the NSVCS the developers of the VEIK also included as part of its VCS component an opportunity for the client and counselor to examine the influence of various sociocultural variables (e.g., race, class, and gender) on the sorting process.

In response to reviews of the VEIK Slaney and MacKinnon-Slaney (1990) concluded that its VCS component represents a career counseling intervention and not a measurement instrument. Reviewers' questions about its psychometric properties should therefore be addressed in terms of validity and reliability as applied to the VCS technique much as Dolliver had discussed in his 1967 paper. These reviews also prompted Slaney and MacKinnon-Slaney to call for further empirical work with the VEIK to determine its efficacy as a treatment method.

Occ-U-Sort

The *Occ-U-Sort* (O-U-S; Jones, 1981) endeavors to reduce sex bias and increase representativeness of educational levels presented in a vocational card sort. Its author therefore developed 180 cards categorized and distributed evenly across three General Educational Levels derived from the *Dictionary of Occupational Titles* (DOT). Jones excluded occupational titles reflecting fields predominated by either females or males, although this attempt to minimize sex bias falls short in the eyes of some reviewers (Dolliver, 1981; Westbrook & Mastie, 1982). To encourage self-directed exploratory behavior a self-guided booklet in which the individual can list reasons for her or his occupational choices and rejections supplements the O-U-S.

Each card in the O-U-S deck lists on the front side an occupational title with its DOT number, General Educational Level, and two-letter Holland code. The reverse side describes the occupation and provides identifying information for the card. Clients can apply the occupations they sort into the "Might Choose" category to obtaining a Holland code via a scheme provided by the O-U-S. The Holland code can then be used to identify occupations of interest from those listed in the accompanying guide to occupations. Jones keyed the 555 occupations in this guide by Holland type as well as by DOT and Guide for Occupational Exploration numbers.

Commentaries on and reviews of the O-U-S suggest that it retains a dubious position as a card sort. At once it is ranked among the most popular card sorts available (Spokane, 1991) and criticized for having insufficient and misleading data that detract from its intended value, particularly as a sex-fair method of assessing interests (Cochran, 1985; Crites, 1985; Westbrook & Mastie, 1982). Considered relative to the VCS as a structured interview and counseling intervention, however, the O-U-S, as with card sorts in general, requires an inherently different approach to its validation than would be taken with traditional interest measures (Dolliver, 1967; Tyler, 1961). Such a perspective led Slaney and MacKinnon-Slaney (1990) to conclude that "the approach to gathering validity data on vocational card sorts may need to be carefully reexamined" (p. 333).

Slaney Vocational Card Sort

For the express purpose of empirically investigating the VCS as a structured interview and career intervention Slaney (1978) devised the *Slaney Vocational Card Sort* (SVCS), which contains 80 occupational titles selected from the *Strong-Campbell Interest Inventory*. The SVCS essentially represents another iteration of the TVCS modified in three important ways. First, rather than obtaining a Holland Code from clients' final occupational rankings, the SVCS prompts clients at the outset of the procedure to rank order descriptions of the six Holland types printed on 5 x 8 cards in terms of how closely each type describes them. The Holland type descriptions come directly from the General Occupational Themes of the *Strong* (Slaney & Croteau, 1994). Revising the TVCS in this way "encouraged clients to think about themselves as whole persons and to examine their career possibilities from an integrated and holistic perspective from the start of the career exploration process" (Slaney et al., 1994, p. 350). A review of research on this modification gave some support to its efficacy as a method for deriving Holland codes, which correlated in one study more highly with expressed vocational interests and college majors than did deriving a code from the *Strong* (Slaney & MacKinnon-Slaney, 1990).

A second departure from the TVCS reflected in the initial SVCS concerns having individuals sort 4 x 6 cards with the Basic Interest Scales from the *Strong* into "Strong Interest," "Little or No Interest," and "Dislike" groups. This change paralleled Slaney's research that indicated stronger associations between measured and sorted basic interests than between measured and sorted occupations. To conserve administration time, later studies with the SVCS eliminated use of the basic interests, although it appears in one other study that they have been retained (Slaney & Croteau, 1994).

The third aspect of Slaney's card sort that differs from Tyler's original VCS but mirrors Dolliver's refinement involves placing 107 occupational titles from the *Strong* on 3 x 5 cards. Clients sort these cards into "Might Choose," "Would Not Choose," and "In Question" categories. Slaney also worked to turn the VCS into a self-directed procedure for assessing interests. Consequently, the SVCS has a companion manual for clients to use as a guide for self-administering the card sort and self-exploring occupations using Holland's Occupations Finder, the DOT, and the *Occupational Outlook Handbook*. While respecting counselors' and researchers' freedom to use the VCS as they see fit, Goldman (1995) also criticized making the VCS self-directed because doing so eliminates the client-counselor relationship so vital to the process-oriented nature of the approach.

Missouri Occupational Card Sort

Concerns about card sorts that lend themselves to self-directed use do not apply to the *Missouri Occupational Card Sort* (MOCS; Krieshok, Hansen, & Johnston, 1989), which by design requires a counselor's administration and involvement. To develop the MOCS Krieshok et al. incorporated the six Holland types, each represented by 15 occupations. Of the resulting 90 occupations most (63%) require a college degree, fewer (12%) require beyond a college degree, and the remainder (25%) require a high school education. A chapter by Gysbers, Heppner, and Johnston (1998) fully describes the MOCS, which is targeted primarily for use with college students.

Missouri Occupational Preference Inventory

Entitled an "inventory" yet designed as a card sort, the *Missouri Occupational Preference Inventory* (MOPI; Moore & Gysbers, 1987) seems aptly named given its differences from other card sorts as described by Slaney and MacKinnon-Slaney (1990), including its complex scoring scheme. The MOPI contains 180 occupations unevenly distributed across Holland types and three educational levels (i.e., high school, high school plus additional training, and college or post-graduate degree). Of note, the MOPI exceeds all other card sorts in terms of the number of occupations it includes at the high school level. Three-letter Holland occupational codes ranked by the client figure into deriving a specific Holland code for the client. On an accompanying worksheet (when the MOPI is not used as a self-directed card sort) the client and counselor summarize the client's (a) reasons for her or his likes and dislikes, (b) top five occupations and their Holland codes, (c) own Holland code, and (d) action plan. Slaney and MacKinnon-Slaney concluded that the MOPI offers a unique approach to the VCS process yet lacks any substantive research support.

Occupational Interest Card Sort

Knowdell (1993) developed the *Occupational Interest Card Sort* (OICS) as a means of clarifying occupations of interest as well as readiness for entering those occupations. The OICS contains 113 occupational title cards and extends the original number of category cards to five labeled "Definitely Interested," "Probably Interested," "Indifferent," "Probably Not Interested," and "Definitely Not Interested." As with various other card sorts that assess interests, the OICS incorporates supplemental activities. Nine specific career exploration exercises augment the OICS and focus on topics ranging from examining role models who have influenced one's vocational choices to preparing to conduct informational interviews.

Deal Me In Cards

Slaney et al. (1994) described the *Deal Me In Cards* (DMI; Farren, Kaye, & Leibowitz, 1985) as a card sort for initial career explorers, career changers, and career advancers. Parallels to a standard deck of playing cards emerge quite obviously in the DMI's title and in its inclusion of 52 interest and skill "playing cards." The DMI spreads these cards evenly over four occupational categories labeled data, people, things, and ideas, yielding 13 color-coded cards per category. Rather than using occupational titles, the face of each DMI card contains the name and a picture of an activity reflecting specific interest and skill areas such as appraising, computing, summarizing, and constructing. On the back of each card is listed the occupational category it represents. A workbook details 22 supplementary career development activities for use with the cards.

The DMI could be used in either individual or group counseling settings and it also lends itself to self-administration. Unlike other card sorts that basically incorporate Tyler's (1961) original procedures, the DMI provides instructions for both "solitaire" and three- to six-player "rummy." Solitaire play begins with the individual shuffling and then dealing the cards face up into four rows of 13 cards each. The "player" then selects 10 cards that best represent her or his interests. Turning over the cards reveals the player's "strong suits" in terms of the number of cards selected that represent each occupational category (i.e., data, people, ideas, or things). Next the player refers to the DMI "question card." This card leads the player to review and explore the choices made and consider possible career options listed on four additional DMI cards containing specific occupational titles for each category. Rummy follows a similar progression, leading all players to select their "suits" of interest and then match those selections with occupations listed on the four accompanying occupational title cards.

CONCLUSION

A central thesis of this chapter holds that the VCS technique by design positions clients actively at the center and in control of the career assessment and counseling process. Because the technique empowers clients to construct and organize their own personal realities about work and career, the VCS can help (a) dispel any preconceived mythic ideas clients, counselors, or counselors-in-training may have about the content and process of career counseling (e.g., career counseling means taking a "test" that will tell the client what type of work she or he should do) and (b) circumvent the potential problems (e.g., race or gender bias and inattention to cultural identity issues) that may accompany measuring a client relative to a normative standard. In essence, then, this chapter elaborates the perspective articulated elsewhere (Goldman, 1983; Gysbers, Heppner, & Johnston, 1998; Slaney & MacKinnon-Slaney, 1990; Slaney & Croteau, 1995) that card sorts provide a useful means of enlivening career counseling generally and vocational interest assessment specifically by revealing how clients organize their occupational preferences and make career choices.

Unlike standardized interest assessment techniques based in a positivist philosophy and designed with predetermined response categories, card sorts derive from a primarily phenomenological perspective that empowers clients to develop their own response categories, construct their own meanings, and reflect on how they personally construe their interests and the career decision-making process. The VCS technique can actively engage client and counselor in collaboratively exploring both career choice content and career choice process. Card sorts focus on career choice content because they prompt clients to idiosyncratically classify occupations relative to their needs, interests, values, abilities, personality styles, and goals. Card sorts focus on career choice process because they reveal clients' task-approach styles, problem-solving methods, and decision-making strategies. The VCS technique can thus help career counselors identify the content of clients' interests *and* understand clients' unique organizing and decision-making styles that reveal how they arrived at their interest choices.

Attending to both content and process individualizes career assessment and counseling while also making it culturally relevant. As Goldman (1995) noted, "the VCS offers flexibility; it can readily be adapted to individuals or groups who differ in language, ethnic identity, age, or mental abilities" (p. 386). This flexibility allows counselors and researchers to design their own card sorts for use specific to their practice and investigative endeavors. For example, Peterson (1998) recently described a card sort technique based in cognitive theory and designed to assess a client's personal, self-generated level of occupational knowledge in terms of its complexity, structure, and integration. Peterson's technique supports constructivist approaches to career counseling and development and advances the VCS "as a means by which individuals actively construct an idiographic representation of their world of work" (p. 51). Developing a card sort to assess clients' mental models of the world of work provides counselors and researchers with an alternative method of exploring and making links between client self-knowledge and occupational knowledge. In terms of potential for other types of vocational card sort development, no known card sorts exist to assess role salience, only one card sort assesses values, and others could be developed to assess cultural values perhaps using Triandis's (1995) work on the cultural syndromes of individualism and collectivism as a guide.

The VCS technique offers an intervention strategy counselors can adapt to their own counseling approaches that by design invites addressing each client's cultural identity concerns while taking account of individual differences that may influence that person's career development and vocational behavior. It also offers a research tool to investigators interested in more idiographic, subjective, or contextual dimensions of vocational interest development and career counseling. In this way the VCS provides both career counseling practitioners and vocational psychology researchers with a versatile complement to standardized interest inventories.

REFERENCES

Bingham, W. V. (1937). *Aptitudes and aptitude testing.* New York: HarperCollins.

Brown, D., & Brooks, L. (1996). Introduction to theories of career development and choice: Origins, evolution, and current efforts. In D. Brown, L. Brooks, & Associates (Eds.), *Career choice and development* (3rd ed.). San Francisco: Jossey-Bass.

Campbell, D., & Hansen, J. C. (1981). *Manual for the SVIB-SCII.* Stanford, CA: Stanford University Press.

Carter, H. D. (1940). The development of vocational aptitudes. *Journal of Consulting Psychology, 4,* 185–191.

Cochran, L. R. (1985). Review of the Occ-U-Sort. In J. V. Mitchell, Jr. (Ed.), *Ninth mental measurements yearbook* (pp. 1076–1078). Lincoln: University of Nebraska Press.

Cochran, L. (1997). *Career counseling: A narrative approach.* Thousand Oaks, CA: Sage.

Collin, A. (1996). New relationships between researchers, theorists, and practitioners: A response to the changing context of career. In M. L. Savickas & W. B. Walsh (Eds.), *Handbook of career counseling theory and practice* (pp. 377–399). Palo Alto, CA: Davies-Black.

Cooper, J. F. (1976). Comparative impact of the SCII and the *Vocational Card Sort* on career salience and career exploration of women. *Journal of Counseling Psychology, 23,* 348–352.

Crites, J. O. (1985). Review of the Occ-U-Sort. In J. V. Mitchell, Jr. (Ed.), *Ninth mental measurements yearbook* (pp. 1077–1079). Lincoln: University of Nebraska Press.

Dewey, C. R. (1974). Exploring interests: A non-sexist method. *Personnel and Guidance Journal, 52,* 311–315.

Dolliver, R. H. (1967). An adaptation of the *Tyler Vocational Card Sort. Personnel and Guidance Journal, 45,* 916–920.

Dolliver, R. H. (1981). Test review: A review of five vocational card sorts. *Measurement and Evaluation is Guidance, 14,* 168–174.

Farren, C., Kaye, B., & Leibowitz, Z. (1985). *Deal me in.* Silver Springs, MD: Career Systems.

Fryer, D. (1931). *The measurement of interests.* New York: Henry Holt.

Goldman, L. (1983). The vocational card sort technique: A different view. *Measurement and Evaluation in Guidance, 16,* 107–109.

Goldman, L. (1995). Comment on Croteau and Slaney. *Career Development Quarterly, 43,* 385–386.

Gysbers, N. C., Heppner, M. J., & Johnston, J. A. (1998). *Career counseling: Process, issues, and techniques.* Needham Heights, MA: Allyn & Bacon.

Gysbers, N. C., & Moore, E. J. (1987). *Career counseling: Skills and techniques for practitioners.* Englewood Cliffs, NJ: Prentice Hall.

Harmon, L. W. (1997). Do gender differences necessitate separate career development theories and measures? *Journal of Career Assessment, 5,* 463–470.

Holland, J. L. (1985). *The Vocational Preference Inventory.* Odessa, FL: Psychological Assessment Resources.

Holland, J. L. (1994). *Self-Directed Search.* Odessa, FL: Psychological Assessment Resources.

Holland, J. L., & Associates. (1980). *Counselor's guide to the vocational exploration and insight kit (VEIK).* Palo Alto, CA: Consulting Psychologists Press.

Jepsen, D. A. (1990). Developmental career counseling. In W. B. Walsh & S. H. Osipow (Eds.), *Career counseling: Contemporary topics in vocational psychology* (pp. 117–158). Hillsdale, NJ: Erlbaum.

Jepsen, D. A. (1994). The thematic-extrapolation method: Incorporating career patterns into career counseling. *Career Development Quarterly, 43,* 43–53.

Jones, L. K. (1981). *Occ-U-Sort professional manual.* Monterey, CA: Publishers Test Service of CTB/McGraw-Hill.

Kelly, G. A. (1955). *The psychology of personal constructs.* New York: Norton.

Knowdell, R. L. (1991a). *Manual for Career Values Card Sort Kit*. San Jose, CA: Career Research and Testing.

Knowdell, R. L. (1991b). *Manual for Motivated Skills Card Sort*. San Jose, CA: Career Research and Testing.

Knowdell, R. L. (1993). *Manual for Occupational Interests Card Sort Kit*. San Jose, CA: Career Research and Testing.

Krieshok, T. S., Hansen, R. N., & Johnston, J. A. (1989). *Missouri Occupational Card Sort Manual*. Columbia: Career Planning and Placement Center, University of Missouri.

Moore, E. J., & Gysbers, N. C. (1987). *Manual for the Missouri Occupational Preference Inventory*. Columbia, MO: Human Systems Consultants.

Peterson, G. W. (1998). Using a vocational card sort as an assessment of occupational knowledge. *Journal of Career Assessment, 6*, 49–67.

Richardson, M. S. (1991). Work in people's lives: A location for counseling psychologists. *Journal of Counseling Psychology, 40*, 425–433.

Richardson, M. S. (1996). From career counseling to counseling/psychotherapy and work, jobs, and career. In M. L. Savickas & W. B. Walsh (Eds.), *Handbook of career counseling theory and practice* (pp. 347–360). Palo Alto, CA: Davies-Black.

Rosenberg, M. (1957). *Occupations and values*. New York: Free Press.

Savickas, M. L. (1992). *New directions in career assessment*. In D. H. Montross & C. J. Shinkman (Eds.), *Career development: Theory and practice* (pp. 336–355). Springfield, IL: Charles C. Thomas.

Savickas, M. L. (1995a). Constructivist counseling for career indecision. *Career Development Quarterly, 43*, 363–373.

Savickas, M. L. (1995b). Examining the personal meaning of inventoried interests during career counseling. *Journal of Career Assessment, 3*, 188–201.

Savickas, M. L. (1997). The spirit in career counseling: Fostering self-completion through work. In D. P. Bloch & L. J. Richmond (Eds.), *Connections between spirit and work in career development* (pp. 3–25). Palo Alto, CA: Davies-Black.

Slaney, R. B. (1978). Expressed and inventoried vocational interests: A comparison of instruments. *Journal of Counseling Psychology, 25*, 520–529.

Slaney, R. B., & Croteau, J. M. (1994). Two methods of exploring interests: A comparison of outcomes. *Career Development Quarterly, 42*, 252–261.

Slaney, R. B., & Croteau, J. M. (1995). Response to Goldman. *Career Development Quarterly, 43*, 387–389.

Slaney, R. B., & MacKinnon-Slaney, F. (1990). The use of vocational card sorts in career counseling. In C. E. Watkins and V. L. Campbell (Eds.), *Testing in counseling practice* (pp. 317–371). Hillsdale, NJ: Erlbaum.

Slaney, R. B., Moran, W. J., & Wade, J. C. (1994). Vocational card sorts. In J. T. Kapes, M. M. Mastie, & E. A. Whitfield (Eds.), *A counselor's guide to career assessment instruments* (3rd ed., pp. 347–360). Alexandria, VA: National Career Development Association.

Spokane, A. R. (1991). *Career intervention*. Englewood Cliffs, NJ: Prentice Hall.

Strong, E. K., Jr. (1938). *Psychological aspects of business*. New York: McGraw-Hill.

Strong, E. K., Jr., Hansen, J. C., & Campbell, D. (1994). *Strong Interest Inventory*. Palo Alto, CA: Consulting Psychologists Press.

Super, D. E. (1954). Career patterns as a basis for vocational counseling. *Journal of Counseling Psychology, 1*, 12–20.

Triandis, H. C. (1995). *Individualism and collectivism*. Boulder, CO: Westview.

Tyler, L. E. (1961). Research explorations in the realm of choice. *Journal of Counseling Psychology, 8,* 195–201.

Tyler, L. E. (1964). Work and individual differences. In H. Borow (Ed.), *Man in a world at work*. Boston: Houghton-Mifflin.

Westbrook, B. W., & Mastie, M. M. (1982). Shall we sort the Occ-U-Sort into the might-choose, would-not-choose, or uncertain pile? *Measurement and Evaluation in Guidance, 15,* 259–266.

Young, R. A., & Valach, L. (1996). Interpretation and action in career counseling. In M. L. Savickas & W. B. Walsh (Eds.), *Handbook of career counseling theory and practice* (pp. 361–375). Palo Alto, CA: Davies-Black.

Young, R. A., Valach, L., & Collin, A. (1996). A contextual explanation of career. In D. Brown, L. Brooks, & Associates (Eds.), *Career choice and development* (3rd ed., pp. 477–512). San Francisco: Jossey-Bass.

SECTION THREE

USING VOCATIONAL INTERESTS IN CAREER INTERVENTION

T HE INFORMATION IN SECTION 2 about the technical problems involved in assessing interests provides a crucial background for appreciating the challenges inherent in best using interest assessments in career intervention, which is the topic of Section 3. The results of an interest inventory must be interpreted by the counselor and communicated to the client in a manner that effectively increases self-knowledge, eases decision making, and informs life planning. In the first chapter Tinsley and Chu report the results of their comprehensive review of 65 studies dealing with the outcomes of test and inventory interpretation. They conclude that although psychologists have been using interest inventories in various types of interventions for more than 60 years, there is little empirical evidence concerning this practice. The evidence that does exist suggests that group interpretation of results seems to be as effective as individual interpretation interviews, yet clients clearly prefer the individual interview. Tinsley and Chu recommend the use of visual aids as adjuncts in inventory interpretation, whether it be to individuals or groups. They also identify important topics that merit further study and offer sage advice on how to design future studies that address these issues.

Despite the lack of empirical guidelines for inventory interpretation, career counselors routinely interpret interest inventories to their clients. Therefore, in the next chapter Zytowski addresses the practical issue of how counselors "should" interpret inventories to clients. He approaches this challenging task by first asking, "How do clients encode, store, and retrieve information from their interest inventory profiles and interpretations?" and answers, "Not well!" He bases his answer on research that shows clients contacted after counseling recall minimal information about their inventory results. Zytowski urges researchers to address this important practice issue by studying how counselors can most effectively and efficiently communicate interest inventory results so that their clients can encode, store, and retrieve the information. This does not mean how to interpret interest inventory profiles; rather it means how to talk to clients about the counselor's interpretation of these profiles. Until researchers clarify the communication dimension of interest inventory intervention, Zytowski has some advice to offer counselors. After reflecting on his more than 30 years' experience as a career counselor and sifting through the research reviewed by Tinsley and Chu, Zytowski offers five principles to guide counselors as they communicate to clients the results of interest measurement. He closes the chapter with a transcript that demonstrates how he applied these principles during one counseling session.

In addition to interpreting interest measurements that identify what a client likes to do, many counselors also attend to what a client can do well. In these discussions client and counselor consider the realism of a client's vocational interests—that is, whether the client possesses or can develop the requisite skills and abilities to pursue all of her or his interests. These conversations are often informed by assessments of the client's work-relevant abilities, ability self-estimates, or skill self-efficacy. Thus the joint interpretation of interest and ability measurements is an important topic in interest inventory intervention. Accordingly, the next two chapters of Section 3 address the topic of joint interpretation of interest and ability measures. The first chapter, written by Prediger, deals with *ability self-estimates,* which have objective, external referents, whereas the second chapter, written by Betz, deals with *ability self-confidence* measures, which have more subjective, internal referents. Both types of self-appraisals can be extremely useful when interpreted in conjunction with interest measures.

In the chapter on ability self-estimates Prediger examines the joint use of interest and ability data in focusing career exploration. He reminds counselors that ability data can be used, like interest assessments are used, to identify fitting occupations for clients to explore. To be a useful guide to occupational exploration, ability assessments must be comprehensive in spanning the diverse occupational fields in the world of work. Unfortunately, most tests miss many work-relevant abilities and hence are poorly coordinated to the structure of the world of work. Prediger solves this problem by making a compelling argument for the use of ability self-estimates because they both comprehensively span the world of work and coordinate with the structure of occupations. Prediger bolsters his argument by presenting evidence that ability self-estimates add unique information to the data provided by interest inventories. He shows that when both interest and ability self-estimate data agree, counselors can have greater confidence in their recommendations concerning which occupations clients should explore first. Prediger concludes the chapter with 10 suggestions for counselors who want to integrate ability self-estimates with interest data. A case study illustrates application of these suggestions.

In the corresponding chapter on ability self-confidence, Betz focuses attention on what should happen after clients learn the results of their interest inventories. In short, they should engage in activities to explore their strongest interests and how to implement them in educational and vocational choices. In thoroughly addressing this critical topic of encouraging clients to act on their interests, Betz draws on the construct of self-efficacy. First she reviews the literature about the role of self-esteem and self-efficacy in vocational behavior, emphasizing their importance for career exploration and decision making. Next she presents a precis of self-efficacy theory and its implications in the vocational realm. Betz offers an important discussion that distinguishes self-efficacy, or self-confidence, from self-estimates of abilities. Then she explains the advantages, and offers two case examples, of career counseling that uses a joint interpretation of self-efficacy and interest measurements. In concluding the chapter, Betz reviews theoretical models that link self-efficacy to interest development and gives examples of intervention research aimed at increasing interests and strengthening confidence in occupational choices.

The final chapter in Section 3 also takes up the topic of encouraging clients to act on their interests, in this case engage in vocational exploratory behavior. Blustein and Flum apply motivational theory to better articulate the link between vocational interests and career exploration. Using a self-determination model, Blustein and Flum explain how interests and exploration interact in charting a career course. They start by defining career exploration as an openness to experiences that fosters self-discovery and prompts reflection about environmental options. Next they define interests as a "central affective synthesis" that assimilates these exploratory experiences into a coherent sense of self. Thus interests link personal needs and environmental action. Blustein and Flum advance their theoretical argument about the interest-exploration nexus by placing it in relational and cultural context. They explain that secure relationships allow individuals to experience and act on their interests. People who experience intrapsychic and interpersonal support from family and friends are better able to explore the world of work and then implement their interests. Individuals with ambivalent attachments to significant others may hesitate to explore interests that could risk their relationships.

Even worse, individuals who are insecurely attached to significant others may lack a secure base from which to venture into the world, thus choosing to avoid career exploration and forego interest implementation. Individuals who do not crystallize intrinsic interests may select activities and jobs because they yield important outcomes, not because they find the activity to be intrinsically interesting. Blustein and Flum provide a theoretical model to explain how activities pursued for extrinsic outcomes may in due course become intrinsically interesting. The proposed developmental pathway that links extrinsic importance to intrinsic interests offers a heuristic new perspective for counselors and researchers committed to fostering interest-based exploration. Furthermore, Blustein and Flum's ideas about interpersonal relationships and interests explicitly articulate a critical dimension of career exploration. Blustein and Flum's views about using the counseling relationship as a secure base for career exploration contributes a central idea to evolving theories of career counseling, one with immediate implications for practitioners who eschew the distinction between personal and career counseling.

CHAPTER TWELVE

Research on Test and Interest Inventory Interpretation Outcomes

Howard E. A. Tinsley and Serena Chu

RESEARCH HAS SHOWN a pervasive hindsight bias ("I knew that all along") that influences our reactions to the findings of psychological research. Perhaps that is because psychologists investigate issues that pertain to everyday life, and our collective body of folk wisdom covers every possibility: "A stitch in time saves nine," or "Haste makes waste." In retrospect the findings of many psychological investigations seem obvious, and therefore trivial. For this reason we suggest that you think about the issues raised in Table 12.1 before reading this chapter. These questions raise important issues about which every practicing psychologist should be knowledgeable, yet they are just a few of the questions that seem important to us. We suggest you jot down your answers to the questions in Table 12.1 and to any additional questions that interest you. Then as you read this chapter, see how accurately you predicted the findings we gleamed from the literature.

REVIEW PROCEDURE

Psychologists have been using tests in various types of interventions for over 60 years, so it seems logical that there would be a significant body of research bearing on the issues raised in Table 12.1. We began with the reviews of Goldman (1971) and Goodyear (1990). We included in our review the 33 references from Goldman's book that were relevant to this topic and all 92 references in Goodyear's review,

TABLE 12.1   Test Your Knowledge of the Outcomes of Test Interpretation

1. The literature now contains more than 400 studies of Holland's theory and more than 300 investigations of the theory of work adjustment. How many studies of test interpretation outcomes have been published?

    a) < 25   b) 50   c) 100   d) 200   e) > 300

2. How many good quality, well-controlled investigations of test interpretation outcomes have been published?

    a) < 10   b) 25   c) 50   d) 100   e) > 150

3. Rank order the following test interpretation approaches in terms of their demonstrated effectiveness.

    a) Individual test interpretation interview
    b) Group test interpretation interview
    c) Computerized test interpretation
    d) Self-interpretation of a test
    e) Use of a standard set of printed materials to guide test interpretation

4. Rank order the five test interpretation approaches listed in question 3 in terms of clients' preferences for the approach.

5. The use of visual aids during test interpretation
    a) Lessens the effectiveness of the test interpretation.
    b) Does not influence the effectiveness of the test interpretation.
    c) Increases the effectiveness of the test interpretation.

6. Involving the client as an active participant in the test interpretation
    a) Lessens the effectiveness of the test interpretation.
    b) Does not influence the effectiveness of the test interpretation.
    c) Increases the effectiveness of the test interpretation.

regardless of whether they were actually cited (75 references) or not cited (17 references) in his review. Next we performed a Silver Platter search on topics related to test and inventory interpretation outcomes using the PsychLIT data bases for (a) journal articles, 1974–1990, (b) journal articles, 1991–May 1997, and (c) chapters and books, 1988–May, 1997. Finally, we did a manual search of every issue of the following journals published in 1990 through May 1997: *Career Development Quarterly, Journal of Career Assessment, Journal of Career Development, Journal of College Student Development, Journal of Consulting and Clinical Psychology, Journal of Counseling and Development, Journal of Counseling Psychology, The Counseling Psychologist, Measurement and Evaluation in Counseling and Development,* and *Psychological Assessment.*

Many of the studies we found focused on related issues such as the Barnum effect and recipient gullibility (e.g., O'Dell, 1972) or recipient preference for a tentative or an absolute interpretation style (e.g., Jones & Gelso, 1988). We found only 65 articles that directly investigated test interpretation outcomes (see Table 12.2). (Parenthetically we note the important distinctions Crites and Walsh draw in this volume between tests and inventories. For convenience's sake we sometimes refer to both tests and inventories as tests in this chapter.) Of these, 19 were published in the 1950s, 17 in the 1960s, and 19 in the 1970s. Only seven relevant studies were published in the 1980s and we found only three that were published in the 1990s.

The total volume of competently done and adequately reported research studies is far less than the 65 studies identified in Table 12.2. We used liberal inclusion criteria, so many of the studies included in Table 12.2 were described inadequately, particularly those done in the 1950s and 1960s. In many instances it was not possible to determine precisely what was done (e.g., the nature of the test or inventory interpretation manipulation) nor to have any confidence in the results. In those instances the reader must take the author's conclusions on faith. Our first conclusion therefore is that the empirical foundation on which to base such an important intervention as psychological assessment and test and inventory interpretation is shockingly inadequate.

PROTOTYPICAL STUDY

Sampling

Sixty-two of the published investigations of test interpretation outcomes used high school or college students as participants. One study used adults, two used elementary or middle school students, and one did not describe the test interpretation recipients. Only eight studies have been published in which actual clients served as participants, and seven of these were published 20 or more years ago. Laboratory analogue research in which volunteers are used is much easier to do than investigations involving actual clients, but actual clients and volunteers can be expected to differ on a number of important dimensions. The use of high school and college student volunteers in this research is a decided advantage for those psychologists working with such clients, but psychologists working with other types of clients will find virtually no guidance in the literature.

TABLE 12.2   Design Features of Test Interpretation Outcome Studies

Authors	Recipients	Randomly Assigned	Control Group Used	Method of Test Interpretation	Visual Aid Used	FU Data Obtained	Measure of Agreement	Description of Interpretation	Interpretation Length Reported
Adamek (1961)	b	Yes	Yes	a,c	a	a	a	a	No
Atanasoff & Slaney (1980)	d	Yes	Yes	c,d,e	b	c	a	a	No
Barak & Friedkes (1981)	d	Yes	No	a,b	a	a	a	b	Yes
Barrett (1967)	b	Yes	Yes	b	a	a,c	b	c	No
Berdie (1954)	d	Yes	Yes	NG	a	d	c	a	No
Bivlofsky et al. (1953)	b	No	No	a,b	b	NG	a	b	No
Brown (1966)	NG	NG	Yes	NG	a	a	b	a	No
Buffer (1967)	b	No	Yes	a	a	b	b	c	Yes
Cooper (1976)	d	Yes	Yes	a	c	c	a	b	No
Crane (1978)	d	No	No	b	a	a	a	a	No
Davidshofer et al. (1976)	d	NG	Yes	b	b	a	a	c	Yes
Dressel & Mattson (1950)	d	No	No	a	b	d	a	e	Yes
Fernald (1964)	d	No	No	a	b	a,d	a	c	Yes
Finn & Tonsager (1992)	c	Yes	Yes	a	b	a,c	a	c	Yes
Folds & Gazda (1966)	d	Yes	Yes	a,b,c	b	c,d	c	e	Yes
Foreman & James (1973)	c	NG	Yes	a,b	a	c,d	a	a	No
Forster (1969)	d	Yes	No	a,d	c	a	a	c	Yes
Froehlich (1954)	d	No	No	a	a	a	c	b	No
Froehlich & Moser (1954)	b	No	No	a,b	b	e	a	b	No
Graff et al. (1972)	c	Yes	Yes	a,b,c	a	a	a	b	Yes

TABLE 12.2 Design Features of Test Interpretation Outcome Studies *continued*

Authors	Recipients	Randomly Assigned	Control Group Used	Method of Test Interpretation	Visual Aid Used	FU Data Obtained	Measure of Agreement	Description of Interpretation	Interpretation Length Reported
Hansen et al. (1994)	d	No	No	b	b	e	a	c	No
Hay et al. (1976)	c	Yes	Yes	a,b	a	a	a	b	Yes
Herman & Ziegler (1961)	e	Yes	Yes	a	a	NG	a	b	Yes
Hewer (1959)	d	Yes	No	a,b	a	a	a	a	No
Hill (1954)	d	No	No	NG	a	a	b	a	No
Hills & Williams (1965)	c	NG	Yes	a	a	a	a	c	No
Hoffman et al. (1981)	d	Yes	No	b,c,f	b	b	a	c	Yes
Holmes (1964)	d	No	No	a	b	a,b	a	c	No
Hoyt (1955)	d	Yes	Yes	a,b	b	d	b	a	No
Johnson (1953)	c	No	No	a	a	a,c	b	a	No
Johnson et al. (1981)	d	No	No	NG	a	a	a	a	No
Kamm & Wrenn (1950)	c	No	No	a	a	b,c,d	a	a	No
Karr (1968)	c	Yes	Yes	a	a	c	b	b	No
Kerr & Ghrist-Priebe (1988)	b	Yes	Yes	a,b	c	d	a	c	Yes
Kivlighan et al. (1981)	d	Yes	No	b	a	a,c	a	a	No
Kivlighan & Shapiro (1987)	d	No	No	c	a	a	a	a	No
Krivatsy & Magoon (1976)	d	Yes	Yes	a,c	a	d	a	a	No
Lallas (1956)	b	No	Yes	a,b	a	NG	c	b	No
Lane (1952)	b	Yes	No	a	a	b,c	a	c	No
Lister & Ohlsen (1965)	a,b	Yes	Yes	a	b	a,d	c	e	No

TABLE 12.2 Design Features of Test Interpretation Outcome Studies *continued*

Authors	Recipients	Randomly Assigned	Control Group Used	Method of Test Interpretation	Visual Aid Used	FU Data Obtained	Measure of Agreement	Description of Interpretation	Interpretation Length Reported
McMahon (1973)	d	Yes	Yes	c	b	c	a	c	No
Miller & Cochran (1979)	b	Yes	Yes	a,b	a	a	c,b	a	Yes
Mules (1972)	d	NG	NG	a,e	a	NG	a	b	No
Mulroy (1974)	b	Yes	NG	e	a	b	a	b	No
Oliver (1977)	d	Yes	No	a,b,e	b	a	a	c	Yes
Pilato & Myers (1975)	b	Yes	Yes	b,e	b	c,d	c	c	No
Power et al. (1979)	b	No	No	c,d	a	c	a	a	No
Randahl et al. (1993)	d	No	Yes	b	a	e	a	b	Yes
Robertson (1958)	b	No	No	a	a	a	a	b	Yes
Robertson (1959)	d	No	No	NG	a	e	c	b	No
Rogers (1954)	d	No	No	a	b	e	c	d	No
Rubinstein (1978)	d	Yes	Yes	a,b	b	c	c	b	No
Seaquist (1970)	d	Yes	No	d,e	b	a,c	a	b	No
Singer & Stefflre (1954)	b	No	No	NG	a	d	c	a	No
Snyder & Clair (1977)	d	Yes	No	a	a	a	a	b	No
Snyder & Shenkel (1976)	d	NG	No	a	a	a	a	b	No
Swanson (1963)	b	NG	No	a,b	b	d	a	b	No
Tipton (1969)	d	Yes	Yes	a	a	a,c	a	c	Yes
Torrance (1954)	d	No	No	b	a	d	c	a	No
Tuma & Gustad (1957)	d	Yes	Yes	a	a	a	a	c	No

TABLE 12.2 Design Features of Test Interpretation Outcome Studies *continued*

Authors	Recipients	Randomly Assigned	Control Group Used	Method of Test Interpretation	Visual Aid Used	FU Data Obtained	Measure of Agreement	Description of Interpretation	Interpretation Length Reported
Walker (1965)	b	NG	Yes	a,b,d,f	b,c	c	a	c	No
Westbrook (1974)	d	Yes	Yes	b	a	a,d	a	b	No
Wilkerson (1967)	a	NG	No	a,b,d	c	NG	a	c	No
Wright (1963)	d	Yes	Yes	a,b	b	a,d	c	c	Yes
Young (1955)	d	No	Yes	a	c	a	a	c	Yes

Recipients: a = grade/middle school students, b = high school students, c = university counseling center clients, d = university students, e = adults, NG = not given; Randomly Assigned: Recipients randomly assigned to treatment conditions (NG = not given); Control group used: NG = not given; Method of Test Interpretation: a = individual test interpretation interview, b = group test interpretation interview, c = participant self-interpretation, d = use of standard printed material, e = computerized interpretation, f = audio interpretation; Visual Aid: a = none used, b = profile used, c = aid in addition to or instead of profile used; Follow-up Data Obtained: a = immediately; b = 1 day to 1 week; c = 1 week to 1 month, d = > 1 month but < 1 year, e = > 1 year; Measure of Agreement Used: a = no measure, b = pre/post-self-estimate taken but no detail given, c = pre/post-self-estimate taken, detail given; Description of Interpretation: a = no explanation given (no mention of interpretation taking place), b = interpretation given, but no details provided, c = list of activities involved in interpretation, but no specific description provided, d = some specific details about the interpretation provided but description not totally adequate, e = detailed description provided; Interpretation Length Reported: Y = yes, N = no.

A convincing evaluation of test interpretation outcomes requires the random assignment of participants to the alternative treatment modalities and the use of a control group against which to compare the results. These basic principles of competent experimental design have been ignored in over half of the research on test interpretation outcomes. Random assignment to treatment and control groups was made in 32 of the 65 studies, and the use of a control group occurred in 31 of the 65 studies.

Type of Test

Almost all of the research used career counseling types of instruments. The modal study of test interpretation interventions has been performed using aptitude and ability scores, followed closely by research in which personality tests were used. There is virtually no research bearing on the communication of interest test results. The use of tests in individual psychotherapy, couples counseling, family counseling, substance abuse counseling, or any of the many other specialty areas in which psychologists function has not been investigated. It seems inarguable that test interpretation in those areas requires special skills and technologies, and that the outcomes of test interpretation interventions may differ from those in career counseling. Therefore psychologists who work in those areas have virtually no guidance from the empirical literature.

WHAT WE KNOW ABOUT THE OUTCOME OF TEST INTERPRETATION INTERVENTIONS

Client Gain

A crucial question is whether test interpretation is associated with greater client gain. Despite the paucity of research on the outcomes of test interpretation, some reviewers have taken the Pollyanna approach, concluding that "counselors can have some confidence that the interpretation of test results to clients has a positive effect" (Goodyear, 1990, p. 246). In drawing this conclusion Goodyear and other reviewers appear to have been unduly influenced by Oliver and Spokane's (1988) meta-analysis, which examined the results of research on individual and group test interpretations. They reported a mean effect size of .62 (standard deviation = .23) for individual test interpretation based on four comparisons from two studies and a mean effect size of .76 (standard deviation = 1.54) for group test interpretation based on 12 comparisons from four studies. The latter effect size is not significantly greater than zero, so the proper interpretation is that the published literature fails to support the efficacy of group test interpretation. The most parsimonious conclusions that we can draw from our review of the literature are that (a) not much research has been done on this issue, (b) the research that has been done is of rather poor quality, and (c) there is no coherent body of evidence demonstrating the efficacy of test interpretation as an intervention.

Method of Interpretation

Another important question concerns the relative effectiveness of the alternative methods of test interpretation. Oliver (1977) reviewed six studies comparing the effectiveness of individual, group, and programmed test interpretations. The research has shown no consistent differences in the effectiveness of these modes of test interpretation. Nevertheless, most studies showed that the individual test interpretation interview was the preferred presentation mode across a wide variety of criteria (e.g., asking clients which presentation mode was favored, most satisfactory, clearest, most helpful, and most liked). Krivatsy and Magoon (1976) reported an analysis in which they concluded that an individual test interpretation is six times more costly than a group test interpretation. Given its greater cost and lack of demonstrated superiority, there appears to be no rational basis for providing individual test interpretations.

One of the major innovations in the last three decades has been the development of self-interpreting interest inventories such as the *Self-Directed Search*. Recently the *Campbell Interests and Skills Survey* (CISS) has been offered for self-interpretation. We have heard numerous expressions of concern that clients will make serious mistakes in attempting to interpret the CISS for themselves, yet we found only seven investigations in which the effectiveness of self-interpretation was considered (see Table 12.2). The specific test interpretation interventions varied across studies, as did the specific research objectives, but investigators typically reported no differences among the modes of test interpretation. Nevertheless, we are struck by the indifference the discipline has shown to evaluating this important innovation in test interpretation. This lack of systematic empirical scrutiny forces psychologists to fall back on their biases and preconceived notions in making decisions about this crucial issue.

We are reminded of the procedure in use at the University of Oregon in the early 1970s. Clients who requested career services were required to complete an interest inventory and participate in a group interpretation session before they could see a counselor for career counseling. Procedures such as this make many psychologists feel a bit uncomfortable. We like to be open, available, and responsive to our clients, and this procedure seems to hold them at a distance. Nevertheless, while recipients prefer the individual test interpretation interview, the evidence suggests that group and self-interpretation procedures are just as efficacious and far more economical than individual interpretations.

Client Variables

Another issue that has stimulated some research interest addresses whether client or counselor attributes are associated with the effectiveness of test interpretation interventions. Typically these studies have been performed using aptitude tests, and a wide variety of attributes have been studied including age, grade, psychological adjustment, and client/ counselor similarity. The only dependable relation identified in this research is that brighter clients are better able to remember test interpretation results. This finding is tautological, of course, because scores on tests of "brightness" typically are heavily influenced by short-term and long-term memory. The lack of a relation between counselor-client similarity and test interpretation effectiveness is particularly noteworthy as it undercuts the position of those who advocate matching clients and counselors.

Degree of Client Participation

Tinsley and Bradley (1986) recommended that counselors engage the client as an active participant in test interpretation, and they suggested several ways to accomplish this. We found nine studies on this issue, most of which were conducted in the 1950s and 1960s. There was no demonstrated empirical relation between degree of client participation and the effectiveness of test or inventory interpretation. Personally we question the conclusion that the client who just sits there like a bump on a log obtains as much benefit from a test interpretation as the client who actively participates in the interpretation process, but that may simply reveal the inflexibility of our preconceived notions. This is an extremely important issue that deserves the attention of the discipline, but virtually no research has been done on this issue in the last 30 years.

Visual Aids

Tinsley and Bradley (1986) also recommended that counselors use both the profile and additional visual aids to communicate test information. For example, figures depicting a series of nine stair steps or a thermometer with values from zero to 100 can be used to communicate concepts such as stanines and percentile ranks, respectively. They argued that visual techniques such as these help clients understand more clearly the meaning of their scores. We found 22 investigations in which recipients were shown the test profile as an aid in test interpretation, but only 6 investigations in which recipients were shown some other type of interpretive aid in addition to or in place of the test profile. The interpretive aids included a wide variety of materials (e.g., a card sort, programmed interpretive manual, personal mapping of future goals, and other handouts). Five of the six studies reported results that suggested that a test or inventory interpretation in which a visual aid is used is more efficacious than an interpretation unaccompanied by a visual aid. While encouraging, it is premature to draw firm conclusions from this sparse literature.

EVALUATION OF THE RESEARCH

The research on test interpretation outcomes is generally flawed in numerous ways. This section discusses the most common and serious flaws and identifies improvements that are needed in future research.

Criterion Issue

An important question that has received very little attention asks, "Precisely what do we expect a test interpretation to accomplish?" This is the heart of the criterion issue, for meaningful research on test and inventory interpretation outcomes cannot be undertaken without considering the desired outcome. For example, reasonable objectives might include learning factual information, changing attitudes or behaviors, or influencing future decision making.

The typical criterion used in research on test and inventory interpretation outcomes has been the recall of specific scores. Change in the accuracy of self-estimates has also been used with some frequency. Often a within-subjects design has been used, in which a pretest is given to measure the client's knowledge or self-estimate; the inventory is then interpreted for the client, and a posttest measure of the criterion is obtained. Follow-up data were obtained immediately following the intervention in 32 of the 65 investigations we found (see Table 12.2). Only four studies have used a one-year follow-up. Contrast this situation with medical research in which the effectiveness of therapies for diseases such as cancer is measured in terms of survival rates after five years. Test interpretations are intended to accomplish immediate, intermediate, and long-term objectives, and research is needed to evaluate each of these.

Berdie (1954) long ago criticized the use of recall of specific test or inventory scores as a criterion because it fails to distinguish between learning (i.e., the ability to reproduce the results verbally—in this instance the mere parroting back of what was said) and accepting (i.e., integrating the information into the self-concept for use in making meaningful life decisions). We would elaborate that distinction by adding "understanding" the meaning of the interpretation as an important objective. One goal of test or inventory interpretation is to stimulate clients to integrate the information into their self-concepts in a manner that it can be used in decision making. It is essential that clients accurately understand the meaning of the inventory results before they integrate them into their self-concept. The criteria that have been used in assessing test interpretation outcomes are totally inadequate for evaluating this issue. Given this, we reiterate our contention that there is absolutely no evidence that any form of test or inventory interpretation intervention produces this type of outcome. It is this lack of attention to the basic effectiveness of test interpretations in producing favorable effects that led Goldman (1972) to characterize tests and counseling as "the marriage that failed" and caused others to decry testing as a fraud.

Another issue that has not even begun to enjoy scrutiny is the effects of test interpretation on the counselor. Most investigators who have studied test or inventory interpretation outcomes seem to have conceptualized the interpretation as an intervention that is intended to do something to the recipient. However, close to four decades ago Goldman (1961) pointed out that the administration and interpretation of tests can also be done to inform the counselor. Thus a second potentially important but totally overlooked set of criteria concerns the effects of test or inventory interpretation on the counselor. Furthermore, Goldman noted that test interpretation may be used as an intervention that is intended to stimulate the client to begin thinking about certain issues. Interpretation objectives such as these may be more difficult to operationalize, but they have great relevance to the work of the psychologist. Therefore a great deal of work is needed to address the criterion issue and to develop ways of measuring the effects of test and inventory interpretation.

Measure of Agreement

Investigators who use a pretest/posttest design must find some way of measuring the level of agreement between the pre- and posttest scores or the level of change from pretest to posttest. There are a variety of ways of doing this, including correlations, distance measures, t-tests, and analysis of variance, but the measure was described clearly in only 12 of the 65 investigations we found (see Table 12.2). Psychologists must consider the strengths and weaknesses of the alternative procedures, select the best procedure for their investigation, and clearly describe the procedure used.

Effective Element

Investigations of test and inventory interpretation outcomes must be designed so that it is possible to determine the element that was the effective agent in producing the outcome. An interpretation outcome can be attributed to at least four elements:

Interpreter competence. One is the competence of the counselor. Goldman (1971) observed that we as a profession may not be very effective in using and interpreting test information. To be informative an investigation must control for or provide some measure of the competence of the interpreter. We suggest that interpreter competence encompasses three elements: the interpreter's technical knowledge of the test and the meaning of the test scores, the clarity of the interpreter's communication skills, and the interpreter's ability to respond to the nonverbal elements of the interaction (i.e., to establish rapport and to perceive and respond effectively to the client). Each of these elements can influence the effectiveness of a test interpretation.

Client motivation. The second important element is the client's motivation. To benefit from a test interpretation the client must be motivated to participate in and gain something from the interpretation. Most prior research on test interpretation has simply assumed that the client is motivated to attend to the interpretation in a meaningful manner, even when volunteers have served as respondents. Investigations of test interpretation outcomes must ensure that at least a minimal level of client motivation is present or must include a measure of client motivation so that it can be related to the outcomes.

Client openness to change. The third important element is the client's openness or resistance to changing his or her self-concept. Tinsley and Bradley (1986) argued that clients are not necessarily always ready for a test interpretation; they may have other more pressing priorities for the counseling session. Even the readiness to hear test results does not mean that the recipient is ready to deal with threatening information, and any personally relevant information can be threatening. The degree of threat involved in the information is likely to be a function of the compatibility of the information with the client's self-concept and the client's openness or resistance to changing his or her self-concept.

A related variable is the client developmental level. Clients at different developmental levels may differ in their ability to process information. Prior research has not shown a relation between psychological adjustment and test interpretation outcomes, but there is evidence linking developmental level to counseling readiness and expectations about counseling (Tinsley, Hinson, Holt, & Tinsley, 1990).

Also important is the client's ability to deal with inaccurate or confusing information. Clients who do not challenge information that they perceive to be inaccurate or confusing may nevertheless reject the information. Measures of the posttest "accuracy" of self-estimates will provide a misleading view of the effects of test interpretation when events such as that occur.

Description of the Intervention

Rigorously designed research cannot be given its proper weight unless the counselor provides a clear, detailed, precise description of the interpretation intervention. It is not adequate to merely state that an individual interpretation interview or a group interpretation procedure was used, but that is the extent of the information that was provided about the interventions in 40 of the 65 studies we found (see Table 12.2). Given the paucity of research on test and inventory interpretation outcomes, we do not know what variables make an important difference. We may be able to identify procedures that are essentially comparable once a sufficient body of research has been published, but for the present it is important that investigators provide a detailed account of the method of interpretation used. Only 3 of the 65 studies we found provided sufficient information (see Table 12.2).

Manipulation Checks

A basic principle of experimental design is that whenever a manipulation is involved, the investigator must perform a check to establish that the intended effect of the manipulation was achieved. We reviewed each of the 65 studies to determine whether they included manipulation checks to eliminate or control for the following possible confounds: counselor competence, clarity of interpretation, client motivation, client resistance to change, threatening content in interpretation, accuracy of interpretation, and regression toward the mean. Only Hay and his colleagues (Hay, Rohen, & Murray, 1976; counselor competence) and Wright (1963; clarity of motivation) reported having performed a manipulation check.

CONCLUSION

The research evidence supports only three conclusions. First, group interpretation methods seem to be about as effective as the individual interpretation interview, given the methodological weaknesses cited above (e.g., flawed criteria, immediate follow-up, lack of random assignment, and lack of a control group). Second, individual interpretations are preferred by those receiving the interpretation. Third, use of a visual aid appears to increase the effectiveness of test or inventory interpretation. Beyond that, there is no coherent body of evidence that can be used to inform the practice of test or inventory interpretation.

Following are some crucial questions that we cannot answer.

1. What percentage of the time do we give clients the wrong advice when we do not use test or interest inventory information? This information is necessary to establish a baseline against which to judge the benefits of test and inventory interpretation.

2. What is the effectiveness of counseling with and without assessment? This is the essential issue. Psychologists use tests because they think their use improves their effectiveness in some way (e.g., improves services, makes more efficient use of the counselor's time, or provides information that would otherwise not be available). There is no coherent body of evidence that supports these beliefs.

3. What is the length of treatment for comparable problems with and without assessment? Holland (1985) argues that the use of self-report measures such as the *Self-Directed Search* can shorten the treatment process and in particular the amount of time that the client needs to spend with a therapist. We have no evidence pertaining to this issue.

4. What is the cost effectiveness of assessment? Everything considered, how much does it cost to provide comparable levels of service to a client when using and not using tests?

In brief, our review of the literature strongly supports Fouad's (this volume) conclusion that there is no evidence that interest inventories possess consequential validity. If the U.S. Food and Drug Administration had regulatory authority over psychological tests, it would ban their use with clients because their effectiveness has not been demonstrated. It is alarming to us to learn that there is no credible body of evidence to document that a test or interest inventory interpretation by a trained counselor is helpful. We think that a skillful interpretation is helpful, yet people think all sorts of things that are wrong.

The following tongue-in-cheek comment seems to accurately describe the attitude of many test users toward test interpretation:

> Actually, we don't like to worry about the validity of our tests because we find it makes us dizzy and it is not billable time. However, we do use multiple methods and cross-validate with tea leaf readings, palmistry, phrenology, and checking the client's horoscope. We take the interpretive statements of the computer completely at face value, especially since we got the new laser printer. (Pullyblank, 1997)

Readers must decide whether they are content to let this parody speak for them or whether the present state of affairs is sufficiently troubling that they will work for change.

REFERENCES

Adamek, G. (1961). The effects of testing and two methods of test interpretation on selected self-perceptions. *Dissertation Abstracts,* 3697. (Order #61-1588).

Atanasoff, G. E., & Slaney, R. B. (1980). Three approaches to counselor-free career exploration among college women. *Journal of Counseling Psychology, 27,* 332–339.

Barak, A., & Friedkes, R. (1981). The mediating effects of career indecision subtypes on career-counseling effectiveness. *Journal of Vocational Behavior, 20,* 120–128.

Barrett, R. L. (1967). A study of the influence of self-regard on changes in accuracy of self-estimates following the reporting of test results. *Dissertation Abstracts, 28,* 465–466.

Berdie, R. F. (1954). Changes in self-rating as a method of evaluating counseling. *Journal of Counseling Psychology, 1,* 49–54.

Bivlofsky, D., McMasters, W., Schorr, J. E., & Singer, S. L. (1953). Individual and group counseling. *Personnel and Guidance Journal, 31,* 363–365.

Brown, R. E. (1966). Acceptance of scholastic ability data and personal adjustment. *Vocational Guidance Quarterly, 14,* 111–114.

Buffer, J. J., Jr. (1967). A study of certain effects of test interpretation in counseling upon achievement and self-perceptions. *Dissertation Abstracts, 27,* 2063.

Cooper, J. F. (1976). Comparative impact of the SCII and the Vocational Card Sort on career salience and career exploration of women. *Journal of Counseling Psychology, 23,* 348–352.

Crane, J. K. (1978). A structured group for career exploration. *Journal of College Student Personnel, 19,* 182.

Davidshofer, C. A., Thomas, L. E., & Preble, M. G. (1976). Career development groups: A program description. *Journal of College Student Personnel, 17,* 413–416.

Dressel, P. L., & Mattson, R. W. (1950). The effect of client participation in test interpretation. *Educational and Psychological Measurement, 10,* 693–706.

Fernald, L. D. (1964). Client recall of test scores. *Personnel and Guidance Journal, 43,* 167–170.

Finn, S. E., & Tonsager, M. E. (1992). Therapeutic effects of providing MMPI-2 test feedback to college students awaiting therapy. *Psychological Assessment, 4,* 278–287.

Folds, J. H., & Gazda, G. M. (1966). A comparison of the effectiveness and efficiency of three methods of test interpretation. *Journal of Counseling Psychology, 13,* 318–324.

Foreman, M. E., & James, L. E. (1973). Vocational relevance as a factor in counseling. *Journal of Counseling Psychology, 20,* 99–100.

Forster, J. R. (1969). Comparing feedback methods after testing. *Journal of Counseling Psychology, 16,* 222–226.

Froehlich, C. P. (1954). Does test taking change self-rating? *California Journal of Educational Research, 5,* 166–169; 175.

Froehlich, C. P., & Moser, W. E. (1954). Do counselees remember test scores? *Journal of Counseling Psychology, 1,* 149–152.

Goldman, L. (1961). *Using tests in counseling.* Englewood Cliffs, NJ: Appleton-Century-Crofts.

Goldman, L. (1971). *Using tests in counseling* (2nd ed.). Santa Monica, CA: Goodyear.

Goldman, L. (1972). Tests and counseling: The marriage that failed. *Measurement and Evaluation in Guidance, 4,* 213–220.

Goodyear, R. K. (1990). Research on the effects of test interpretation: A review. *The Counseling Psychologist, 18,* 240–257.

Graff, R. W., Danish, S., & Austin, B. (1972). Reactions to three kinds of vocational-educational counseling. *Journal of Counseling Psychology, 19,* 224–228.

Hansen, J. C., Kozberg, J. G., & Goranson, D. (1994). Accuracy of student recall of *Strong Interest Inventory* results 1 year after interpretation. *Measurement and Evaluation in Counseling and Development, 26,* 235–242.

Hay, N. M., Rohen, T. M., & Murray, R. E. (1976). Three approaches to vocational counseling: A multifactor evaluation. *Journal of College Student Personnel, 17,* 475–479.

Herman, L. M., & Ziegler, M. L. (1961). The effectiveness of interpreting freshman counseling-test scores to parents in a group situation. *Personnel and Guidance Journal, 40,* 143–149.

Hewer, V. H. (1959). Group counseling, individual counseling, and a college class in vocations. *Personnel and Guidance Journal, 37,* 660–665.

Hill, J. M. (1954). The effects of artificially measured low aptitude test scores on change in vocational interest. *Dissertation Abstracts, 14,* 78.

Hills, D. A., & Williams, J. E. (1965). Effects of test information upon self-evaluation in brief educational-vocational counseling. *Journal of Counseling Psychology, 12,* 275–281.

Hoffman, M. A., Spokane, A. R., & Magoon, T. M. (1981). Effects of feedback mode on counseling outcomes using the *Strong-Campbell Interest Inventory:* Does the counselor really matter? *Journal of Counseling Psychology, 28,* 119–125.

Holland, J. L. (1985). *The Self-Directed Search professional manual* (Rev. ed.). Odessa, FL: Psychological Assessment Resources.

Holmes, J. E. (1964). The presentation of test information to college freshmen. *Journal of Counseling Psychology, 11,* 54–58.

Hoyt, D. P. (1955). An evaluation of group and individual programs in vocational guidance. *Journal of Applied Psychology, 39,* 26–30.

Johnson, D. G. (1953). Effect of vocational counseling on self-knowledge. *Educational and Psychological Measurement, 13,* 330–338.

Johnson, J. A., Smither, R., & Holland, J. L. (1981). Evaluating vocational interventions: A tale of two career development seminars. *Journal of Counseling Psychology, 34,* 326–329.

Jones, A. S., & Gelso, C. J. (1988). Differential effects of style of interpretation: Another look. *Journal of Counseling Psychology, 35,* 363–369.

Kamm, R. B., & Wrenn, C. G. (1950). Client acceptance of self-information in counseling. *Educational and Psychological Measurement, 10,* 32–42.

Karr, B. (1968). A proposed model for test interpretation. *Dissertation Abstracts International,* 3473-B. (Order #68-2006).

Kerr, B. A., & Ghrist-Priebe, S. L. (1988). Intervention for multipotentiality: Effects of a career counseling laboratory for gifted high school students. *Journal of Counseling and Development, 66,* 366–369.

Kivlighan, D. M., Hageseth, J. A., Tipton, R. M., & McGovern, T. V. (1981). Effects of matching treatment approaches and personality types in group vocational counseling. *Journal of Counseling Psychology, 28,* 315–320.

Kivlighan, D. M., & Shapiro, R. M. (1987). Holland type as a predictor of benefit from self-help career counseling. *Journal of Counseling Psychology, 34,* 326–329.

Krivatsy, S. E., & Magoon, T. M. (1976). Differential effects of three vocational counseling treatments. *Journal of Counseling Psychology, 23,* 112–118.

Lallas, J. E. (1956). A comparison of three methods of interpretation of the results of achievement tests to pupils. *Dissertation Abstracts, 16,* 1842.

Lane, D. (1952). A comparison of two techniques of interpreting test results to clients in vocational counseling. *Dissertation Abstracts, 12,* 591–592.

Lister, J. L., & Ohlsen, M. M. (1965). The improvement of self-understanding through test interpretation. *Personnel and Guidance Journal, 43,* 804–810.

McMahon, M. P. (1973). Effects of knowledge of ability test results on academic performance and text anxiety. *Journal of Counseling Psychology, 20,* 247–279.

Miller, M. J., & Cochran, J. R. (1979). Evaluating the use of technology in reporting SCII results to students. *Measurement and Evaluation in Guidance, 12,* 166–173.

Mules, W. C. (1972). A comparison of conventional modes of interpreting *Strong Vocational Interest Blank* results to modes which employ a computer generated, prose interpretation. *Dissertation Abstracts International,* 1445-A. (Order #72-26267).

Mulroy, J. P. (1974). A comparison of differential modes of interpretation of the *Strong Vocational Interest Blank* with high school juniors. *Dissertation Abstracts International, 34.* (Order #747-2689).

O'Dell, J. W. (1972). Barnum explores the computer. *Journal of Consulting and Clinical Psychology, 38,* 270–273.

Oliver, L. W. (1977). Evaluating career counseling outcome for three modes of test interpretation. *Measurement and Evaluation in Guidance, 10,* 153–161.

Oliver, L. W., & Spokane. A. R. (1988). Career intervention outcome: What contributes to client gain? *Journal of Counseling Psychology, 35,* 447–462.

Pilato, G. T., & Myers, R. A. (1975). The effects of computer mediated vocational guidance procedures on the appropriateness of vocational preference. *Journal of Vocational Behavior, 6,* 61–72.

Power, P. G., Holland, J. L., Daiger, D. C., & Takai, R. T. (1979). The relation of student characteristics to the influence of the *Self-Directed Search. Measurement and Evaluation in Guidance, 12,* 98–107.

Pullyblank, J. (1997). Message to Psychological Assessment—Psychometrics Electronic Discussion List (assess-p@maelstrom.stjohns.edu).

Randahl, G. J., Hansen, J. C., & Haverkamp, B. E. (1993). Instrumental behaviors following test administration and interpretation: Exploration validity of the *Strong Interest Inventory*. *Journal of Counseling and Development, 71,* 435–439.

Robertson, M. H. (1958). A comparison of counselor and student reports of counseling interviews. *Journal of Counseling Psychology, 5,* 276–280.

Robertson, M. H. (1959). Results of a pre-college testing and counseling program. *Personnel and Guidance Journal, 37,* 451–454.

Rogers, L. B. (1954). A comparison of two kinds of test interpretation interview. *Journal of Counseling Psychology, 1,* 224–231.

Rubinstein, M. R. (1978). Integrative interpretation of vocational interest inventory results. *Journal of Counseling Psychology, 25,* 306–309.

Seaquist, D. L. (1970). An investigation of the effectiveness of a programmed interpretive guide to the *Strong Vocational Interest Blank*. *Dissertation Abstracts International,* 3278-A. (Order #70-27166).

Singer, S. L., & Stefflre, B. (1954). Analysis of the self-estimate in the evaluation of counseling. *Journal of Counseling Psychology, 1,* 252–255.

Snyder, C. R., & Clair, M. S. (1977). Does insecurity breed acceptance? Effects of trait and situational insecurity on acceptance of positive and negative diagnostic feedback. *Journal of Consulting and Clinical Psychology, 45,* 843–850.

Snyder, C. R., & Shenkel, R. J. (1976). Effects of "favorability," modality, and relevance upon acceptance of general personality interpretations prior to and after receiving diagnostic feedback. *Journal of Consulting and Clinical Psychology, 44,* 34–41.

Swanson, R. A. (1963). A study of factors related to the distortion of interest inventory information interpreted to individuals and to groups. *Dissertation Abstracts, 304.* (Order #64-4214).

Tinsley, D. J., Hinson, J. A., Holt, M. S., & Tinsley, H.E.A. (1990). Level of psychosocial development, perceived level of psychological difficulty, counseling readiness and expectations about counseling: Examination of group differences. *Journal of Counseling Psychology, 37,* 143–148.

Tinsley, H.E.A., & Bradley, R. W. (1986). Test interpretation. *Journal of Counseling and Development, 64,* 462–466.

Tipton, R. M. (1969). Relative effectiveness of two methods of interpreting ability test scores. *Journal of Counseling Psychology, 16,* 75–80.

Torrance, E. P. (1954). Some practical uses of a knowledge of self-concepts in counseling and guidance. *Educational and Psychological Measurement, 14,* 120–127.

Tuma, A. H., & Gustad, J. W. (1957). The effects of client and counselor personality characteristics on client learning in counseling. *Journal of Counseling Psychology, 4,* 136–141.

Walker, J. L. (1965). Four methods of interpreting test scores compared. *Personnel and Guidance Journal, 44,* 402–405.

Westbrook, F. D. (1974). A comparison of three methods of group vocational counseling. *Journal of Counseling Psychology, 21,* 502–506.

Wilkerson, C. D. (1967). The effects of four methods of test score presentation to eighth grade students. *Dissertation Abstracts International,* 1318-A. (Order #67-12661).

Wright, E. W. (1963). A comparison of individual and multiple counseling for test interpretation interviews. *Journal of Counseling Psychology, 10,* 126–135.

Young, F. C. (1955). Evaluation of a college counseling program. *Personnel and Guidance Journal, 33,* 282–286.

CHAPTER THIRTEEN

How to Talk to People About Their Interest Inventory Results

Donald G. Zytowski

W<small>ILLIAM</small> C<small>OHEN</small>, the Secretary of Defense in the Clinton administration, former Republican Senator from Maine, and published novelist and poet, remarked while discussing aptitude tests for military recruits, "Those aptitude tests said back in high school that I should be a farmer. So here I am" ("Defense's Cohen," 1997).

Secretary Cohen may or may not be remembering his test results correctly, but he has apparently misunderstood their implications. I'm confident that the test did not say he *should* be a farmer. It might have said he had interests *like* those of farmers or that he had aptitudes consistent with a career in farming, that farmer was an occupation that might, from his high school perspective, provide a fair measure of job satisfaction or present some opportunity for success, and that he should consider carefully that occupation before rejecting it. (And how does anyone know that farming might not have been more rewarding than his career thus far?)

Results of psychological assessments ordinarily are first simply communicated to test- or inventory-takers or to interested others on a report form or verbally, e.g.: "You scored 68 on Scale A." Then the meaning for the individual must be derived by placing the results in a "frame of reference" (Levy, 1963). That is, they must be *interpreted*. For example, test results might be interpreted to answer a question of treatment modality: "I believe this score indicates that this individual would benefit from hospitalization," or "We regret to inform you that we cannot offer you admission to our program." In the case of interest inventories, results are typically communicated to the inventory-taker, who is helped in some way to discern their implications: "Your score of 68 indicates that your interests are very like those of city managers," or, "Your score of 68 on this scale suggests that you might find a career in public administration satisfying."

We don't know how Secretary Cohen's test results were communicated to him or what help he had in interpreting them. They might have come from a profiled report handed out in homeroom, with information on the back of the form explaining its most salient features. There might have been a teacher or a counselor present to call attention to these features and answer questions. There might even have been a psychometrically sophisticated counselor discussing the implications of his test results with him in a private session.

Experienced counselors know that such recollections as Cohen's are not uncommon. Their former clients often mistake the kind of assessment—interest or aptitude—that they had, remember results selectively or erroneously, or interpolate the imperative "should" into their assessment results. We also know that interest inventory profiles are less than perfectly stable over time, so that a recollection from one administration of an inventory may differ from a second one.

There are a few recent studies of accuracy of recall of interest inventory results. They are not encouraging. Toman and Savickas (1997), using a videotaped interpretation in small groups of the *Strong Interest Inventory* (SII; Harmon, Hansen, Borgen, & Hammer, 1994) with college students, found between 13% and 95% correct responses to the *Strong Interest Inventory* Retention Test (Miller & Cochran, 1979). Toman and Zytowski (1997), using an in-person large group interpretation with classroom discussion of the Kuder Occupational Interest Survey (Kuder & Zytowski, 1991), found 98% correctly remembered their highest Vocational Interest Estimate, but only 69% could recall correctly a college major ranking in the top range of their report. Hansen, Kozberg, and Goranson (1994), with an unspecified interpretation, found that college students contacted one year after receiving their SII results recalled them uncertainly: 36% could correctly remember their highest General Occupational Theme and 56% their highest Basic Interest Scale. (It is interesting to speculate why Basic Scales were better remembered than the simpler General Occupational Themes.) None of these studies addressed understanding of their results, such as the implications of a high score.

Accurate recall and appropriate interpretation of assessment results are but two consequences of test interpretation. Goodyear (1990) has reviewed studies of other outcomes—client satisfaction, exploratory behavior, and enhanced vocational identity or career maturity—and concluded that there is little evidence that they are differentially affected by one or another method of reporting but that individual interpretations are generally preferred over group procedures. As well, self-interpretations seem as effective—or should we say as ineffective—as counselor-mediated interpretations, while offering a significant cost saving.

As Goodyear's (1990) survey suggests, there are a variety of modes in which assessment results are communicated: without counselor interaction—a score report or profile with printed explanation; a narrative report; video or computer interactive supplement (e.g., Gati, 1987; Gati & Blumberg, 1991)—or with counselor interaction—individually; small group, with discussion; large group, with little or no discussion.

The makeup of the score report is fundamental, particularly in the case of self-interpretation, yet there is little empirical guidance for report authors. Strahan and Kelly (1994) have taken up the question recently, suggesting several alternative means of graphical presentation of inventory results. They assert that what you learn may depend on what you are shown and particularly *how* you are shown. This is a potentially fruitful focus of inquiry, especially with instruments that offer parallel graphic and narrative reports.

When counselors mediate the presentation of assessment results, their expertise must certainly be a crucial variable as well. For instance, they must know what is being measured and be prepared with vocabulary with which to report it sensibly to a person who is hearing about it for the first time. One should not describe a scale named "Conventional" without explaining that it incorporates "preferences for activities that entail the explicit, ordered, systematic manipulation of data" (Holland, 1997, p. 26).

As examples of other challenges that must be addressed, one popular instrument offers 253 scores of five kinds, in three different types of scaling. Another gives its results in terms of scores that are not described in any standard reference on psychometrics. A third presents its results in raw scores without particular note that gender differences occur on some of its scales.

Similarly there appear to be no universally accepted guidelines for what verbal descriptions attach to what score levels. One instrument's "high" description is assigned to t-scores of 60 or more (the equivalent of the 84th percentile in a normal distribution of scores), while another instrument's "high" begins at the 75th percentile. Yet a third instrument asks us to attend not to whether a score is in the "high" range but to its rank in an ordering by scores of all the scales.

Counselors also need sufficient grasp of the concept of standard error of measurement in order that they may say confidently, "You scored higher on Scale A than you did on Scale B," since interest inventory scores tend not to be accompanied by error bands. Holland's "Rule of 8" (Holland, Powell, & Fritzsche, 1994, p. 20) is a welcome exception.

It is ironic that we insist on the highest standards of test construction (*Standards for Educational and Psychological Testing, American Psychological Association,* 1985) and application (Eyde et al., 1993; *Responsibilities of Users of Standardized Tests, American Counseling Association,* 1989), but there is little generally approved guidance for how assessment results are to be communicated to facilitate appropriate interpretation and other desirable outcomes.

Counselors must do nothing less than strive to transmit to their clients as effectively as possible the results of assessments in general and interest inventories in particular. Guidance for this task can be found in some test manuals and in the journal literature: Crites (1981); Harmon, Hansen, Borgen, and Hammer (1994); Healy (1990); Kuder and Zytowski (1991); Shertzer and Linden (1979); Tinsley and Bradley (1986); and Zytowski and Borgen (1983), among others.

The following combines suggestions from the above sources that may be most relevant for interest inventories into a set of general principles, with examples added from my own counseling experience of how they may be realized. Bear in mind that interest inventory results do not tell you what career path a client *should* choose. They suggest options that may result in certain satisfactions and longevity, but other variables that go into a choice of one or another occupation should be incorporated into one's planning and decision making. Clients should gather more information about possibilities before committing to a course of action.

FIVE PRINCIPLES OF INTEREST INVENTORY INTERPRETATION

1. *Prepare for the discussion of results.* Tinsley and Bradley (1986) and Shertzer and Linden (1979) emphasize particularly that counselors take time ahead of the interview to familiarize themselves with the large and small details of the inventory results, select key points that require emphasis, and integrate them with information from other sources, such as previous interviews or records. Swanson (1992) suggests that we should generate hypotheses to be tested in the interpretation, paying attention to consistencies and inconsistencies within the profile as well as between the profile and case information.

Hood and Johnson (1997) advocate being sure that we have vocabulary ready for all the concepts that the inventory covers, including special scales. Garfield and Prediger (1994) even suggest that from time to time we discuss our intended interpretation with colleagues as a check to assure that we have not incorporated erroneous material.

2. *Involve clients in communicating results.* If there is one imperative that is supported by research, this is it. Dressel and Mattson (1950) established this principle early in the post-World War II surgence of career counseling, and it has been affirmed repeatedly since then. Anastasi (1988) suggests that we report results as answers to specific questions raised by the counselee. Crites (1981) and Healy (1990) state it more forcefully: The client and counselor should take the role of collaborators in understanding the results of an assessment. Clients should structure the interview by saying what they would like to hear about first (although Harmon et al. [1994] endorse an orderly sequence from simple to complex). Tinsley and Bradley suggest that we review what the inventory asked for (likes and dislikes for occupational titles or activities) and how it asked it (free or forced choice, etc.). I don't tell clients these things; I ask them to recall it for me—e.g., "What kinds of things did this inventory ask you about?"

In the computer-administered form of the *Kuder Occupational Interest Survey* DD/PC (Kuder & Zytowski, 1993), survey-takers are presented with a multiple-choice question about how they expect to use their results, perhaps thereby clarifying for them the possibilities involved. Alternatively, the counselor could present the various options orally before beginning the inventory interpretation process.

Gustad and Tuma (1957) found that asking clients to forecast their results produced better learning, not unlike Weinrach's (1980) technique of presenting clients with an alphabetical list of scales on the inventory and asking them to name their top- and bottom-ranking scales. When there are as few as 6 or 10 general interest scales to be discussed, their names and brief descriptions can be printed on cards and clients asked to sort them in the order they expect the inventory to reveal. The counselor then can rearrange their order, thereby presenting results in a physical mode that underlines the verbal meaning.

Almost all the sources so far mentioned suggest that clients be asked for reactions to their results. I have observed that this sometimes takes the form of asking clients to explain *why* they scored as they did. But this practice tends to place the inventory in the authoritative role and may cause the client to invent reasons that may or may not be valid. Rather, I prefer Healy's (1990) and Garfield and Prediger's (1994) perspective of helping the counselee to think of assessment interpretations as hypotheses to be checked against prior experience, compared with feedback from others, tested via mutually planned activities, and periodically reviewed and modified. I might ask, "What kinds of things like this have you done in the past?" or "How does this fit with what your friends say about you?"

3. *Use simple, emphatic communication.* Shertzer and Linden (1979) and Hood and Johnson (1997) both suggest the use of vivid, concrete communication—e.g., "You hit a home run on Scale A." They would avoid using acronyms (RIASEC or BIS, for instance), while Crites (1981) would substitute descriptive phrases ("Very High," "Average," etc.) for all numerical scores. Krumboltz and Vosvick (1996) advise that we match the language of the client, asserting that it speeds the process of access to deeper issues.

We might use alternative modes of communication. Emphasis can be added by colloquial speech or body language, or by graphics: making checkmarks or circling scores in colored pencils and drawing stick figures or faces. Having an illustration of the bell curve at hand to emphasize a high or low score is usually understood and helpful. Note that the local weather forecast on television is generally delivered verbally as well as in the form of graphics of sun, clouds, and raindrops. What analog to such graphics can test interpretation use?

Tinsley and Bradley (1986) urge counselors to let clients see their profiles or other report forms. I once asked a visually impaired counselor how she dealt with test interpretations. She replied that she simply gave the reports to her clients and asked them to find their top scores and tell her what they were. Although this sometimes results in too much attention to less to-the-point "special" scales, it does help emphasize that the clients should take a share of the responsibility for understanding their inventory results.

Also we can develop custom-made summary reports on the order of the SII Snapshot (Harmon et al. 1994) if a report form is too extensive or complex for the developmental level of our clients.

4. *Ask clients to recapitulate their results in their own words.* This very important strategy is advanced by Hood and Johnson (1997). The end purpose of an interpretation interview is to get counselees to incorporate interest inventory information into their working self-concepts. Consider carefully the

content of the self-statement and be prepared to make adjustments. Which of the following statements would you reinforce: "The test says I should be a plumber," or, "I have interests similar to those of plumbers," or "I might be pretty satisfied working in the plumbing trade."

I often use role-playing techniques for this purpose. I ask inventory-takers to pretend to call a parent or friend and tell them about their results. I hold my hand to my ear as though speaking on a phone and cue them by asking, "How did your tests come out?" I further develop the conversation with questions like, "Does that mean you're going to change majors?" or "Oh, I'm so glad you're making concrete plans." Alternatively, I will play the role of the client and ask the inventory-taker to explain my (actually his or her) results to me.

5. *Stimulate continuing career development.* Garfield and Prediger (1994) suggest that the counselor can help by identifying steps (or methods) for exploring the career options suggested in the assessment results and assisting in their evaluation. I often ask clients what they plan to do next, even suggesting a visit to the career information section of the library or to someone in an occupation of interest, or a query on the Internet. Working up balance sheets of pluses and minuses of various alternatives can clarify possibilities, despite the artificiality of quantifying nonobjective attributes. Follow up by asking what immediate and intermediate steps the client thinks are necessary to realize newly identified career goals.

Undoubtedly most counselors would endorse my exhortations. However, only a few are derived from empirical findings. I believe that we would do well to heed Spokane's (1991, p. 271) suggestion for refining how we communicate assessment results: "We need research and theory on how clients encode, store, and retrieve information they are presented with or scan on their own." Who will accept this challenge and advance the practice of interest inventory interpretation with further definitive guidelines?

ROB: AN INTEREST INVENTORY INTERPRETATION

Background

Rob,* a six-foot-plus, well-muscled young man, settled into the chair and said, "I guess I need some help from you."

---

*A pseudonym. In addition, certain biographical details have been altered to preserve the privacy of the client.

"Tell me more," I replied.

Rob had graduated from a city high school and completed a year and a half of college in a neighbor state. He had adequate but variable grades in high school, good written and oral language skills, but a D in an ill-advised physics class. He played end on the school's undistinguished football team and allowed himself to be recruited for a part in a school play in his senior year. He enjoys a good relationship with his father, a trucking company manager, and his school secretary mother, sharing their passion for Chicago's big league sports. I got the impression in this initial interview of an articulate, slightly shy, but not introspective individual.

Rob went to college mainly because everyone else did. Two years ago he dropped out because he couldn't see what it was doing for him and began a series of jobs in youth-oriented enterprises—pizza parlor, copy center, video rentals—mostly to earn money to live independently of his parents, for his classic old BMW coupe, and for scuba-diving. An older sister had been a more serious student, completing a community college program in data processing. She is now a computer operations supervisor for a local credit union.

Rob was referred to me at the state university counseling service because the admissions counselor thought he would do well to declare a major before he selected courses with which to resume his studies.

In our initial meeting I tried to ascertain the state of development of his career-related thinking, his vocational maturity. Mostly his demonstrated interests appeared to be recreational, which he seemed reluctant to translate into occupations. No chain retailer career path into management, of which he had seen plenty, appealed to him either. We concluded that he might first profit from a systematic exploration of his interests via the *Kuder Occupational Interest Survey* (KOIS; Kuder & Zytowski, 1991), an assessment I frequently use.

In order to introduce Rob to a framework for thinking about interests, I asked him to complete an estimate of the relative strength of 10 interest areas, to which we would later compare his KOIS Vocational Interest Estimates results (see Gustad & Tuma, 1957; Weinrach, 1980). His results are shown in Fig. 13.1.

Rob described himself (shown under the "My Ranks" heading) as most interested in Literary activities, followed by Outdoor and Mechanical. Artistic, Musical, and Computational activities were least preferred.

Rob filled out the KOIS the next day in the testing room; I received his results, shown in Figs. 13.2 and 13.3, a week later. I saw him the following day, having spent a few minutes previewing the results in preparation.

HOW WELL DO YOU KNOW YOUR INTERESTS?

Name: *Rob*   Date:

Directions: Read the descriptions of the following types of
interests. In the left hand column write "1" next to the one
that you think is most attractive to you. Then a "2" for the
next most, and so on until you have rank ordered all ten
interests.

My Ranks		Interest Inventory
_8_	ARTISTIC - Creative work involving attractive design, color, form, and materials.	_8_
_4_	CLERICAL - Tasks that require precision and accuracy.	_2_
_10_	COMPUTATIONAL - Working with numbers.	_9_
_1_	LITERARY - Reading and writing.	_1_
_3_	MECHANICAL - Woring with machines and tools.	_5_
_9_	MUSICAL - Going to concerts, playing musical instruments, singing, reading about music and musicians.	_6_
_2_	OUTDOOR - Activities that keep you outside most of the time and usually deal with plants and animals.	_3_
_5_	PERSUASIVE - Meeting and dealing with people and promoting projects, or selling things and ideas.	_7_
_6_	SCIENTIFIC - Discovering new facts and solving problems.	_10_
_7_	SOCIAL SERVICE - Helping people.	_4_

FIGURE 13.1   Rob's anticipated and actual ranks on the KOIS Vocational Interest Estimates.
Definitions from the *Kuder Occupational Interest Survey* Report Form, by F. Kuder. Copyright 1985 by The
McGraw-Hill Companies, Inc. Reproduced with permission.

I was gratified to see that Rob's results appeared interpretable, although his occupational scale scores were rather low (40s), indicating less strong similarity levels
(interests less coherent?) than I might wish for (50–60). His estimate of his interests
was well in accord with his inventoried results, suggesting that he is in good touch
with his preferences but that he does not appreciate how they translate into occupations or college majors. The interpretation interview, slightly edited in the interests of readability, begins on page 287. My after-the-fact comments are in italics.

Kuder Occupational Interest Survey Report Form	Compared with men MOST SIMILAR, CONT.

Name ROB

Sex MALE   **Date**

Numeric Grid No.   **SRA No.**

1 **Dependability:** How much confidence can you place in your results? In scoring your responses several checks were made on your answer patterns to be sure that you understood the directions and that your results were complete and dependable. According to these:

YOUR RESULTS APPEAR
TO BE DEPENDABLE

Compared with men, MOST SIMILAR, CONT.

LAWYER	.40
PRINTER	.39
POLICE OFFICER	.39
COUNSELOR, HS	.37
AUDIOL/SP PATHOL	.37
PAINTER, HOUSE	.37
BOOKKEEPER	.36
BRICKLAYER	.36
WELDER	.36

THE REST ARE LISTED IN ORDER OF SIMILARITY:

PHOTOGRAPHER	.35

2 **Vocational Interest Estimates:** Vocational interests can be divided into different types and the level of your attraction to each type can be measured. You may feel that you know what interests you have already — what you may not know is how strong they are compared with other people's interests. This section shows the relative rank of your preferences for ten different kinds of vocational activities. Each is explained on the back of this report form. Your preferences in these activities, as compared with other people's interests, are as follows:

Compared with men		Compared with women	
HIGH		HIGH	
LITERARY	98	LITERARY	98
CLERICAL	84	OUTDOOR	87
OUTDOOR	81	MECHANICAL	80
AVERAGE		AVERAGE	
SOCIAL SERVICE	64	CLERICAL	74
MECHANICAL	36	SOCIAL SERVICE	32
LOW		PERSUASIVE	27
MUSICAL	20	LOW	
PERSUASIVE	19	MUSICAL	22
ARTISTIC	11	ARTISTIC	05
COMPUTATIONAL	01	COMPUTATIONAL	03
SCIENTIFIC	01	SCIENTIFIC	01

3 **Occupations:** The KOIS has been given to groups of persons who are experienced and satisfied in many different occupations. Their patterns of interests have been compared with yours and placed in order of their similarity with you. The following occupational groups have interest patterns *most* similar to yours:

Compared with men		Compared with women	
JOURNALIST	.48	POLICE OFFICER	.46
ELEM SCH TEACHER	.46	JOURNALIST	.45
BOOKSTORE MGR	.46	PERSONNEL MGR	.43
LIBRARIAN	.45		
		THESE ARE NEXT MOST SIMILAR:	
THESE ARE NEXT MOST SIMILAR:		MINISTER	.39
NURSE	.41	FILM/TV PROD/DIR	.39
SOCIAL WORKER	.41	BOOKSTORE MGR	.39
FORESTER	.40	SOCIAL WORKER	.37
FILM/TV PROD/DIR	.40	SECRETARY	.36

FIGURE 13.2   Portion of Rob's *Kuder Occupational Interest Survey* Report Form

Report form by F. Kuder. Copyright 1985 by The McGraw-Hill Companies, Inc. Reproduced with permission.

FIGURE 13.3   College majors scores from Rob's *Kuder Occupational Interest Survey* Report Form

Report form by F. Kuder. Copyright 1985 by The McGraw-Hill Companies, Inc. Reproduced with permission.

The Interpretation Interview

Counselor: Hi, Rob! I've got your interest inventory report here. I've looked it over already. *1. Prepare for the discussion of the results.* You want to go over it?

Client: Sure. What does it say I should (*N.B.*) major in?

Co: Well, it's not going to give you any "shoulds," just "coulds." Got that? *It's guidance; not authority.* You remember what you had to do to answer it?

Cl: Yeah, my interests are in a lot of things I could do. But that most and least was different.

Co: Do you think it let you paint a good picture of yourself on the answer sheet?

Cl: Hmm? Oh well, yeah, pretty much.

Co: OK, now, here's your copy of your report. We'll do highlights now. You can read everything when you want to take the time—(pointing) you just go 1, 2, 3, down the report in sections. And (turning the form over) there's more to check on the back of the report.

Cl: OK.

Co: Remember you estimated last week how you'd score on the 10 interest areas?

Cl: Oh, yeah.

Co: Why don't you write in on the other side of the form how the inventory ranks them—compared with males, that is? 2. *Involve clients in communicating results.* (Rob takes the ranks off his report form and writes them opposite on his estimate sheet.) How do they look?

Cl: Hey, I think I did pretty good, didn't I?

Co: Yeah, except you were off a little on helping people—Social Service, I mean.

Cl: Huh? I don't figure that! I don't think I'm—

Co: Well, it might have to do with that "compared with" phrase just above the computer-printed lines.

Cl: Yeah?

Co: You may think of yourself as not liking Social Service, helping people very much, so you put it down pretty far, but guys in general think about the same, and compared to them, it ranks you higher among the 10 interests than you think. 3. *Use simple, empathic communication. I think I could have said this better. How would you have said it?*

Cl: (no response.)

Co: OK, so we could summarize—

Cl: (interrupting) Say, you know one time when I was at my old school, our dive club volunteered swimming lessons to some handicapped kids for a while, and, you know, I really had fun doing that. They were so . . . they really had a great time. I wasn't thinking about it when I filled out that form!

Co: So! As a name on a form it's one thing, but when you relate it to things you've actually done and compare that with other people, maybe working with people is more important than you think. *I'm trying to modify a self-perception. Do you agree that it is important?* So, in summary, your top-ranked interests are reading and writing, using words, say, and the clerical interests, that's being precise, accurate. Outdoor interests are important to you, too.

Cl: I can see where that being precise comes from; you know, in diving you have to keep track of how many minutes at how deep you've gone so you don't get the bends when you come up.

Co: I imagine that your preference for being precise is one of the reasons you enjoy scuba diving. You know, pilots are the same way. *Clients often cite some present behavior as the reason for their interest. I try to persuade them that the basic interest underlies their liking for some activity.*

Cl: That right?

Co: Then there are five interest areas that you're not hot for at all: music and art, selling, and math and science.

Cl: Yeah, that's what happened to that high school physics class. Say, what's this "compared with women"?

Discussion of the particular attributes of the interest survey employed here have been omitted, but counselors must be prepared to deal with the idiosyncrasies of each that they use.

Co: Now, are you ready to go over what kinds of people your interest patterns make you look like?

Cl: What d'ya mean?

Co: I mean, a lot of people in different occupations have taken this interest survey, and their answers are stored in the computer. So their interests are known. Then the computer kind of holds your answer sheet up against how each occupation in general answers and figures out how similar you are to each one. It prints out the most similar occupation, the next most, and—

Cl: I got it! Sort of like—

Co: *I should have let him finish his sentence to see if he really got it.* So what do you see at the top of the list in that box marked 3?

Cl: Here? Journalist? Newspaper. Oh, wow! (long, quiet pause) Wow, I never thought of that. (long pause) There was a journalism class in high school, but I took the media class instead. That was neat, TV stuff and all. But I didn't think . . . It was just an elective.

Co: And what's next on your most similar list? *Let's get back to the inventory results.*

Cl: I don't want to be a grade school teacher!

Co: This doesn't say you have to be; you just have interests that are like theirs. OK? *I'm trying to soften the "should," the imperative.*

Cl: I see. And then bookstore manager and librarian. Huh! (I remain silent.) Bookstore manager . . . You know, when I was working at the copy place, there was this bookstore on the same block, and I used to . . . the magazine racks, I could . . .

Co: I'm getting the idea that something about books, or writing, or the language arts feels right to you. After all, you seemed to know about Literary being your top interest.

Cl: Yeah, well . . . What are these down under "These are next most similar?" *Does Rob not want to deal with this insight? Perhaps we would explore his associations with being "literary."*

Co: Well, you could say that the top four occupational groups all tied for first in the race for your attention, and the next group all came in second—nurse, social worker, forester—forester?—film and TV director or producer, lawyer, on down the list. *I use the metaphor of a race to make an interpretation vivid. Is it effective?*

Cl: 'S funny. Nurse? Social worker?

Co: Yes, kind of hangs with elementary teacher, and your social service interests aren't low at all.

Cl: I guess.

Co: You could sort of merge these different occupations into some families or clusters on account of their similarities. What kind of names would you give 'em? *4. Ask clients to recapitulate their results in their own words.*

Cl: Yeah, that's a good idea. (pause) Well, there's the writing, or language maybe, I don't know. And oh yeah, I see it, the teacher and the nurse and stuff are the helping people . . . And the forester, what about the forester?

Co: Maybe reflects your outdoor interests?

Cl: Yeah, I dunno . . .

Co: But see I'm trying to get you to use some words that describe the main things in your high rankers.

Cl: (pause) Hey, you know, my old school had a major called "communications." Would that be a major I could do?

Co: That might be a good way to describe some of your interests. And the TV and film jobs, and lawyer, are in that ballpark, too.

Cl: (looking further down in the "Next Most Similar" column) Well, I'm not sure I go for any of these—printer, police officer, painter? I mean, they're all OK, just I don't think for me, that's all. *Rob might have benefited from exploring this resistance. Instead, I push the communications theme.*

Co: OK. And if you notice, over on the right-hand side, under "College Majors," your top score is English major.

Cl: Yeah, I saw that.

Co: Looks to me like you got some prospects to follow up on that could lead to a major. So tell me, is there anybody else who is gonna be interested in what your interest inventory says?

Cl: Well, (shyly) there's this girl. She's kind of the reason I decided to come back to school.

Co: Oh, I get it. So what are you going to tell her about your report?

Cl: I guess . . . I guess I can tell her the test says I should do something like go into journalism. *Again, the "should." We'll take it on more directly.*

Co: Nah, the test isn't saying you *should* do anything. It maybe says that your interests are kind of glued together around literary—reading and writing—kinds of activities, plus things that call for attention to details, and the out-of-doors. And that you *could* do things that journalism, teaching, books, or something like that need.

Cl: So I could tell her I'm thinking about journalism, right?

Co: Yeah, thinking, but hold it! Only journalism? We have majors here in advertising, PR, speech communication, um, English, theater, linguistics . . . You know what I mean? I mean . . . *I'm trying to expand his concept of the implications of his literary interests.*

Cl: What d'ya mean?

Co: Here, this is a coincidence, but today this publishing company sent us a sample of a new career book of theirs. It's called *Real People Working in Communications* (Goldberg, 1997). Here's the table of contents: newspaper publishing—that's your regular journalism—magazines, books, radio and TV, advertising, PR work, even communications educators—I think she means journalism teachers. Say, you know with your social service interests . . . Well . . . See, it's got a bunch of interviews with people who are actually in jobs in these fields. Like one of the newspaper people is actually a photojournalist. Well, how about I loan this to you? 5. *Stimulate continuing career development. Is this an effective method?*

Cl: OK.

Co: We'll want it back. So when you return it, I want to know what major you declared. OK?

Cl: Deal!

Epilogue

Rob did return the book and with it a note telling me that he did not have to declare a major after all, but that he did sign up for Journalism 101, which included a survey of all the ways the degree could be used in occupations. I hope he is also looking into some of the other specialties available to him, like technical writing, teaching English, and the like, from other departments.

I don't know if he is still saying "should."

REFERENCES

American Counseling Association (1989). *Responsibilities of users of standardized tests* (Rev. ed.). Washington, DC: Author.

American Psychological Association (1985). *Standards for educational and psychological testing.* Washington, DC: Author.

Anastasi, A. (1988). *Psychological testing.* Old Tappan, NJ: Macmillan.

Crites, J. O. (1981). Integrative test interpretation. In D. H. Montross & C. S. Shinkman (Eds.), *Career development in the 1980s: Theory and practice* (pp. 161–168). Springfield, IL: Charles C. Thomas.

Defense's Cohen is a different breed of cat for Clinton's Cabinet. (1997, March 22). *Minneapolis Star and Tribune,* p. A4.

Dressel, P. L., & Mattson, R. W. (1950). The effects of client participation in test interpretation. *Educational and Psychological Measurement, 10,* 693–706.

Eyde, L. D., Robertson, G. J., Krug, S. E., Moreland, K. L., Robertson, A. G., Shewan, C. M., Harrison, P. L., Porch, B. E., Hammer, A. L., & Primoff, E. S. (1993). *Responsible test use: Case studies for assessing human behavior.* Washington, DC: American Psychological Association.

Garfield, N. J., & Prediger, D. J. (1994). Assessment competencies and responsibilities: A checklist for counselors. In J. T. Kapes, M. M. Mastie, & E. A Whitfield (Eds.), *A counselor's guide to career assessment instruments* (pp. 41–48). Alexandria, VA: National Career Development Association.

Gati, I. (1987). Description and validation of a procedure for the interpretation of an interest inventory profile. *Journal of Counseling Psychology, 34,* 141–148.

Gati, I., & Blumberg, D. (1991). Computer vs. counselor interpretation of interest inventories: The case of the *Self-Directed Search. Journal of Counseling Psychology, 38,* 350–366.

Goldberg, J. (1997). *Real people working in communications.* Lincolnwood, IL: VGM Career Horizons.

Goodyear, R. K. (1990). Research on the effects of test interpretation: A review. *The Counseling Psychologist, 18,* 240–257.

Gustad, J. W., & Tuma, A. H. (1957). The effects of different methods of test introduction and interpretation on client learning in counseling. *Journal of Counseling Psychology, 4,* 313–317.

Hansen, J. C., Kozberg, J. G., & Goranson, D. (1994). Accuracy of student recall of *Strong Interest Inventory* results 1 year after interpretation. *Measurement and Evaluation in Counseling and Development, 26,* 235–242.

Harmon, L. W., Hansen, J. C., Borgen, F. H., & Hammer, A. L. (1994). *Strong Interest Inventory: Applications and technical guide.* Stanford, CA: Stanford University Press.

Healy, C. C. (1990). Reforming career appraisals to meet the needs of clients in the 1990s. *The Counseling Psychologist, 18,* 214–226.

Holland, J. L. (1997). *Making vocational choices: A theory of vocational personalities and work environments* (3rd ed.). Odessa, FL: Psychological Assessment Resources.

Holland, J. L., Powell, A. B., & Fritzsche, B. A. (1994). *Self-Directed Search: Professional user's guide.* Odessa, FL: Psychological Assessment Resources.

Hood, A. B., & Johnson, R. W. (1997). *Assessment in counseling: A guide to the use of psychological assessment procedures* (2nd ed.). Alexandria, VA: American Counseling Association.

Krumboltz, J. D., & Vosvick, M. A. (1996). Career assessment and the *Career Beliefs Inventory. Journal of Career Assessment, 4,* 345–361.

Kuder, F., & Zytowski, D. G. (1991). *Kuder Occupational Interest Survey: General manual.* Monterey, CA: CTB/McGraw-Hill.

Kuder, F., & Zytowski, D. G. (1993). *Kuder DD/PC: User's guide.* Monterey, CA: CTB/McGraw-Hill.

Levy, L. H. (1963). *Psychological interpretation.* New York: Henry Holt.

Miller, M. J., & Cochran, J. R. (1979). Comparison of the effectiveness of four methods of reporting interest inventory results. *Journal of Counseling Psychology, 26,* 263–266.

Shertzer, B., & Linden, J. D. (1979). *Fundamentals of individual appraisal: Assessment techniques for counselors.* Boston: Houghton Mifflin.

Spokane, A. (1991). Career intervention. Englewood Cliffs, NJ: Prentice Hall.

Strahan, R. F., & Kelly, A. E. (1994). Showing clients what their profiles mean. *Journal of Counseling and Development, 72,* 329–331.

Swanson, J. L. (1992). Generating hypotheses from Rachael's profile. *Career Development Quarterly, 41,* 31–35.

Tinsley, H. E., & Bradley, R. W. (1986). Test interpretation. *Journal of Counseling and Development, 64,* 462–466.

Toman, S. M., & Zytowski, D. (1997, January). Interpreting interest inventories to groups. Paper presented at the annual convention of the National Career Development Association, Daytona Beach, FL.

Toman, S. M., & Savickas. M. L. (1997). Career choice readiness moderates the effects of interest inventories. *Journal of Career Assessment, 5,* 275–291.

Weinrach, S. G. (1980). Discrepancy identification: A model for the interpretation of the *Kuder Occupational Interest Survey* and other interest inventories. *Vocational Guidance Quarterly, 29,* 42–50.

Zytowski, D. G., & Borgen, F. E. (1983) Assessment. In W. B. Walsh & S. H. Osipow (Eds.), *Handbook of vocational psychology* (pp. 6–32). Hillsdale, NJ: Erlbaum.

CHAPTER FOURTEEN

Integrating Interests and Abilities for Career Exploration

General Considerations

Dale J. Prediger

THIS CHAPTER IS INTENDED for those who support (through instruction and instrument development) or practice the tandem (joint) use of interest and ability measures to stimulate and facilitate self-career exploration, planning, and replanning—developmental tasks faced by each of us. Specifically this chapter presents considerations (things to keep in mind) when using interest and ability measures in a comprehensive, structured search for occupations that have counselee-compatible work tasks and workers. The criterion-related validity data reported herein were obtained because of their relevance for this use of scores—as versus predicting success, satisfactoriness, or satisfaction as a blivot maker at General Motors.

Procedures that facilitate self-career exploration and planning for the many also apply to problem-oriented career counseling with individuals. The focus here, however, is on general measurement and career counseling considerations, not considerations unique to a counselee. Hence counselors will need to adapt the general considerations in a clinically tailored way. For example, see the discussion of Goldman's (1971) clinical bridge under Consideration 1, below.

This chapter does not review research, theory, and thinking on the use of interest measures in career counseling. Other chapters address those topics. With respect to ability measures, several volumes would be required to cover the vast literature on ability structure and criterion-related validity alone, not to mention the use of various ability measures in career counseling. The purpose here is to identify and make a selective case for *general* considerations in the use of interest measures with measures of specialized abilities (e.g., numerical, leadership, mechanical, sales, clerical). Measures of specific skills (e.g., rotating factors, rolling kayaks, spinning news releases) are not addressed.

Regarding interests, the focus is on basic interest scales rather than occupational scales. Although the general considerations have implications for occupational scales, such as those on the *Strong Interest Inventory* (Harmon, Hansen, Borgen, & Hammer, 1994) and the *Campbell Interest and Skill Survey* (Campbell, Hyne, & Nilsen, 1992), the chapter does not directly address the use of ability measures in tandem with occupational interest scales. There are three reasons. First, scores on occupational scales and basic interest scales have different bases and meanings (e.g., see Harmon, this volume). Second, there are no measures of ability that parallel occupational interest scales; and third, interest inventories with occupational scales almost always have basic interest scales (Kapes, Mastie, & Whitfield, 1994).

Regarding abilities, the chapter's focus is on ability tests and on ability assessments obtained via informed self-estimates (Prediger, 1992). The latter draw on lifetime experiences, including ability test results, if relevant. Measures of confidence in abilities and/or skills (Betz, Borgen, & Harmon, 1996; Campbell et al., 1992), specific (work task, occupational, etc.) self-efficacy beliefs (Osipow & Temple, 1996; Tracey, 1997), and so forth are not addressed because no one appears to claim that they measure abilities. In fact, some hold that they do not (Betz et al., 1996; Campbell et al., 1992). Ability self-confidence measures have internal, psychologically based uses such as understanding counselee behavior, building confidence, and managing anxiety. Ability measures have external, real-world uses such as determining what counselees can do, whether it is "good enough," how they can to do better. Although evidence is lacking at this time, it appears that measures of work-relevant abilities differ sufficiently from measures of ability self-confidence for both to be helpful when used in conjunction with measures of interests. In any case, employers may be more interested in worker abilities than ability self-confidence. (Considerations 4–6 are relevant to ability self-confidence measures as well as ability measures.)

Finally, on a personal note, you should know that *auf Deutsch* ("in German"—my ancestral heritage), Prediger means preacher. So perhaps you will excuse whatever resemblance the general considerations that follow have to preaching. It's where I came from. Also I have been engaged with this chapter's topic for 30 years.

CONSIDERATIONS REGARDING ABILITY MEASURES USED IN CAREER EXPLORATION

Consideration 1: A Similarity-Based, Work-World Search for Occupational Options

Ideally ability measures should be used as one would use interest measures—to identify occupations with counselee-compatible work tasks and workers. The goal is to translate scores into occupational suggestions based on a comprehensive, structured, work-world search—to bridge the gap between scores and occupational options. In a classic and still helpful text on using tests in counseling, Goldman (1971) described four "bridges" between test scores and their implications for counselees. Three bridges are objective: the norm (comparison), regression (success prediction), and discriminant (similarity) bridges. One bridge is subjective: the clinical (build-a-counselee-model) bridge.

Goldman notes that the norm bridge is incomplete because it essentially stops with statements of relative standing, not their implications. Hence it is not discussed here. Goldman also notes that the strength of the clinical bridge depends on the availability of information based on the three objective bridges, plus counselor skills and insights. Because the clinical bridge is labor intensive and expensive, whereas the focus of this chapter is on developmental career counseling for the many, use of the clinical bridge with ability and interest measures is not discussed. Readers may wish to refer to Lowman (1991), Seligman (1994), and Zunker (1994)—in addition to Goldman (1971), of course.

Regression (Success Prediction) Bridge. This bridge, which takes its name from the statistical procedures on which it is based (correlation and regression analysis), provides predictions of level of performance ("success") in some endeavor (e.g., grades in college). But for many reasons ability tests cannot predict occupational success in any way useful for comprehensive career exploration (Goldman, 1972, 1982; Prediger, 1974; Prediger & Swaney, 1992; Thorndike, 1982). For example, there is no common scale on which counselees can compare success predictions across occupations. Success itself is variously defined across occupations (e.g., sous-chef, life insurance agent, carpenter, social worker) and persons (e.g., personnel psychologists, counselees). Even if common indicators of success could be agreed upon, predictor-success correlations would not be available for the vast majority of occupations considered in comprehensive career exploration. (Correlations based on representative samples would be even rarer.)

The correlations that are available are generally low, unless they have been inflat-ed by various "adjustments" that don't actually reduce the large prediction errors noted by Goldman (1972, 1982). Finally, the least-demanding occupations tend to have the highest success predictions. For reasons such as these, Zytowski (1994) noted that the regression model (bridge) "is the failed relationship [between tests and counseling]. A new one, based on membership or *similarity* [italics added] . . . has replaced it" (p. 222).

Sometimes the regression bridge is crossed via ability test cut-offs that persons must presumably exceed in order to be "successful" (e.g., to be hired, to meet supervisor expectations). U.S. Department of Labor multiple aptitude cut-offs for the *General Aptitude Test Battery* (U.S. Department of Labor, 1980) provide a good example. When applied to career exploration, one ability at a time, the multiple cut-off bridge becomes the sequential elimination model (SEM; Lichtenberg, Shaffer, & Arachtingi, 1993) for using assessment results in a structured search for occupations. The main assumptions for a given occupation are that (a) there are critical values for certain abilities that must be exceeded in order to ensure success, regardless of the specific job or employer; (b) high scores cannot com-pensate for low scores, despite performance realities; and (c) overqualification (substantially exceeding the cut-offs) is of no concern to the counselee. These assumptions may apply to the selection of blivot makers by General Motors, but they are not warranted in career counseling. Also counselees typically have time to build abilities important to occupations they may never consider if the SEM is used. Nevertheless, the multiple cut-off version of the regression bridge is popu-lar, especially in computer-based career planning systems drawing on data in U.S. Department of Labor publications. Katz (1993) provided an overview of such systems.

Discriminant (Similarity) Bridge. This bridge, which also takes its name from the statistical procedure on which it is based (discriminant analysis), provides estimates of a counselee's similarity to members of various groups (e.g., success-ful and satisfied social workers). The underlying assumption, which is addressed by discriminant analysis, is that occupational groups differ from each other in sensible ways on the measures being used. As applied in career counseling, sim-ilarity estimates based on the discriminant bridge can be used to survey the work world in order to identify occupations that may be counselee-compatible. In what is now called person–environment fit counseling (Rounds & Tracey, 1990), the goal is not to find the ideal match. Rather, the goal is to say, for example,

"Here are some occupations that attract persons who are similar to you in important ways. You might want to check them out." Generally, use of the discriminant bridge has been motivated by well-documented differences in the interests and abilities characterizing occupational groups.

This common-sense, "You look like people who—" approach to test interpretation does not require the use of discriminant analysis statistics. Counselee-occupation profile comparisons (the discriminant bridge's profile similarity model) have long been used in career counseling based on interest and ability measures (Goldman, 1971). For over 65 years the *Strong Interest Inventory* Occupational Scales (Harmon et al., 1994) have used this model at the item level. Regarding basic interest scales, counselors use the profile similarity model when they suggest that counselees look into mechanical engineering or automotive technology on the basis of a profile peak on a mechanical interest scale. The underlying assumption (supported by data, one would hope) is that persons in such occupations have (as a group) a profile peak on that scale.

Comparisons of interest-occupation profile shapes via Holland three-letter codes (the three highest RIASEC types; Holland, 1997) probably represent the most widespread use of the profile similarity model. Simultaneous, visual comparisons of interest, ability, and occupational group similarities are provided by the World-of-Work Map (American College Testing, 1988; Prediger & Swaney, 1995), as illustrated in the case study at the end of this chapter. Profile comparison procedures such as these overcome tedious, inexact, "squint-and-tell" comparisons of a counselee's score profile with profiles for multiple occupational groups, one at a time. The advantages of the profile similarity model and limitations of the regression bridge recommend use of ability measures in a similarity-based work-world search for occupational options.

Consideration 2: Comprehensive Assessment of Abilities

Almost universally, interest assessment is work-world comprehensive. A comprehensive assessment of work-relevant abilities is also essential. Especially when used in tandem, interest and ability measures need to be coordinated with each other and with a work-world structure (e.g., Holland's, 1997, RIASEC types). If there is no interest, ability, and work-world coordination, counselors may be forced to relate psychological apples and kumquats to work-world bananas. Even the load limit of the labor-intensive clinical bridge could be exceeded.

A number of instruments assess both interests and abilities with varying degrees of coordination. Since they are described elsewhere, they are not described here. Kapes and his colleagues (1994) provided reviews for eight paper-based instruments and one that is computer-based. In addition they identified 12 computer-based career planning systems (e.g., CHOICES, DISCOVER, SIGI) that have interest and ability measures as major components. Murphy, Conoley, and Impara (1994) list reviews and reference citations for instruments assessing both interests and abilities. Other sources of information include counselor-oriented measurement texts (e.g., Hood & Johnson, 1997; Walsh & Betz, 1995).

One Ability or Many? Common sense and research involving ability test scores and job analysis data (Dawis, Dohm, Lofquist, Chartrand, & Due, 1987; Desmarais & Sackett, 1993; Prediger, 1989) indicate that occupations differ on a wide range of specialized abilities relevant to their work tasks. (Also see the discussion of the many-ability approach, below.) That is, a measure of general mental ability (g), formerly called intelligence (IQ), is insufficient for career counseling. Whereas specialized abilities reveal work-relevant ability differences across occupations, g conceals these differences. Since g can be well estimated from a combination of specialized abilities (Jensen, 1986; Hunter, 1986), it is also redundant.

Problems with the One-Ability Approach. As implied above, more than general mental ability needs to be considered in career exploration and planning. Nevertheless, g is routinely used in work-world searches for occupational options. For example, the U.S. *Department of Defense Career Exploration Program* (U.S. Department of Defense, 1995a), probably the most widely used assessment of interests and abilities, each year provides nearly 1,000,000 students in 14,000 high schools with occupational suggestions based on a match between their g-score and interest scores. That is, "OCCU-FIND" (U.S. Department of Defense, 1995b) focuses student attention on occupations that match their *Armed Services Vocational Aptitude Battery* (ASVAB) "Code." Occupations congruent with interest scores, alone, are repeatedly excluded from student consideration (U.S. Department of Defense, 1995b, pp. 5.6–5.7).

Unfortunately, the five-level, g-based ASVAB Code provides substantially different occupational suggestions to Blacks, Whites, and Hispanics, as documented for ASVAB national norm group members (Prediger & Swaney, 1992). For example, the percentage of White students referred to Level 1 and 2 occupations (e.g., engineer, physician, lawyer, financial manager) is nearly six times that of Black students.

Although reported to students, the 10-score ASVAB profile is not used in OCCU-FIND's every-student search for occupational options. With respect to abilities, only the ASVAB code is used by OCCU-FIND. There are alternatives to g-based career explanation, however. For example, Prediger and Swaney (1992) developed and validated a way to use 8 of the 10 ASVAB scores, together with self-estimates for other work-relevant abilities, in a work-world search for occupational options. Ability patterns provide the basis for the search (as do interest patterns). Once options are tentatively identified, exploration of their feasibility can include information from a variety of ability indicators. (This two-step approach is discussed under Suggestion 8 at the end of the chapter.) The driving rationale is "Be all you can be"—not what a g-test says you can be.

Problems with the Many-Ability Approach. Because ability test batteries typically assess only three to six abilities beyond the three R's (Kapes et al., 1994), they may have limited usefulness in a comprehensive, work-world search for occupations with counselee-compatible work tasks. Research indicates that there are many more work-relevant abilities (social interaction, leadership, sales, being organized, etc.). For example, Holland, Fritzsche, and Powell (1994) identified 12 work-relevant abilities; Lowman (1991) identified 11; Prediger (1989) and American College Testing (1998) identified 15; and Jones (1996) cited 17 on the basis of work by the U.S. Department of Labor "Secretary's Commission on Achieving Necessary Skills." Tests and assessment centers cannot assess multiple work-relevant abilities unless tremendous time and effort are expended. What's more, norm groups and score scales are likely to differ across abilities, thus making the identification of strengths and weaknesses difficult at best.

For all of these reasons, nontest abilities may be dealt with haphazardly in developmental career counseling—or simply ignored. A measurement-based alternative to "If you can't test it, forget it" is suggested under Consideration 3. But first another reason for a comprehensive assessment of abilities deserves attention:

An Identical Interest-Ability Structure? Integrating interests and abilities for the purpose of career exploration would be greatly facilitated if interests, abilities, and occupations had the same basic structure. This is not guaranteed, of course, by having interest scales, ability scales, and occupational groups with the same names. Regarding measures of ability self-confidence, Campbell and his colleagues (1992) noted that "Little is known about the structure of skills compared with the structure of interests" (p. 65). Regarding tested abilities, there appears to be general agreement that ability structure (e.g., see Anastasi & Urbina, 1997) differs substantially from interest structure (e.g., see Rounds & Day, this volume). But as noted above, ability test batteries seldom, if ever, provide a comprehensive assessment of work-relevant abilities. In contrast, measures of basic interests are almost always work-world comprehensive. Measures of Holland's (1997) RIASEC interest types are perhaps the most noteworthy examples. Regarding Holland's hexagonal arrangement of interest types, structural analyses of interest score intercorrelations support the Data/Ideas and People/Things Dimensions proposed by Prediger (1982), as does research *external* to those analyses (see Prediger, 1996, for a summary; also see Rolfhus & Ackerman, 1996, pp. 183–184). But what about work-relevant abilities?

Consideration 3 makes a case for the use of ability self-estimates to obtain a comprehensive assessment of work-relevant abilities. The *Inventory of Work-Relevant Abilities* (IWRA; American College Testing, 1998) obtains informed self-estimates (Prediger, 1992) for 15 abilities shown by research to differentiate occupations spanning Holland's types. Prediger (1989) and American College Testing (1998) described how IWRA abilities were identified and assigned to Holland types. Only 7 of IWRA's 15 abilities are typically assessed by ability tests.

Ability self-estimates obtained from two samples via IWRA were subjected to a principal components analysis (Prediger, in press). Sample A consisted of 618 12th-graders in an urban, suburban, and rural cross-section of six schools in six states. Sample B consisted of 4,387 12th-graders in a nationally representative sample of 49 schools (Swaney, 1995). For both samples, all 15 IWRA abilities loaded on the first principal component (median loadings of .48 for both samples), thus indicating a general factor but not necessarily *g*. The total variance accounted for (VAF) in both samples was 50%. The four abilities (e.g., mechanical versus meeting people) with loadings of .40 or higher on the second component (same abilities and VAFs of 14% in both samples) clearly indicated a People/Things dimension (factor). The five abilities (e.g., numerical versus artistic) with loadings of .40 or higher on the third component (same abilities in both samples; VAFs of 11% and 10%) provided good support for a Data/Ideas dimension. Thus, when there is a comprehensive assessment of abilities (and general factor variance is not allowed to contaminate subsequent dimensions through a rotation procedure such as varimax), ability dimensions highly similar to interest dimensions emerge. (This research was recently extended by Prediger [in press], through use of targeted factor extraction procedures.)

Results of research involving job analysis data for a large cross-section of occupations (see Prediger, 1996, for a summary) indicate the presence of Data/Ideas and People/Things Work Task Dimensions. Occupations, of course, are defined by their work tasks. Structural analyses of mean interest profiles for workers in cross-sections of occupations indicate that occupations are differentiated by Data/Ideas and People/Things Dimensions (Prediger, 1982). Furthermore, the mean interests of workers in cross-sections of occupations are highly related to work tasks (Prediger, 1982). Tracey (1997) obtained Data/Ideas and People/Things factors in a principal components analysis of self-efficacy beliefs regarding work tasks. Given these findings, basic interests, work-relevant human abilities, work tasks, work task self-efficacy beliefs, and occupations all appear to have the same general structure. If so, the foundation for a coordinated use of interest and ability measures in career counseling would be substantially strengthened.

Consideration 3: Self-Estimates as Alternatives to Ability Tests

Consideration 2 makes a case for a comprehensive assessment of work-relevant abilities yet notes that many work-relevant abilities are not assessed by ability tests. Thus ability-based career exploration that relies solely on tests misses important abilities. Also it does not take into account the powerful role of self-concepts in career development. What might be called Donald Super's Dictum states, "In choosing an occupation one is, in effect, choosing a means of implementing a self-concept" (Super, 1957, p. 196). Notice that Super did not say, "In choosing an occupation one is, in effect, choosing a means of implementing test scores."

What to do? One alternative (probably the only feasible one) is to use easily accessible self-estimates of work-relevant abilities. Ability self-estimates bring important, work-relevant self-concepts to the attention of the counselor and counselee. They can be discussed, perhaps revised, and then used in a work-world search for occupational options in the same way that interest results are used. As documented below, the validity of self-estimates for career exploration applications can exceed that of test scores.

Various procedures for obtaining ability self-estimates are illustrated by the *Ability Explorer* (Harrington & Harrington, 1996), the computer-based CHOICES (Careerware, 1992), IWRA (American College Testing, 1998), and the *Self-Directed Search* (SDS; Holland et al., 1994). In selecting a procedure for obtaining ability self-estimates, counselors need to be alert to the many problems that must be addressed (Mabe & West, 1982). The procedure recommended here is to obtain informed self-estimates of abilities (Prediger, 1992), which draw on first-hand and vicarious experience. Whereas test scores can be based on narrow or abstract exercises (consider the typical clerical perception and spatial visualization tests), *informed* self-estimates can be broadly defined in work-relevant terms. For example, clerical ability is described in IWRA as follows: *"Quickly and accurately doing tasks such as looking up information in catalogs or tables, sorting things, recording addresses or expenses, etc.* [italics in original]. Consider your ability to handle paperwork; to complete forms accurately and neatly (for example, an application); to catch errors" (American College Testing, 1998, Appendix C).

Almost every measurement text states that test results should be viewed and used in the context of other relevant information. When available and relevant, ability test results can be used to inform self-estimates. Thus they can be viewed in context. Whether test results should replace self-estimates is debatable, however. When ability self-estimates are replaced by test results in a structured search for occupational options, one (in effect) says to the counselee, "Your self-concept is so flawed it cannot be trusted for career exploration. So—we'll use test scores and leave you to your flawed self-concept. Someday we may find time to correct it."

Comparability of Self-Estimates Across Abilities. So that counselors and counselees can determine highest abilities (or interests), scores must be on a uniform scale. It is well known that raw ability test scores cannot be compared. Hence comparisons are typically based on normative standing. (For a summary of validity data documenting the advantage of normed interest scores over raw interest scores, see Swaney, 1995, Chapter 2.) Regarding self-estimates, people tend to overestimate standing on many abilities. More important for comparisons across abilities, the extent of overestimation differs across abilities. For example, Harrington and Harrington (1996) reported ability level cumulative percentage distributions for the 14 ability self-estimates obtained via their *Ability Explorer.* The distributions were based on self-estimates provided by approximately 750 11th-graders. Across the 14 abilities the percentages of students with summary self-estimates of "a little above average" or higher ranged from lows of 36% and 48% for scientific and musical/dramatic abilities to highs of 80% and 84% for clerical and interpersonal abilities.

Because one would expect less than 50% of a representative group to be "a little above average" or higher, it is evident that the extent of overestimation differed substantially across the abilities. (Also see data provided by Holland et al., 1994, and Westbrook, Buck, Wynne, & Sanford, 1994). Thus the determination of highest abilities from raw self-estimates is difficult at best. In addition, the Harrington and Harrington data indicate that when occupational suggestions are based on raw self-estimates, large numbers of students, especially females (given the sex differences in *Ability Explorer* item responses), will be referred to inter-personal (e.g., personal service) and clerical occupations.

For the above reasons validity may suffer when raw self-estimates are com-pared across abilities. Just as with ability tests, ability self-estimates need to be scaled (Swaney, 1987). When they are scaled, career groups generally score as expected (Prediger & Swaney, 1992), a commonly used indicator of validity for career exploration applications.

Accuracy of Self-Estimates. The use of ability self-estimates in career exploration is sometimes denigrated because self-estimates are assumed to be inaccurate. However, research reviewed by Mabe and West (1982) indicates that, just as with ability test scores, the accuracy of ability self-estimates depends on how they are obtained. Because the assumption that every test score and every self-estimate is accurate is not warranted, *both* may be the problem when correlations between self-estimates and test scores are low. Also tests and self-estimates with the same name may not assess the same construct. Compare, for example, the self-estimate defin-ition for clerical ability cited above with the items on a typical clerical ability test.

This is not the place for an update of the Mabe and West (1982) review of 55 studies of the relationship between ability self-estimates and test scores. (For a recent, well-done study see Westbrook et al., 1994.) The point is that test scores do not provide Truth regarding work-relevant abilities, despite gospel to the contrary.

Validity for Career Exploration. Given that ability test scores and self-estimates both have problems, the key question appears to be, Do ability tests or self-estimates have the greater validity for use in career exploration? A common way to investigate an instrument's validity for career exploration is to determine the percentage of occupational group members who score highest on the scale appropriate to their group—that is, to determine the instrument's "hit rate." The results of four studies comparing ability test and self-estimate hit rates are reported in Table 14.1.

In each of the four studies, self-estimates were based on an early edition of IWRA (American College Testing, 1988). For Data Sources 1, 2, and 4 the six *Career Planning Program* (American College Testing, 1988) ability test scores (e.g., numerical, mechanical) were used. For Data Source 3 the 10 ASVAB (U.S. Department of Defense, 1995a) aptitude test scores were used. For Data Sources 1, 3, and 4 each student was assigned to one of Holland's (1997) RIASEC types on the basis of occupational choice screened on certainty. For Data Source 2, students were assigned to RIASEC types on the basis of vocational program, after being screened for success and satisfaction. In each study, hit rates were determined from discriminant functions following a discriminant analysis. Because the six criterion groups (RIASEC types) were treated as being of equal size (i.e., importance) when hit rates were determined, base and chance hit rates both equal one-in-six, or 17%.

Table 14.1 reports hit rates for 6 to 10 ability tests in Column 1. Hit rates for ability test and self-estimate composites for Holland's six types are reported in Column 3. For Data Sources 1–3, self-estimates were combined with ability test scores in order to obtain six composites. Hence incremental validity is addressed. For Data Source 4, only self-estimates were used. As shown by the last column, the use of ability self-estimates led to improvements over ability test hit rates of 8% to 48%, depending on the study.

It might be argued that the ability self-estimates had higher hit rates than test scores because the former influence interests—hence occupational choice. For Data Source 2, however, students chose their vocational program one to two years prior to the assessment of abilities. Also the joint studies of ability self-estimates and interests summarized under Consideration 5 show the limited extent to which ability self-estimates and interests overlap.

The four studies that compare the validity of ability self-estimates and test scores for career exploration appear to be unique. Regarding the prediction of "success," Baird (1976) cites massive evidence favoring ability self-estimates over test scores as predictors of school and college grades, a common application of test batteries. (For an update see Katz, 1993.) No doubt, additional studies comparing the validity of ability self-estimates and test scores will be needed before informed self-estimates of ability are accepted as an alternative to gospel.

CONSIDERATIONS REGARDING THE TANDEM USE OF INTEREST AND ABILITY MEASURES

Consideration 4: Comparison of Interest and Ability Scores

Ability test profile level clearly indicates strength (amount) of ability, given that ability test scores are based on right/wrong answers and that there are voluminous data showing a relationship between ability score level and external criteria such as college grades. However, one cannot assume interest profile level indicates strength of interest.

TABLE 14.1　Career Exploration Validity of Ability Tests, Ability Self-Estimates, and a Comprehensive Combination

Data source	Sample size			Hit rates for Holland-type criterion groups				
				Abilities typically assessed by tests		Tested abilities plus self-estimates[a]	Advantage of self-estimates:	
	Grade	Schools	Students[b]	Test scores	Self-estimates			
				(Col. 1)	(Col. 2)	(Col. 3)	(Col. 3 minus 1)	
1. Prediger (1987, Study 2)	12	31	3,768	34%	–	42%	+8%; 08/34 = +24%[c]	
2. Prediger & Brandt (1990)	12	19	2,101	36%	–	39%	+3%; 03/36 = +8%	
3. Prediger & Swaney (1992)	11 & 12	13	1,669	29%	–	43%	+14%; 14/29 = +48%	
4. Prediger & Swaney (1992, Appendix C)	11	3	529	39%	41%	42%	+3%; 03/39 = 8%	

[a]Scores for 15 abilities combined into composites for Holland's six types, as per American College Testing (1998). For Data Source 4, ability self-estimates replaced the six test scores.

[b]Sample size prior to criterion group screening.

[c]Advantage reported as a percentage of the test score hit rate (Column 1).

Meaning of Interest Profile Level. As reported by Prediger (1998), basic interest scales using Likert-type responses typically have a large response style ("yea-/naysaying") component that directly affects score profile level. For each of 23 diverse samples (total N of 53,429; 10 widely used interest inventories), principal components analyses were conducted on Holland-type intercorrelations. Across samples the median VAF for the first component was 42%. All Holland types had high, positive correlations with this component (median of about .65).

To determine whether interest profile level indicates strength of interest in addition to response style, occupational group hit rates were compared for high and low profile groups matched on profile differentiation and shape (Prediger, 1998). The study was replicated across three samples. Two of the samples consisted of 12th-graders for whom certainty-screened occupational choice was obtained concurrently with scores on the *Unisex Edition of the ACT Interest Inventory* (UNIACT; Swaney, 1995). The first sample was labeled Sample B under Consideration 2. The second sample included 386,836 college-bound students who registered for the ACT Assessment (American College Testing, 1997a). The third sample consisted of 3,612 college alumni for whom occupation was determined an average of eight years after UNIACT scores were obtained.

If the highest scores in high profiles indicate stronger interests than the highest scores in low profiles, then one would expect a higher hit rate for the high profile group. However, the high and low profile groups had essentially the same hit rates. Thus there is no reason to believe that interest profile level indicates strength of interest. These results suggest that when interest inventories are used in tandem with ability measures, comparisons of interest profile level with ability profile level are not warranted. Such comparisons may lead to career counseling based on interest inventory yea-/naysaying (response style). The same may apply to comparisons of interest profile level and ability self-confidence (self-efficacy, etc.) profile level.

Validity of Interest Profile Shape. Hit rate data for basic interest scales (e.g., see Donnay & Borgen, 1996; Prediger, 1998; Swaney, 1995) support the widespread interpretation of profile shape. These validity data and the profile level data cited above indicate that when interest and ability measures are used in tandem, profile shapes should be compared—unless there is evidence that profile levels can be compared. When interest and ability profile shapes are compared, unique and valid information can be obtained (see Considerations 5 and 6). Whether self-estimate profile level indicates strength of ability and not response style is an open question. But the question is irrelevant to interest-ability comparisons based on profile shape.

Consideration 5: Provision of Unique Information

When using interest and ability scores in tandem, it is important to determine whether the ability scores provide new information. It may appear that ability scores add a "can-do" dimension to interest scores. But if the scores are largely redundant, time and money are wasted. Career suggestions will differ largely due to measurement error.

Inter-individual Correlations. There have been a number of studies of the correlations between pairs of interest and ability scales (to be called inter-individual correlations in order to distinguish them from the *intra*-individual correlations). In such studies, level and direction of correlation depend on which abilities and interests are paired; if the match is not good, correlations will be low. In probably his most comprehensive discussion of "Abilities vs. Interests," Strong (1955, p. 146) concluded that "most [inter-individual] correlations range between .30 and -.30 with a few higher coefficients. Both positive and negative correlations are in the expected direction. . . . [The] correlations are seldom high enough to be of practical significance" (p. 146). Strong's 1995 summary statement still appears to be accurate (e.g., see American College Testing, 1988; Lowman, 1991; Randahl, 1991).

As noted above, interest scores have a large response style component that affects score level, independent of interests. In addition the constructs assessed by interest and ability measures usually differ, even when they have similar names. Hence low correlations should not be surprising. Regarding construct differences, mechanical reasoning test items (for example) may define mechanical ability much more narrowly than the items on a mechanical interest scale. When there is an effort to match interest and ability constructs, correlations between corresponding interest–ability pairs tend to be higher, as correlations based on assessments of Holland's RIASEC types show (American College Testing, 1988; Holland et al., 1994; Swanson, 1993). For Samples A and B (described under Consideration 2), the median interest–ability (UNIACT–IWRA) correlations across Holland's six types were .43 and .45, respectively (American College Testing, 1998). The chief difference between these studies and the studies cited by Strong (1955) appears to be the greater degree of match between interest and ability constructs.

Intra-individual Correlations. Interest–ability correlations, as normally reported, address one pair of scales at a time. This is surprising because career counseling is based on multiscore *profiles*. Even if the correlation between each interest–ability scale pair is zero, everyone could score highest on the same scale (e.g., Social Service) for both interests and abilities. Thus inter-individual correlations appear to be irrelevant to career counseling. In contrast, *intra*-individual correlations— the relationship, obtained one individual at a time, between the individual's scores on corresponding scales in pairs of interest and ability profiles (i.e., profile shape)—*are* relevant for the tandem use of interest and ability measures. Such correlations indicate the extent to which counselees receive unique information. What then is the relationship between interest and ability profile shapes?

As noted above, intra-individual correlations are obtained one person at a time. Typically the median value and some measure of range are reported for persons in the sample under study. Randahl (1991) cited and summarized results obtained from several early studies of intra-individual correlations. For Samples A and B the median intra-individual correlations for UNIACT interests and IWRA abilities were .53 and .54, respectively (American College Testing, 1998). Across sample members the correlations ranged from about -1.00 to +1.00. The relatively low medians and extreme range of correlations indicate substantial differences in interest and ability profile shapes.

Overlap of Occupational Suggestions. From a career counselor's perspective intra-individual correlations are much more informative than inter-individual correlations. But they do not directly address the occupational suggestions counselees receive when interest and ability measures are used in tandem. One way to compare the information provided by interest and ability measures is to determine the extent of agreement between highest interest and ability scores. For both Samples A and B the agreement rate was 38% (American College Testing, 1998). That is, 38% of the sample members were referred to the same RIASEC type on the basis of their interest and ability scores; their scores were redundant. However, unique results were provided to 62% of the sample members. Especially since the tandem use of interest and ability measures (including ability self-confidence, etc., measures) is increasing (Betz & Hackett, 1997), having information on the extent to which counselees receive unique results appears to be important.

Consideration 6: Provision of More Valid Information

When using interest and ability measures in tandem, it is not sufficient to determine the extent to which they provide unique information. It is also important to know whether the ability measures have validity (for career exploration applications) beyond that of the interest measures (and vice versa). Two sets of scores are not necessarily more valid (useful) than one. Ability score interpretations that are unique (that differ from interest score interpretations) may lack validity (and vice versa).

Three validity-related questions appear to be relevant. First, do ability and interest scores have *independent validity?* This question can be addressed by determining whether ability scores have a substantial hit rate for persons who are interest-score misses and vice versa. Second, do ability and interest scores have *agreement validity?* This question can be addressed by determining whether the hit rate, when highest ability and interest scores agree, is substantially higher than the hit rate for either alone. Third, do ability and interest scores have *incremental validity?* This question can be addressed by determining whether the hit rate for ability and interest scores combined is higher than the hit rate for either alone.

In incremental validity studies hit rates are determined for the total sample. However, independent validity studies involve only those cases for whom interest (or ability) predictions were incorrect (misses). Although psychometrically important, independent validity has no direct application in career counseling because one never knows whether a given counselee is an interest miss or an ability miss. Agreement validity studies involve only those cases for whom interest and ability results agree. Because the hit rate for "disagrees" must go down if the hit rate for "agrees" goes up, the total sample hit rate can never exceed that of the more valid measure. Incremental validity studies, in contrast, ask whether some combination of interest and ability scores is more valid than either alone. Hit rates for the total sample are examined. By way of analogy, high school grades and test scores have incremental validity for the prediction of college grades (for example, see American College Testing, 1997a). That is, predictions are more accurate when grades and test scores are used in combination.

Evidence of Independent Validity. I am aware of only one published study addressing the independent validity of interest and ability measures. In an analysis of longitudinal data for 2,101 vocational high school students (see discussion of Data Source 2 under Consideration 3), Prediger and Brandt (1990) obtained membership predictions for Holland-type criterion groups consisting of successful and satisfied students in various vocational programs. Rather than being based on highest interest and ability scores, the predictions were based on computer-implemented decision rules intended to simulate a counselor interpretation. Since one to three of the six Holland types could be predicted for a student, the chance hit rate for interests alone was 28% instead of 17% (1/6). The actual hit rate for interests alone was 64%. The ability hit rate for interest misses (chance equaled 29%) was 44%. Thus independent validity was demonstrated.

Evidence of Agreement Validity. In a recent study (American College Testing, 1998) of agreement validity for UNIACT interest and IWRA ability measures, students in Samples A and B (described under Consideration 2) were assigned to Holland types on the basis of occupational preference screened on certainty. Criterion group membership predictions were based on highest score for Holland type (high-point code). Hence the chance hit rate was 17% (1/6). The Sample A and B hit rates for interests alone were 44% and 41% respectively. When the interest and ability high-point codes agreed, hit rates were 57% and 50% respectively. Thus, for these instruments, counselors can have more confidence in career suggestions when interest and ability scores agree. Conversely, validity is lower when scores disagree.

Evidence of Incremental Validity. Studies of the incremental validity of interest and ability measures appear to be rare. A few studies have used discriminant analysis (DISANL) to determine the extent to which combinations of disparate interest and ability measures differentiate occupational groups (Austin & Hanisch, 1990), occupational plan groups (Cooley & Lohnes, 1968), or vocational education program groups (Prediger, 1971). However, only Cooley and Lohnes reported data for interests and abilities separately. Of course the determination of incremental validity requires such data.

In their study, Cooley and Lohnes used 11 "motive" scores (largely based on interests) and 11 ability scores to differentiate six occupational plan groups and to predict group membership for persons in a cross-validation sample. Cross-validated predictions are needed because DISANL (like regression analysis) capitalizes on chance. Hence, for the analysis sample, one would expect two sets of scores (i.e., 22 predictors) to do better than one set of scores (i.e., 11 predictors) by chance alone.

The Cooley-Lohnes sample consisted of 5,857 ninth-graders who had completed the motive and ability measures. Occupational plans were obtained one year after they graduated from high school. Cross-validated hit rates for the six plan groups were 27%, 30%, and 33% for motives, abilities, and their combination, respectively. Thus the hit rate for motives and abilities combined was about 10% higher than for abilities alone (33 - 30 = 3; 3/30 = 10%). For motives the increment was about 22%.

Other ways of combining interest and ability scores appear to have more practical relevance for career counseling, especially since they do not preclude the separate consideration of interests and abilities. For example, interest and ability scores may be mentally combined in the clinical bridge (Goldman, 1971) to counselee implications. Miller (1997) recently suggested a simple procedure for combining interest, ability, etc., three-letter codes for RIASEC types; and of course interest and ability scores can simply be added together in order to obtain total scores, as in the SDS Summary Score (Holland et al., 1994).

In an incremental validity study involving the additive approach to combining interest and ability scores Gottfredson and Holland (1975) obtained hit rates for RIASEC criterion groups separately for each of the five SDS components and the SDS Summary Score (total score). For a sample of 192 liberal arts college males, one interest component and one ability component did as well as or better than the SDS Summary Score. Hence incremental validity was not demonstrated.

Gottfredson and Holland also obtained validity data for a sample of 432 liberal arts females. Perhaps because of the unusual nature of the sample (72% were in the Social-type criterion group), none of the six hit rates (five SDS components and Summary Score) beat the base rate (72%). That is, none of the SDS hit rates was higher than the hit rate for predictions based solely on knowledge of criterion group size. Thus for the female sample the data on incremental validity were irrelevant.

Given the increasing use of interest and ability measures in tandem, I find it surprising that evidence of incremental validity appears to be lacking (with the exception of the 30-year-old Cooley-Lohnes study). Perhaps this is because few assessment instruments actually combine interest and ability scores. (Recall that validity data must be relevant to use.) But, independent and agreement validity also appear to have received little attention. Hence we don't know whether practitioners and their clients are wasting time and dollars on one or the other type of measure, all the while attending to interest-ability profile differences that may be irrelevant to career exploration and planning.

SUMMARY OF CONSIDERATIONS

It is important to keep in mind that the considerations presented here apply to the use of interest and ability measures in an every-person, comprehensive search for occupations that have counselee-compatible work tasks and workers. Considerations regarding the use of ability measures in career exploration include (a) a similarity-based search for occupational options (rather than a prediction-based research), (b) a comprehensive assessment of work-relevant abilities (rather than a narrow, test-based assessment), and (c) use of informed self-estimates of work-relevant abilities as valid alternatives to ability tests. Considerations regarding the tandem use of interest and ability measures include (a) interest-ability score comparisons based on profile shape rather than profile level, (b) evidence of the extent to which interest and ability scores provide unique information, and (c) evidence of independent, agreement, and incremental validity for career exploration applications. Regarding the last three considerations, the results of recent research involving five samples (Ns of 690, 3,612, 4,679, 53,429, and 386,836) were summarized. Betz and Hackett (1997) note that the tandem use of interest and ability measures (including ability self-confidence, etc., measures) is increasing. Counselors should expect evidence that interest and ability measures provide unique information and have independent, agreement, and incremental validity.

SOME SUGGESTIONS FOR COUNSELORS

The following suggestions apply to the use of interest and ability measures in developmental career counseling—particularly, stimulating and facilitating self-career exploration and planning. They are drawn from the considerations noted above. Because the suggestions are not intended to be comprehensive, readers may wish to consult the career assessment textbooks cited under Consideration 1.

1. Use ability measures as you would use interest measures—to identify occupations with counselee-compatible work tasks and workers. That is, use the similarity (discriminant) bridge between scores and counselee implications rather than the success (regression) bridge.

2. Seek a comprehensive assessment of work-relevant abilities and a coordinated basis for linking abilities and interests to occupational options. That is, use informed self-estimates of work-relevant abilities rather than ability test scores. When it comes to *comprehensive assessment for the many* and work-world linkage of assessment results, ability tests appear to be a "crock" (to coin a psychometric term).

3. Don't assume interest profile level indicates strength of interest. Compare interest and ability profile shapes, not levels—*unless* there is evidence that profile levels can be compared. Give special attention to the highest scores, regardless of profile level.

4. Whatever the measure, use scaled (e.g., normed) scores to determine profile shapes and highest scores.

5. When using interest and ability measures in tandem, require that ability scores provide new information (and vice versa).

6. When using interest and ability measures in tandem, require that ability scores add validity to interest scores (and vice versa).

7. When ability measures are comprehensive and well coordinated with interest measures, seek a simple procedure for relating them to occupational options. If the interests and abilities correspond to RIASEC types, three-letter codes can be used (Holland et al., 1994) or, as illustrated in the case study that follows, occupational options can be identified visually via the World-of-Work Map (American College Testing, 1988; Prediger & Swaney, 1995). Once occupational options are identified, ability measures can be used to sort them out.

8. When ability measures are not comprehensive and/or not well coordinated with interest measures and work-world structure, change ability measures. If this is not possible, do the "two-step." First, identify counselee-compatible occupations via interest inventories, job values inventories, etc. Second, use a combination of ability measures tailored to counselee needs to identify counselee-compatible occupations that (a) are currently attainable and/or (b) require a reasonable amount of ability development. Of course ability scores should be considered in the context of other information (e.g., achievement test scores, school/college grades, quality of education, time and financial resources for ability development). Thus, in the "two-step," interest measures are used to stimulate and focus career exploration, and ability measures are one of the many things considered during the process of exploration.

9. If counselees lack abilities relevant to occupations that interest them, suggest ways they can build those abilities (e.g., see Jones, 1996). One of a career counselor's primary concerns is helping persons develop occupational possibilities into realities.

10. Use ability self-estimates to help counselees clarify self-concepts (e.g., via a review of experiences, accomplishments, grades, ability test scores, etc.). As noted by Goldman (1972), "The main contribution of tests in counseling is not making predictions but facilitating the clarification of self-concept" (p. 219).

CASE STUDY

Context

In order to illustrate career counseling applications of this chapter's considerations, a case study reported by Prediger and Swaney (1995) is summarized and extended below. The summary and extension provide information about the assessments that were used, how they were linked to occupational options for the purpose of career exploration, and how they were used in career planning. Readers are urged to consult the case study source for specifics. Because the case study is in the form of a summary report, the counselor-counselee interactive process (e.g., see Healy, 1990) is not addressed. Also the use of assessment results may appear to be directive. In fact, I am impressed with the personal-story, life-theme approach to career counseling advanced by Savickas (1997), especially because of the way it facilitates the integration of assessment results with life events and with needs, work-relevant values, and life goals.

Counselee Background

Jessica Vundering (she prefers Jess) is a 22-year-old, first-year student at University A. Jess grew up on a farm in the rural Midwest. After high school graduation she continued to help with the family farm's record keeping and other responsibilities. Later she took a "big-city job" as a clerk in a large insurance company.

Being displeased with her job and its location, Jess sought career counseling at her local community college. There Jess completed ability tests and was later admitted to a nearby state university (formerly a teacher's college) with a tentative major in elementary education. She is the only one in her family to attend college. During her first semester Jess enrolled in "Exploring Teaching: A Field Experience." During her second semester she sought help from the counseling center regarding choice of major (the presenting problem).

Measures for Which Results Are Available

Formal assessment at Jess's small, rural high school was limited to state-mandated achievement tests, on which she recalls "scoring above average." As part of her career counseling contact at the community college, Jess completed the *Differential Aptitude Tests* (DAT; Psychological Corporation, 1992). On the basis of her DAT results, especially her Scholastic Aptitude score, Jess decided to complete the four academic ability tests included in the ACT Assessment (the ACT;

American College Testing, 1997a). The universities in her state require applicants to submit ACT scores.

At her university's counseling center, Jess was introduced to DISCOVER (American College Testing, 1995b), a computer-based career planning system that includes UNIACT, IWRA, the *Inventory of Work-Relevant Experiences* (IWRE; American College Testing, 1988) and the *Inventory of Job Values* (IJV; Prediger & Staples, 1996). On her own, Jess decided to complete all of these assessments online.

Basis for Linking Measures to Occupational Options

The empirically based World-of-Work Map (American College Testing, 1988; Prediger, 1996; Prediger & Swaney, 1995), an extension of Holland's (1997) hexagon, was used to link all six of the measures cited above to occupational options. Holland's hexagon and its underlying, research-based Data/Ideas and People/Things Work Task Dimensions form the core of the map (Fig. 14.1). The periphery shows the locations of Holland's (1997) RIASEC types and the corresponding titles used with UNIACT, IWRA, and IWRE. Any set of scores for RIASEC types can be linked to occupations via the World-of-Work Map and the accompanying Job Family Charts (American College Testing, 1997b). The Job Cluster and Job Family List (Fig. 14.2) provides an overview of the map's 23 job families. Together the job families encompass all occupations in the *Dictionary of Occupational Titles* (U.S. Department of Labor, 1991).

World-of-Work Map results for interests (UNIACT), abilities (IWRA), and experiences (IWRE) are reported via "map regions," as shown by Fig. 14.1, and counselees are encouraged to look into job families in their map regions. For reasons noted by Prediger and Staples (1996), job values (which counselees report via the IJV) cannot be translated into map regions. Hence a best-fit approach is used to link IJV results to job families, which are also map locations. Thus, as shown by Fig. 14.1, results for all four types of measures can be located on the World-of-Work Map and thereby compared. Prediger and Swaney (1995) suggested counseling approaches when the map locations for various combinations of measures are problematic.

Because the DAT and ACT do not provide a comprehensive assessment of work-relevant abilities, their results cannot be used directly in a *comprehensive* search for occupational options. However, Jess did use her DAT and ACT scores, along with other relevant information (e.g., her grades, experiences), to inform her self-estimates for 7 of IWRA's 15 abilities (e.g., numerical, mechanical, scientific).

Results for UNIACT, IWRA, and IWRE are linked to World-of-Work Map regions via three-letter codes based on the three highest, norm-based scores for

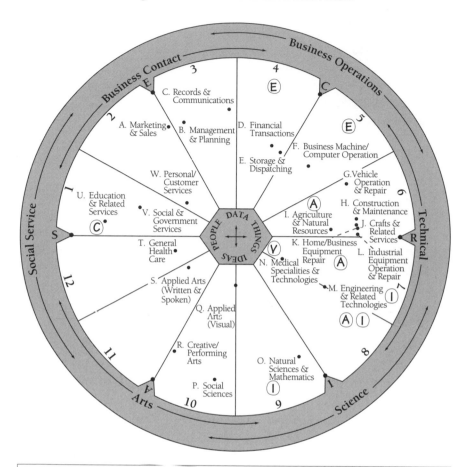

About the Map

The World-of-Work Map arranges job families (groups of similar jobs) into 12 regions. Together, the job families cover all U.S. jobs. Although the jobs in a family differ in their locations, most are located near the points shown.

A job family's location is based on its primary work tasks—working with DATA, IDEAS, PEOPLE, and THINGS.

Six general areas of the work world and related Holland types are indicated around the edge of the map. Job Family Charts (available from ACT) list over 500 occupations by general area, job family, and preparation level. They cover more than 95% of the labor force.

FIGURE 14.1   World-of-Work Map

Case study results are represented by circled initials. C = current occupational choice, I = interests, E = experiences, A = abilities, and V = job values.

BUSINESS CONTACT JOB CLUSTER

A. MARKETING AND SALES JOB FAMILY
Sales workers in stores; route drivers (milk, etc.); buyers; travel agents; sales workers who visit customers (real estate and insurance agents; stock brokers; farm products, office and medical supplies sales workers)

B. MANAGEMENT AND PLANNING
Store, motel, restaurant, and agribusiness managers; office supervisors; purchasing agents; managers in large businesses; recreation/parks managers; medical records administrators; urban planners

BUSINESS OPERATIONS JOB CLUSTER

C. RECORDS AND COMMUNICATIONS
Office, library, hotel, and postal clerks; receptionists; computer tape librarians, office, medical, and legal secretaries; court reporters; medical record technicians

D. FINANCIAL TRANSACTIONS
Bookkeepers; accountants; grocery check-out clerks; bank tellers; ticket agents; insurance underwriters; financial analysts

E. STORAGE AND DISPATCHING
Shipping and receiving clerks; mail carriers; truck, cab, and airline dispatchers; cargo agents; air traffic controllers

F. BUSINESS MACHINE/COMPUTER OPERATION
Computer console, printer, etc., operators; office machine operators; typists; word-processing equipment operators; statistical clerks

TECHNICAL JOB CLUSTER

G. VEHICLE OPERATION AND REPAIR
Bus, truck, and cab drivers; auto, bus, and airplane mechanics; forklift operators; merchant marine officers; airplane pilots

H. CONSTRUCTION AND MAINTENANCE
Carpenters; electricians; painters; custodians (janitors); bricklayers; sheet metal workers; bulldozer and crane operators; building inspectors

I. AGRICULTURE AND NATURAL RESOURCES
Farmers; foresters; ranchers; landscape gardeners; tree surgeons; plant nursery workers; pet shop attendants

J. CRAFTS AND RELATED SERVICES
Cooks; meatcutters; bakers; shoe repairers; piano/organ tuners; tailors; jewelers

K. HOME/BUSINESS EQUIPMENT REPAIR
Repairers of TV sets, appliances, typewriters, telephones, heating systems, photocopiers, etc.

L. INDUSTRIAL EQUIPMENT OPERATION AND REPAIR
Machinists; printers; sewing machine operators; welders; industrial machinery repairers; production painters; laborers and machine operators in factories, mines, etc.; firefighters

SCIENCE JOB CLUSTER

M. ENGINEERING AND OTHER APPLIED TECHNOLOGIES
Engineers and engineering technicians in various fields; biological and chemical lab technicians; computer programmers; computer service technicians; drafters; surveyors; technical illustrators; food technologists

N. MEDICAL SPECIALTIES AND TECHNOLOGIES
Dental hygienists; EEG and EKG technicians; opticians; prosthetics technicians; X-ray technologists; medical technologists; dentists; optometrists; pharmacists; veterinarians

O. NATURAL SCIENCES AND MATHEMATICS
Agronomists; biologists; chemists; ecologists; geographers; geologists; horticulturists; mathematicians; physicists

P. SOCIAL SCIENCES
Marketing research analysts; anthropologists; economists; political scientists; psychologists; sociologists

ARTS JOB CLUSTER

Q. APPLIED ARTS (VISUAL)
Floral designers; merchandise displayers; commercial artists; fashion designers; photographers; interior designers; architects; landscape architects

R. CREATIVE/PERFORMING ARTS
Entertainers (comedians, etc.) actors/actresses; dancers; musicians, singers; writers; art, music, etc. teachers

S. APPLIED ARTS (WRITTEN AND SPOKEN)
Advertising copywriters; disk jockeys; legal assistants; advertising account executives; interpreters; reporters; public relations workers; lawyers; librarians; technical writers

SOCIAL SERVICE JOB CLUSTER

T. GENERAL HEALTH CARE
Orderlies; dental assistants; licensed practical nurses; physical therapy assistants; registered nurses; dieticians; occupational therapists; physicians; speech pathologists

U. EDUCATION AND RELATED SERVICES
Teacher aides; preschool teachers; athletic coaches; college teachers, guidance/career/etc., counselors; elementary and secondary school teachers; special education teachers

V. SOCIAL AND GOVERNMENT SERVICES
Security guards; recreation leaders; police officers; health/safety/food/etc., inspectors; child welfare workers; home economists; rehabilitation counselors; social workers

W. PERSONAL/CUSTOMER SERVICES
Grocery baggers; bellhops; flight attendants (stewards, stewardesses); waitresses and waiters; cosmetologists (beauticians); barbers; butlers and maids

FIGURE 14.2   Job Cluster and Job Family List

each of the measures. (Prediger & Swaney, 1995, provide a look-up table.) Thus profile shape rather than profile level is used for a comprehensive search for occupational options. Regarding abilities (IWRA) and experiences (IWRE), profile level may also be relevant to career exploration and planning. Hence Jess's counselor referred to her complete score profiles (including her DAT and ACT profiles) when helping her consider certain occupations and the preparation they required. Jess's complete IWRE profile was helpful in determining whether her interests and abilities had an adequate experience base, something counselors need to consider.

Occupational Options Explored by the Counselee

As shown by Fig. 14.1, Jess's interest and ability results converge on job families involving things and ideas work tasks. However, her IWRE-assessed experiences suggest Map Regions 4 and 5, which primarily involve data work tasks. This is in keeping with Jess's work experience (which she disliked). Jess's counselor observed that, although Jess did not score highest on the IWRE Technical Scale, the *level* of her score was substantially above average, as one would expect for someone growing up on a farm. Jess's score on the IWRE Science Scale was also above average, thus indicating that her UNIACT and IWRA results were informed. Jess recalled that she was the only girl (of 22 in her high school class) who took general science, biology, and chemistry. Regarding job values, DISCOVER reported the three job families that best fit what Jess wanted in a job. Job Family N (Medical Specialties and Technologies) ranked the highest and seemed especially appealing to Jess. So she entered a V (for values) by its name in Region 7.

After surveying the occupations in various job families and the type of preparation typically required, as shown by the Job Family Charts, Jess settled on two occupations in Job Family N and two in Job Family K (Home/Business Equipment Repair) for further exploration, the latter two because less education was required. DISCOVER provided her with specific information for each occupation. Her counselor suggested additional sources. At this stage, counseling entered Step 2 in the "two-step" described under Suggestion 8 above.

Career Plans Made by Counselee

Jess was certain that she did not want to become an elementary school teacher. Veterinarian (in Job Family N) became her first choice after she talked with a woman vet who worked with farm animals. (Where she grew up, the vets were men.) However, Jess had misgivings about qualifying for a veterinary medicine program, which was also at a different university (University X). Her second choice was medical technologist, which did not require education beyond four years of college. However, that program was offered at University Y.

Jess recalled that she had sent her ACT scores to Universities X and Y and hence had received grade predictions on her score report. Based on her ACT scores and high school grades, her chances in 10 of earning a C or higher during the first year were 7 and 8 at Universities X and Y, respectively. Jess's counselor reviewed this information, Jess's ACT scores, high school grades, first-term college grades, and ability self-estimates (her ability self-concepts appeared to be accurate) in light of his knowledge of Universities X and Y. As he and Jess discussed the "big picture," Jess came to see she would have a good chance of completing a four-year degree at either of the universities. Hence she set aside the Job Family K occupations she was considering.

Using ACT score profiles for veterinary medicine and health sciences/services (American College Testing, 1995a), Jess's counselor showed her that her ACT Science score ranked in the upper quarter of first-year college students planning to major in veterinary medicine. Her other ACT scores also ranked high. Jess's standing among students planning to major in health sciences/services (which includes medical technology) was even higher. Jess recalled that she had received an A and two B's in the high school science courses she had taken.

What to do now? Jess had a good part-time job at University A and needed the money. Also she discovered that the biology and chemistry course prerequisites for the two programs she was considering were similar and that most of the courses were offered by her current institution. Hence Jess decided to spend at least another year there and take several of the course prerequisites. She viewed this as "testing the waters." Also she planned to learn more about medical technology (veterinary medicine she had observed firsthand), perhaps via job-shadowing or a summer internship arranged through her university's experiential education office. Jess is no longer wondering why she went to college.

Final Comment

The scores available for Jess covered a wide range of personal characteristics. Much more could have been said about their interaction and their use in the clinical (build-a-counselee-model) bridge (Goldman, 1971) to score implications. Also Suggestion 9 (ability building) was not addressed in the case summary, and Suggestion 10 (self-concept clarification) was only briefly addressed. (Suggestions 5 and 6 were addressed earlier in the chapter.) Finally, readers not already suffering from test scores overload may find informative a case study example (Prediger and Schmertz, 1998) of how interest, ability, and skill self-confidence scores from five widely used instruments (total of nine sets of scores) can be integrated for the purpose of career exploration.

REFERENCES

American College Testing. (1988). *Interim psychometric handbook for the 3rd edition ACT Career Planning Program.* Iowa City, IA: Author.

American College Testing. (1995a). *College student profiles: Norms for the ACT assessment* (Rev. ed.). Iowa City, IA: Author.

American College Testing. (1995b). *DISCOVER for Colleges and Adults: Professional Manual.* Hunt Valley, MD: Author.

American College Testing. (1997a). *ACT Assessment technical manual.* Iowa City, IA: Author.

American College Testing. (1997b). *VIESA job family charts.* Iowa City, IA: Author.

American College Testing. (1998). *Career Planning Survey technical manual.* Iowa City, IA: Author.

Anastasi, A., & Urbina, S. (1997). *Psychological testing* (7th ed.). Englewood Cliffs, NJ: Prentice Hall.

Austin, J. T., & Hanisch, K. A. (1990). Occupational attainment as a function of abilities and interests: A longitudinal analysis using Project TALENT data. *Journal of Applied Psychology, 75,* 77–86.

Baird, L. (1976). *Using self-reports to predict student performance* (Research Monograph No. 7). New York: College Entrance Examination Board.

Betz, N. E., Borgen, F. H., & Harmon, L. W. (1996). *Skills Confidence Inventory: Applications and technical guide.* Palo Alto, CA: Consulting Psychologists Press.

Betz, N. E., & Hackett, G. (1997). Applications of self-efficacy theory to the career assessment of women. *Journal of Career Assessment, 5,* 383–402.

Campbell, D. P., Hyne, S. A., & Nilsen, D. L. (1992). *Manual for the Campbell Interest and Skill Survey.* Minneapolis: National Computer Systems.

Careerware: ISM Systems Corporation. (1992). *CHOICES* [Computer software]. Ottawa, Ontario, Canada: Author.

Cooley, W. W., & Lohnes, P. R. (1968). *Predicting development of young adults.* Pittsburgh, PA: American Institutes for Research and School of Education, University of Pittsburgh.

Dawis, R. V., Dohm, T. E., Lofquist, L. H., Chartrand, J. M., & Due, A. M. (1987). *Minnesota Occupational Classification System II: A psychological taxonomy of work.* Minneapolis: University of Minnesota Department of Psychology.

Desmarais, L. B., & Sackett, P. R. (1993). Investigating a cognitive complexity hierarchy of jobs. *Journal of Vocational Behavior, 43,* 279–297.

Donnay, A. C., & Borgen, F. H. (1996). Validity, structure, and content of the 1994 *Strong Interest Inventory. Journal of Counseling Psychology, 43,* 75–291.

Goldman, L. (1971). *Using tests in counseling* (2nd ed.). Englewood Cliffs, NJ: Appleton-Century-Crofts.

Goldman, L. (1972). Tests and counseling: The marriage that failed. *Measurement and Evaluation in Guidance, 4,* 213–220.

Goldman, L. (1982). Assessment in counseling: A better way. *Measurement and Evaluation in Guidance, 15,* 70–73.

Gottfredson, G. D., & Holland, J. L. (1975). Vocational choices of men and women: A comparison of predictors from the *Self-Directed Search. Journal of Counseling Psychology, 22,* 28–34.

Harmon, L. W., Hansen, J. C., Borgen, F. H., & Hammer, A. L. (1994). *Strong Interest Inventory: Applications and technical guide*. Stanford, CA: Stanford University Press.

Harrington, J. C., & Harrington, T. F. (1996). *Ability Explorer: Preliminary technical manual*. Chicago: Riverside Publishing.

Healy, C. C. (1990). Reforming career appraisals to meet the needs of clients in the 1990's. *The Counseling Psychologist, 18,* 214–226.

Holland, J. L. (1997). *Making vocational choices* (3rd ed.). Odessa, FL: Psychological Assessment Resources.

Holland, J. L., Fritzsche, B. A., & Powell, A. B. (1994). *The Self-Directed Search technical manual*. Odessa, FL: Psychological Assessment Resources.

Hood, A. B., & Johnson, R. W. (1997). *Assessment in counseling: A guide to the use of psychological assessment procedures* (2nd ed.). Alexandria, VA: American Counseling Association.

Hunter, J. E. (1986). Cognitive ability, cognitive aptitudes, job knowledge, and job performance. *Journal of Vocational Behavior, 29,* 340–362.

Jensen, A. R. (1986). g: Artifact or reality? *Journal of Vocational Behavior, 29,* 301–331.

Jones, L. K. (1996). *Job skills for the 21st century: A guide for students*. Phoenix: Oryx Press.

Kapes, J. T., Mastie, M. M., & Whitfield, E. A. (Eds.). (1994). *A counselor's guide to career assessment instruments* (3rd ed.). Alexandria, VA: National Career Development Association.

Katz, M. R. (1993). *Computer-assisted career decision-making: The guide in the machine*. Hillsdale, NJ: Erlbaum.

Lichtenberg, J. W., Shaffer, M., & Arachtingi, B. M. (1993). Expected utility and sequential elimination models of career decision making. *Journal of Vocational Behavior, 42,* 237–252.

Lowman, R. L. (1991). *The clinical practice of career assessment: Interests, abilities, and personality*. Washington, DC: American Psychological Association.

Mabe, P. A., III, & West, S. G. (1982). Validity of self-evaluation ability: A review and meta-analysis. *Journal of Applied Psychology, 67,* 280–296.

Miller, M. J. (1997). Extending Prediger's 4-2-1 formula: Practical applications for career counselors. *Journal of Employment Counseling, 34,* 40–43.

Murphy, L. L., Conoley, J. C., & Impara, J. C. (Eds.). (1994). *Tests in print IV: An index to tests, test reviews, and the literature on specific tests*. Lincoln, NE: Buros Institute of Mental Measurements.

Osipow, S. H., & Temple, R. D. (1996). Development and use of the Task-Specific Occupational Self-Efficacy Scale. *Journal of Career Assessment, 4,* 445–456.

Prediger, D. J. (1971). Converting test data to counseling information: System trial—with feedback. *Journal of Educational Measurement, 8,* 161–169.

Prediger, D. J. (1974). The role of assessment in career guidance. In E. L. Herr (Ed.), *Vocational guidance and human development* (pp. 325–349). Boston: Houghton Mifflin.

Prediger, D. J. (1982). Dimensions underlying Holland's hexagon: Missing link between interests and occupations? *Journal of Vocational Behavior, 21,* 259–287.

Prediger, D. J. (1987). *Career counseling validity of the ASVAB Job Cluster Scales used in DISCOVER* (ACT Research Report No. 87-2). Iowa City, IA: American College Testing.

Prediger, D. J. (1989). Ability differences across occupations: More than g. *Journal of Vocational Behavior, 34,* 1–27.

Prediger, D. J. (1992, March). Conditions related to the accuracy of ability self-estimates. In D. Prediger (Chair), *Beyond the "ASVAB code": Using the other ASVAB aptitude scores to expand career exploration.* Symposium conducted at the meeting of the American Association for Counseling and Development, Baltimore.

Prediger, D. J. (1996). Alternative dimensions for the Tracey-Rounds interest sphere. *Journal of Vocational Behavior, 48,* 59–67.

Prediger, D. J. (1998). Is interest profile level relevant to career counseling? *Journal of Counseling Psychology, 45,* 204–211.

Prediger, D. J. (in press). Basic structure of work-relevant abilities. *Journal of Counseling Psychology.*

Prediger, D. J., & Brandt, W. E. (1990). *Project CHOICE: Validity of interest and ability measures for student choice of vocational program* (ACT Research Report No. 90-2). Iowa City, IA: American College Testing.

Prediger, D. J., & Schmertz, E. (1998). Ellenore Flood's UNIACT results. *Career Development Quarterly, 46,* 352–359.

Prediger, D. J., & Staples, J. S. (1996). *Linking occupational attribute preferences to occupations* (ACT Research Report No. 96-3). Iowa City, IA: American College Testing.

Prediger, D. J., & Swaney, K. B. (1992). *Career counseling validity of DISCOVER's job cluster scales for the revised ASVAB score report* (ACT Research Report No. 92-2). Iowa City, IA: American College Testing.

Prediger, D. J., & Swaney, K. B. (1995). Using UNIACT in a comprehensive approach to assessment for career planning. *Journal of Career Assessment, 3,* 429–451.

Psychological Corporation. (1992). *Differential Aptitude Tests technical manual* (5th ed.). San Antonio, TX: Author.

Randahl, G. J. (1991). A typological analysis of the relations between measured vocational interests and abilities. *Journal of Vocational Behavior, 38,* 333–350.

Rolfhus, E. L., & Ackerman, P. L. (1996). Self-report knowledge: At the crossroads of ability, interest, and personality. *Journal of Educational Psychology, 88,* 174–188.

Rounds, J. B., & Tracey, T. J. (1990). From trait-and-factor to person-environment fit counseling: Theory and process. In W. B. Walsh & S. J. Osipow (Eds.), *Career counseling: Contemporary topics in vocational psychology* (pp. 1–44). Hillsdale, NJ: Erlbaum.

Savickas, M. L. (1997). The spirit in career counseling: Fostering self-completion through work. In D. P. Bloch & L. J. Richmond (Eds.), *Connections between spirit and work in career development* (pp. 3–26). Palo Alto, CA: Davies-Black.

Seligman, L. (1994). *Developmental career counseling and assessment* (2nd ed.). Thousand Oaks, CA: Sage.

Strong, E. K., Jr. (1955). *Vocational interests 18 years after college.* Minneapolis: University of Minnesota Press.

Super, D. E. (1957). *The psychology of careers.* New York: HarperCollins.

Swaney, K. B. (1987). *The DISCOVER self-estimated abilities study: Methods and results.* Unpublished manuscript, American College Testing, Research Division, Iowa City, IA.

Swaney, K. B. (1995). *Technical manual: Revised Unisex Edition of the ACT Interest Inventory (UNIACT).* Iowa City, IA: American College Testing.

Swanson, J. L. (1993). Integrated assessment of vocational interests and self-rated skills and abilities. *Journal of Career Assessment, 1,* 50–65.

Thorndike, R. L. (1982). *Applied psychometrics*. Boston: Houghton Mifflin.

Tracey, T.J.G. (1997). The structure of interests and self-efficacy expectations: An expanded examination of the spherical model of interests. *Journal of Counseling Psychology, 44*, 32–43.

U.S. Department of Defense. (1995a). *Counselor manual for the Armed Services Vocational Aptitude Battery Career Exploration Program*. North Chicago, IL: U.S. Military Entrance Processing Command.

U.S. Department of Defense. (1995b). *Exploring careers: The ASVAB workbook*. North Chicago, IL: U.S. Military Entrance Processing Command.

U.S. Department of Labor. (1980). *Manual for the USES General Aptitude Test Battery: Section IV. Specific aptitude test batteries*. Washington, DC: U.S. Government Printing Office.

U.S. Department of Labor. (1991). *Dictionary of occupational titles* (4th ed., rev.). Washington, DC: U.S. Government Printing Office.

Walsh, W. B., & Betz, N. E. (1995). *Tests and assessment* (3rd ed.). Englewood Cliffs, NJ: Prentice Hall.

Westbrook, B. W., Buck, R. W., Wynne, D. C., & Sanford, E. (1994). Career maturity in adolescence: Reliability and validity of self-ratings of abilities by gender and ethnicity. *Journal of Career Assessment, 2*, 125–161.

Zytowski, D. G. (1994). Tests and counseling: We are still married, and living in discriminant analysis. *Measurement and Evaluation in Counseling and Development, 26*, 219–223.

Zunker, V. G. (1994). *Using assessment results for career development* (4th ed.). Pacific Grove, CA: Brooks/Cole.

CHAPTER FIFTEEN

Getting Clients to Act on Their Interests

Self-Efficacy as a Mediator of the Implementation of Vocational Interests

Nancy E. Betz

THIS CHAPTER WILL DISCUSS the possibility that self-concept barriers, in particular low self-esteem and low self-efficacy, may prevent individuals from exploring or pursuing—that is, acting on—possible areas of vocational interest. The chapter begins by reviewing some of the vocational theory and research that has emphasized the importance of self-esteem to vocational development in general and to vocational interest exploration in particular. I will then proceed to a discussion of a theory I believe to have particularly important implications for interest exploration: Bandura's (1977, 1986) self-efficacy theory. Finally, I will discuss joint use of vocational interests and self-efficacy expectations in career counseling, with special consideration of how to handle possible interest areas accompanied by low self-efficacy.

SELF-ESTEEM AND VOCATIONAL DEVELOPMENT

The importance of the self-concept in general to career development has of course long been recognized by vocational psychologists. One of the first theorists to explicitly incorporate the self-concept into vocational theory was Donald Super, whose work helped to define the field of vocational psychology and career development. Super originally suggested the importance of the self-concept in a 1949 speech made in Fort Collins, Colorado, and later published (Super, 1951). Major statements in 1953 and 1963 defined the "vocational self-concept" (Super, 1963, p. 20) and posited that the process of vocational development was that of implementing the vocational self-concept. Much later Super (1990) particularly emphasized the metadimensions of self-esteem and self-efficacy in influencing how effectively the vocational self-concept can be implemented.

Although Super's theory has generated a vast body of research on self-concept implementation, vocational maturity, and career exploratory behavior (see a recent comprehensive review by Osipow & Fitzgerald, 1996), most relevant to this chapter is the work of Korman and others on self-esteem and career preferences. In an attempt to elaborate on and refine some of the postulates of Super's theory, Korman (1966, 1967) postulated that "self-esteem operates as a moderator of the vocational choice process in that individual's high in self-esteem would seek those vocational roles which would be congruent with one's self-perceived characteristics, whereas this would be less likely the case for those individuals with low self-esteem" (Korman, 1967, p. 65). In a series of studies, Korman found that high self-esteem individuals were more likely to implement their vocational self-concepts in their occupational choices than were low self-esteem individuals and that high self-esteem individuals were more likely to make choices that fulfilled their needs than were low self-esteem individuals (Korman, 1969).

Osipow and his colleagues pursued similar ideas. For example, Resnick, Fauble, and Osipow (1970) examined the relationship between self-esteem (as measured by the *Tennessee Self-Concept Scale*) and vocational crystallization, as indicated by the number of high scores (above the 75th percentile) on the *Kuder Preference Record*. Although high self-esteem individuals did not have more high scores than did low self-esteem individuals, high esteem individuals of both sexes expressed more certainty about their career plans.

Leonard, Walsh, and Osipow (1973) found that high self-esteem individuals were more likely to make a second vocational choice (an alternative choice if they could not implement their first choice) consistent with, rather than inconsistent with, their primary vocational preference as measured by Holland's *Vocational Preference Inventory*. In contrast, individuals low in self-esteem were as likely to make inconsistent as consistent vocational choices.

Also suggestive of the importance of self-esteem in career choices is the 30-year-old body of research on women's career development, reviewed by Betz and Fitzgerald (1987) and, more recently, Fitzgerald, Fassinger, and Betz (1995) and

Phillips and Imhoff (1997). In general this research suggests that women with higher levels of self-esteem are more likely to select occupations congruent with their abilities and talents (often traditionally male-dominated occupations) than are women with lower levels of self-esteem.

Although the work mentioned has suggested the moderating effect of self-esteem on the general choice process, other theorists have connected this concept more directly to vocational interest development and exploration. Two important themes emerge from this work, that of low self-esteem as a barrier to the exploration of possible vocational interests and, second, the potentially helpful (indeed necessary) role of experiences that can both increase self-esteem and facilitate interest exploration.

Holland, in both his theory (1973, 1985) and the instruments he has developed (e.g., the *Self-Directed Search*), has long acknowledged the essential role of both the self-concept and a full versus restricted range of experience if career decisions are to be informed and adaptive. Holland's *Self-Directed Search* (Holland, 1994) contains a section for self-estimates of ability as part of the overall assessment of the six RIASEC types. In a 1991 symposium Holland expressed the view that individuals with low self-esteem may not act on their interests, and he suggested that interventions designed to increase an individual's range of experiences would be useful in increasing self-efficacy.

Also emphasizing both experiential background and self-perceptions is social learning theory, first applied to career development by Krumboltz and his colleagues (see reviews by Krumboltz & Nichols, 1990; Osipow & Fitzgerald, 1996). Although the theory is too large in scope to be reviewed here, the concepts postulated included self-observation generalizations (SOGs) and task approach skills, which both refer to an individual's self-perceptions and are influenced by learning histories as well as genetic factors and current environment. Both SOGs and task approach skills are thought to be related to action outcomes important in making and implementing career decisions.

Thus there is ample evidence from previous theory and research in vocational psychology to suggest the potentially important role of self-perceptions in the exploration and implementation of vocational interests, as well as other aspects of effective career decision making. Along with other researchers, such as Lapan (Lapan, Boggs, & Morrill, 1989), I suggest in particular that the construct of self-efficacy expectations and the theory in which it is embedded, Bandura's (1977) self-efficacy theory, may provide a bridge from Super's theory to vocational interest exploration. Self-efficacy theory may have considerable utility not only for understanding the failure to act on one's interests but as a framework for the design of interventions that can increase self-efficacy and therefore possibly facilitate vocational interest exploration. Accordingly, the next section describes self-efficacy theory.

SELF-EFFICACY THEORY

Self-efficacy theory may be viewed as one approach to the more general study of the applicability of social learning or social cognitive theory (e.g., Krumboltz, Mitchell, & Jones, 1976; Krumboltz & Nichols, 1990; Lent, Brown, & Hackett, 1994) to vocational behavior.

Briefly, as originally proposed by Bandura (1977), self-efficacy expectations refer to a person's beliefs concerning his or her ability to successfully perform the tasks or behaviors of a specific domain of activity: for example, mathematics, drawing, public speaking. Efficacy beliefs are important because they are postulated by at least three behavioral indicators to be major mediators of behavior: (1) approach versus avoidance behavior; (2) quality of performance of behaviors in the target domain; and (3) persistence in the face of obstacles or disconfirming experiences. Low self-efficacy expectations regarding a behavior or behavioral domain are postulated to lead to avoidance of those behaviors, poorer performance, and a tendency to give up at the first sign of difficulty.

In the context of career development, "approach behavior" versus avoidance may refer to the implementation of vocational interests or to an individual's willingness to choose, or even consider, a given educational or career option. Self-efficacy beliefs can thus act as either facilitators of a given career choice, if they are strong, or barriers to career choices, when they are low or weak. Avoidance is especially detrimental to the pursuit of vocational interests, because it is difficult to develop or pursue activity areas that the individual fears. Further, avoidance is a vicious cycle, in that avoidance prevents learning experiences that could engender a feeling of competency. Low self-efficacy thus engenders further avoidance. If approach behavior is desired, then somehow this vicious cycle must be broken. One approach to doing this would utilize interventions based on Bandura's four sources of efficacy information.

More specifically, Bandura postulated that efficacy expectations are both learned originally and potentially modified later on by what he called sources of efficacy information. These four sources of information are as follows: (1) performance accomplishments—that is, experiences of successfully performing the behaviors in question; (2) vicarious learning or modeling; (3) verbal persuasion—for example, encouragement and support from others; and (4) lower levels of emotional arousal—that is, lack of anxiety—in connection with the behavior. Thus the theoretical context of the self-efficacy construct provides not only a means for understanding the development of self-efficacy beliefs but also the means for their modification through interventions incorporating positive "applications" of the four sources of efficacy information.

In 1981 Hackett and Betz (1981) proposed that self-efficacy expectations relative to career domains might be related to, or moderate, the processes of career choice and adjustment. Fifteen years of research on such related concepts as mathematics self-efficacy, self-efficacy for scientific and technical careers, and career decision-making self-efficacy (see reviews by Betz & Hackett, 1997; Betz & Luzzo, 1996; Lent, Brown, & Hackett, 1994; Multon, Brown, & Lent, 1991) supports this hypothesis. However, I now urge more attention to its role in interest exploration, and this is the subject of the next section.

SELF-EFFICACY AND INTEREST EXPLORATION

As mentioned in the previous section, the relationship of low self-efficacy to avoidance behavior may be particularly crucial if clients are to "act on" their interests. Conversely, the necessity of some degree of self-efficacy for approach behavior leads me to emphasize the need for attention to clients who express some degree of interest in a particular area but a concomitant lack of confidence in their abilities in that domain. In some cases their lack of confidence may be related to an actual lack of ability, but in many cases it is due to a lack of experience; these are cases where, if interventions based on self-efficacy theory are made, the counselor may assist a client in turning a possible interest area into a real vocational option. Thus it may be useful to consider joint use of interests and self-efficacy beliefs in career counseling.

Before proceeding, it may be helpful to distinguish the concept of self-efficacy from that of self-rated abilities. As discussed by Brown, Lent, and Gore (1994), the concept of self-efficacy beliefs evolved from social cognitive theory and is usually operationalized by asking individuals to indicate their confidence in their ability to complete a given task (see also Lent, Brown, & Hackett, 1994). For this reason the terms *self-efficacy* and *confidence* are in some cases used interchangeably, and I will do so herein. The term *confidence* has the advantage of being more familiar and layperson friendly, but I urge retention of its connection to self-efficacy theory because the theory provides a rich network of hypotheses concerning both the origins and the consequences of low confidence and, most importantly, has embedded within it a blueprint for the design of interventions.

In contrast, the concept of self-estimates of ability evolved from trait-and-factor theory and is usually assessed normatively, by asking the respondent to compare his/her abilities to those of others (e.g., as in Holland's *Self-Directed Search* or in the research of Swanson & Lease, 1989).

Brown, Lent, and Gore (1994) reported analyses that indicated that self-efficacy and self-estimates of ability in relationship to the Holland (1985) types are empirically distinct, although correlated, concepts. Correlations among the latent constructs representing self-efficacy and self-estimates of ability ranged from .52 (for Realistic and Conventional) to .73 (Artistic). Brown and his colleagues also reported that self-efficacy beliefs were more highly related to vocational interests than were self-estimates of ability. Research by Lowman and Williams (1987) reported moderate correlations between self-estimates of ability and measured ability, but Hall, Kelly, Hansen, and Gutwein (1996) reported unimpressive relationships between these two sets of variables.

Although the conceptual and operational distinctions between self-efficacy beliefs and self-estimates of ability should be noted, they are both considered to be potentially useful in counseling when used in conjunction with interest measures. Some of the inventories to be mentioned herein use self-efficacy (or confidence) measures—for example, the *Strong Interest Inventory/Skills Confidence Inventory* and *Kuder Occupational Interest Survey* and *Kuder Task Self-Efficacy Scale* (Lucas, Wanberg, & Zytowski, 1997)—while others, such as the *Self-Directed Search* (Holland, 1994) and the UNIACT (see Prediger & Swaney, 1995), use self-estimates of ability. The *Campbell Interest and Skill Survey* (Campbell, Hyne, & Nilsen, 1992) uses self-estimates of skill, which Campbell urges be viewed as confidence estimates.

Regardless of the means of measuring interests and self-efficacy or self-estimates of ability, what is needed in order to use these jointly in career counseling is measures of both interest and confidence with respect to parallel, or least related, activity or occupational domains such as Holland types or basic interests. The pattern that is especially important for present purposes is one where there is some indication of interests, yet low confidence in relationship to that domain. In the next section I will use self-efficacy theory with respect to the Holland types to illustrate how these ideas can be used in counseling, and I will conclude the section by mentioning the many other interest inventories and measures of self-efficacy that likewise permit joint use of interest and efficacy data in career counseling.

SELF-EFFICACY AND INTERESTS WITH RESPECT TO THE HOLLAND TYPES: USE IN COUNSELING

There are now several measures of self-efficacy with respect to one or more of the six Holland (1985) types; these six themes—Realistic, Investigative, Artistic, Social, Enterprising, and Conventional (RIASEC)—have been among the major individual differences variables used in career theory, assessment, and counseling.

The *Skills Confidence Inventory* (SCI; Betz, Borgen, & Harmon, 1996a) is a 60-item measure of self-efficacy, with 10 items assessing self-efficacy for each of the six RIASEC areas. As described in Betz et al. (1996a) and Betz, Harmon, and Borgen (1996b), the SCI was developed using a sample of over 1,800 employed adults and college students. Each General Confidence Theme (GCT) consists of 10 activities, tasks, or school subjects associated with the relevant Holland theme. Sample activities and school subjects items are as follows: Build a doll house, Industrial Arts (R); Perform a scientific experiment, Calculus (I); Design sets for a play, Art (A); Meet new people, Counseling Methods (S); Sell a product to a customer, Public Speaking (E); Organize systems for filing information, Accounting (C). Respondents are asked to indicate their degree of confidence in their ability to complete the activity or task on a scale ranging from 1 ("No Confidence at All") to 5 ("Complete Confidence").

Administration of both the *Strong Interest Inventory* (Harmon, Hansen, Borgen, & Hammer, 1994) and the *Skills Confidence Inventory* would yield scores for interests and confidence in the six RIASEC themes or General Occupational Themes (GOTs) on the *Strong*. Although a detailed profile showing the interest/confidence patterns for each of the six types, with counseling implications, is available as part of the overall *Strong* profile, the present discussion is intended to be general rather than specific to one interest inventory/measure of confidence and will thus be illustrated using patterns of high and low interest and efficacy scores for the Holland RIASEC themes obtainable from the SII/SCI or other similar measures.

In a general sense the career assessment should lead to some type of cross classification of levels of interest (e.g., high, medium, and low) with levels of confidence (high, medium, low), with concomitant counseling implications. A client worksheet provided in the manual for the SCI is shown in Fig. 15.1 completed

Name KAREN

SKILLS CONFIDENCE

INTEREST		MORE CONFIDENCE	LESS CONFIDENCE
	MORE INTEREST	These occupational areas are high priorities for exploration: 1. INVESTIGATIVE 2. ___ 3. ___ 4. ___	These occupational areas are good options to consider if I can increase my skills confidence: 1. REALISTIC 2. ___ 3. ___ 4. ___
	LESS INTEREST	These occupational areas are possible options to consider if my interest in them develops: 1. SOCIAL 2. CONVENTIONAL 3. ___ 4. ___	These occupational areas are low priorities for exploration: 1. ARTISTIC 2. ENTERPRISING 3. ___ 4. ___

FIGURE 15.1 Illustration of the joint use of Holland type interest and confidence scores in career counseling: The case of Karen.

for a client named Karen. This worksheet yields four possible categories of Holland type. It should be noted that operationalizing levels of high and low depends on the specific inventory and measures used, and is usually described in the test manual.

In the present example the upper left quadrant shows those Holland types for which both interests and confidence are high, indicating high priorities for occupational exploration. Holland types for which there is some interest but low confidence (upper right quadrant) may well be possible options if confidence can be increased using Bandura's four sources of efficacy information. Areas of low interest but higher confidence (lower left quadrant) may provide options if interests can be strengthened, but consideration of these areas may not be necessary if the previous two cells provide options. Finally, areas of low interest and low confidence (lower right quadrant) are generally considered low priorities for exploration. Those familiar with the *Campbell Interest and Skills Survey* may note the resemblance of the interpretations suggested in this figure to the fourfold interpretive system of the CISS: Pursue (high interest, high skills), Develop (high interest, lower skills), Explore (high skills, lower interest), Avoid (low skills, low interest). For the recommendation to Develop, the report suggests that "Respondents should be encouraged to further develop their skills in this area or, failing that, to appreciate this area as an avocational focus" (Campbell, 1995, p. 403).

Assuming that increases in confidence are necessary before the "approach behavior" needed to facilitate the exploration of interests can occur, here are suggestions based on Bandura's theory. For the performance accomplishments source of efficacy information the counselor might recommend classes, workshops, community education programs providing *beginning* (elementary) instruction in the area. Programs through technical schools, county colleges, adult education in the community, as well as four-year colleges and universities, should be considered. It is essential to ensure initial success experiences in order to build confidence. Recalling the third consequence of perceived self-efficacy—that is, persistence in the face of obstacles or disconfirming experiences—one cannot expect the client to endure failure experiences until some degree of confidence has been built through successful experiences.

Interventions focusing on the vicarious learning or modeling source of efficacy information might include encouraging the client to spend a few hours at the worksite of someone who works in an occupation in this area and/or talk with people in the occupation, especially people of the same gender and/or race/ethnicity, and, especially for younger clients, providing videos or occupational information showing similar others performing successfully in the occupation/area.

Emotional arousal (anxiety) may be addressed through traditional anxiety management techniques such as relaxation and systematic desensitization. For example, Deffenbacher (1992) provides an extensive review of various approaches to intervention for anxiety reduction, including systematic desensitization based on the pairing of anxiety responses with relaxation derived from progressive relaxation training, self-managed relaxation coping skills, and exposure.

Finally, the verbal persuasion component of efficacy information implies that the support and encouragement of the counselor and/or others in the individual's life can serve a vital confidence-building function. Most obviously, the counselor can assist the client in structuring new experiences and can then serve as "cheer-leader" and supporter as new behaviors are tried out.

The cases summarized by Figs. 15.1 (Karen) and 15.2 (Richard) illustrate con-cretely the use of these ideas in counseling. Karen illustrates the case of a woman in her late 20s, with a B.S. in horticulture but working as an administrative assis-tant for a publishing company. Karen's scores on the GOTs and SCI General Confidence Themes are as shown below:

Holland Type	Interests	Confidence
Realistic	Very High (60)	Lower (2.2)
Investigative	High (60)	High (3.9)
Artistic	Average (59)	Lower (2.8)
Social	Average (45)	High (3.7)
Enterprising	Average (50)	Lower (2.3)
Conventional	Average (54)	High (3.9)

Given her high Investigative Interest scores and average scores on every other Holland type except Realistic, it is not surprising that Karen is dissatisfied with her current career path and would like to get on a track more consistent with her interests.

The joint consideration of interests and confidence reveals Investigative to be a desirable area for exploration because of high interests and high confidence, suggesting careers in the sciences. But Karen's Realistic interests, if accompanied by some confidence, could open up the area of Investigative-Realistic careers, which include many engineering and technical fields. These fields appealed to Karen, but her lack of Realistic confidence prevented her from exploring them. Accordingly, interventions were called for. Karen decided to take some beginning courses in electronics and computer programming through a community adult education program in order to build up her confidence in Realistic areas. At the same time she explored degree-related options in engineering and computer sci-ence, possibly electrical engineering to combine the two. Left to her own devices, Karen's low self-efficacy relative to the Realistic theme probably would have led to continued avoidance rather than the "approach" behaviors she began to exhib-it with the efficacy-based interventions and support of the counselor.

Richard's case is that of an undecided, indeed floundering, college student. Administration of the *Strong Interest Inventory* and *Skills Confidence Inventory* yielded the following pattern of scores:

Name __RICHARD__

SKILLS CONFIDENCE

	MORE CONFIDENCE	LESS CONFIDENCE
MORE INTEREST	These occupational areas are high priorities for exploration: 1. NONE 2. _____ 3. _____ 4. _____	These occupational areas are good options to consider if I can increase my skills confidence: 1. ENTERPRISING 2. _____ 3. _____ 4. _____
LESS INTEREST	These occupational areas are possible options to consider if my interest in them develops: 1. REALISTIC 2. _____ 3. _____ 4. _____	These occupational areas are low priorities for exploration: 1. CONVENTIONAL 2. INVESTIGATIVE 3. ARTISTIC 4. SOCIAL

INTEREST

FIGURE 15.2   Illustration of the joint use of Holland type interest and confidence scores in career counseling: The case of Richard.

Modified and reproduced by special permission of the Publisher, Consulting Psychologists Press, Inc., Palo Alto, CA 94303 from *Skills Confidence Inventory Applications and Technical Guide,* by Nancy E. Betz, Fred H. Borgen, & Lenore W. Harmon. Copyright 1996 by Consulting Psychologists Press, Inc. All rights reserved. Further reproduction is prohibited without the Publisher's written consent.

Holland Type	Interests	Confidence
Realistic	Little	High (4.0)
Investigative	Average	Lower (3.1)
Artistic	Average	Lower (3.4)
Social	Little	Lower (3.4)
Enterprising	Very High	Lower (3.0)
Conventional	Average	Lower (2.4)

As shown, there are no areas of high interest and high confidence and thus no obvious areas for exploration. Enterprising, for which Richard has some interest, is also an area where he lacks confidence; this pairing is shown in the upper right quadrant. Only Realistic, where Richard reports confidence but little interest (lower left quadrant), represents another occupational possibility.

If confidence in the Enterprising area could be increased, then enterprising occupations could become viable vocational options. Accordingly, Richard enrolled in an adult education course called "Practically Painless Public Speaking" and a college counseling center class on assertiveness training. Additional experiences, like Toastmaster's Club and elective courses in the Department of Communication, eventually led to a more socially confident, self-assured young man able to pursue a business major and ultimately a career in that field.

Although the cases of Karen and Richard use the SII/SCI to illustrate the joint use of interest and efficacy data in career counseling, there are many other measures that can be used for this purpose. For example, the *Campbell Interest and Skill Survey* (Campbell et al., 1992) contains seven orientations, 29 Basic Interest and 60 Occupational Scales, all accompanied by skills measures, which Campbell says are more appropriately interpreted as measures of confidence. Holland's *Self-Directed Search* (Holland, 1994) asks respondents to provide self-estimates of ability for each RIASEC type as well as to indicate preferences for activities and occupations. Holland (1985) suggested that an individual's pattern of self-estimates of ability on the SDS can in some cases be used to help clients, women especially, plan for more adventurous goals. American College Testing's Career Planning Program, which includes the UNIACT (Prediger & Swaney, 1995), also yields assessments of ability self-estimates. Lucas, Wanberg, and Zytowski (1997) describe the development of a 30-item scale measuring self-efficacy for tasks corresponding to Kuder's 10 vocational interest areas (Kuder & Zytowski, 1991). They discuss the benefits of using this task self-efficacy scale along with the *Kuder Occupational Interest Survey*. Thus the conjoint use of interest and efficacy measures seems to be gaining increased acceptance in career assessment and counseling.

SELF-EFFICACY AND VOCATIONAL INTEREST DEVELOPMENT

Although this chapter has focused on the use of self-efficacy theory to assist clients in acting on their interests, there is also evidence that efficacy-based interventions may lead to increased levels of interest—that is, to interest development. Beginning with Strong (1943) and Bordin (1943), many vocational theorists have suggested the dynamic (Bordin, 1943) or fluid (Spokane, 1991) nature of vocational interests even in the context of overall interest stability. More specifically, these theorists acknowledge the overall stability of interests but at the same time suggest that new interests can develop with new experiences. For example, an individual may have lifelong avocational interests in music, reading, and sports yet in retirement also have the time and opportunity to develop interests in computers, woodworking, and photography.

A fairly large body of research suggests that task success (akin to the performance accomplishment source of efficacy information) can increase interest and/or task liking (e.g., Locke, 1965; Korman, 1968; Osipow & Scheid, 1971; Osipow, 1972; Campbell & Hackett, 1986). Strong (1943) wrote that an interest may emerge following recognition of successful use of one's abilities (see also Savickas, 1995).

Holland (1985) writes about ways in which a person's RIASEC type may become more differentiated and/or change somewhat over the years. For instance, persons of a particular type may become more like that type with age as they experience more and more activities and acquire more and more associated competencies and rewards. In contrast, a person of a particular type may get an opportunity, or be forced, to perform the activities and acquire the competencies of a different type and discover that this experience (prevented earlier because of traditional sex-role socialization, racial discrimination, poverty, or other factors) is congenial, so that a shift in disposition may occur. Such shifts are usually expected to be minor rather than major because of the cumulative learning and environmental barriers that must be overcome. Thus Holland suggests that the probability of change becomes smaller with age, because the impact of cumulative learning and of environmental resistance to change grows stronger (Holland, 1985).

Barak and his colleagues (Barak, 1981, in press; Barak, Librowsky, & Shiloh, 1989) formulated a cognitive theory of the development of interests in which perceived abilities are one of the major determinants of interest development. In a study by Barak, Shiloh, and Haushner (1992) children receiving an intervention designed to increase their perceived abilities on a task also showed increased preferences for the tasks subject to manipulation. Likewise, Lapan and his colleagues (Lapan, Boggs, & Morrill, 1989; Lapan, Shaughnessy, & Boggs, 1996) have been pursuing research based on the presumption that increasing self-efficacy can increase interests. Lapan and his colleagues (1989) found evidence that lower self-efficacy with respect to Realistic and Investigative areas may explain women's lower Realistic and

Investigative interests. And Lapan and his colleagues (1996) used path analysis to support the importance of both math self-efficacy and math interests in predicting entry into math/science majors and in the mediation of gender differences in these decisions.

The most recent theory attempting to relate self-efficacy theory to vocational interest development, also based on the more general social-cognitive model originally formulated by Bandura (1986), is that of Lent, Brown, and Hackett (1994). Their (1994) model highlights three "person" mechanisms—self-efficacy, outcome expectations, and goals—that form the core of a social-cognitive approach to career behavior. In contrast to efficacy expectations, which involve the belief that one can successfully perform a behavior, outcome expectations involve beliefs in the consequences of performing those behaviors. Efficacy and outcome expectations must be distinguished because "correct" performance does not always lead to the desired outcome.

Efficacy and outcome expectations are postulated to influence the development both of interests and of goals related to the career choice and decision process, with plans, decisions, aspirations, and behavioral choices all involving goal mechanisms. Lent, Lopez, and Bieschke (1993) provided the first empirical test of the social-cognitive model. Their results suggested that self-efficacy mediates the effects of prior performance on interests, which in turn mediate the effect of self-efficacy on choice intentions. Fouad and Smith (1996) tested the social cognitive model with respect to math and science self-efficacy in a sample of inner-city middle school students in the Midwest. They reported a strong relationship between self-efficacy and interests, which in turn related to choice intentions. Finally, Lopez, Lent, Brown, and Gore (1997) reported the results of a comprehensive test of the social-cognitive model for predicting math-related interests and performance in a sample of 296 students enrolled in math courses at a predominantly white, middle-class high school. Both self-efficacy and outcome expectations predicted subject matter interest, and self-efficacy partially mediated the effects of measured ability on course grades. Thus they conclude good support for a model in which ability relates to self-efficacy, which in turn facilitates greater outcome expectations and stronger interests.

Thus there is both empirical and theoretical support for the possible role of increased self-efficacy, achieved through successful task performance, in increasing interests. One of the most important applications of this body of research is the possibilities for interventions capable of increasing self-efficacy, interests, and therefore career options. Although a number of successful interventions in the domain of career decision-making self-efficacy have been reported (see a review by Betz & Luzzo, 1996), studies of interventions in other areas are just beginning. For example, Luzzo, Hasper, Albert, Bibby, and Martinelli (1998) studied the effectiveness of a math-science self-efficacy intervention on math self-efficacy, math and science interests, and choice of majors and careers, in a sample of undecided college students. Schifano and Betz (1998) demonstrated the effectiveness of an intervention focused on Realistic self-efficacy in increasing Realistic confidence among college women. In this latter study an all-day intervention, including classes for college women on architecture and the construction trades, and the use of hand tools and hardware, was developed and examined.

SUMMARY

This chapter has outlined the possible importance of variables related to self-esteem, and in particular the more specific concept of self-efficacy expectations, to clients' tendency to explore, act on, and implement their vocational interests. Examples of the joint interpretation of interests and efficacy, or confidence, with regard to Holland's types have been provided, but the ideas are intended to be applicable to any situation where assessments of both vocational interests and confidence/efficacy/self-estimates of ability with respect to the same or a related activity domain are available.

It should be noted that there is as yet insufficient research focused on the extent to which efficacy-based interventions can lead a client to "act on" hitherto unexplored interest areas, so the suggestions made herein should be considered somewhat speculative at this time, even though based on a solid history of theory, related research, and clinical practice. More generally there is ample basis to suggest that increases in self-efficacy expectations may not only assist clients to "act on" their interests but may also lead to the development of new interests in areas previously unexplored. However, this possibility too awaits empirical verification. Also needing more research is the operational (as opposed to conceptual) distinctiveness of self-efficacy beliefs versus global self-esteem (see, e.g., Tracey, 1997). Overall, however, the reciprocal relationships between efficacy beliefs and vocational interests are one of the most interesting, and potentially useful, areas of vocational research.

REFERENCES

Bandura, A. (1977). Self-efficacy: Toward a unifying theory of behavioral change. *Psychology Review, 84,* 191–215.

Bandura, A. (1986). *Social foundations of thought and action.* Englewood Cliffs, NJ: Prentice Hall.

Barak, A. (1981). Vocational interests: A cognitive view. *Journal of Applied Psychology, 75,* 77–86.

Barak, A. (in press). A cognitive view of the nature of vocational interests: Implications for career assessment, counseling, and research. In F.T.L. Leong & A. Barak (Eds.), *Contemporary models in vocational psychology: A volume in honor of Samuel H. Osipow.* Hillsdale, NJ: Erlbaum.

Barak, A., Librowsky, I., & Shiloh, S. (1989). Cognitive determinants of interests: An extension of a theoretical model and initial empirical examinations. *Journal of Vocational Behavior, 34,* 318–334.

Barak, A., Shiloh, S., & Haushner, O. (1992). Modification of interests through cognitive restructuring: Test of a theoretical model in preschool children. *Journal of Counseling Psychology, 39,* 490–497.

Betz, N. E. (1992). Counseling uses of career self-efficacy theory. *Career Development Quarterly, 41,* 22–26.

Betz, N., Borgen, F., & Harmon, L. (1996). *Skills Confidence Inventory applications and technical guide.* Palo Alto, CA: Consulting Psychologists Press.

Betz, N. E., & Fitzgerald, L. F. (1987). *The career psychology of women.* Orlando: Academic Press.

Betz, N., & Hackett, G. (1997). Applications of self-efficacy theory to the career assessment of women. *Journal of Career Assessment, 5,* 383–402.

Betz, N., Harmon, L., & Borgen, F. (1996). The relationships of self-efficacy for the Holland themes to gender, occupational group membership, and vocational interests. *Journal of Counseling Psychology, 43,* 90–98.

Betz, N., & Luzzo, D. (1996). Career assessment and the Career Decision-Making Self-Efficacy Scale. *Journal of Career Assessment, 4,* 313–328.

Bordin, E. S. (1943). A theory of vocational interests as dynamic phenomena. *Educational and Psychological Measurement, 3,* 49–65.

Brown, S. D., Lent, R. W., & Gore, P. A. (1994, August). *Self-rated abilities and self-efficacy beliefs: Same or different constructs?* Paper presented at the annual meeting of the American Psychological Association, Los Angeles.

Campbell, D. P. (1995). The *Campbell Interest and Skill Survey:* A product of ninety years of psychometric evolution. *Journal of Career Assessment, 3,* 391–411.

Campbell, D. P., Hyne, S. A., & Nilsen, D. L. (1992). *Manual for the Campbell Interest and Skill Survey.* Minneapolis: National Computer Systems.

Campbell, N. K., & Hackett, G. (1986). The effects of mathematics task performance on math self-efficacy and task interest. *Journal of Vocational Behavior, 28,* 149–162.

Deffenbacher, J. (1992). Counseling for anxiety management. In S. B. Brown & R. W. Lent (Eds.), *Handbook of Counseling Psychology* (2nd ed., pp. 719–756). New York: Wiley.

Fitzgerald, L., Fassinger, R., & Betz, N. (1995). Theoretical issues in the vocational psychology of women. In S. H. Osipow & W. B. Wash (Eds.), *Handbook of Vocational Psychology* (2nd ed., pp. 67–109). Hillsdale, NJ: Erlbaum.

Fouad, N., & Smith, P. L. (1996). Test of a social-cognitive model for middle school students: Math and science. *Journal of Counseling Psychology, 43,* 338–346.

Hackett, G., & Betz, N. E. (1981). A self-efficacy approach to the career development of women. *Journal of Vocational Behavior, 18,* 326–339.

Hall, A. S., Kelly, K., Hansen, K., & Gutwein, A. K. (1996). Sources of self-perceptions of career related abilities. *Journal of Career Assessment, 4,* 331–343.

Harmon, L., Hansen, J. C., Borgen, F. H., & Hammer, A. L. (1994). *Strong Interest Inventory: Applications and technical guide.* Stanford, CA: Stanford University Press.

Holland, J. L. (1973). *Making vocational choices.* Englewood Cliffs, NJ: Prentice Hall.

Holland, J. L. (1985). *Making vocational choices: A theory of vocational personalities and work environment* (2nd ed.). Englewood Cliffs, NJ: Prentice Hall.

Holland, J. L. (1994). *Self-Directed Search Form R: 1994 Edition.* Odessa, FL: Psychological Assessment Resources.

Holland, J. L. (1997). *Making vocational choices: A theory of vocational personalities and work environments* (3rd ed.). Odessa, FL: Psychological Assessment Resources.

Korman, A. K. (1966). Self-esteem as a moderator of the relationship between self-perceived abilities and vocational choice. *Journal of Applied Psychology, 51,* 65–67.

Korman, A. K. (1967). Self-esteem as a moderator of the relationship between self-perceived abilities and vocational choice. *Journal of Applied Psychology, 1,* 65–67.

Korman, A. K. (1968). Task success, task popularity, and self-esteem influences on task liking. *Journal of Applied Psychology, 52,* 484–490.

Korman, A. K. (1969). Self-esteem as a moderator in vocational choice: Replications and extensions. *Journal of Applied Psychology, 53,* 180–192.

Krumboltz, J. D., Mitchell, A. M., & Jones, G. B. (1976). A social learning theory of career selection. *The Counseling Psychologist, 6,* 71–81.

Krumboltz, J. D., & Nichols, C. W. (1990). Integrating the social learning theory of career decision-making. In W. B. Walsh & S. H. Osipow (Eds.), *Career counseling* (pp. 159–192). Hillsdale, NJ: Erlbaum.

Kuder, G. F., & Zytowski, D. G. (1991). *Kuder Occupational Interest Survey, Form DD, general manual.* Monterey, CA: CTB MacMillan/McGraw-Hill.

Lapan, R. T., Boggs, K. R., & Morrill, W. H. (1989). Self-efficacy as a mediator of Investigative and Realistic General Occupational Themes on the *Strong Interest Inventory. Journal of Counseling Psychology, 36,* 176–182.

Lapan, R. T., Shaughnessy, P., & Boggs, K. (1996). Efficacy expectations and vocational interests as mediators between sex and choice of math/science college majors: A longitudinal study. *Journal of Vocational Behavior, 49,* 277–291.

Lent, R. W., Brown, S. D., & Hackett, G. (1994). Toward a unifying social cognitive theory of career and academic interest, choice, and performance. *Journal of Vocational Behavior, 45,* 79–122.

Lent, R. W., Lopez, F. G., & Bieschke, K. J. (1993). Predicting mathematics-related choice and success behaviors: Text of an expanded social cognitive model. *Journal of Vocational Behavior, 42,* 223–236.

Leonard, R. L., Jr., Walsh, W. B., & Osipow, S. H. (1973). Self-esteem, self-consistency, and second vocational choice. *Journal of Counseling Psychology, 20,* 91–93.

Locke, E. (1965). The relationship of task success to task liking and satisfaction. *Journal of Applied Psychology, 49,* 379–385.

Lopez, F. G., Lent, R. W., Brown, S. D., & Gore, P. A. Jr. (1997). Role of social-cognitive expectations in high school students' mathematics related interest and performance. *Journal of Counseling Psychology, 44,* 44–52.

Lowman, R. L., & Williams, R. (1987). Validity of self-ratings of abilities and competencies. *Journal of Vocational Behavior, 31,* 1–13.

Lucas, J. L., Wanberg, C. R., & Zytowski, D. G. (1997). Development of a career task self-efficacy scale: The Kuder Task Self-Efficacy Scale. *Journal of Vocational Behavior, 50,* 432–459.

Luzzo, D., Hasper, P., Albert, Bibby, M. A., & Martinelli, M. A., Jr. (1998, August). *Increasing math and science self-efficacy and interests of career undecided college students.* Paper presented at annual convention of the American Psychological Association, San Francisco.

Multon, K. D., Brown, S. D., & Lent, R. W. (1991). Relation of self-efficacy beliefs to academic outcomes: A metaanalytic investigation. *Journal of Counseling Psychology, 38,* 30–38.

Osipow, S. H. (1972). Success and preference: A replication and extension. *Journal of Applied Psychology, 56,* 179–180.

Osipow, S. H., & Fitzgerald, L. F. (1996). *Theories of career development* (4th ed.). Needham Heights, MA: Allyn & Bacon.

Osipow, S. H., & Scheid, A. B. (1971). The effect of manipulated success ratios on task preference. *Journal of Vocational Behavior, 1,* 93–98.

Phillips, S. D., & Imhoff, A. R. (1997). Women and career development: A decade of research. *Annual Review of Psychology, 48,* 31–59.

Prediger, D. J., & Swaney, K. B. (1995). Using UNIACT in a comprehensive approach to assessment for career planning. *Journal of Career Assessment, 3,* 429–452.

Resnick, H., Fauble, M. L., & Osipow, S. H. (1970). Vocational crystallization and self-esteem in college students. *Journal of Counseling Psychology, 17,* 465–467.

Savickas, M. L. (1995). Examining the personal meaning of inventoried interests during career counseling. *Journal of Career Assessment, 3,* 188–201.

Schifano, R., & Betz, N. (1998, August). *Increasing realistic self-efficacy and interests in college women.* Paper presented at the annual convention of the American Psychological Association, San Francisco.

Spokane, A. R. (1991). *Career intervention.* Englewood Cliffs, NJ: Prentice Hall.

Strong, E. K. (1943). *Vocational interests of men and women.* Stanford, CA: Stanford University Press.

Super, D. E. (1951). Vocational adjustment: Implementing a self-concept. *Occupations, 30,* 88–92.

Super, D. E. (1963). Self-concepts in vocational development. In D. E. Super (Ed.), *Career development: Self-concept theory* (pp. 1–16). New York: College Entrance Examination Board.

Super, D. E. (1990). A life-span, life-space approach to career development. In D. Brown, L. Brooks, & Associates (Eds.), *Career choice and development* (2nd ed., pp. 197–261). Hillsdale, NJ: Erlbaum.

Swanson, J. L., & Lease, S. H. (1989). Gender differences in self-ratings of abilities and skills. *Career Development Quarterly, 38,* 347–359.

Tracey, T.J.G. (1997). The structure of interests and self-efficacy expectations: An expanded examination of the spherical model of interests. *Journal of Counseling Psychology, 44,* 32–44.

CHAPTER SIXTEEN

A Self-Determination Perspective of Interests and Exploration in Career Development

David L. Blustein and Hanoch Flum

WITHIN THE CAREER development community, the last few decades of the end of the 20th century may be known by some scholars and practitioners as the "Age of Interests." The focus on measuring, understanding, and expressing individual interests in the world of work is certainly evident in our major theories and practice efforts (Brown & Brooks, 1996). Yet at the same time, the later part of the 20th century has been characterized by profound and pervasive changes evoked by postindustrial economies, the growing spread of democracy within the world, rapid social developments, and expanding educational and vocational opportunities. When considered collectively, these major social and economic changes also have resulted in the rising significance of individual initiative and self-direction within career development, as manifested by the increasingly accepted notion that one can attain satisfaction at work. For increasing proportions of citizens in the Western world (although clearly not all citizens), attaining adult status has been characterized by the option of selecting a line of work that is of "interest." Nested within this framework of changes is the assumption that individuals can select satisfying work. The attainment of an intrinsically satisfying career naturally is enhanced by the exploration of one's self and environment (Jordaan, 1963; Super, Savickas, & Super, 1996). If we view interests as the "tip of the iceberg" in this vast sea of changes in our relationship to work, it may be more accurate to consider the current era as the "Age of Self-Determination." In this chapter we describe a conceptual infrastructure for this

Age of Self-Determination by delineating key relationships between interests and exploration.

Embedded within the complex and rich relationships between interests and exploration is a perspective of career development that we believe is prototypical of postindustrial life. This perspective is based on the supposition that individuals seek to determine their own career futures. As the literature across a wide domain of psychological discourse reveals (e.g., Deci & Ryan, 1985; Jordaan, 1963; Super, 1980), the inherent human tendency to determine the course of life experience involves attention to both interests and exploration. In this chapter we initially review the important themes that have been considered to date in the literature on interests and exploration. After examining the literature on interests and exploration, we consider some of the outstanding questions in this area from a self-determination perspective (e.g., Deci, 1992; Deci & Ryan, 1985, 1991). We use the self-determination perspective as the scaffolding for a comprehensive conceptualization of the central roles of interests and exploration in contemporary vocational behavior. Concluding this discussion are suggestions for counseling practice that emerge from the self-determination perspective on interests and exploration.

CONCEPTUAL AND DEFINITIONAL ASPECTS OF INTERESTS AND EXPLORATION

Exploration: A Context-Rich Perspective

One of the objectives of our scholarly agenda is to delineate a more refined yet encompassing definition of exploration (Blustein, 1997; Flum, 1995). In our view, definitions of career exploration that emphasize the review of various sources of educational and vocational information do not capture the essence or scope of a process that has both deeper intrapsychic qualities as well as broader psychosocial features. In addition to the very real demands of reviewing one's environmental options, exploration involves a process of self-discovery and openness to experience that is lifelong and, when optimally functioning, allows one to learn from the natural vicissitudes of life experience. Thus in this chapter we adopt the context-rich view of exploration that was proposed by Blustein (1997). This context-rich perspective is based on selected aspects of Super's lifespan, life-space theory that emphasize the interrelationships of life roles across the life space (Super, 1980; Super et al., 1996). By adopting a life-span, life-space perspective, Blustein sought to highlight the embeddedness of exploration; according to this view, exploration takes place naturally across life roles, resulting in feedback that is potentially relevant throughout various junctures of the life span.

Building on the work of Blustein (1992, 1997) and other scholars within and outside of vocational psychology (Bowlby, 1988; Deci & Ryan, 1985; Erikson, 1968; Grotevant & Cooper, 1988; Jordaan, 1963; Krapp, 1994), we propose a definition of career exploration that seeks to capture the breadth, depth, and cultural boundaries of the natural human tendency to explore oneself and one's context. Drawing from these diverse sources, we view career exploration as encompassing the appraisal of one's internal psychological attributes, such as values, personality characteristics, interests, and abilities. In addition to this self-exploration, career exploration includes the consideration of information gleaned from one's environment, including options and constraints from relevant educational, vocational, and relational contexts. Furthermore, we believe that optimal career exploration is characterized by an openness to the ebb and flow of natural life experiences, thereby facilitating learning and adaptation to changing social circumstances.

Consistent with the position that we are advancing here is the awareness that exploration is necessarily a social activity that is bound by relational, cultural, and economic factors. Following the context-based views that are increasingly redefining the intellectual landscape in career development (Blustein, 1997; Richardson, 1993; Savickas, 1995a; Young & Collin, 1992), we propose that a more thorough understanding of career exploration needs to encompass the following factors:

Social elements: Social elements include the influence of family and relational support for exploration, which affects both the process and content of exploration (Grotevant & Cooper, 1988). In relation to the initiation of exploration, social support functions to facilitate exploratory activity in a number of domains, including identity formation (Grotevant & Cooper, 1985) and career development (Ketterson & Blustein, 1997; Kracke, 1997). In addition, the content of exploration generally encompasses interpersonal and social factors that provide feedback to individuals about themselves and their attributes (Flum, 1995). Furthermore, the initiation and direction of exploration has been linked to socially defined expectations (Erikson, 1968; Super et al., 1996).

Cultural elements: It has become clear that career development theories and practices are bound by cultural factors that vary across diverse groups of potential

clients (Fouad & Bingham, 1995). As such, the way in which adaptive exploration is defined within a given culture influences how an individual engages in
the process of self-discovery and information gathering (Blustein, 1997; Flum,
1994, 1997). In addition, cultural affordances and constraints shape the opportunities and the content of one's exploration.

Political and economic elements: The degree to which an individual has access
to the opportunity structure is a fundamentally important factor that needs to be
incorporated into a comprehensive understanding of exploration. Therefore it is
critical to acknowledge the reality that the distribution of resources is not equal,
thereby leaving many individuals at a disadvantage in terms of their opportunities for exploration and the implementation of meaningful career lives (Blustein,
1997; Marshall & Tucker, 1992).

Interests: Historical and Contemporary Definitions

Traditionally, definitions of interests in career development have maintained a
common focus on the identification and classification of the natural preferences
that individuals have for a given set of activities or tasks (Crites, 1969; Holland,
1997; Osipow & Fitzgerald, 1996). This parsimonious definition is consistent
with the reliance upon psychometric appraisal as the primary means of defining
and exploring interest patterns. One useful elaboration of this definition is the
distinction between expressed and inventoried interests (Crites, 1969; Spokane,
1994). Expressed interests can be obtained simply by asking people directly to
identify the activities they prefer, while inventoried interests are derived from
psychometric scales or tests (Spokane, 1994). One of the latent functions of this
schema is that it has allowed scholars and practitioners to think more broadly
and expansively about the development, expression, and function of interests
within human development (Savickas, 1995b; Spokane, 1994).

In a highly integrative and innovative recent article, Savickas (1995b)
advanced the intellectual study of interests within career development by incorporating ideas from a diverse and relevant array of sources to describe the personal
or psychological meaning of interests. Building on the work by Darley and
Hagenah (1955) and Angyal (1941), Savickas described interests as a means by
which individuals relate meaningfully to their social roles. Savickas then integrated Adlerian theory with perspectives derived from narrative and life theme
approaches to personality development in suggesting that interests link the individual with the necessary activities and tasks that allow for personally meaningful

interactions within one's social world. In detailing the personal meaning of inventoried interests, Savickas has established a broad and intellectually rich framework from which to consider the role of interests in career development.

In this chapter, we have sought to follow the inclusive thinking of Savickas (1995b) in applying relevant ideas from outside of vocational psychology to our discussion of interests and exploration. In contrast to the richly descriptive perspectives and taxonomies of interests within the realm of vocational appraisal and person–environment fit models (Holland, 1997; Spokane, 1994), we are concerned with examining *how* interests function within the broad array of human experiences. Given our concern with the relationship between interests and exploration, we have elected to emphasize those aspects of interests that are conceptually related to motivational and exploratory behaviors (see Savickas, 1995b).

In order to construct a conceptually rich definition of interests, we have reviewed discussions of interests from such areas as education, motivation, and related conceptions of curiosity and exploration (Dewey, 1913; Fink, 1994; Krapp, 1994; Renninger, Hidi, & Krapp, 1992; Todt, Drewes, & Heils, 1994). Because of the diversity of perspectives that have characterized the scholarly literature on interests, it is difficult to derive a universally accepted definition. However, a number of themes seemed to emerge consistently in our review of this literature that help to construct a framework for understanding the psychological meaning and function of interests. First, interests have been viewed as a fundamental aspect of affective experience that promotes meaningful interactions with one's environment (Deci, 1992; Savickas, 1995b; Todt et al., 1994). Second, considerable research and theory suggests that interests influence an individual's value system and self-concept (Deci, 1992; Renninger et al., 1992). As such, interests are thought to form a central component of an individual's inner psychological world, affecting one's values and identity.

Given the self-determination framework that we are adopting in this chapter, we have elected to rely on the definitional groundwork of interests advanced by Deci (1992), who has considered interests within his overall thinking about human motivation (Deci & Ryan, 1985). According to Deci, interests are intertwined into a socially bound system in which the person interacts with an activity in his/her life space that generates intrinsically motivated behavior. For Deci, interests represent a core component of one's affective system connecting individual experience with activities and objects within one's social and environmental context. Deci's conception of interests contains many parallels with other prominent views of interests (see Krapp, 1994; Savickas, 1995b; Todt et al., 1994), particularly in his connection of interests to broader conceptualizations of exploration, curiosity, and motivation. Our view is that by explicating the motivational framework of interests, we will be more appropriately positioned to understand the nature of the relationships between interests and exploration. As we shall detail later in this chapter, the weaving together of interests and exploration that has been eloquently detailed in the self-determination theory provides a conceptual framework for the consideration of the highly complex interrelationships between interests and exploration in the vocational domain.

INTERESTS AND EXPLORATION: A RECURSIVE RELATIONSHIP

In our view, the nexus of relationships between interests and exploration provides a focal point for understanding some of the fundamental aspects of the human tendency to engage meaningfully with one's environment. To a great extent, human beings historically have been curious about and interested in the world; some scholars have even argued that this inherent exploratory quality has been a key ingredient in our evolutionary success (Keller, Schneider, & Henderson, 1994). The intellectual landscape pertaining to interests and exploration therefore provides an informative glimpse into the complex motivational systems that may in fact underlie many aspects of vocational behavior in Western cultures.

Prior to reviewing the literature on interests and exploration, it is important to detail the nature of the relationships between these two phenomena. In the career development literature, it has been common to consider interests as furnishing a guide for exploration; that is, individuals may explore means of manifesting or expressing their interests in various domains of life experience, including the work domain (Borgen & Bernard, 1982; Holland, 1997). However, a closer look at these two phenomena reveals a more complex set of relationships. For example, exploratory activity can occur as an outcome after an interest-based intervention. Furthermore, exploration can yield changes in the nature, complexity, and expressiveness of one's interests.

One also can construe exploratory activities along a dimension of intrinsic interest. If exploration can be viewed as intrinsically interesting, it may be possible for individuals to engage in an open and curious relationship with their surroundings.

This openness to new experiences and growth, which is akin to an exploratory attitude (see Blustein, 1997), is likely to be highly adaptive in negotiating career transitions. As this brief discussion has suggested, the relationship between interests and exploration is inherently reciprocal. In general, interests may serve to facilitate exploration, and exploration may function to influence and change interests. The complexity of this recursive relationship between interests and exploration is detailed further in the following review of the literature from career development.

INTERESTS AND EXPLORATION: A VIEW FROM THE CAREER DEVELOPMENT LITERATURE

Numerous studies have been conducted over the past few decades examining the interrelationships between interests and exploration in the career development field. The first set of studies that merits our attention pertains to the degree to which exposure to interest-based counseling interventions promotes exploratory behavior. The second set of studies examines how exploration fosters gains in the awareness and crystallization of one's interest.

Promoting Exploration via Interest-Based Interventions

Career development practitioners and researchers have had a long and often passionate relationship with interest assessment (Betz, 1992; Hackett & Watkins, 1995). The promise of interest inventories has led some theorists to consider the interpretation of an inventory protocol to be the *essence* of a career intervention (e.g., Holland, 1997). Furthermore, other career development scholars have proposed that presenting clients with interest inventories followed by an interpretation will, in and of itself, facilitate exploratory behavior (Randahl, Hansen, & Haverkamp, 1993). The importance of exploration as a meaningful outcome in interest assessment has been viewed by some authors as evidence of exploration validity, which is thought to represent a highly coveted source of validity for the developers of interest inventories (Borgen & Bernard, 1982; Tittle, 1978). Exploration validity represents the objective that the use of interests inventories in career interventions ought to evoke exploratory activity (Tittle, 1978). Thus, in addition to the other types of validity (such as criterion validity and construct validity), an interest inventory could be evaluated based on its capacity to prompt exploration, particularly for those individuals whose career goals are unfocused. This notion of exploration validity also fits into the life-span, life-space perspectives of career development (Super et al., 1996), which have detailed an array of developmental tasks that ought to precede the actual specification and implementation of career choices. As such, instead of considering an interest inventory as a means of promoting or confirming choices, exploration validity is based on the contention that interest inventories can ideally serve to encourage exploration prior to decision making. Given the importance of exploration validity, it would be wonderful if we could report a large number of highly confirmatory studies. In actuality, the research evidence is far less clear.

The literature on the degree to which interest-based interventions foster exploration is replete with the complications that are evident in most lines of inquiry in our field. That is, the definitions of exploration tend to vary, with many of the operational definitions focusing exclusively on behaviorally based information-seeking activities (e.g., Krivatsky & Magoon, 1976; Zytowski, 1977). Moreover, the studies are diverse with respect to the nature of the interventions and the measures that are used to assess changes in exploratory behavior. Nevertheless, the existing research does yield a number of important trends that merit our attention.

In most of the studies, exploration is assessed by a simple index of how often an individual reports engaging in a given information-seeking task. Some of the studies in fact have reported that exposure to the interpretation of an interest inventory is associated with greater levels of information-seeking behavior than comparable groups of clients who did not receive such interventions (Prediger & Noeth, 1979; Randahl et al., 1993; Toman & Savickas, 1997). In contrast, many studies reported equivocal findings wherein exposure to interest inventories did not foster environmental exploration (Cooper, 1976; Krivatsy & Magoon, 1976; Zener & Schnuelle, 1976; Zytowski, 1977).

A few highly creative studies have assessed the extent to which interest-based interventions foster self-exploration. Here again the findings are inconclusive. For example, one notable study by O'Neil, Price, and Tracey (1979) concluded that exposure to the *Self-Directed Search* engendered more thinking about career issues, perhaps reflecting a sort of self-exploration focusing on self-appraisal and introspection. In contrast, Hansen, Kozberg, and Goranson (1994) observed that college students who received feedback on the *Strong Interest Inventory* were able to recall their profiles with a low accuracy rate a year later. Hansen and her colleagues suggested that "a brief presentation of the profile results does not sufficiently promote self-knowledge of interests over the long-term" (p. 240).

In sum, the studies that have examined the exploration validity of interest-based interventions have yielded equivocal results. In the section that follows, we briefly review the studies that have assessed the extent to which exploration-based interventions promote interest crystallization.

Promoting Interest Crystallization via Exploration-Based Interventions

A very rich literature has examined the impact of career exploration and career decision-making interventions on the crystallization of self-attributes and self-definition. Given the purported stability of interests, perhaps the most useful question to raise is how effective career exploration-based interventions are in promoting an *awareness* of interests. Numerous studies have considered the impact of career exploration-based interventions with respect to such outcome indexes as vocational identity and vocational self-concept crystallization (Rayman, Bernard, Holland, & Barnett, 1983; Remer, O'Neil, & Goh, 1984). These outcomes typically are derived from self-reports of one's level of self-knowledge about various self-concept dimensions, including interest crystallization.

In reviewing the career outcome literature, Phillips (1992) concluded that more extensive, in-depth interventions seem to be most effective in fostering gains in self-definition. Typically the more effective interventions included "some form of self-assessment and feedback, information about specific and general aspects of the world of work, and advice on how career decisions are made" (Phillips, 1992, p. 516). In effect, when clients receive *comprehensive* interventions that foster exploration of both the self and the environment, they tend to experience significant gains in their self-definition.

In addition, a number of innovative studies have demonstrated that providing individuals with an opportunity to explore work roles in depth fosters self-concept crystallization (Brooks, Cornelius, Greenfield, & Joseph, 1995; Ducat, 1980; Taylor, 1988). A close look at these interventions, many of which were based on internships or actual work experiences, suggests that their success is based in part on their ability to enhance the level of client competence and confidence in career exploration. As we will see shortly, enhancing competence is considered to be a critical feature in fostering intrinsically motivated activity, including many aspects of exploration (Deci & Ryan, 1985).

When considering the existing career literature on self-definition in relation to the review of those studies on the exploration validity of interest inventories, we can derive a more insightful look at the nature of the relationships between interests and exploration. The first point that arises from this review is that the relationship between interests and exploration is complex; simple exposure to interests-based material does not by itself seem to be sufficient to foster exploratory activity or self-appraisal. Following this observation, the next question that emerges is what sort of interventions do promote exploratory activity? Given the predominant findings in the career intervention outcome literature (Phillips, 1992), we can assume with some confidence that self-awareness of one's interests can be enhanced by more in-depth and systematic interventions that foster both self-exploration and exploration of relevant aspects of the environment. As the outcome literature has indicated, clients who are provided with comprehensive opportunities to learn about themselves and their educational and vocational opportunities, while also expanding their skills in decision making, planfulness, and exploration, are likely to exhibit significant gains in their awareness of their interest structure (Remer et al., 1984). However, following the suggestion of scholars both in career development (Toman & Savickas, 1997) as well as those who are examining these processes in other domains of psychological discourse (Deci, 1992; Fink, 1994; Krapp, 1994), the relationship between interests and exploration is likely mediated by an array of intrapersonal and contextual factors.

One means of examining this unequivocal set of findings may be to expand our theoretical search to encompass ideas emerging from outside of the purview of vocational psychology. The following section reviews some of the more promising new directions in research and theory in interests and exploration.

INTERESTS AND EXPLORATION: A VIEW FROM THE SELF-DETERMINATION PERSPECTIVE

An Overview of Self-Determination Theory

As we have suggested earlier, the self-determination theory by Deci and Ryan (1985) is highly relevant to considerations of interests and exploration. Moreover, the self-determination perspective encourages us to place both interests and exploration into a broader motivational perspective, thereby yielding potentially important implications for theory development and counseling practice. Deci and Ryan (1991) have advanced a comprehensive and interrelated theory of human motivation and the self in which the inherent properties of the self are considered to be motivational and agentic. Another critical aspect of self-determination theory is that those aspects of human behavior that are intrinsically motivated tend to be characterized by interest. In this theoretical system, human nature is understood as being motivated by internal and external factors to develop an inherent active agency, thus helping individuals form and maintain a coherent self (Deci & Ryan, 1985, 1991).

By emphasizing the agentic aspects of human behavior and by highlighting the importance of interests in motivating behavior, Deci and Ryan (1985, 1991) have developed a motivational perspective that contrasts with other motivational models that have emerged from cognitive expectancy and behavioral theories. Deci (1971) initiated his discussion of self-determination and intrinsic motivation in an attempt to explain human behavior that seemed to occur outside of the influence of external reinforcements and cognitive expectations. Building on the initial findings from studies that identified various classes of human behavior that were not contingent upon external reinforcers and social demands, Deci and Ryan have fashioned a comprehensive motivational model based on their observations that self-determination guides much of human behavior and experience. In short, self-determination refers to the natural human striving to take initiative that allows individuals to attain freely experienced choices and goals that are consistent with their interests and values (see Deci & Ryan, 1985, 1991, for more detailed reviews of this theory).

While interests clearly guide some aspects of self-determined behavior, behaviors that are intrinsically motivated also reflect innate psychological needs. The three innate and primary psychological needs that have been detailed in the Deci and Ryan (1985) perspective are the need for autonomy (or self-determination), the need for competence (or effectance), and the need for relatedness. As such, certain classes of behaviors, such as exploratory behavior, as well as inherent strivings to develop interests and capacities, may be explained in part by needs for competence, autonomous self-determination, and relational bonds.

Self-determination theory considers interests to be critical in understanding intrinsic motivation. Interests are described as a thread that ties up "the self to external and internal experiences" (Deci & Ryan, 1991, p. 241). In other words, interests are regarded as a "central affect of synthesis" (Deci & Ryan, 1991, p. 241); as such, interests play an assimilatory role in the construction and maintenance of the self. As an affect-based function, interests link needs and action and serve as a guide and regulator of intentional action. Derived from this model, exploration can be construed as an intentional action, with interests energizing and directing exploratory behavior. At the same time, identification and clarification of

TABLE 16.1   The Development of High and Low Levels of Interests:
             A Self-Determination Perspective

Individual's Experiences	High Interest	Low Interest
Activity Level: Challenge	Optimal	Too-high challenge—a threat Too low—not challenging
Self-Experience: Competent	High (with a sense of competency that could be developed)	Low
Relational Context	Secure	Insecure [no support or threat to relationship(s)]

interests can be the objective of exploratory behavior. We may conclude that the experience of interest promotes development. Interests are critical and instrumental in making choices and hence in advancing coherence and the individual's sense of self-determination.

A Self-Determination Perspective of Interests and Exploration

Given the underlying assumptions of self-determination theory that we have outlined, we propose the following rubric for considering how interests and exploration interact within the broader framework of motivational theory. The rubric that we have derived from Deci and Ryan's work (see Table 16.1) offers a conceptually expansive view of interests and exploration that embraces intrapsychic factors as well as contextual factors. (To illustrate this rubric, we find it useful to consider these factors as pertaining to a bimodal categorization of "High" and "Low" interest.)

When considered collectively, this table describes the set of factors that influences the relationships between interests and exploration. Beginning at the top of the table, we see that the level of challenge that individuals experience is likely to affect their interest level in a given activity. As in so many other areas of human experience, the optimal level is typically somewhere between the very high or low levels, thereby offering individuals an opportunity to both learn something new and potentially master it. A challenge that is too high might be perceived as a threat. When an interest is overshadowed by a threat—for example, it is interpreted as being far too demanding or is experienced as being overwhelming—the threat may become the dominant effect and the interest is likely to diminish. Likewise, when there is no challenge, the intrinsic desire is likely to remain silent and unstimulated and a high level of interest is unlikely to develop.

The level of competency that an individual experiences also provides an important internal crucible for considering one's level of interest in an activity. Those individuals who feel competent are naturally able to approach a new task or object with a greater level of interest than those individuals who do not feel competent in that particular domain. The sense that one has the capability or can learn the appropriate skills to carry out the relevant action and to cope competently with the task is an important facilitative factor in developing a high level of interest.

The final factor that is delineated in this table refers to the relational context. Consistent with other theoretical perspectives both in career development (Blustein, Prezioso, & Schultheiss, 1995) and in other lines of psychological theory (Bowlby, 1988; Josselson, 1992; Mitchell, 1988), the availability of secure relationships in one's intrapsychic and interpersonal contexts serves to enhance one's potential for experiencing interest. The individual may feel supported by significant others and confident that the pursuit of his or her interest would not risk relationships. The availability of trustful relationships allows for the emotional reservoir that is required for investment in the exploration and development of high interest. Conversely, a sense of insecurity in relationships may pose an obstacle in the development of high interest. Moreover, the individual might be afraid that a pursuit of an interest could risk the relationship and therefore elect to forgo further exploration. In addition, the lack of support makes it difficult to experiment with new tasks and activities, hence diminishing one's potential for developing high levels of interest.

As summarized in the career development literature (Blustein, 1997), there is considerable individual variability in self and environmental exploration, with some individuals seeming to find exploration simply unappealing or uninteresting. Thus career development scholars and practitioners have sought means to enhance the degree to which exploration can be construed as an intrinsically motivated activity. The same factors that apply to the development of high interest, as summarized in Table 16.1, also very likely apply to the specific case of *interest in exploration*. When an individual feels challenged to explore and experiences the self as having the internal and relational resources to do so, it would seem likely that an interest in exploration would develop. With the optimal configuration of internal and contextual factors that have been derived from self-determination theory and research (Deci & Ryan, 1985), new interventions may be developed that help individuals experience a greater interest in exploration throughout their lives.

Intrinsic and Extrinsic Motivation

The distinction in the Deci and Ryan (1985) model between intrinsic and extrinsic motivation seeks to capture a fundamental aspect of human motivation and behavior with significant implications for our understanding of interests and exploration. Certain classes of behavior are seemingly enacted for spontaneous interest and enjoyment, while other behaviors are undertaken not so much for satisfaction but because these behaviors are instrumental in reaching an outcome or because they are regarded as being important for some extrinsic goal. While this may seem like a sharp, dichotomous distinction, the reality of motivational behavior suggests that the picture is far more complicated. Although intrinsic motivation is the prototype of self-determination (Deci, 1992), behavior also can be self-determined in instances of extrinsic motivation. When behavior is controlled and regulated by external rewards and contingencies, it is generally not self-determined. However, behavior that was originally undertaken because it served to win an extrinsic reward, such as to gain parental approval, may develop into a self-determined behavior.

The manner by which extrinsically motivated behavior becomes self-determined can be understood via the process of internalization (Schaefer, 1968). Deci and Ryan (1991) describe different forms of internalized extrinsic motivation. The first type is *introjected* regulatory processes, representing processes that have been internalized to the extent that the activity is experienced as something that "should" or "ought" to be done. Introjected regulatory processes might be engaged in to obtain approval or avoid disapproval from others, yet these processes are not owned by the person himself or herself. We may add here that in the case of a behavior of this type, the individual may perceive the activity as being important to somebody else (i.e., externally important), but this behavior is not yet accepted as the individual's own.

Gradually, though, the individual may come to *identify* with the importance of a given activity and accept it as his or her own, representing the next developmental phase of the internalization process. In this case, the individual may experience less conflict, and guilt or anxiety can be expected to be less salient. In our view, the more internal sense of importance that occurs as one identifies with a set of tasks and behaviors is analogous to the concept of values as they have been articulated in the career developmental literature (see Super et al., 1996). The regulation of the activity is more integrated and thus represents greater self-determination.

Developmentally the next level of internalization is an *integrated* regulatory process, which is characterized by greater coherence of the self. It is not only the full self-endorsement of the importance of the activity that is involved here, but the individual has developed a sense of authorship and thus the integrated activity feels authentic and fits relatively harmoniously with other regulatory processes or structures.

In self-determination theory, interest is primarily associated with activities that are intrinsically motivated but can be allied with extrinsically motivated activities if their regulation has been integrated with the person's intrinsic self (Deci & Ryan, 1991). Though according to Deci (1992), importance continues to be more central than interest even in the case of self-determined extrinsic motivation, we suggest that a person is more likely to experience high interest as a higher level of internalization is reached. Moreover, exploration could be instrumental in the enhancement of internalization and in the development of an integrated and coherent self.

One of the major distinctions between intrinsic and extrinsic motivation that is pertinent to the present discussion pertains to the parallel distinction between interest and importance. As is evident in the definitions that we have provided of the two major types of motivation, *interest* tends to play a role in intrinsically motivated behavior; alternatively, extrinsically motivated behavior tends to be associated with activities that are considered to be *important* as opposed to intrinsically interesting. In our view, a comprehensive motivational-based perspective of exploration will necessarily encompass both intrinsic *and* extrinsic motivation. In the realm of career exploration, for example, some activities may in fact be intrinsically *interesting* and other activities may be engaged in because they lead to *important* outcomes, hence tapping into extrinsically motivated functions (see Blustein, 1988). Moreover, the vast differences in individuals and their contexts suggests that what may be intrinsically motivating for one person may be extrinsically motivating or not motivating at all for other individuals. For example, an individual who is optimally interested in a given set of activities or issues and experiences both competence and social support may be more likely to initiate an often challenging set of exploration tasks, such as informational interviews. In contrast, individuals who experience considerable social anxiety and who face their exploration with little sense of support or competence may find informational interviewing to be a daunting activity.

Conclusion: Self-Determination Theory and Career Development

In our view, the self-determination perspective complements existing notions in career development theory that postulate that individuals seek to express themselves creatively and meaningfully in the world of work (Holland, 1997; Super et al., 1996). Moreover, the Deci and Ryan (1985) perspective enhances these traditional notions by highlighting motivational processes that, with few exceptions (see, for example, Savickas, 1995b), have not been central in career development theory and practice. By deriving relevant implications from the self-determination perspective of Deci and Ryan (1985), we are attempting to place the individual's motivational system at the center of the interest-exploration relationship.

One of the primary inferences that can be derived from the self-determination model is that the exploration of various interests may be intrinsically motivated. In this light, an individual may find many of the actual exploratory tasks to be interesting. Moreover, intrinsically motivated exploration may occur as a means of finding an outlet for an interest. A second inference is that selected aspects of extrinsically motivated behavior can be internalized in a manner that fosters self-determination, thereby allowing individuals to develop and express their own interests and values. When considered collectively, intrinsic motivation and the internalized modes of extrinsic motivation serve to provide individuals with the means of expressing their interests, values, and overall identity in the world of work.

From the vantage point of self-determination theory, some of the equivocal findings that we described earlier may relate to differences in how individuals have experienced their exploratory tasks. As detailed earlier, individuals are likely to experience some noteworthy changes in their self-definition when they are involved in comprehensive, systematic interventions (Phillips, 1992). When clients engage in intensive and comprehensive interventions, they are likely to become increasingly competent in career decision making and exploration, thereby experiencing tasks as optimally challenging. In addition, the use of counselors and group support in many of the psychoeducational interventions may be construed as furnishing an explicit level of relational support, which is also central in attaining self-determination.

Another implication of the Deci and Ryan perspective (e.g., 1985) pertains to the role of exploration in facilitating the internalization process that helps extrinsically motivated behavior become an important component of self-determination. While exploration may be initially triggered because one is led to believe that one should explore, it is conceivable that the sense of importance combined with one's experience with exploration can be transformed to a sense of effectance. As individuals explore, they have an opportunity to develop greater levels of competence, which may help them to understand the importance of their exploratory activity and of the outcomes of their behavior. Hence exploration is an activity that could lead by experiential means to greater internalization, thereby facilitating the reformulation of external regulation into internalized regulation. In effect, by engaging in active exploration, individuals will be able to experience greater ownership of an increasing proportion of adaptive career behaviors and attitudes.

Furthermore, the role of extrinsically motivated factors in the self-determination model provides a means of understanding how individuals can engage in career development tasks that may not be immediately gratifying or rewarding. The developmental sequence of internalization outlined by Deci and Ryan (1985) may be applied to our understanding of how individuals employ a wide array of behavior and attitudes that may not be intrinsically interesting in their striving toward self-determination. In particular, the literature on the internalization of extrinsic motivation may be relevant to individuals who are forced to confront career choices that are not inherently interesting or compelling, such as in the case of individuals who have lost access to their desired vocational options or who cannot obtain employment at a given time. Based on the self-determination perspective, extrinsically motivated behaviors and attitudes that are viewed as central to one's life goals and identity are more likely to be inherently viable and self-generating. In this light, exploratory activities may not necessarily be intrinsically interesting or directly connected to the implementation of vocational interests in order to be considered self-determined. Thus individuals who are able to understand how extrinsically motivated behavior or attitudes fit into their broader life plan will likely be able to initiate and sustain a wide array of career development tasks, including exploration, thereby maximizing their overall level of adaptiveness.

In the next section we pursue the application of the self-determination model in further depth by examining how practitioners can facilitate progress in the career development tasks of their clients.

IMPLICATIONS FOR COUNSELING PRACTICE

As we indicated earlier, one of the key elements of self-determination involves tasks that are optimally challenging. In general, we propose that interventions that promote an optimal level of challenge are more likely to result in self-determined exploration, encompassing both intrinsic and extrinsic motivational factors. Like many other activities in life experience, exploratory tasks are more likely to be self-motivating if they are challenging and provide an opportunity for both new learning and mastery. The application of the "optimal level of challenge" in the realm of career exploration can be manifested in the design of career materials that are both relevant and evocative. In addition, counselors may help to foster self-exploration by developing interventions that are psychologically challenging yet supportive, such as group or individual counseling experiences that build on existing strengths while developing new growth areas.

In addition, interventions that help clients to develop competence in their career development tasks are likely to result in positive outcomes. Consistent with the life-span, life-space perspectives of career development (Super et al., 1996), we believe that interventions need to help clients attain a readiness to make career decision and clarify their interests. In short, we believe that clients would be best served by experiencing interest-based material within the context of interventions that are tailored to their impending developmental tasks as well as their unique individual attributes. Furthermore, skill development in the domain of exploration would need to address the traditional domain of environmental exploration; as such, interventions that furnish individuals with clear and relevant instructions on how to look for, process, and use educational and occupational information would seem most useful (Blustein, 1992). In addition, interventions that help clients to engage in the honest self-appraisal that characterizes self-exploration would seem optimal. Furthermore, enhancing the level of competence in career exploration can be instrumental in facilitating the transition from a more external regulation to a more internal mode of self-regulation, thereby enhancing self-determination.

The third major factor in fostering self-determination according to Deci and Ryan (1985) is relational support, which represents an increasingly important factor in current career development theory and practice (Blustein et al., 1995; Kracke, 1997). The emotional risks involved in exploring and implementing one's interests have been detailed in the literature (Blustein, 1992). Therefore, helping clients to access the natural support systems in their families and peer groups would be useful. Also, for those clients who are struggling with their relationships, integrative interventions that address their relational concerns in tandem with their career issues may be indicated. Furthermore, within the therapeutic relationship counselors can provide an additional source of emotional and relational sustenance, which would help in fostering exploration of interests and values.

Naturally it would be wonderful if clients experienced exploration as an intrinsically interesting activity that required no prompting or special effort. In our view, it may be possible to increase the proportion of exploration that is in fact part of an overall self-determination process, encompassing both intrinsic and extrinsic motivation. Thus interventions that are designed to promote the internalization of extrinsic motivation clearly need to form a significant component of a comprehensive treatment system. In applying the Deci and Ryan (e.g., 1985) perspective to the realm of extrinsically motivated activities, it would seem useful to provide clients with a clear sense of the connection between short-term activities and long-term goals. Clients may be able to understand that although selected activities may not seem immediately interesting, they are potentially very *important* to the creation and implementation of a life plan that allows for self-determination and interest expression in one's work life. A potentially useful heuristic is to help clients to feel that they are the authors of their career life story and that their efforts in exploration can contribute to the goal of a "happy ending" (see Savickas, 1995b).

In our attempt to adopt the context-rich perspective of Deci and Ryan as well as other scholars in career development (Blustein, 1997; Flum, 1995; Richardson, 1993), we believe that career exploration interventions also need to be sensitive and affirming of cultural and social differences. The question of what individuals construe as important is very much influenced by their culture (Flum, 1997). As such, counselors need to maintain an awareness of how culture affects the formation of interests. The development of interests clearly occurs in a cultural context where various activities and experiences are viewed with varying degrees of affective valence given the prescribed priorities within particular cultural groups (Deci & Ryan, 1991). In addition, cultural factors will influence the construction of what is considered exploratory. For example, it might be particularly useful to take into account the interdependent nature of relational bonds within given cultures in order to design career interventions that are meaningful and effective (Flum, 1997; Markus & Kitayama, 1994). Other examples include the use of culturally sensitive occupational materials as well as assessment instruments that are open to and affirming of cultural variations.

Another important contextual element that needs to be addressed is access to the opportunity structure. A context-rich perspective of the career interests-exploration linkage encourages us to consider the social and political aspects of one's context that clearly affect vocational behavior. We propose that counselors need to be aware of the limitations that social and economic differences play in career development. By maintaining this notion in "bolder relief," counselors may be able to help clients negotiate social and economic barriers while also reducing any "blame the victim" types of inferences that may be attributed to clients who are struggling with interest crystallization and career exploration.

CONCLUSION

This chapter has attempted to provide a conceptual structure in which to consider the complex relationships between interests and exploration. By adopting the self-determination perspective of Deci and Ryan (1985), we have placed both interests and exploration in the broader framework of motivational psychology. As our discussion has proposed, the sort of questions that have been raised in the career literature to date regarding the nature, structure, and measurement of interests can be enhanced considerably by placing these processes into a conceptual umbrella that situates individuals at the navigational helm of their career. From a self-determination perspective, interests and exploration represent interrelated processes that have a reciprocal and highly complex effect on one's overall career development.

The exploration, specification, and implementation of one's career clearly represent a fundamental means by which individuals can exercise self-determination in contemporary life. Of course, it is clear to us that the sort of self-determination that we have described in this chapter is not available to every worker or potential worker. Large cohorts of citizens throughout the world do not exercise much if any control in their work lives; instead they are faced with the need to find ways to support themselves and their families by whatever expedient means are available. Following the notion that opened this chapter wherein we considered the recent era as the Age of Self-Determination, we would like to propose that the 21st century be the era where opportunities for genuine self-determination are expanded. The vast inequities that exist in the workforce only serve to highlight the fact that not all people are in a position to self-determine their career lives. When considering these inequities in light of the pervasive changes in the labor market where greater levels of skills and knowledge are needed, it is easy to imagine a future where these distinctions become even more dramatic.

In response to the gaps in the opportunity structure, a number of viable suggestions are currently being considered in public policy, education, applied psychology, and other disciplines wherein these problems and proposed solutions are being discussed (e.g., Marshall & Tucker, 1992; Rifkin, 1995). From the perspective of the more macro-level disciplines such as economics and public policy, the vantage point of the individual is often overlooked (see, for example, Blustein, Phillips, Jobin-Davis, Finkelberg, & Roarke, 1997). In our view, the self-determination model that has been detailed here offers a means of considering individuals in direct relation to their context. Our position is that by maintaining the prominence of both the person and the broader social context in tandem, counselors will be able to contribute meaningfully to the experiences of clients while also maintaining a viable commitment to expanding opportunities for the vast majority of our citizens. Thus we hope that the material presented in this chapter forms part of the knowledge base for the individual and systemic interventions that will make the 21st century the true "Age of Self-Determination."

We acknowledge the assistance of the following students who helped in reviewing the literature reported in this paper: Ann Capobianco, Erin Christopher, Linda Fama, Sheryl Gonzalez, Michelle Gruhn, Selcuk Sirin, Marianne Skau, Heidi Warm, and Lauren Wisely.

REFERENCES

Angyal, A. (1941). *Foundations for a science of personality.* New York: The Commonwealth Fund.

Betz, N. E. (1992). Career assessment: A review of critical issues. In S. D. Brown & R. W. Lent (Eds.), *Handbook of counseling psychology* (2nd ed., pp. 453–484). New York: Wiley.

Blustein, D. L. (1988). The relationship between motivational processes and career exploration. *Journal of Vocational Behavior, 32,* 345–357.

Blustein, D. L. (1992). Applying current theory and research in career exploration to practice. *Career Development Quarterly, 41,* 174–184.

Blustein, D. L. (1997). A context-rich perspective of career exploration across the life roles. *Career Development Quarterly, 45,* 260–274.

Blustein, D. L., Phillips, S. D., Jobin-Davis, K., Finkelberg, S. L., & Roarke, A. E. (1997). A theory-building investigation of the school-to-work transition. *The Counseling Psychologist, 25,* 364–402.

Blustein, D. L., Prezioso, M. S., & Schultheiss, D. P. (1995). Attachment theory and career development: Current status and future directions. *The Counseling Psychologist, 23,* 416–432.

Borgen, F. H. & Bernard, C. B. (1982). Test reviews: Strong-Campbell Interest Inventory. *Measurement and Evaluation Guidance, 14,* 208–212.

Bowlby, J. (1988). *A secure base: Parent-child attachment and healthy human development.* New York: Basic Books.

Brooks, L., Cornelius, A., Greenfield, E., & Joseph, R. (1995). The relation of career-related work or internship experiences to the career development of college seniors. *Journal of Vocational Behavior, 46,* 332–349.

Brown, D., & Brooks, L. (Eds.). (1996). *Career choice and development* (3rd ed., pp. 121–178). San Francisco: Jossey-Bass.

Cooper, J. F. (1976). Comparative impact of the SCII and the *Vocational Card Sort* on career salience and career exploration of women. *Journal of Counseling Psychology, 23,* 348–352.

Crites, J. O. (1969). *Vocational psychology.* New York: McGraw-Hill.

Darley, J. G., & Hagenah. T. (1955). *Vocational interest measurement: Theory and practice.* Minneapolis: University of Minnesota Press.

Deci, E. L. (1971). Effects of externally mediated rewards on intrinsic motivation. *Journal of Personality and Social Psychology, 18,* 105–115.

Deci, E. L. (1992). The relation of interest to the motivation of behavior: A self-determination perspective. In K. A. Renninger, S. Hidi, & A. Krapp (Eds.), *The role of interest in learning and development* (pp. 43–70). Hillsdale, NJ: Erlbaum.

Deci, E. L., & Ryan, R. M. (1985). *Intrinsic motivation and self-determination in human development.* New York: Plenum.

Deci, E. L., & Ryan, R. M. (1991). A motivational approach to self: Integration in personality. In R. Dienstbier (Ed.), *Nebraska symposium on motivation* (pp. 237–288). Lincoln: University of Nebraska Press.

Dewey, J. (1913). *Interest and effort in education.* Boston: Riverside Press.

Ducat, D. E. (1980). Cooperative education, career exploration, and occupational concepts for community college students. *Journal of Vocational Behavior, 17,* 195–203.

Erikson, E. (1968). *Identity: Youth and crisis.* New York: Norton.

Fink, B. (1994). Interest and exploration: Exploratory action in the context of interest genesis. In H. Keller, K. Schneider, & B. Henderson (Eds.), *Curiosity and exploration* (pp. 101–120). New York: Springer-Verlag.

Flum, H. (1994, June). *Evolutive identity formation: Developmental and cultural issues.* Paper presented at the thirteenth biennial meeting of the International Society for the Study of Behavioral Development, Amsterdam, The Netherlands.

Flum, H. (1995). Career development and adolescence. In H. Flum (Ed.), *Adolescents in Israel: Personal, familial, and social aspects* (pp. 201–223). Israel: Reches Publishing Co. (Hebrew)

Flum, H. (1997). *Identity formation in adolescence: Notes from a cultural perspective.* Manuscript submitted for publication.

Fouad, N. A., & Bingham, R. P. (1995). Career counseling with racial and ethnic minorities. In W. B. Walsh & S. H. Osipow (Eds.), *Handbook of vocational psychology* (2nd ed., pp. 331–365). Hillsdale, NJ: Erlbaum.

Grotevant, H. D., & Cooper, C. R. (1985). Patterns of interaction in family relationships and the development of identity exploration in adolescence. *Child Development, 56,* 415–428.

Grotevant, H. D., & Cooper, C. R. (1988). The role of family experience in career exploration: A life-span perspective. In P. Baltes, R. H. Lerner, & D. Featherman (Eds.), *Life-span development and behavior* (Vol. 8, pp. 231–258), Hillsdale, NJ: Erlbaum.

Hackett, G., & Watkins, C. E. (1995). Research in career assessment: Abilities, interests, decision making, and career development. In W. B. Walsh & S. H. Osipow (Eds.), *Handbook of vocational psychology* (2nd ed., pp. 181–215). Hillsdale, NJ: Erlbaum.

Hansen, J. C., Kozberg, J. G., & Goranson, D. (1994), Accuracy of student recall of *Strong Interest Inventory* results 1 year after interpretation. *Measurement and Evaluation in Counseling and Development, 26,* 235–242.

Holland, J. L. (1997). *Making vocational choices: A theory of vocational personalities and work environments* (3rd ed.). Odessa FL: Psychological Assessment Resources.

Jordaan, J. P. (1963). Exploratory behavior: The formation of self and occupational concepts. In D. E. Super (Ed.), *Career development: Self-concept theory* (pp. 42–78). New York: College Entrance Examination Board.

Josselson, R. (1992). *The space between us: Exploring dimensions of human relationships.* San Francisco: Jossey-Bass.

Keller, H., Schneider, K., & Henderson, B. (Eds.). (1994). *Interest and curiosity.* New York: Springer-Verlag.

Ketterson, T. U., & Blustein, D. L. (1997). Attachment relationships and the career exploration process. *Career Development Quarterly, 46,* 167–178.

Kracke, B. (1997). Parental behaviors and adolescents' career exploration. *Career Development Quarterly, 45,* 341–350.

Krapp, A. (1994). Interest and curiosity: The role of interest in a theory of exploratory activity. In H. Keller, K. Schneider, & B. Henderson (Eds.), *Interest and curiosity* (pp. 79–99). New York: Springer-Verlag.

Krivatsky, S. E., & Magoon, T. M. (1976). Differential effects of three vocational counseling treatments. *Journal of Counseling Psychology, 23,* 112–118.

Markus, H. R., & Kitayama, S. (1994). A collective fear of the collective: Implications for selves and theories of selves. *Personality and Social Psychology Bulletin, 20,* 568–579.

Marshall, R., & Tucker, M. (1992). *Thinking for a living: Education and the wealth of nations.* New York: Basic Books.

Mitchell, S. A. (1988). *Relational concepts in psychoanalysis.* Cambridge, MA: Harvard University Press.

O'Neil, J. M., Price, G. E., & Tracey, T. J. (1979). The stimulus value, treatment effects, and sex differences when completing the *Self-Directed Search* and *Strong-Campbell Interest Inventory. Journal of Counseling Psychology, 26,* 45–50.

Osipow, S. H., & Fitzgerald, L. F. (1996). *Theories of career development* (4th ed.). Needham Heights, MA: Allyn & Bacon.

Phillips, S. D. (1992). Career counseling: Choice and implementation. In S. D. Brown & R. W. Lent (Eds.), *Handbook of counseling psychology* (2nd ed., pp. 513–548). New York: Wiley.

Prediger, D. J., & Noeth, R. J. (1979). Effectiveness of a brief counseling intervention in stimulating vocational exploration. *Journal of Vocational Behavior, 14,* 352–368.

Randahl, G. J., Hansen, J. C., & Haverkamp, B. E. (1993). Instrumental behaviors following test administration and interpretation: Exploration validity of the *Strong Interest Inventory. Journal of Counseling and Development, 71,* 435–439.

Rayman, J. R., Bernard, C. B., Holland, J. L., & Barnett, D. C. (1983). The effects of a career course on undecided college students. *Journal of Vocational Behavior, 23,* 346–355.

Remer, P., O'Neil, C. D., & Goh, D. E. (1984). Multiple outcome evaluation of a life-career development course. *Journal of Counseling Psychology, 31,* 532–540.

Renninger, K. A., Hidi, S., & Krapp, A. (Eds.). (1992). *The role of interest in learning and development* (pp. 43–70). Hillsdale, NJ: Erlbaum.

Richardson, M. S. (1993). Work in people's lives: A location for counseling psychologists. *Journal of Counseling Psychology, 40,* 425–433.

Rifkin, J. (1995). *The end of work: The decline of the global labor market force and the dawn of the post-market era.* Los Angeles: Tarcher.

Savickas, M. L. (1995a). Current theoretical issues in vocational psychology: Convergence, divergence, and schism. In W. B. Walsh & S. H. Osipow (Eds.), *Handbook of vocational psychology* (2nd ed., pp. 1–34). Hillsdale, NJ: Erlbaum.

Savickas, M. L. (1995b). Examining the personal meaning of inventoried interests during career counseling. *Journal of Career Assessment, 3,* 188–201.

Schaefer, R. (1968). *Aspects of internalization.* Madison, CN: International Universities Press.

Spokane, A. R. (1994). The resolution of incongruence and the dynamics of person-environment fit. In M. L. Savickas & R. W. Lent (Eds.), *Convergence in career development theories* (pp. 119–137). Palo Alto, CA: Consulting Psychologists Press.

Super, D. E. (1980). A life-span, life-space approach to career development. *Journal of Vocational Behavior, 16,* 282–298.

Super, D. E., Savickas, M. L., & Super, C. M. (1996). The life-span, life-space approach to careers. In D. Brown & L. Brooks (Eds.), *Career choice and development* (3rd ed., pp. 121–178). San Francisco: Jossey-Bass.

Taylor, S. M. (1988). Effects of college internships on individual participants. *Journal of Applied Psychology, 73,* 393–401.

Tittle, C. K. (1978). Implications of recent developments for future research in career interest measurement. In C. K. Tittle & D. G. Zytowski (Eds.), *Sex-fair interest measurement: Research and implications.* Washington, DC: National Institute of Education.

Todt, E., Drewes, R., & Heils, S. (1994). The development of interests during adolescence: Social context, individual differences, and individual significance. In R. K. Silbereisen & E. Todt (Eds.), *Adolescence in context: The interplay of family, school, peers, and work in adjustment.* New York: Springer-Verlag.

Toman, S. M., & Savickas, M. L. (1997). Career maturity moderates the effects of interest inventory interpretation. *Journal of Career Assessment, 5,* 275–291.

Young, R. A., & Collin, A. (Eds.). (1992). *Interpreting career: Hermeneutical studies of lives in context.* New York: Praeger.

Zener, T. B., & Schnuelle, L. (1976). Effects of the *Self-Directed Search* on high school students. *Journal of Counseling Psychology, 23,* 353–359.

Zytowski, D. G. (1977). The effects of being interest inventoried. *Journal of Vocational Behavior, 11,* 153–157.

CURRENT STATUS AND FUTURE DIRECTIONS

THIS FOURTH AND FINAL SECTION of the book presents two chapters that first assess the current status and then identify future directions for interest theory, research, and practice. The chapter authors independently reflect on the main themes represented in the first 16 chapters and then suggest future directions for the study of vocational interests. In the first of these two chapters Walsh briefly outlines the history of interest measurement as a prelude to stating seven conclusions that can be drawn from the empirical literature about interests. Next he recommends that researchers intensify their investigations into (a) how interest inventory interpretations foster career development, (b) the negative implications of homogeneity among occupational incumbents arising from selection of employees who "fit" the existing occupational environment, and (c) issues relevant to interest measurement for diverse cultural and socioeconomic groups preparing to work in manifold settings. Walsh concludes the chapter by reflecting on how the role of vocational interests in career decision making may change as North America becomes a postindustrial society in need of workers who are occupational generalists and team players rather than vocational specialists.

In the second chapter Borgen identifies the major themes represented in the book and then organizes and analyzes them using a heuristic model that relates domains of individuality to venues for living. Borgen ends this volume with an important recommendation for the future of interest theory, research, and practice. He wisely suggests that practitioners and researchers view interests as the facet of individuality that enables people to passionately express their individuality in all of life's venues.

CHAPTER SEVENTEEN

What We Know and Need to Know

A Few Comments

W. Bruce Walsh

THE ASSESSMENTS OF INTERESTS was introduced in 1927 when E. K. Strong, Jr., developed the *Strong Vocational Interest Blank* for Men (SVIB). The SVIB was an empirically based inventory that showed how an individual's likes and dislikes resembled the likes and dislikes of people employed in a variety of occupations. More than 60 years later, evidence indicates that the *Strong* inventory is the fifth most frequently researched assessment instrument, accounting for some 1,720 papers and empirical studies. Watkins, Campbell, and McGregor (1988), in their survey of assessment instruments, found the *Strong* inventory to be the third most frequently used assessment inventory. There is no question that E. K. Strong's work has had a profound impact on interest measurement since the year 1927 (Walsh & Betz, 1995).

In the early years of assessment Strong (1927) thought that interests were tied to abilities. He theorized that people participated in activities because of their abilities; if in fact their performance was successful, they grew to like the activity. The liking of the successful performance Strong viewed as an interest. Thus Strong thought that interests were on a liking-to-disliking dimension. This liking-disliking continuum, in time, became the basic response format for the initial *Strong Vocational Interest Blank*. However, to this very day the evidence tends not to be very supportive of the relationship between abilities and interests. Therefore the links among ability, activity, success, liking, and interest have not been validated.

A second milestone in the area of interest measurement was the work of G. F. Kuder. In 1934 Kuder introduced the *Kuder Preference Record,* made up of a series of content scales assessing one's preferences for outdoor activities, mechanical activities, and so forth. Kuder's early work was not empirically based, but in 1966 he introduced the *Kuder Occupational Interest Survey* (KOIS), which used empirically defined occupational scales. The most recent revision (second edition) of the *Kuder Occupational Interest Survey* occurred in 1979 (Kuder & Diamond, 1979). In 1985 a new report form was designed for the KOIS.

During the next two decades a number of theoretical notions were discussed, but none were translated into measurement and application. In 1940 H. D. Carter introduced the concept of the dynamic character of interests and took into account the social forces that influence adolescents in the process of developing interests and an acceptable self-concept and in choosing a career. Carter also thought that one's value system influenced one's range of possible occupations. In 1941 John Darley suggested that differential interests reflect the process of personality development. He, like Carter, believed that interests are dynamic factors and should be viewed as a phase of personality development. Consistent with this dynamic theme, E. S. Bordin suggested in 1943 that in answering an interest inventory a person is guided by self-concept and occupational stereotypes. Thus people who see themselves as lawyers respond as they believe a lawyer would respond. In 1940 Donald Super suggested that interests were the products of interaction between inherited aptitudes and glandular factors, on the one hand, and opportunity and social evaluation, on the other. Not unlike E. K. Strong, Super seemed to be suggesting that abilities and opportunities were related to the development of interest patterns. A second definition of interests by Super (1949) reflected even greater precision. Super identified four ways of defining interests: expressed interest (verbal statement), manifest interest (evidenced), tested interest (information), and inventoried interest (likes and dislikes). Super further pointed out that the concept of interest has been used to mean degree of interest, strength of motivation, drive, and need.

In 1959 John Holland theorized that behavior is a function of interests, personality, and social environments. In this context Holland suggested that the choice of an occupation is an expression of personality and that interest inventories are therefore personality inventories. Thus Holland thought that the choice of an occupation represented the individual's motivation, knowledge of the occupation, insight and understanding of self, and abilities. In fact Holland was convinced that people entered vocational environments because of their interests and personalities. In any event, over the years Holland's theory has led to considerable research on a number of new assessment techniques. To measure the interest and personality types Holland himself developed the *Vocational Preference Inventory* (1985) and more recently the *Self-Directed Search* (1994). Other inventories that have drawn upon his theoretical concepts include the *Strong Interest Inventory,* the *Unisex Edition of the ACT Interest Inventory* (Swaney, 1995), the *Career Assessment Inventory* (Johansson, 1982), and the Harrington and O'Shea *System for Career Decision Making* (1993). It is clear that Holland's theory and subsequent assessment techniques have had considerable impact on the field of interest measurement over the past two decades.

About the same time Anne Roe (1956) introduced a theory of vocational choice based on a series of studies exploring the personalities of research scientists in different fields. The results of these investigations demonstrated differences in the personality needs and childhood experiences of people doing research in different scientific areas. Based on these findings, Roe concluded that a major distinction among the scientists was on a dimension of interest toward persons or not toward persons (that is, toward things). Or, stated differently, the evidence was suggesting that early rewarded social activities seem to be related to later person orientation. The person-to-thing dimension has been viewed as a basic interest dimension since its inception by Roe some years ago.

A theme running through all of the above interest perspectives is the trait-and-factor approach, with its long history of extensive use focused on personal characteristics that tend to link the individual to different environments. The trait-and-factor approach, in the main, is based on the idea that human behavior may be ordered and measured along dimensions of defined traits, or factors, and that individuals may be reasonably well characterized and described in terms of these defined traits. There is no question that the evidence to some extent tends to support the validity of the trait-and-factor approach, but at the same time we need to keep in mind the concepts of human development and environment and their subsequent impact and interaction with the concept of interests.

A second theme running through the above interest perspectives is the overall positive direction of interest inventories. As noted by Sundberg (1977), interest inventories look for directions of positive effort, while personality inventories, in contrast, measure maladjustments. That is, interest inventories attempt to measure motivations that determine life decisions (Tyler & Walsh, 1979).

WHAT WE KNOW

In the context of this historical background I now comment on a few things that we know and need to know in the meaning, measurement, and practice in the assessment of vocational interests. First and foremost, information about a person's interests, likes, or preferences for different kinds of activities, events, or people may be obtained in a variety of different ways as suggested by Donald Super in 1949. Probably the most direct and simplest method of collecting such information is to ask individuals what they are interested in or what they want to do when they grow up. This is called an *expressed interest,* and the individual is simply asked to make a verbal statement of liking or disliking for various activities, tasks, or occupations. The method is consistent with the idea that if you want to know something about someone, simply ask them. A second method of assessing interests involves observing a person's behavior in different situations. This is called *manifest* or *evidenced interest* and involves participation in an activity, situation, or occupation. The reasoning behind this method is that individuals tend to participate in the activities they like and find somewhat satisfying. *Tested interests,* a third method of assessment, infers interests from an individual's knowledge of special terminology or relevant information about a given topic. It is assumed that interest in a vocation should result in an accumulation of relevant information about the vocation. Thus the reasoning is that the more specific knowledge an individual has about a given occupation, the more the individual is interested in pursuing that occupation. Inventoried interest is the fourth way of collecting information about, or assessing, an individual's interests. This method of assessment asks individuals to report their likes, dislikes, and preferences among items in a list of activities, occupations, or people. This method of inventoried interest is the most popular and widely used and permits a broader sampling of behaviors, likes, and preferences. In addition, the inventoried interest method provides objective scores that permit individual and occupational group comparisons. Thus, for example, interest inventories give us some idea how an individual's likes and dislikes are similar to the likes and dislikes of individuals in specific occupations.

A second item we know is that, surprisingly, interests and abilities are not that highly correlated. For example, a person may have interests very similar to those of artists but achieve in only a mediocre way in the artistic profession. A person may have a high degree of accounting ability but not have interests similar to those of individuals in the profession of accounting. The person simply may not like the activities associated with accounting. So, although interests and abilities tend not to be highly related, keep in mind that they do interact. An individual's interests and abilities may be influenced by environmental variables such as education, experience, and learning.

A third known item is that interest patterns do seem to be quite stable within broad interest categories for young adults and on into life for many people, but there certainly are exceptions. The stability of interests of individuals was repeatedly studied by Strong and others. Strong (1943) used a cross-sectional method that compared the interests of several age groups tested at about the same time. His findings indicated interest correlations of .88 between 25- and 55-year-old men, .82 between 15- and 25-year-old men, and .73 between 15- and 55-year-old men. Thus Strong concluded that an individual's interests stabilized by age 25, were minimally changed by adult experiences, and were not greatly influenced by age. A more recent study by Swanson and Hansen (1988) used a longitudinal design to examine the stability of interests over 4-year, 8-year, and 12-year intervals. For a sample of men and women and using the *Strong Interest Inventory*, they reported correlation coefficients of .81 for 4 years, .83 for 8 years, and .72 for 12 years. Thus interests were found to be remarkably stable over these three time intervals.

Hansen (1988) also studied the stability of interests for occupational groups and society in general. She used archival data from the *Strong Interest Inventory* that spanned a 50-year period. In order to study changes in occupational groups, she selected six occupations that were tested at least three times between the 1930s and 1980s, and that had archival data for men and women in those occupations. Findings indicate that both women and men exhibited stability of interests within occupations over extended periods of time. Stated differently, the configuration of an interest profile for a particular occupation remained quite similar across time. Overall, the stability of interests of individuals, occupational groups, and society in general is well documented by the findings.

A fourth known fact is that interest inventories work. For example, Harmon, Hansen, Borgen, and Hammer (1994) reported that between one-half and two-thirds of all college students enter occupations that are predictable from their earlier scores on the *Strong Interest Inventory*. Zytowski (1976) found that 51% of 882 men and women who had taken the *Kuder Occupational Interest Survey* were in an occupation predicted by Kuder. A series of studies by Walsh and his associates explored the concurrent validity of Holland's theory for White and Black employed adults (college and noncollege degreed) using the *Vocational Preference*

Inventory (VPI) and the *Self-Directed Search*. In general, the findings indicate that White and Black men and women (college and noncollege degreed) tend to be working in congruent occupational environments. The hit rate for White men and women was 71% and for Black men and women 79%. In general, people enter and remain in college majors congruent with their interests and personality style. In addition, people enter and remain in occupational environments congruent with their interests and personality style. Stated differently, people enter and remain in occupations where individuals have similar likes and dislikes.

A fifth item that we know is that people in occupations where individuals have similar likes and dislikes tend to be more satisfied. The evidence indicates that people in occupational environments congruent with their interests tend to be happier and more satisfied than are people who work in incongruent environments. Their behavior tends to be rewarded. Furthermore, the evidence indicates that person/job congruence and job satisfaction increase with age and that the majority of the population maintains stable work histories (Holland & Gottfredson, 1976).

A sixth known fact involves occupational levels. A characteristic of newly developed or recently revised interest inventories is the expansion of the occupational levels they cover. At the outset interest inventories focused on professional careers, with a smattering of occupations requiring less than a college education. In contrast, we now find several inventories offering a substantial number of scales for vocational/technical occupations that do not require a college degree. Such developments tend to reflect, at least in part, a growing recognition of the importance of effective career choices at all occupational levels as well as the crucial role of interests in successful and personally satisfying work experience in all types of jobs.

WHAT WE NEED TO KNOW

Above I have discussed some of what we know in regard to the assessment of vocational interests. There continue to be a number of areas in need of significant exploration. For example, what effect does the interest inventory have on the test-taker? One alternative is that the interpretation can support and strengthen existing vocational aspirations for the individual. In another person the interpretation may stimulate a comprehensive exploration of the world of work, with attention to previously unconsidered options. For yet another it may provide increased self-understanding. In sum, we need to explore the outcome effects in the use of vocational interest inventories.

Another area in which we need to know more is hypothesized by Schneider and Smith (in press) regarding the dark side consequences of person–environment congruence. They hypothesize that person-environment congruence may contribute to homogeneity in thinking, decision making, and action, resulting in an organization's inability to adapt to changing demands of the environment. Additional characteristics may include lack of motivation, increased group thinking, low risk taking, limited boundary spanning, strategic and competitive predictability, as well as an inability to absorb diversity in persons, places, or processes. Schneider and Smith call into question the assumption of all positive consequences of good fit or person–environment congruence. They note that it is important, as usual, to remember that nothing is all black and white. We need to look more closely at the issue, exploring potential moderators of these effects, to gain a better understanding of the bad side of good person–environment fit.

In terms of need to know, as noted by Tinsley (1994) we have just begun to scratch the surface in investigating the complex relations among race, vocational assessment, and vocational behavior. Major problems continue to impede significant research in this area. For example, few existing theoretical frameworks attempt to relate racial identity to vocational assessment and behavior. In addition, investigators pursuing research on racial issues find few reliable and valid instruments to use in their research. In sum, in future research it is important to have participants from diverse ethnic backgrounds.

Another need to know area involves school-to-work transition. Although there are no firm statistics on how many of the United States' 27 million teens run small businesses, the numbers are well into the thousands and growing. Teenagers are selling handmade crafts, moving furniture, detailing cars, and designing clothes, among other things. A 1994 Gallup Poll suggests that in response to the shifting economy, 7 out of 10 high school students want to start a business. The main motive is to be their own boss, not to earn a lot of money. Despite this strong interest, 86% of the teens surveyed said they lacked the skills and interests needed to start even the simplest business. One would think this is an area in which we would be able to productively shape some behavior and empower some individuals to pursue their thirst for practical information.

We also need to know about poverty. Who are the poor in America? About 70% are women and children. The evidence indicates that the poor tend to be single mothers, living in a city, and African American. Whatever happened to the war on poverty? It was stalemated in the 1970s and called off completely in the early 1980s. But it did reduce poverty rates between 1960 and 1971: The rate fell from 23% to 12%. According to the 1994 figures, it is now at about 14.5%. What positive steps could be taken to deal with poverty? Vocational assessment and training programs, vocational counseling, education, college scholarships would seem to be some viable options.

And we need to know about the interests and preferences of older workers. Over the next 20 years or so some occupations and industries might not find sufficient labor due to expected lower rates of expansion in the pool of younger workers. Employers in these interest industries will have to draw a greater than usual percentage of their employees from among the older, faster-growing segment of the population. Service sector jobs appear to be a prime target in which older workers will be employed. For example, in 1989, 42% of all workers age 65 and older were employed in the service sector compared with 35% of workers of all ages. Again, this trend suggests opportunity for programs of vocational assessment, recruitment, and training of older workers.

OTHER INTEREST INVENTORIES

This volume has focused primarily on the following interest inventories: the *ACT Interest Inventory,* the *Campbell Interest and Skill Survey,* the *Kuder DD Interest Inventory,* the *Self-Directed Search,* and the *Strong Interest Inventory.* There are a number of other interest inventories, and I would like to comment briefly on a few of these. For example, the *Picture Interest Inventory* (PII), published by the California Test Bureau (Weingarten, 1958), asks individuals to mark the activity they would most like to perform and the one that they would least like to perform in each of 53 triads of pictures. On a second part of the inventory individuals are asked to report whether they like or dislike each of the activities illustrated in 30 pictures. The PII was developed for grade seven through adulthood and takes about 30 to 40 minutes to complete. It is scored in six fields of interest (Personal-Social, Natural, Mechanical, Business, Arts, and the Sciences) and for three supplemental scales (Verbal, Computational, and Time Perspective). The test-retest reliabilities for the PII range from a low of .76 to a high of .92; validity data are clearly limited, however.

Another way to assess interests is through the use of a card sort. This assessment procedure was originally developed by Tyler (1969) and extended by a number of other authors (Cooper, 1976; Jones, 1979). Initially Tyler simply asked individuals to cluster the occupations into categories based on similarities and differences. She then inquired as to the basis or underlying constructs of the clusters that could subsequently be used for considering additional occupations. In sum, the Tyler card sort does seem to be a sensitive, ideographic assessment technique that may be used to aid client self-understanding.

Another ideographically oriented interest assessment technique is Hall's (1976) *Occupational Orientation Inventory*. This inventory samples needs, job characteristics, and worker traits. The items are empirically assigned to three kinds of scales: 13 directional scales reflecting values and needs; the data, people, things orientations of the *Dictionary of Occupational Titles*; 8 degree scales that assess the individual's concerns about job factors such as co-workers and location; and a verification scale that assesses a defensive response. Counselors are subsequently encouraged to investigate with clients the personal meanings assigned to different items and to discuss scores on the various need scales. In addition, scores on the data, people, things scales are explored.

The *Vocational Interest Inventory* (VII; Lunneborg, 1981) is the outcome of a research program started by Lunneborg in 1968. The VII is a 112-item inventory with eight scales designed to measure the occupational types structured by Anne Roe in her theory of careers. The eight types are Service, Business Contact, Organizational, Technical, Outdoor, Science, General Cultural, and Arts and Entertainment. As noted by Borgen (1986), the VII has several distinctive features. From the outset it has been organized by Roe's Occupational Classification System. Secondly, the VII has attempted to minimize sex differences at the item level, and it was the first to attempt such an effort. Finally, the VII permits high school students to compare themselves with students of like age who later went on to specific career fields in college.

The *Jackson Vocational Interest Survey* (JVIS; 1991) is an inventory consisting of 34 Basic Interest Scales that assess either an individual's preferences for specific work roles (e.g., Creative Arts, Skill Trades, and Social Work) or preferences for work environments requiring specific behaviors (e.g., Planfulness, Independence, and Interpersonal Confidence). The latter preferences Jackson calls *work styles*. The JVIS consists of 289 items and may be hand or machine scored. The availability of hand scoring is a distinct advantage. It takes about one hour to complete, and items are at the seventh-grade reading level. A very distinctive feature of the JVIS is the emphasis on work styles rather than interests. Jackson notes that work styles are not personality dimensions but preferences in working in environments placing a premium on certain required behaviors. The work style scales include Dominant Leadership, Job Security, Stamina, Accountability, Academic Achievement, Independence, Planfulness, and Interpersonal Confidence.

SUMMARY

We need to remember that our society and the workforce have changed since vocational interests were first investigated. And our society and the workforce will continue to change. Over the next 20 years or so some occupations and industries might not find sufficient labor due to expected lower rates of expansion in the pool of younger workers. Employers in these occupations and industries will have to draw a greater than usual percentage of their employees from among the older, faster-growing segment of the population. Women and racial/ethnic minorities continue to enter and advance in the workforce. Unfortunately, as noted above, we have just begun to scratch the surface in investigating the relations among race, occupational interests, and vocational behavior. In addition, increased technology continually results in evolution and change in occupations and industries. In some occupations the need for vocational specialization is being tempered by the necessity for occupational generalists. In some respects the concept of work itself is changing and evolving. Thus, as we move to the 21st century, it will be important to keep an eye on the role of vocational interests in the career decision-making process.

REFERENCES

Bordin, E. S. (1943). A theory of vocational interests as dynamic phenomena. *Educational and Psychological Measurement, 3,* 49–65.

Borgen, F. H. (1986). New approaches to the assessment of interests. In W. B. Walsh & S. H. Osipow (Eds.), *Advances in vocational psychology: The assessment of interests, Vol. 1.* Hillsdale, NJ: Erlbaum.

Cooper, J. E. (1976). Comparative impact of the SCII and the Vocational Card Sort on career salience and career exploration of women. *Journal of Counseling Psychology, 23,* 348–351.

Darley, J. G. (1941). *Clinical aspects and interpretation of the Strong Vocational Interest Blank.* New York: Psychological Corporation.

Hall, L. G. (1976). *Occupational Orientation Inventory* (3rd ed.). Bensenville, IL: Scholastic Testing Service.

Hansen, J. C. (1988). Changing interests of women: Myth or reality? *Applied Psychology: An International Review, 37*(2), 133–150.

Harmon, L. W., Hansen, J. C., Borgen, F. H., & Hammer, A. L. (1994). *Strong Interest Inventory: Applications and technical guide.* Stanford, CA: Stanford University Press.

Harrington, T. F., & O'Shea, A. T. (1993). *Manual for the Career Decision Making System* (Rev. ed.). Circle Pines, MN: American Guidance Service.

Holland, J. L. (1959). A theory of vocational choice. *Journal of Counseling Psychology, 6,* 35–45.

Holland, J. L. (1985). *Professional manual for the Vocational Preference Inventory.* Odessa, FL: Psychological Assessment Resources.

Holland, J. L. (1994). *Professional manual for the Self-Directed Search.* Odessa, FL: Psychological Assessment Resources.

Holland, J. L., & Gottfredson, G. D. (1976). Using a typology of persons and environments to explain careers: Some extensions and clarifications. *The Counseling Psychologist, 6*(3), 20–29.

Jackson, D. N. (1991). *Manual for the Jackson Vocational Interest Survey.* Port Huron, MI: Research Psychologist Press.

Johansson, C. B. (1982). *Manual for the Career Assessment Inventory* (2nd ed.). Minneapolis: National Computer Systems Interpretative Scoring System.

Jones, L. K. (1979). Occu-Sort: Development and evaluation of an occupational card sort system. *Vocational Guidance Quarterly, 28,* 56–62.

Kuder, G. F. (1934). *Kuder General Interest Survey.* Chicago: Science Research Associates.

Kuder, G. F., & Diamond, E. E. (1979). *Occupational interests survey, general manual* (2nd ed.). Chicago: Science Research Associates.

Lunneborg, P. W. (1981). *The Vocational Interest Inventory manual.* Los Angeles: Western Psychological Services.

Roe, A. (1956). *The psychology of occupations.* New York: Wiley.

Schneider, B., & Smith, D. B. (in press). Attraction-selection-attrition: Toward a person-environment psychology of organizations. In W. B. Walsh, K. H. Craik, & R. H. Price (Eds.), *New Directions in Person-Environment Psychology.* Hillsdale, NJ: Erlbaum.

Strong, E. K., Jr. (1927). Vocational interests tests. *Educational Record, 8,* 107–121.

Strong, E. K., Jr. (1943). *Vocational interests of men and women.* Stanford, CA: Stanford University Press.

Sundberg, N. D. (1977). *Assessment of persons.* Englewood Cliffs, NJ: Prentice Hall.

Super, D. E. (1940). *Avocational interest patterns.* Stanford, CA: Stanford University Press.

Super, D. E. (1949). *Appraising vocational fitness.* New York: HarperCollins.

Swaney, K. B. (1995). *Technical manual: Revised Unisex Edition of the ACT Interest Inventory (UNIACT).* Iowa City, IA: American College Testing.

Swanson, J. L., & Hansen, J. C. (1988). Stability of vocational interests over four year, eight year, and twelve year intervals. *Journal of Vocational Behavior, 33,* 185–202.

Tinsley, H.E.A. (1994). Racial identity and vocational behavior. *Journal of Vocational Behavior, 44,* 115–117.

Tyler, L. E. (1969). Research explorations in the realm of choice. *Journal of Counseling Psychology, 8,* 195–202.

Tyler, L. E., & Walsh, W. B. (1979). *Tests and measurements* (3rd ed.). Englewood Cliffs, NJ: Prentice Hall.

Walsh, W. B., & Betz, N. E. (1995). *Tests and assessment* (3rd ed.). Englewood Cliffs, NJ: Prentice Hall.

Walsh, W. B., & Holland, J. L. (1992). A theory of personality types and work environ-
    ments. In W. B. Walsh, K. H. Craik, & R. H. Price (Eds.), *Person–environment
    psychology: Models and perspectives.* Hillsdale, NJ: Erlbaum.
Watkins, C. E., Jr., Campbell, V. L., & McGregor, P. (1988). Counseling psychologists' uses
    of the opinions about psychological tests: A contemporary perspective. *The
    Counseling Psychologist. 16,* 476–486.
Weingarten, K. P. (1958). *The Picture Interest Inventory.* Monterey, CA: CTB/McGraw-Hill.
Zytowski, D. G. (1976). Predictive validity of the Kuder Occupational Interest Survey.
    Journal of Counseling Psychology, 23, 221–233.

CHAPTER EIGHTEEN

New Horizons in Interest Theory and Measurement
Toward Expanded Meaning

Fred H. Borgen

THIS IS A LANDMARK BOOK. Never before has the topic of vocational interests been so extensively examined from such a large and diverse number of expert perspectives. In this final chapter I stand on the shoulders of the preceding experts to distill some of the exciting themes they have addressed in their chapters. From this horizon, it is apparent that they have infused the construct of vocational interests with expanded meaning. Their new perspectives are helping to elaborate an integrative nomological network that embraces vibrant areas of psychology. The meaning of vocational interests today is informed by such lively topics as genetics, developmental psychology, personality, individuality, abilities, agency, and self-efficacy.

Nearly a century of empiricism and counseling use attest to the potency of vocational interests. Interests show some of the largest effect sizes in psychology. Peoples' interests drive how they live. How people live probably drives what interests them. This book documents the state of the art in researching interest constructs and adapting them to effective counseling. It also suggests, as this chapter highlights, that the theoretical linkage of interests is now expanding to encompass the whole person, across domains of individuality and venues of living.

The editors of this book originally asked me to write about the future of interest measurement, akin to parts of a chapter I wrote previously (Borgen, 1986). However, I have found the role of soothsayer too daunting, so I have not pretended to exhaustively or explicitly predict the future. Instead, I wrote this chapter from the perspective of my over 30 years of involvement with interest measurement research. It is a topic that has passionately interested me, from my graduate years to my current work with graduate students. I have had great fun seeing how new ideas can be grafted on the sturdy base that has long typified interest measurement. I hope to share some of that excitement.

BIG BOOKS OF INTEREST

This book is the most comprehensive treatment of vocational interests that has ever been published. It is the most comprehensive because it includes the largest number of authors, representing a wide array of thinking and perspectives. It also has the widest variety of topics. Traditional topics such as validating interests measures, developmental changes in interests, and applying interests in counseling are covered. But the book also deals with diverse material that has never previously been covered so comprehensively. For example, I am not aware of anyone who has written previously about definitions of interests with the breadth, scope, and historical scholarship that Savickas brings to Chapter 2. The scope of the book is also wide because many new topics have emerged out of the recent interest measurement literature; many of them are linked to exciting leading edges of psychology.

Whether this book will be seen as one of the most important books on vocational interests is a question for the future. It stands a good chance, yet the competition is formidable. Strong's (1943) *Vocational Interests of Men and Women* continues to be the classic treatment of the topic. Campbell's (1971) *Handbook for the Strong Vocational Interest Blank* makes the interest hall of fame, especially as an updating of Strong' s earlier empiricism. Another 1970s book on interests is Zytowski's (1973) edited volume, with chapters written by the authors of the major inventories. In the more recent era Walsh and Osipow's (1986) book may rival this book as a comprehensive edited volume, but it focuses more on specific interest inventories with a smaller set of expert perspectives.

The present volume focuses broadly on general issues in meaning, measurement, and use. Meaning is equivalent to construct validity, a continuing process that maps the lawful linkages with a larger psychology. In the 1990s, interest theory and measurement is a broader topic than ever before because so many diverse ideas and perspectives are jousting for inclusion in the arena.

Holland can be seen in the modern era as the guru of interest measurement. He is usually typecast as a vocational theorist, but his powerfully simple hexagon, with its six dimensions, is also centrally a taxonomy of interests. The six dimensions, or Holland types, are typically measured with interest inventories. The majority of influential inventories today use some variation of Holland interest scales. These include Holland's *Self-Directed Search* and *Vocational Preference Inventory,* the *Strong Interest Inventory,* the *Unisex Edition of the ACT Interest Inventory,* and the *Campbell Interest and Skill Survey.*

With Holland's measures one also gets Holland's meaning, which is his widely influential theory. Holland (1997) presents his theory, and its current state of evolution, in a pithy yet seminal book, *Making Vocational Choices,* now in its third edition. Much of what we know today about the meaning, measurement, and use of interests is tied to Holland's theoretical statement. Thus his book must be a leading contender for the most influential book in interest measurement. Recently his peers acknowledged his preeminence with the Distinguished Professional Contribution Award of the American Psychological Association. In this book Holland (this volume) continues to lead the field with ideas and empiricism about how interests are integrated with personality.

IMPRINTING ON INTERESTS

As a graduate student over 30 years ago, I had the distinct good fortune, as a research assistant to David Campbell at the University of Minnesota, to be imprinted on interest measurement. Our research team developed the 1968 Basic Interest Scales of the *Strong* inventory (Campbell, Borgen, Eastes, Johansson, & Peterson, 1968). They were the first set of content scales to be added to the *Strong,* beginning a series of later expansions of Strong's (1943) venerable inventory. Then in my first professional position, as a research psychologist at National Merit Scholarship Corporation, I had the good fortune to inherit a rich longitudinal data set of National Merit scholars who had taken the *Strong* before entering college. Thus I was able to study the validity of the Basic Interest Scales as well as the traditional Occupational Scales for predicting college major and career choice at the end of college (e.g., Borgen & Helms, 1975). Then my final good fortune related to the Basic Interest Scales was that in 1992 I was invited by the publisher to join in revising the *Strong,* presumably to "tweak" the Basic Interest Scales.

My 1990s cathexis to the *Strong* quite soon expanded and intensified. The most fun I had with the 1994 *Strong* (Harmon, Hansen, Borgen, & Hammer, 1994) was working with Lenore Harmon in developing the new Personal Style

Scales. They continue to be the aspect of the *Strong* I find the most fascinating. Perhaps this is because, while working with David Campbell to create the Basic Interest Scales, I could not convince him there was any valid personality variance in the *Strong* items beyond the Adventure scale. Today there are four putative personality scales in the *Strong*, and I am scheming to get more. Perhaps it is also due to Mischel's (1968) paradigm-rattling argument that personality dimensions as traits were moribund, or opinion-makers such as Guion (Guion & Gottier, 1965), who asserted that personality had little demonstrated relationship to work performance.

My good fortunes continued as the publishers of the *Strong* encouraged Nancy Betz, Lenore Harmon, and me to develop the 1996 *Skills Confidence Inventory* (Betz, Borgen & Harmon, 1996a & b). The General Confidence Themes based on the six Holland dimensions (Harmon et al., 1996) are self-efficacy counterparts to the interest measures of the six General Occupational Scales of the *Strong*. Here is a new inventory begging for more investigations of its meaning and implications for practice and theory (see Betz, Borgen, Kaplan, & Harmon, in press; Betz, Harmon, & Borgen, 1996; Harmon et al., 1996).

Suddenly my students, my research colleagues, and I are rich with data and ideas about relations among interests, personality, and self-efficacy as well as how they influence important life decisions and outcomes. In this chapter I illustrate the kinds of questions and issues that we have been addressing in the 1990s. By inference these issues lead to agendas for the future and reflect directions in which I would like the field of interest measurement to move.

CONSTRUCTING MEANING

Construct validation gives meaning to measures (Clark & Watson, 1995; Cronbach & Meehl, 1955; Fouad, this volume; Messick, 1995). The ultimate objective of my research program with the *Strong* inventory aims at construct validity. The centerpiece of construct validity is meaning. Meaning makes test scores useful in both counseling and theory. If counselors clearly know and understand what a test score means, then they can weave a narrative picture of the client. When counselors translate quantitative information into qualitative understanding, their clients gain useful self-knowledge to inform both present and future actions (Borgen, 1995; Tinsley & Chu, this volume; Zytowski, this volume). For the theorist, construct validity, the meaning of constructs within a nomological network of scientific relationships or laws, is the ultimate objective of science (Cronbach & Meehl, 1955; Messick, 1995).

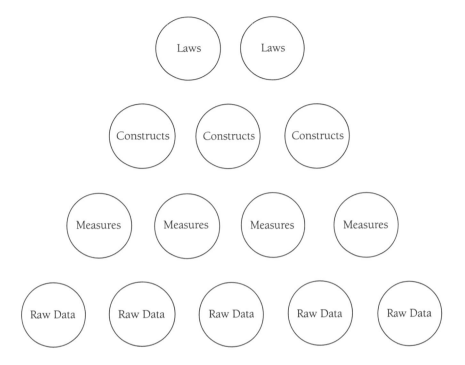

FIGURE 18.1   Schematic for a nomological net

True to my (alleged) atheoretical bias, I often consider construct validity from the "bottom" of the nomological network as portrayed in Fig. 18.1. Instead of beginning with a comprehensive theoretical conception, I often start with the measure and then move from that measure toward abstractions by reflecting on the implications the measure holds for the nomological network. The Minnesota mantra is, "What do the data say?" Working with a venerable instrument such as the *Strong*, this is a natural perspective to adopt. Paradigms wax and wane, yet the implacable *Strong* persists. The *Strong* is not going away, so why not explore the limits of what responses to it mean? It also fits comfortably with the goal of trying to make the *Strong* more useful for counselors and clients. Practical questions prevail: What is the meaning of a particular score on the Learning Environment Personal Style Scale of the *Strong*? What are the implications of a score of, say, 60 on the Learning Environment Scale? As we pursue such practical questions, we quickly encounter questions of large theoretical importance: How are personality and interests related? Is personality related to the work experience?

Messick (1995) has comprehensively explained how the validity of psychological measures is expressed in their meaning. The meaning of test results has both practical and theoretical implications. Practically, the meaning of a test result refers to the range of useful interpretations that can be made from it for action by clients. Theoretically, the meaning of a test result relates to how the construct it taps is woven into a larger nomological network that may contain many constructs and abstractions (Cronbach & Meehl, 1955). Despite the shibboleths, there are Minnesotans such as Meehl who look at the nomological network from all directions. Messick emphasizes that validity is not a fixed property of a test but a property of the inferences that are made with the test across a variety of contexts. Because test use evolves into different contexts, and because theoretical perspectives and paradigms also evolve, the study of validity itself is an evolving process. As science and practice evolve, so too should our understanding of the construct validity and meaning of a particular test.

Savickas (this volume) presents a compelling scholarly treatment of conceptions of interest measurement, especially over its early historical period. One lesson I draw from the Savickas chapter is that the way we talk about interests is highly contextual, a product of the thinking of the times. His suggestion that Strong's parsing of interests reflected the four major viewpoints of American psychology is especially telling. By reading Savickas, I have come to see how much my foci in interest measurement and theory are a product of my time. I am most interested in how interests are related to personality and self-efficacy, two of the hot topics of the 1980s and 1990s.

SVEN AND THE ART OF MODEL MAINTENANCE

Our theories and taxonomies tell us that people who maintain motorcycles (Realistic types) are a stoic, nonverbal lot, and not likely to wax poetic or fanciful about philosophy and values (Artistic types). Yet occasionally folks such as Pirsig (1974) stretch across the hexagon in surprising ways. Likewise, it is possible for a dustbowl empiricist to have some fancies of theory, however brief.

This chapter presents a nascent model of some of the issues that drive the research program my students and I are pursuing. When my students read this chapter, they will not recognize what follows as our research program. They never guessed we were following a model. This will look like a programmatic menu bearing little resemblance to the ad hoc cacophony and chaos that have been our everyday fare over the past half dozen years. Our real life has been an untidy variant of dustbowl empiricism. Usually we Minnesotans are perfectly happy with a data set and a computer. We don't need models. So this is the tidied-up model I would write if I were asked to describe my research program.

A unifying goal structuring my research program has been to understand the meaning, the validity of interpretations, of the 1994 *Strong* and the 1996 *Skills Confidence Inventory*. This quest has both practice and science implications, and each reciprocally influences the other. The practice implications are not given the attention in this chapter that they deserve, yet they are really the initiating force in my research. This personalized model has much in common with nearly all of the other chapters in this book. My attempts to bridge interests with the larger life experience seem especially close to the underlying messages in the chapters in this volume by Gottfredson, Holland, Rounds and Day, Prediger, and Blustein and Flum. I especially see in each of these chapters a message, either direct or indirect, that vocational interests relate to other domains of individuality, such as abilities, cognitions, personality, genes, and developmental processes. The core premise for my sketch of a model is a 1990s version of Parsons' (1909) person–job matching model, or more broadly the person–environment (P–E) fit model (Chartrand, 1991). The match between characteristics of people and the arenas where they live has important implications for their lives. I want to think about this broadly. We have a whole array of psychological assessment devices for helping people understand their individuality. Their individuality interacts with a whole array of their life experience. So I frame this as relationships between one's *individuality* and one's experiences in *living*, as suggested in Fig. 18.2. Individuality and living connect within a complex nomological network that describes how individual differences interact with life experiences. Tyler (1959, 1978) used the term *individuality* to denote how counseling psychology incorporates an individual differences approach to assessing, understanding, and helping people (see Dawis, 1992; Hartung, this volume; Lubinski & Dawis, 1995; Spokane & Decker, this volume).

Next I focus on aspects of individuality and living environments that are part of my current thinking and research. This is primarily heuristic, rather than prescriptive. It is useful for stimulating thinking, but does not pretend to be comprehensive. First, on the left side of Fig. 18.3, there are four domains of individuality that I emphasize: *interests, personality, self-efficacy,* and *values*. These are depicted as venn-like diagrams to suggest that these are likely overlapping

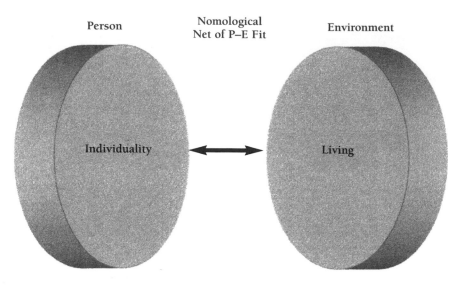

Person   Nomological   Environment
                Net of P–E Fit

Individuality ⟷ Living

FIGURE 18.2   Linking individuality and living through the nomological net of P–E fit

domains or constructs and that a crucial part of our research agenda is to determine the extent of that overlap. It is possible we are measuring the same phenomenon and merely calling it different things. Excessive overlap among our measures of individuality can (and should) embarrass us as both practitioners and theoreticians. Two currently hot topics are the overlap between interests and personality, and the overlap between interests and self-efficacy. The diagram reminds me that the overlap between personality and self-efficacy is a neglected topic, one deserving more attention. Values are a somewhat different domain in this figure; it is not an area of my current research; I put values here to remind me that this is a largely unexplored research area, especially the questions of overlap of values with the other three domains of individuality. I leave abilities out of the picture, so that many readers will be stimulated to draw their own pictures of their research agenda. I think abilities should be included in any comprehensive picture of human attributes (see Lubinski & Dawis, 1995).

As if these questions of overlap in our measures of individuality were not vexing enough, we have not even mentioned the issue here that is the most theoretically compelling: the issue of causal relationships among these domains. For example, are interests precursors to self-efficacy, as Lent, Brown, and Hackett

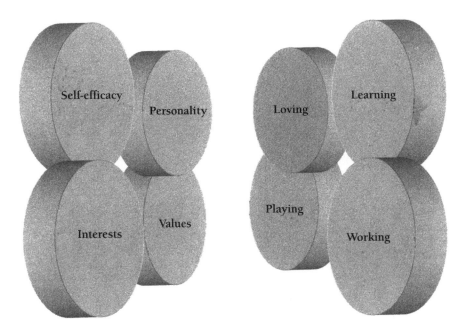

FIGURE 18.3 A potential nomological space of individuality and living
On the left, four overlapping domains of individuality; on the right, four overlapping venues of living

(1994) assert? Or is it even more complex, with reciprocal, spiraling causality between interests and self-efficacy? Another example of a pressing causal question waiting in the wings is the role of genetics (see Gottfredson, this volume).

Next there is the question of all the psychological environments where we live our lives. People in the 1990s work hard, but they also want to live passionately in all the venues of their lives. So, as depicted on the right side of Fig. 18.3, in my P–E fit model four major venues of living are *loving, working, learning,* and *playing.* Freud believed that a healthy person is able to love and to work. A century later we have expanded our priorities. No doubt, important venues of living are missing; worshiping is one that comes to mind. Again the venn diagram helps to remind us that these spheres of living overlap. These concepts borrow from Super's ideas about life space and life career (Super, 1980, 1994). How one arena of living overlaps and affects another is an important topic, although not my current focus. Rather, I view these areas of living as different criterion spaces. Thus I am interested in how the different constructs of individuality show validity generalization across interpersonal, work, educational, and leisure environments. For example, I want to know more about the meaning of various interest scales and self-effi-cacy scales across these environments. Taking liberties with Rounds and Day (this volume), I want to know if you can teach an engineer to say "I love you."

The totality of Fig. 18.3 is my version of how I am thinking about the nomo-logical network linking individuality and living. I don't even want to draw more than two or three lines of the nomological network and will leave that to some eager path analyst. But the potential linkages must be faced, so that is done in Table 18.1. This shows an expanded matrix between individuality and living. The table has been framed as three boxes of P–E fit (see Bolles, 1977). Box A con-tains person or individuality variables; box B contains variables across the venues of living, often viewed as criterion variables; and box C represents the fit and causal relations between individuality and living. Each of the 36 cells within the boxes is a potential place to seek meaning through nomological relationships. How shall we choose the ones we will investigate?

Table 18.1 portrays an overall picture of some research possibilities prompt-ed by an expanded view of interests within domains of individuality and venues of living. It deserves some scrutiny to highlight the possibilities of what has been heavily researched and what has been neglected thus far. The cells of the Table 18.1 matrix are numbered sequentially to reflect some of the usual sequence by which research is appropriately conducted. First are the cells in the diagonal. These represent research only within one general class of variables. Cells 1 through 4 in box A refer to studies about the dimensionality of domains of indi-viduality, such as studies of interests within cell 1. Next, cells 5 through 8 in box B refer to studies about dimensionality of venues of living. These might be con-sidered studies of the criterion space. Especially in counseling psychology, where our focus is so much on individuality, this is relatively unexplored terrain. Other areas of psychology focus on a portion of this nomological space as they explore questions such as the relationship among job satisfaction, work commitment, and work performance.

Cells 9 through 14 in box A represent relationships between domains of indi-viduality, while cells 15 and 20 in box B represents relationships across venues of living. Finally, the intersection of person and environment occurs in box C, where domains of individuality are paired with venues of living. This is the traditional domain for studying validity, where an assessed person variable is related to some behavioral outcome. Here is where our measures get their ultimate meaning in terms

TABLE 18.1   The Three Boxes of P–E Fit

| | | Individuality | | | | Living | | | |
		Interests	Personality	Self-Efficacy	Values	Loving	Working	Learning	Playing
Individuality	Interests	1 Person							
	Personality	9 Person	2 Person						
			Box A: Person						
	Self-Efficacy	10 Person	11 Person	3 Person					
	Values	12 Person	13 Person	14 Person	4 Person				
Living	Loving	21 Fit	22 Fit	23 Fit	24 Fit	5 Life			
	Working	25 Fit	26 Fit	27 Fit	28 Fit	15 Life	6 Life		
			Box C: Fit				Box B: Life		
	Learning	29 Fit	30 Fit	31 Fit	32 Fit	16 Life	17 Life	7 Life	
	Playing	33 Fit	34 Fit	35 Fit	36 Fit	18 Life	19 Life	20 Life	8 Life

Note: Pairwise relationships between four domains of individuality and four venues of living.

of real-world outcomes. This book and the long legacy of interest measurement are testaments to the huge amount of research done in cell 25, relating interests to work behavior. Many of the other cells in box C have barely been examined. Incidentally, in Table 18.1 I use the term *fit* as a shorthand for the P–E fit perspective. Increasingly I think about these matters as more than the psychometric matching of parallel profiles of interests and work environments. Writers such as Blustein and Flum (this volume) and even Gottfredson (this volume) on genetics, and several others in this volume, have encouraged me to think of this as the mutual engagement of individuality and living, each reciprocally determining the other (Bandura, 1989, 1997).

Cell 1 represents only studies relating interests to other interests. Typical questions that are asked here are the following: How many dimensions of interests are there; what are the more potent dimensions of interests; how are these dimensions organized? These questions usually fall under the rubric of research on the structure of interests. It is instructive to note that this is the most vigorous area of published research on interests in the 1990s, most notably by Gati (1991) and by Tracey and Rounds (1993) (see Rounds & Day, this volume). It also gives perspective to note that the structure of interests research is primarily constrained within cell 1. With methods like factor analysis and multidimensional scaling, most of this research is only relating interests to other interests; rarely has the prominent research related interests to other domains of individuality or to other criterion variables in the environment. Partially parallel things could be said about cell 2, representing the flurry of advocacy for the Big Five personality model (Digman, 1990; Goldberg, 1993) in the past decade. However, the Big Five model has also generated influential work on the validity of the five dimensions in relationship to work performance, as depicted in cell 26 (Barrick & Mount, 1991).

But many of the important questions are even more complex than suggested by Table 18.1. Important questions are those of divergent validity, namely does one measure give us meaningful information not conveyed by a similar measure? For example, on the new *Skills Confidence Inventory* does Investigative Confidence (self-efficacy) provide valid information beyond the Investigative GOT interest scale on the *Strong* (see Betz, this volume)? Unlike each cell in Table 18.1, which represents a pair of variable sets, this is a three-variable problem involving two measures of individuality and a criterion variable in the environmental space.

Yet another wrinkle of complexity not even mentioned in Fig. 18.3 and Table 18.1 is that the relationships conveyed must be tested over contexts and groups (Messick, 1995). Does the meaning of an assessment generalize over groups that differ by, say, gender, ethnicity, and age (see Harmon, this volume)? Little wonder that Messick (1995) stresses that construct validation is a never-ending process.

Also missing in Fig. 18.3 and Table 18.1 is any explicit mention of developmental processes. The figures are apt to be seen as merely a cross-sectional slice of events frozen in time. A figure that reflected developmental reality would be animated, bouncing across time and showing reciprocal and changing influences between individuality and living (see Blustein & Flum, this volume; Swanson, this volume).

QUESTIONS ABOUT INTERESTS, PERSONALITY, AND WORK BEHAVIOR

As an illustration, this section addresses just a fraction of the conceptual space in the expanded model of individuality and living in Fig. 18.3 and Table 18.1. Here the focus is on the role of interests and personality in work behavior. This topic involves three of the circles, interests and personality on the individuality side, and working on the environment side. As denoted in cells 9, 25, and 26 in Table 18.1, with three elements there are at least three pair-wise questions to be addressed conceptually and empirically: (1) Are interests and personality related? (cell 9); (2) Are interests related to work behavior? (cell 25); and (3) Is personality related to work behavior? (cell 26). As we pursue this agenda, we will see there is also another central question if we find that both interests and personality relate to work behavior. This question, affecting both our counseling and our theory, is (4) Does the joint consideration of interests and personality add to our understanding of work behavior? This more complex question transcends any single cell in Table 18.1.

Space is devoted to this topic to highlight the theme that historically there have been many leaders in vocational psychology who would not think it useful to grandly draw pictures like Fig. 18.3 and Table 18.1. Specifically, personality has not been a part of vocational psychology for many leaders, especially if one suggested that there are occupational differences related to personality. If one only read Holland (1976, 1996, 1997), one would learn that interests and personality are similar and that both are related to vocational choice. Questions 1 through 3 would be answered affirmatively and one could go on to other things. Alas, the literature is full of influential naysayers on both questions 1 and 3. Some influential writers have claimed the relation between personality and interests is minimal. Others have claimed in various ways that personality is not an important variable in work behavior.

The Relationship of Interests and Personality

Historically many leaders in vocational psychology have been skeptical about the overlap between interests and personality (e.g., Dawis, 1991; Osipow, 1983; Super & Crites, 1962). Curiously, Dawis (1991) reviewed some of the same evidence Holland (1976, 1996, 1997) examined to support his claim of the overlap of between interests and personality, but Dawis concluded the evidence for linkage was unimpressive. Both Dawis (1991) and Holland (1976) draw on a seminal factor analysis by Guilford (Guilford, Christensen, Bond, & Sutton, 1954). Given some of the skepticism about the role of personality at work, especially in the 1960s, it is surprising to read Guilford and see how clearly he believed that personality and interests are linked within the motivational domain.

> An interest is defined as a generalized behavior tendency an individual has to be attracted to a certain class of incentives or activities. . . . The definition adopted indicates an obvious relation to motivation. This is as it should be. Published interest inventories and previous factor analyses have not paid sufficient attention to this relationship . . . The variables analyzed included both those referring directly to activities of a vocational nature and those having broad meanings that transcend vocations . . . many motivational variables not obviously associated with recognized interests were included in the list of possibilities. Several different manifestations of motivation such as needs, drives, attitudes, character traits, and temperament traits, as well as interests, were also considered. (Guilford et al., 1954, pp. 1–2)

As personality psychology has experienced a rebirth in the last two decades, so too has the focus on the relation between interests and personality. The Big Five personality model has come to dominate conceptualizing and research (Digman, 1990; Goldberg, 1993). Recently, the relation between interests and personality has been framed as a relation between the Big Five of personality and the Big Six of Holland's interest model. A series of studies (e.g., Fox, 1995; Gottfredson, Jones, & Holland, 1993; Holland, Johnston, & Asama, 1994; Tokar & Swanson, 1995; Tokar, Vaux, & Swanson, 1995; see Holland, 1996, 1997 for reviews) have generally shown that certain of the personality dimensions moderately relate to certain of the interest dimensions. For example, one consistent finding is that personality extraversion correlates with enterprising interests, often about .40 or more. The number of such studies has grown to the point where a meta-analysis of the Big Five and Big Six correlations would be useful.

My reading of the data concludes that the global dimensions of the Big Five and the Big Six share a moderate relationship. It is well established that interests and work behaviors, such as career choice, share a strong and extensive link. It follows that there is likely some relation between personality and work behaviors. Although this relation has a checkered history in the literature, there is recent interest in this topic and emerging evidence that there are important influences of personality at work. The most famous of these is the work by Barrick and Mount (1991), who related the Big Five to work performance within occupations. Another line of evidence is developing because of the addition of the Personal Style Scales to the 1994 *Strong* inventory. Although Harmon et al.

(1994) expected the Personal Style Scales to relate most to behaviors within occupations, they found surprisingly strong differences across occupations (see also Donnay & Borgen, 1996). Also, the fact that Harmon et al. could develop Personal Style Scales from Strong's interest items is reminiscent of Guilford and colleagues' (1954) claim that interests and personality tap similar motivational domains.

THE STIMULUS OF THE *STRONG:* RECENT RESEARCH ON INTERESTS, PERSONALITY, AND SELF-EFFICACY

My colleague Don Zytowski fondly reminds us that the *Strong* is the only inventory that has more scales than items. Over the years the *Strong* has undergone remarkable innovation (Campbell & Hansen, 1981; Hansen & Campbell, 1985) so that today it includes a variety of scales beyond E. K. Strong's (1943) classic Occupational Scales. The latest additions to the *Strong* (Harmon, Hansen, Borgen, & Hammer, 1994) are the Personal Style Scales. An observer such as Zytowski might rightly ask whether there is any incremental validity or counseling utility for yet another set of scales. His challenge is being put to the test.

Initial Validation of the 1994 Personal Style Scales

The 1994 *Strong Interest Inventory* (Harmon et al., 1994) is the first version of the *Strong* to explicitly feature personality-type scales. Called Personal Style Scales, these four new scales are Work Style, Learning Environment, Leadership, and Risk Taking/Adventure. Harmon et al. (1994) described the development of these scales. They reflect a repackaging of some prior scales in the *Strong* and the creation of at least one scale that is quite new. Risk Taking/Adventure is essentially the old Adventure scale that in prior versions of the *Strong* was classified as a Basic Interest Scale. The Learning Environment Style scale represents an explicit attempt to improve on the old Academic Comfort scale of the *Strong*. The Leadership Style scale emerged out of factor analytic work with the *Strong* items; this clear factor dimension turned out to be highly correlated with the old Introversion-Extraversion scale in prior *Strong* inventories ® = .xx in 1994 *Strong* norm group. So it turned out, in part by chance, that Work Style is the most conceptually new of the four Personal Style Scales. It could be developed because the four terms *data, ideas, people,* and *things* were paired in six items in the new *Strong,* and respondents in the norm group of 18,951 were asked to indicate which they preferred in each pair. The scale was developed by the empirical, contrasted-groups

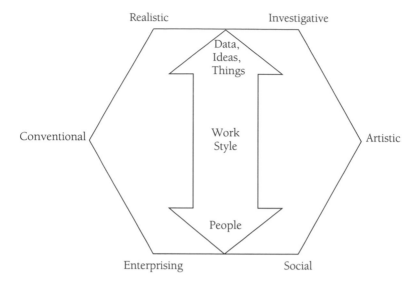

FIGURE 18.4   Relationship of the Work Style scale to Holland's RIASEC hexagon

method pioneered by E. K. Strong, Jr. One anchoring group included those who always preferred people, and the polar opposite group included those who never preferred people.

The Work Style scale has turned out to be a potent scale, as subsequent studies have examined its correlates and behavioral implications. Was this just luck by some inveterate dustbowl empiricists? Lenore Harmon was the creator of the Work Style scale, and she was in fact more a conceptualizer than a number cruncher yet also talented at applying Strong's contrasted groups method. Although Harmon did not post a theoretical manifesto, she knew that preferences for data, ideas, people, or things have a long and potent history in vocational psychology. Most directly these concepts are tightly and richly linked with Holland's (1997) hexagon and have been explicitly linked with the hexagon in Prediger's (1976) and Swaney's (1995) widely used World-of-Work Map in the American College Testing (ACT) counseling materials. Thus we should not have been surprised to see how nicely the Work Style scale fits across two sides of the hexagon, correlating positively with two Holland themes, and negatively with two Holland themes. In the 1994 *Strong* norm group of 9,467 women, Work Style correlates .64 and .60, respectively, with Social and Enterprising and –.39 and –.46, respectively, with Realistic and Investigative. Similar correlations occur for men. Fig. 18.4 illustrates this relationship.

Here are some other examples of the external validity implications of scores on the new Work Style scale. As shown in the *Strong* manual (Harmon et al., 1994, p. 168), occupations are sharply demarcated by Work Style, separated by two standard deviations, or an effect size of 2.0. For example, this is shown graphically where community service organization directors score 57 on Work Style, but physicists score 37. A more formal test of this occupational separation is the article by Donnay and Borgen (1996). For the 50 occupations in the 1994 norm group of 18,951 the analysis of variance effect size for Work Style is the largest of the four Personal Styles, exceeded only by Investigative and Enterprising of six Holland GOTs.

The Meaning of the Personal Styles Scales of the 1994 *Strong Inventory*

Lindley (1997) recently examined the validity of the Personal Style Scales in a sample of 1,064 college students. She sought to elaborate the meaning of the scales by examining their relation to other established personality dimensions. In terms of Table 18.1 she focused on cell 9, the conjunction of interests and personality. The *Adjective Checklist* (ACL; Gough & Heilbrun, 1983) provided the concurrent validation measures of personality, both at the item level and at the scale level. Fig. 18.5 shows an example of the kind of meaning that is given to these scales by looking at item endorsements on the ACL. Here various levels of the Learning Environment scale are shown in terms of the probability that college students would describe themselves as artistic on the ACL. One can see the clear relationship, with the probabilities being fourfold greater at a score above 60 than below 40. Lindley was also interested in the very important practical and scientific issue of whether such interpretative implications differ by gender. Her conclusion was that most relations between items and scales were similar across the genders, as is apparent in the illustration in Fig. 18.5, and therefore similar interpretations can be made for women and men on the Personal Style Scales. Imagine the possibilities of applying this kind of information to clients in a computerized, interactive format for test interpretation.

Lindley (1997) also was able to examine relations between the Personal Style Scales and the Big Five personality dimensions. She scored the ACL data for the Big Five ACL scales developed by John (1990). Her results clearly linked the Personal Style Scales to Big Five dimensions in theoretically expected ways. In addition, the linkages, and therefore meaning, were quite similar across genders as well as across her validation and cross-validation samples. For genders combined,

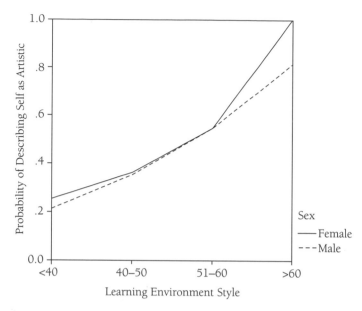

FIGURE 18.5   Probabilities of describing oneself as artistic for four score levels
of the Learning Environment Style scale

across the validation and cross-validation samples the strongest correlations were
between Leadership Style and Extraversion, .49 and .54 respectively. Again as
expected, Learning Environment correlated .35 and .42 with Openness, and Work
Style correlated .30 and .32 with Agreeableness. The one unexpected link involved
Leadership Style correlating .32 and .48 to Openness. This finding awaits further
clarification. Risk Taking/Adventure correlated .30 in the cross-validation sample,
but just .17 in the validation sample with Openness. These results help to map the
overlap between the Personal Style Scales and the Big Five. The Personal Styles link
in meaningful ways with Extraversion, Agreeableness, and Openness. The Personal
Styles are not linked to Conscientiousness and Neuroticism, raising the tantalizing
possibility that future revisers of the *Strong* may want to consider new Personal Style
Scales in these, or related, domains.

Synergy of Interests and Self-Efficacy Predicting Occupation

Donnay (1998) has recently done pioneering work on the relationship between
vocational interests and vocational self-efficacy, and especially their discriminant
validity for external criteria. His work reveals important information about how
much interests and self-efficacy on Holland themes are independent or overlapping

dimensions, most notably against a behavioral criterion of occupational membership. Are they measuring similar predictive variance or fully independent variance, or are they providing information that is interactive or synergistic? This work addresses some of the questions raised so well by Prediger (this volume). In terms of Table 18.1 this work addresses the links of interests and self-efficacy in cell 10, the validity relations of interests to work in cell 25, and the validity relations of self-efficacy to work cell 25. But it also transcends these individual cells by addressing all of these relationships jointly.

Donnay's work was possible because of the recent development of the *Skills Confidence Inventory* (Betz, Borgen, & Harmon, 1996a & b) as a companion to the *Strong Interest Inventory* (Harmon et al., 1994). Now career counselors and researchers have parallel measures of the six Holland dimensions for self-efficacy (or confidence) and interest on, respectively, the General Confidence Themes (GCTs) and General Occupational Themes (GOTs).

Betz et al. (1996a & b) developed the Skills Confidence Inventory by using a subset of the same national sample of employed adults that was used by Harmon et al. (1994) to develop the 1994 *Strong Interest Inventory*. For their subsample Betz et al. sampled from women and men in 21 different occupations that were distributed across the six Holland occupational themes. Thus this group is diverse in interests, and they also turned out to be equally diverse in self-efficacy (Betz et al., 1996b). For his research Donnay (1998) was able to match up 1,105 individuals who had taken the *Strong* in 1992–93 and the Skills Confidence Inventory in 1993–94. This was the sample that enabled his study of the relationships of interests and self-efficacy.

Using a concurrent validity perspective with this national sample of employed adults, Donnay's research strategy was to look at interests and self-efficacy as predictors of membership in their current occupations. The dependent variable was membership in one of the 21 occupations held by these working adults. Following his earlier work with interests alone (Donnay & Borgen, 1996), one of Donnay's primary approaches was to use discriminant analysis as a multivariate prediction of occupation from the six GOTs (interests), and six GCTs (confidence or self-efficacy) separately, and then together as a set of 12 predictors. To evaluate the stability of these multivariate results Donnay randomly split the sample into a validation sample of 564 and a cross-validation sample of 541. Discriminant analysis provided two indexes of strength of predictive relationships. In the first index the portion of variance accounted for is shown by 1 – Wilk's lambda (Betz, 1987). Hit rate from discriminant prediction is another

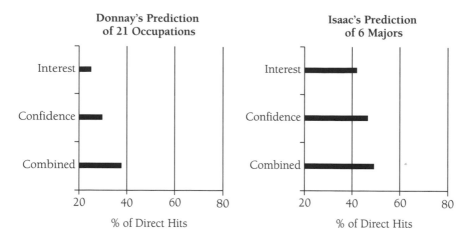

FIGURE 18.6   Synergistic effects of interests and self-efficacy
                 for predicting working and learning outcomes

Note: Discriminant function hit rates for Donnay's (1998) prediction of 21 occupations and Isaac et al.'s (1997)
prediction of 6 college major families.

index, interpreted relative to the chance rate; in this case the base rate was 4.8% hits
by chance. Donnay's results are illustrated here for his validation sample; similar
results were found for the cross-validation sample. As shown on the left side of Fig.
18.6, Donnay found that interests and self-efficacy, on the six Holland themes, each
substantially predicted membership in the 21 occupations. The combined, or synergistic, effect was also striking, indicating that interests and self-efficacy each contributed important independent variance. As displayed in the figure, hit rates were
26% and 30% for interests and self-efficacy, respectively, but 38% for the two
domains of individuality combined. This is a big effect, more than seven times the
chance hit rate. Using the multivariate index of effect size of 1 – lambda, Donnay
found that interests accounted for 79% of the variance and self-efficacy accounted
for 82% of the variance, but together they accounted for 91% of the variance.
Donnay's results clearly suggest both our counseling and our theory will be
improved if we integrate interests and self-efficacy in our models.

Synergy of Interests and Self-Efficacy Predicting College Major

Isaacs, Borgen, Donnay, and Hansen's (1997) research question and approach
resembled Donnay's (1998), but their outcome variable was college major rather
than adult occupation. For their college sample of 760 they shifted the criterion
space from working to learning. Within a concurrent validity perspective they

asked whether interests and self-efficacy, as measured by the six GOTs and six GCTs, could predict college major within one of the six Holland themes. Thus Isaacs et al. tested the validity generalization of these measures in the *Strong Interest Inventory* and *Skills Confidence Inventory* to a new outcome, namely college major. They also examined the combined synergistic effect of using both kinds of measures to predict college major. Following Table 18.1, this research merges the links of interests and self-efficacy (cell 9), the validity relations of interests and learning (cell 29), and the validity relations of self-efficacy and learning (cell 31).

Like Donnay (1998), Isaacs et al. used discriminant analysis with 6 measures of interests, 6 measures of self-efficacy, and the 12 measures combined. While Donnay predicted membership in 21 occupations, Isaacs et al. predicted 6 Holland major fields. Overall predictive accuracy, in terms of Wilks's lambda, should not be expected to be as high with these more molar groups, because there will be more variability within each group. On the other hand, the absolute level of predictive hit rate should be higher because with only six groups to predict, the chance rate is higher, 1/6 or 16.7%. The right side of Fig. 18.6 shows the hit rates for predicting major: 42% for interests, 47% for confidence, and 49% for interests and confidence combined. Again there is a synergistic effect of combining both interest and self-efficacy measures, but the effect is only a 2% increment, as compared to 7.5% for Donnay's prediction of 21 specific occupations. Here, in this example for predicting major, the incremental effect is more apparent for the 1 – lambda effect size, which is 47% variance explained by interests, 48.5% for confidence, and 57% for interests and confidence combined. The Isaac et al. study clearly shows the potential for our models, in the extended venue of the learning environment, to incorporate both interests and self-efficacy measures to capture important dimensions of individuality.

Personality, Self-Efficacy, and Working

A final empirical example illustrates the kinds of integrative questions that can be addressed with data sets containing multiple measures of individuality and living. In Table 18.1, this example shows relations between personality, self-efficacy, and work: jointly considering cells 11, 26, and 27. The sample is the one constructed by Donnay (1998), containing the 1,105 working adults in 21 occupations drawn from the national norm groups for the 1994 *Strong* and the 1996 *Skills Confidence Inventory*. This is a simple yet compelling graphic illustration of

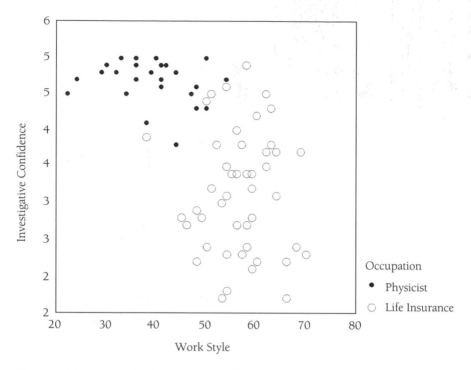

FIGURE 18.7 Example of occupational differences on self-efficacy and personal style
Note: 48 life insurance agents and 27 physicists plotted on Investigative Confidence and Work Style

how personality and self-efficacy relate to work. Fig. 18.7 shows a scatter plot of 48 life insurance agents and 27 physicists on the Work Style scale and the Investigative Confidence scale. We know from the interest measurement literature that life insurance agents and physicists live on different psychological continents. Their passions and aversions are mirror images. One adores science, the other loathes it; one is passionate about selling and persuading, the other would rather have a root canal. They are classic exemplars of the outer reaches of Holland's hexagon and the various meanings he draws from it (Holland, 1996, 1997). Fig. 18.7, by my intraocular trauma test, shows that life insurance agents and physicists are also very different people in terms of self-efficacy and personality. Do these variables add to our understanding beyond knowing their interest scores? Research such as Donnay's (1998) suggests that the answer is yes, but the question has yet to be fully explored.

BRINGING PASSION AND INTEGRATION TO INTEREST THEORY AND MEASUREMENT

Historically interest measurement often has been isolated from much of larger psychology (see Savickas, this volume). The concepts of interests have also reflected a scientific objectivity and detachment that have rendered them at times dispassionately arid. The time has come to bring more passion and integration to interest measurement.

There is a temptation, given the long proximity of interest measurement to mythical Lake Wobegon, Minnesota, to call attention to the Lake Wobegon effect in interest measurement. These Lake Wobegon folks are dogmatic about never doing anything to excess, so one could say that all their interests are about average. The limits of their exultation extend to "you betcha." Thus it is fitting that the *Strong* inventory, long associated with Minnesota, asks people about their interests with a modest three-point LID scale, ranging from "Like" to "Indifferent" to "Dislike." (Please indulge my narrative for a moment and ignore the empirical facts about how well this response format works.) The people in the real world I know, even in Iowa, have a stronger set of words for describing how they react to stimulus materials. Among the younger set most of these terms are unprintable for mature readers.

In the real world people think about their lives with a range of reactions from passion to aversion. They make choices and plans to "pursue their passions," to "fulfill their bliss." Advertisers know this, and passion is the language of advertising. Publishers of self-help career books know this, and this is the language of these books. Business guru Tom Peters does not call his best-selling book "A Preference for Excellence"; he is passionate about everything he does and his book titles reflect it (Peters & Austin, 1985). Many people in the 1990s are bullish on life in all its venues.

I have suggested in this chapter that interest measurement is ripe for more integration with other domains of individuality, such as personality and self-efficacy. Holland has long taken the position that his interest inventories *are* personality inventories. In recent years a series of studies have empirically confirmed links between Holland Big Six dimensions and the Big Five personality model.

We now need to know more about the links between interests and self-efficacy, and between personality and self-efficacy. We have a promising knowledge base about the former, but we know very little about the latter. Betz and her colleagues have shown that, on the Holland dimensions, there are moderate relations between interests and self-efficacy. Donnay's (1998) and Isaac et al.'s (1997) work show interests and self-efficacy each have valid independent variance, leading to synergistic results when combined in prediction.

I am itching to learn more about the relations between personality and self-efficacy because I have seen enough profiles on the *Skills Confidence Inventory* to suspect that it may reflect personality dimensions. My first clue came in trying out the inventory on the "Viking family" on the deck in Lake Wobegon. One of my brash, clearly extraverted relatives scored near the top in confidence on all six scales. (He is not a native of Lake Wobegon.) Prediger (1998, this volume) has shown that level of interest profiles is not important, but my hunch is that level of skills confidence profiles will turn out to be importantly related to other variables, including personality.

As we start integrating interest measurement with the whole person and the whole of counseling, we see how it links to vast, deeply held aspects of the person. As we see the links between work interests and personality, we tap into the core of human resilience and perhaps even passion. As president of the American Psychological Association (APA), Seligman recently took a natural step beyond his advocacy for learned optimism (Seligman, 1991) and established an APA project to focus on what healthy, thriving people are all about. In words that are reminiscent of long traditions in counseling psychology, he suggests, "We have discovered that there is a set of human strengths that are the most likely buffers against mental illness: courage, optimism, interpersonal skill, work ethic, hope, honesty and perseverance" (Seligman, 1998, p. 2). Beyond viewing Seligman's list of attributes as buffers against mental illness, I prefer to see them as a beginning list of the characteristics of thriving, coping, resilient people. In keeping with my theme herein, I would add passion to the list. One could also argue that many of the things in Seligman's list add up to living passionately. One could take what we currently know about interests, personality, and self-efficacy and map those dimensions into nearly all the terms in Seligman's list.

A number of writers now view interests as a part of studying and understanding the whole person. These themes echo throughout the chapters of this book. Lowman (1991), writing from the practice perspective, argues that assessment for work should attend to multifaceted individuality. Scholars are actively examining how domains of individuality overlap in human action (Ackerman & Heggestad, 1997; Bandura, 1989, 1997; Donnay, 1998; Holland, 1996, 1997; Lent, Brown, & Hackett, 1994; Lubinski & Dawis, 1995; Swanson, 1993).

Csikszentmihalyi has even created the concept of flow to describe the passionate engagement that people bring to their everyday living (Csikszentmihalyi, 1997; Csikszentmihalyi & LeFevre, 1989.)

FINAL COMMENTS ABOUT THIS BOOK

Interest measurement is one of psychology's most enduring and potent areas of individual differences (Lubinski & Dawis, 1995). Its legacies span most of a century, anchored by icons such as Strong (1943) and Kuder (1977), and in the last half of the century our icon is the world's most meaningful and well-traveled hexagon (Holland, 1996, 1997). This book chronicles where we have been and what is happening at the horizons of the field at the end of the century. As the title of the book suggests, and as Savickas and Spokane (this volume) explicate, measurement of interests and their application in counseling have a long and fruitful history of application. Many of the experts in this volume are continuing those applications.

Although conceptually interests have sometimes been "what the interest test measures" (see Savickas, this volume), the field is advancing toward enhanced meaning in our measures. Across the chapters in this book one can see evidence. The number and diversity of authors in this book exemplify that today there are more people working actively in interest measurement with a wider variety of conceptual diversity than ever before. New topics have intersected with interests in ways that promise more integration and stimulation of new research directions. At the moment there is a segmentation where a very small cadre of thinkers and researchers are relatively isolated in their perspective on a piece of the puzzle. This book puts all of that diversity together in one place and invites the next generation to produce a John Holland to advance the field.

Holland (1996, 1997) wrote the book on interest measurement. His creative contributions have been integrative for more than 35 years but not always fully appreciated or understood by the field. His assertion that interests and personality are related stakes out the center ground of theoretical and counseling integration. His conceptual position means that he does not leave out much about the fully functioning person in a variety of life roles. He could use my too-complex Table 18.1 to show me how his theory and research has already addressed most of its 36 cells. His genius also keeps it simple so that the ideas translate to workable theory and counseling.

People's interests at work are confronting a whole array of what else makes their individuality and lives passionate and tightly intertwined. Interests emerge as a centerpiece of what enables us passionately to engage in life as emotionally healthy, thriving, coping, and even joyful human beings in all of life's venues.

REFERENCES

Ackerman, P. L., & Heggestad, E. D. (1997). Intelligence, personality, and interests: Evidence for overlapping traits. *Psychological Bulletin, 121,* 219–245.

Bandura, A. (1989). Human agency in social cognitive theory. *American Psychologist, 44,* 1175–1184.

Bandura, A. (1997). *Self-efficacy: The exercise of control.* New York: Freeman.

Barrick, M. R., & Mount, M. K. (1991). The Big Five personality dimensions and job performance: A meta-analysis. *Personnel Psychology, 44,* 1–26.

Betz, N. E. (1987). Use of discriminant analysis in counseling psychology research. *Journal of Counseling Psychology, 34,* 393–403.

Betz, N. E., Borgen, F. H., & Harmon, L. W. (1996a). *Skills Confidence Inventory.* Palo Alto, CA: Consulting Psychologists Press.

Betz, N. E., Borgen, F. H., & Harmon, L. W. (1996b). *Skills Confidence Inventory Applications and Technical Guide.* Palo Alto, CA: Consulting Psychologists Press.

Betz, N. E., Borgen, F. H., Kaplan, A., & Harmon, L. W. (in press). Gender as a moderator of the validity and interpretive utility of the *Skills Confidence Inventory. Journal of Vocational Behavior.*

Betz, N. E., Harmon, L. W., & Borgen, F. H. (1996). The relationship of self-efficacy for the Holland themes to gender, occupational group membership, and vocational interests. *Journal of Counseling Psychology, 43,* 90–98.

Bolles, R. N. (1977). *Three boxes of life.* Berkeley, CA: Ten Speed Press.

Borgen, F. H. (1986). New approaches to the assessment of interests. In W. B. Walsh & S. H. Osipow (Eds.), *Advances in vocational psychology: Vol. I. The assessment of interests* (pp. 31–54). Hillsdale, NJ: Erlbaum.

Borgen, F. H. (1995). Leading edges of vocational psychology: Diversity and vitality. In W. B. Walsh & S. H. Osipow (Eds.), *Handbook of vocational psychology: Theory, research. and practice* (2nd ed., pp. 427–441). Hillsdale, NJ: Erlbaum.

Borgen, F. H., & Helms, J. E. (1975). Validity generalization of the men's form of the *Strong Vocational Interest Blank* with academically able women. *Journal of Counseling Psychology, 22,* 210–216.

Campbell, D. P. (1971). *Handbook for the Strong Vocational Interest Blank.* Stanford, CA: Stanford University Press.

Campbell, D. P., Borgen, F. H., Eastes, S., Johansson, C. B., & Peterson, R. A. (1968). A set of Basic Interest Scales for the *Strong Vocational Interest Blank for Men. Journal of Applied Psychology, 52,* 2.

Campbell, D. P., & Hansen, J. C. (1981). *Manual for SVIB-SCII (3rd ed.).* Stanford, CA: Stanford University Press.

Chartrand, J. M. (1991). The evolution of trait-and-factor career counseling: A person X environment fit approach. *Journal of Counseling and Development, 69,* 518–524.

Clark, L. A., & Watson, D. (1995). Constructing validity: Basic issues in objective scale development. *Psychological Assessment, 7,* 309–319.

Cronbach, L. J., & Meehl, P. E. (1955). Construct validity in psychological tests. *Psychological Bulletin, 52,* 281–302.

Csikszentmihalyi, M. (1997). *Finding flow: The psychology of engagement with everyday life.* New York: Basic Books.

Csikszentmihalyi, M., & LeFevre, J. (1989). Optimal experience in work and leisure. *Journal of Personality and Social Psychology, 56,* 815–822.

Dawis, R. V. (1991). Vocational interests, values, and preferences. In M. D. Dunnette & L. M. Hough (Eds.), *Handbook of industrial and organizational psychology, Vol. 2* (2nd ed., pp. 833–871). Palo Alto, CA: Consulting Psychologists Press.

Dawis, R. V. (1992). The individual differences tradition in counseling psychology. *Journal of Counseling Psychology, 39,* 7–19.

Digman, J. M. (1990). Personality structure: Emergence of the five-factor model. *Annual Review of Psychology, 41,* 417–440.

Donnay, D.A.C. (1998). *Assessing careers: Vocational interest and vocational self-efficacy.* Unpublished doctoral dissertation, Iowa State University.

Donnay, D.A.C., & Borgen, F. H. (1996). Validity, structure, and content of the 1994 *Strong Interest Inventory. Journal of Counseling Psychology, 43,* 275–291.

Fox, M L. (1995). *Assessment of personality and vocational interests: Redundant versus complementary.* Unpublished doctoral dissertation, Iowa State University.

Gati, I. (1991). The structure of vocational interests. *Psychological Bulletin, 109,* 309–324.

Goldberg, L. R. (1993). The structure of phenotypic personality traits. *American Psychologist, 48,* 26–34.

Gottfredson, G. D., Jones, E. M., & Holland, J. L. (1993). Personality and vocational interests: The relation of Holland's interest dimensions to five robust dimensions of personality. *Journal of Counseling Psychology. 40,* 518–524.

Gough, H. G., & Heilbrun, A. B., Jr. (1983). *The Adjective Checklist manual.* Palo Alto, CA: Consulting Psychologists Press.

Guilford, J. P., Christensen, R. R., Bond, N. A., & Sutton, M. A. (1954). A factor analytic study of human interests. *Psychological Monographs, 68* (4, No. 375).

Guion, R. M., & Gottier, R. F. (1965). Validity of personality measures in personnel selection. *Personnel Psychology. 18,* 135–164.

Hansen, J. C., & Campbell, D. P. (1985). *Manual for the Strong Interest Inventory* (4th ed.). Stanford, CA: Stanford University Press.

Harmon, L. W., Borgen, F. H., Berreth, J. M., King, J. C., Shauer, D., & Ward, C. C. (1996). The *Skills Confidence Inventory:* A measure of self-efficacy. *Journal of Career Assessment, 4,* 457–477.

Harmon, L. W., Hansen, J. C., Borgen, F. H., & Hammer, A. L. (1994). *Strong Interest Inventory: Applications and technical guide.* Stanford, CA: Stanford University Press.

Holland, J. L. (1976). Vocational preferences. In M. D. Dunnette (Ed.), *Handbook of industrial and organizational psychology* (pp. 521–570). Chicago: Rand McNally.

Holland, J. L. (1996). Exploring careers with a typology: What we have learned and some new directions. *American Psychologist, 51,* 397–406.

Holland, J. L. (1997). *Making vocational choices* (3rd ed.). Odessa, FL: Psychological Assessment Resources.

Holland, J. L., Johnston, J. A., & Asama, N. F. (1994). More evidence for the relationship between Holland's personality types and personality variables. *Journal of Career Assessment. 18,* 91–100.

Isaacs, J., Borgen, F. H., Donnay, D.A.C., & Hansen, T. A. (1997). *Self-efficacy and interests: Relationships of Holland themes to college major.* Poster presentation at the 105th Annual Convention of the American Psychological Association, Chicago.

John, O. P. (1990). The Big Five factor taxonomy: Dimensions of personality in the natural language and in questionnaires. In L. A. Pervin (Ed.), *Handbook of Personality: Theory and research* (pp. 66–100). New York: Guilford Press.

Kuder, F. (1977). *Activity interests and occupational choice.* Chicago: Science Research Associates.

Lent, R.W., Brown, S. D., & Hackett, G. (1994). Toward a unifying social cognitive theory of career and academic interest, choice, and performance. *Journal of Vocational Behavior, 45,* 79–122.

Lent, R. W., Larkin, K. V., & Brown, S. D. (1989). Relation of self-efficacy to inventories vocational interests. *Journal of Vocational Behavior, 34,* 279–288.

Lindley, L. D. (1997). *Validity of the* Strong Interest Inventory: *Gender and personal styles.* Unpublished master's thesis, Iowa State University.

Lowman, R. L. (1991). *The clinical practice of career assessment: Interests. abilities. and personality.* Washington, DC: American Psychological Association.

Lubinski, D., & Dawis, R. (Eds.) (1995). *Assessing individual differences in human behavior.* Palo Alto, CA: Davies-Black.

Messick, S. (1995). Validity of psychological assessment: Validation of inferences from persons' responses and performances as scientific inquiry into score meaning. *American Psychologist, 50,* 741–749.

Mischel, W. (1968). *Personality and assessment.* New York: Wiley.

Osipow, S. H. (1983). *Theories of career development* (3rd ed.). Englewood Cliffs, NJ: Prentice Hall.

Parsons, F. (1909). *Choosing a vocation.* Boston: Houghton Mifflin.

Peters, T., & Austin, N. (1985). *A passion for excellence.* New York: Time Warner Books.

Pirsig, R. M. (1974). *Zen and the art of motorcycle maintenance: An inquiry into values.* New York: Morrow.

Prediger, D. J. (1976). A world of work map for career exploration. *Vocational Guidance Quarterly, 24,* 198–208.

Prediger, D. J. (1998). Is interest profile level relevant to career counseling? *Journal of Counseling Psychology, 45,* 204–211.

Seligman, M.E.P. (1991). *Learned optimism.* New York: Knopf.

Seligman, M.E.P. (1998). Building human strength: Psychology's forgotten mission. *APA Monitor, 29*(1), 2.

Strong, E. K., Jr. (1943). *Vocational interests of men and women.* Stanford, CA: Stanford University Press.

Super, D. E. (1980). A life-span, life-space approach to career development. *Journal of Vocational Behavior, 16,* 282–298.

Super, D. E. (1994). A life-span, life-space perspective on convergence. In M. L. Savickas & R. W. Lent (Eds.), *Convergence in career development theories: Implications for science and practice* (pp. 63–74). Palo Alto, CA: Davies-Black.

Super, D. E., & Crites, J. O. (1962). *Appraising vocational fitness* (2nd ed.). New York: HarperCollins.

Swaney, K. B. (1995). *Technical manual: Revised Unisex Edition of the ACT Interest Inventory (UNIACT).* Iowa City, IA: American College Testing.

Swanson, J. L. (1993). Integrated assessment of vocational interests and self-rated skills and abilities. *Journal of Career Assessment, 1,* 50–65.

Tokar, D. M., & Swanson, J. L. (1995). Evaluation of the correspondence between Holland's vocational personality typology and the five-factor model of personality. *Journal of Vocational Behavior, 46,* 89–108.

Tokar, D. M., Vaux, A., & Swanson, J. L. (1995). Dimensions relating Holland's vocational personality typology and the five-factor model. *Journal of Career Assessment. 3,* 57–74.

Tracey, T. J. (1997). The structure of interests and self-efficacy expectations: An expanded examination of the spherical model of interests. *Journal of Counseling Psychology, 44,* 32–43.

Tracey, T.J.G., & Rounds, J. (1993). Evaluating Holland's and Gati's vocational-interest models. A structural analysis. *Psychological Bulletin, 113,* 229–246.

Tyler, L. E. (1959). Toward a workable psychology of individuality. *American Psychologist, 14,* 75–81.

Tyler, L. E. (1978). *Individuality: Human possibilities and personal choice in the development of men and women.* San Francisco: Jossey-Bass.

Walsh, W. B., & Osipow, S. H. (Eds.). (1986). *Advances in vocational psychology: Vol. I. The assessment of interests.* Hillsdale, NJ: Erlbaum.

Zytowski, D. G. (Ed.). (1973). *Contemporary approaches to interest measurement.* Minneapolis: University of Minnesota Press.

Contributors

Presenters at Lehigh Conference: Seated (left to right): James Rounds, John Crites, David Blustein, Fred Borgen, Nancy Betz, Howard Tinsley, Dale Prediger. Standing (left to right): Karen O'Brien, Hanoch Flum, Lenore Harmon, Arnold Spokane, Jeffrey Prince, Nadya Fouad, John Holland, Mark Savickas, Jane Swanson, Bruce Walsh, Linda Subich, Linda Gottfredson, Donald Zytowski, Edward Schmertz.

Nancy E. Betz, Ph.D., is professor of psychology at The Ohio State University. She received her Ph.D. degree in psychology from the University of Minnesota in 1976. Since joining the faculty at Ohio State in 1976, her research and teaching interests have focused on the areas of psychological testing, barriers to women's and minorities' pursuit of many career fields, and the applications of self-efficacy theory to career choice and adjustment. Betz is a recipient of the John L. Holland Award for Research in Career and Personality Psychology. She served as editor of the *Journal of Vocational Behavior* from 1984 to 1990 and has also served on the editorial boards of the *Journal of Counseling Psychology, Journal of Vocational Behavior, Journal of Career Assessment,* and *Psychology of Women Quarterly.* She is a fellow of both the American Psychological Association and the American Psychological Society. Betz can be reached at betz.3@osu.edu.

David L. Blustein, Ph.D., received his doctoral degree in counseling psychology from Teachers College, Columbia University, in 1985. He is currently associate professor in the Department of Counseling Psychology at the University at Albany, State University at New York. Blustein is a fellow of the American Psychological Association and the recipient of the 1991 Division 17 Early Career Scientist-Practitioner Award. His research interests include work-based transitions (such as the school-to-work transition), career exploration and decision-making processes, and the contribution of human relationships to vocational behavior. Blustein has lectured in several universities in Portugal. He currently serves on the editorial board of the *Journal of Counseling Psychology*. He can be reached at DLB71@CNSIBM.Albany.edu.

Fred H. Borgen, Ph.D., is professor of psychology at Iowa State University, where he previously directed the counseling psychology program. His psychology doctorate is from the University of Minnesota, where he worked with David Campbell in the 1960s to develop the Basic Interest Scales for the *Strong Interest Inventory*. Collaborating with the revision team at Consulting Psychologists Press, Borgen was one of the developers of the 1994 *Strong*. He is coauthor (with Nancy E. Betz and Lenore W. Harmon) of the 1996 *Skills Confidence Inventory*. Borgen can be reached at fhborgen@iastate.edu.

Serena Chu is a doctoral candidate in counseling psychology at Southern Illinois University. She is a recipient of numerous undergraduate honors including the American Psychological Association Undergraduate Students of Excellence in Psychology Award in 1995. She has presented posters and conducted interactive sessions on issues related to ethnic identity development at the annual meetings of the Midwestern Psychological Association and the Asian American Psychological Association.

John O. Crites, Ph.D., is president of Crites Career Consultants in Boulder, Colorado. He is author of *Vocational Psychology: The Study of Vocational Behavior* and *Development and Career Counseling: Models, Methods, and Materials,* and coauthor (with D. E. Super) of *Appraising Vocational Fitness*. He has constructed and developed the *Career Maturity Inventory* and the *Career Mastery Inventory*. Crites served as president of the Counseling Psychology Division (17) of the American Psychological Association in 1972 and in 1973. He has received the Eminent Career Award (1984) from the National Career Development Association and the Walter F. Storey Award (1985) from the American Society for Training and Development. His career in higher education included positions as professor of counseling psychology at the University of Iowa, the University of Maryland, Kent State University, and Northwestern University.

Susan X Day received her master's degree in psychology from Illinois State University and is now completing her Ph.D. degree in counseling psychology at the University of Illinois at Urbana-Champaign. Her current research focuses on the structure of vocational interests and on evaluating psychotherapy delivered through distance technology.

Alysia R. Decker received her master's degree in counseling psychology from Lehigh University. She is currently pursuing professional opportunities in the field of career development.

Hanoch Flum, Ph.D., is a senior lecturer in the Department of Education at Ben Gurion University in Beer Sheva, Israel. He has taught courses in adolescent psychology, adult development, and career development and counseling. He is editor of *Adolescents in Israel: Personal, Familial, and Social Aspects*. Flum's research interests focus on identity development in adolescents and young adults and include the role of culture and career development, especially in light of social change. Flum can be reached at flum@bgumail.ac.il.

Nadya A. Fouad, Ph.D., is professor in the Department of Educational Psychology and associate dean in the School of Education at the University of Wisconsin–Milwaukee. She has published numerous articles and chapters on cross-cultural vocational assessment, career development, interest measurement, and cross-cultural counseling. She serves as coeditor of "Legacies and Traditions" for *The Counseling Psychologist* and as an editorial board member for the *Journal of Career Assessment* and the *Journal of Vocational Behavior*. Fouad is a fellow of the Counseling Psychology Division (17) of the American Psychological Association and serves Division 17 as vice president for Diversity and Public Interests and as chair of the Society for Vocational Psychology. Fouad can be reached at nfouad@soe.uwm.edu.

Linda S. Gottfredson, Ph.D., is professor of educational studies at the University of Delaware. She is best known for her 1981 theory of vocational aspirations, "Circumscription and Compromise." She is also widely known for her work analyzing the implications of individual and group differences in intelligence, including guest editing three special journal issues on the subject: "The g Factor in Employment" (*Journal of Vocational Behavior*, December 1986), "Fairness in Employment Testing" (*Journal of Vocational Behavior*, December 1988), and "Intelligence and Social Policy" (*Intelligence*, January/February 1997). Gottfredson is a fellow of the American Psychological Association, the American Psychological Society, and the Society for Industrial and Organizational Psychology. She can be reached at gottfred@udel.edu.

Lenore W. Harmon, Ph.D., is professor of educational psychology at the University of Illinois in Urbana-Champaign. She served as editor of the *Journal of Vocational Behavior* from 1975 to 1984 and as editor of the *Journal of Counseling Psychology* from 1988 to 1993. Harmon received the 1993 Leona Tyler Award from the Division of Counseling Psychology of the American Psychological Association. Her research interests include the career development of women and athletes and the development of interest inventories. She can be reached at l-harmon@uiuc.edu.

Paul J. Hartung, Ph.D., is assistant professor of behavioral sciences at Northeastern Ohio Universities College of Medicine in Rootstown and an adjunct faculty member of the Counseling and Special Education Department at the University of Akron. His research interests include developmental career theory and assessment, career decision making, multicultural career counseling, and physician career development. Hartung serves on the editorial boards of *Career Development Quarterly* and *Journal of Career Assessment*. He is the communications officer of the Society for Vocational Psychology, a section in the Counseling Psychology Division (17) of the American Psychological Association. Hartung can be reached at phartung@neoucom.edu.

John L. Holland, Ph.D., has been a researcher-practitioner, research supervisor, and teacher for 45 years. He is best known for the *Self-Directed Search*, the leading interest inventory in the world. In 1994, Holland received the Award for Distinguished Professional Contributions from the American Psychological Association.

Dale J. Prediger, Ed.D., is vocation research psychologist at American College Testing (ACT). He directed the development and validation of the *Unisex Edition of the ACT Interest Inventory* (UNIACT), which is completed by more than four million people each year. Prediger continues to seek better ways to integrate the results of work-relevant measures (e.g., interests, experiences, abilities, job values) used in career exploration and planning. Currently, the World-of-Work Map (an extension of Holland's hexagonal model of interest structure) serves that purpose. Prediger can be reached at prediger@act.org.

James Rounds, Ph.D., is professor of educational psychology and psychology at the University of Illinois in Urbana-Champaign. He received his Ph.D. degree in psychology from the University of Minnesota. His scholarship focuses on the development and evaluation of structural hypotheses in personality. Rounds can be reached at j-rounds@uiuc.edu.

Mark L. Savickas, Ph.D., is professor and chair in the Behavioral Sciences Department at the Northeastern Ohio Universities College of Medicine and adjunct professor of counselor education at Kent State University. He has served as editor of the *Career Development Quarterly* (1991–1998) and is now editor for the *Journal of Vocational Behavior*. He also serves on the editorial boards of the *Journal of Counseling Psychology*, the *Journal of Career Assessment*, the *Australian Journal of Career Development*, and the *Educational Research Journal* (Hong Kong). He edited (with R. Lent) *Convergence in Career Development Theories* (1994) and (with B. Walsh) *The Handbook of Career Counseling Theory and Practice* (1996). He is a recipient of the John L. Holland Award for Outstanding Achievement in Career and Personality Research (1994) from the Counseling Psychology Division of the American Psychological Association and the Eminent Career Award (1996) from the National Career Development Association. Savickas can be reached at ms@neoucom.edu.

Arnold R. Spokane, Ph.D., is professor of education and psychology and coordinator of the Counseling Psychology Program at Lehigh University. A practicing career counselor for nearly 20 years, Spokane is the author of *Career Intervention* (Prentice Hall, 1991) and specializes in the study of the full range of career interventions, the overlap between career and mental health issues (including occupationally induced stress), and the interactions of persons and environments at work. Spokane is on the editorial boards of the *Journal of Career Development, Career Development Quarterly,* and the *Journal of Career Assessment,* and is the author or coauthor of more than 50 journal articles, book chapters, and technical reports on career development.

Jane L. Swanson, Ph.D., is professor of psychology at Southern Illinois University. She has served as associate editor of the *Journal of Vocational Behavior* and on the editorial boards of the *Journal of Counseling Psychology, Career Development Quarterly,* and *The Counseling Psychologist.* Swanson's research focuses on career assessment, interest measurement, perceptions of career-related barriers, and women's career development. Swanson can be reached at swanson@siu.edu.

Howard E. A. Tinsley, Ph.D., is professor in the Department of Psychology at the University of Florida and at the WLRA International Center of Excellence at Waugeningen Agricultural University, The Netherlands. He is a guest editor for the *Journal of Counseling Psychology,* a former editor of the *Journal of Vocational Behavior,* and a former member of the editorial advisory board of the Test Corporation of America. Tinsley has authored more than 120 publications dealing with vocational psychology, psychological measurement, and leisure psychology. He is a recipient of the research award of the American Rehabilitation Counseling Association and of the Allen V. Sapora Research Award for Excellence in Leisure Psychology. Tinsley is a diplomate of the American Board of Vocational Experts, and has served as chair of the American College Personnel Association Commission on Assessment and as president of the Academy of Leisure Sciences. He can be reached at tinsley@psych.ufl.edu.

W. Bruce Walsh, Ph.D., is professor in the Department of Psychology at The Ohio State University, where he has served as coordinator of the counseling psychology program for the last nine years. Walsh is the founder and charter editor of the *Journal of Career Assessment.* He coauthored *Tests and Assessments* and *Tests and Measurements* and coedited *Career Counseling for Women, Career Counseling, The Handbook of Vocational Psychology,* and *Person-Environment Psychology.* Walsh has also served on the editorial boards of the *Journal of Counseling Psychology, Journal of Vocational Behavior, Journal of Professional Psychology,* and *Journal of College Student Development.* In 1998, he served as president of the Counseling Psychology Division (17) of the American Psychological Association.

Donald G. Zytowski, Ph.D., served as a counseling psychologist on the staff of the Student Counseling Service and on the psychology faculty of Iowa State University from 1965 to 1990. His first publication on the *Kuder Occupational Interest Survey* appeared in 1968. He has served as developer of the Kuder inventories since 1983. Zytowski is a former president of the Counseling Psychology Division (17) of the American Psychological Association and has been recognized by Division 17 as a Distinguished Contributor to Counseling Psychology. He has received the Extended Research Award from the American Counseling Association and the Eminent Career Award from the National Career Development Association. Zytowski can be reached at DZytowski@aol.com.

Name Index

Subject Index

abilities, 23, 214
  heritability of, 72–74
  integration with interests, 254–255, 295–296
    bridging scores and options, 297–299, 313–314
    case study, 316–321
    comprehensive assessment, 299–303, 314
    counseling suggestions, 314–321
    information analysis, 309–314
    score comparisons, 306–308, 314
    self-estimates, 296, 303–307, 314
    relationship to interests, 7, 48, 374–375
    self-determination theory on, 357, 361
    self-efficacy theory on, 39–41
Ability Explorer, 303–305
achievement,
  heritability of, 72–74
  See also intelligence; success
ACL *(Adjective Checklist),* 399
ACT. *See* American College Testing
activities, 266
  exploration as social activities, 347, 373
  and functionalist view of interests, 23, 31–33
adaptations, characteristic, defined, 153
Adjective Checklist (ACL), 399
affection,
  and structuralist view of interests, 23, 25–27
  See also emotions
African Americans, 119, 121–122, 377–378
age,
  and intelligence,
    changes in IQ, 74–75
    heritability of IQ, 62–66
    shared vs. nonshared environments, 68–72
  and interests, 184
    changes, 145–146
    stability, 138, 143–144, 148, 152
American College Testing (ACT), 91–92, 104, 121, 299, 301–307, 310, 315–321, 398
  See also names of measurement tools from ACT

American Counseling Association,
  Responsibilities of Users of Standardized Tests, 280
American Indians, 119, 121–122
Analysis of Work Interests, 167
anxiety, 91, 335–336
  heritability of, 64, 73, 79
APA, 16, 90, 385, 406
  Standards for Educational and Psychological Testing, 280
Appraising Vocational Fitness by Means of Psychological Tests (Super), 23
approach behavior, vs. avoidance behavior, 330–331
aptitudes. *See* abilities
Armed Services Vocational Aptitude Battery (ASVAB), 300–301, 305–306
Asian Americans, 119, 121–122
associationist view of interests, 23–26
ASVAB. *See Armed Services Vocational Aptitude Battery*
attention,
  associationist view of, 23–26
  and definition of interests, 22–23
  purposivist view of, 27–28
attributes. *See* traits
autonomy needs. *See* self-determination
Aviation Psychology Program, 166
avoidance behavior, vs. approach behavior, 330–331

Barnum effect, 259
behavioral genetics, 38, 57–59
  and guidelines for counseling, 76–81
  heritability,
    current studies, 62–76
    of personality and interests, 152–153
    previous studies, 59–62
Bell Adjustment Inventory, 88
bias,
  in assessments, 104, 127

425